Chauncey's Creek

Mc Clary

Logy Ledge   Beacon
B.

Gooseberry I.

7¼   8¾   4½

1¼   11½   3¼

6½   10½   10¾   4¾   3¾

11½   10¼   4¼

9   11½   11½   BUOY   8
B.No.6

8¾   8¾   3¼   *Fishing Ids.*

9¼   9¼   11½

8½   8½   *rocky*   5½

8½   8¾   3½   4½

6½   7¼   8½   *Cod Rock Buoy*   10¾
B.No.5

17½   7¼   7½   8

Ft. Constitution
Portsmouth Lt.Ho.

6¼

Clay   17   4½   7   *rocky*   4

9½   *Clay*

3¼   5½   7¼   6½

BUOY   *rocky*
B.No.3
Stielman's Rocks   7½

3½   *Clay*

5½   9   9½

9¼   6½

10½   5½   8   *Wood I.*   7¾

10½   16   7¾

13½   *rocky*   12½

9¼   4½   10   *r cky*   5

7½   6½   *White I.*

8¼   *Whale's Back*   5½
Light Ho.

Beacon   *Ferry's Pt.*
B

3½   7   7½

3½   5¼   *rocky*   4½   7¼

rocky   6½   7½   *Sand*   BUOY
B.No.1   *Kitt's Rocks*

N. ¼ E.

Horn I.

Sand

Philips Rocks

Sand

rocky

"Constructing Munitions of War"

Amid great fanfare, the long-delayed USS Franklin *slid down the ways at the Yard on September 17, 1864. A gathering of Portsmouth citizens viewed the festivities from across the Piscataqua River. The man wearing a top hat and seated in a carriage (upper center) has been tentatively identified as Frank Jones. PNSVC*

"Constructing Munitions of War": The Portsmouth Navy Yard Confronts the Confederacy, 1861–1865

Richard E. Winslow III

The Portsmouth Marine Society
Publication Twenty-One

Published for the Society by

Peter E. Randall
PUBLISHER

Designed and produced by
Peter E. Randall Publisher
Box 4726, Portsmouth, NH 03802

A publication of
The Portsmouth Marine Society
Box 147, Portsmouth, NH 03802

ISBN 0915819-20-1

Front Endleaf: The 1866 Coast Survey "Portsmouth Harbor" map pinpoints many of the localities associated with the Portsmouth Navy Yard during the Civil War. Note the town of Portsmouth (far left), Piscataqua River (left center), and Navy Yard Island (center), the entire economically and militarily vital area, in turn, defended against potential enemy threat from the sea by Fort McClary (far right) and Fort Constitution (Lower right). Portmouth Room. PPL

Back Endleaf: Individual pages of Civil War-era Portsmouth Navy Yard Log Book(s) detail the daily (Sundays and holidays included) record of the Yard's muster, weather, and other useful categories. In addition to filling in the pertinent data on the printed form, the Yard clerk also noted, under the "Remarks" column, any significant information. PNSYC

In appreciation for their unstinting support
during the researching, writing, revising, and publishing of this book,
I honor eight friends:

Kathleen Brandes, Ray Brighton, Fred Crawford, Jim Dolph,
Nancy Hunt, Peter Randall, and Joe and Jean Sawtelle.

Other Portsmouth Marine Society Publications:

Contents

Acknowledgments

As with the building and outfitting of a vessel, a book is only as good as the materials and the specialized skills that go into it. In the preparation of this study, I have enjoyed the help of scores of people: archivists, librarians, historians, writers, photographers, curators, editors, compositors, researchers, collectors, indexers, and publishers. Many are longtime friends who have worked with me on my other Portsmouth Marine Society books.

For superb materials, I thank Sherman Pridham, Portsmouth Public Library, Portsmouth, NH; Kevin Shupe, Carolyn Eastman, Jeanette Mitchell, and Jane Porter, Portsmouth Athenaeum; Robyn Mason, Cumings Library, Strawbery Banke, Portsmouth; Joseph and Jean Sawtelle, Portsmouth Marine Society; Deborah Watson and Peter Crosby, Reference Department, William Ross, Frank Wheeler, and Roland Goodbody, Special Collections, Dimond Library, University of New Hampshire, Durham; Jacquelyn Thomas and Edouard Desroches, Rockefeller Library, Phillips Exeter Academy, Exeter, NH: Stephen Cox, William Copeley, Deborah Tapley, Jim and Donna-Belle Garvin, and Betsy Hamlin-Morin, New Hampshire Historical Society, Concord; Frank Mevers, John Page, and Andrew Taylor, Division of Records Management and Archives, Concord; Kenneth Cramer and Philip Cronenwett, Baker Memorial Library, Dartmouth College, Hanover, NH; Gerald Davis, Douglas Stein, and Paul O'Pecko, G.W. Blunt White Library, Mystic Seaport Museum, Mystic, CT; John Koza, Phillips Library, Kathy Flynn and Mark Sexton, Photography Department, Peabody Essex Museum, Salem, MA; Dean Allard, William Dudley, Michael Crawford, Charles

Brodine, Charles Haberlein, Bernard Cavalcante, and Katherine Rohr, Naval Historical Center, Washington Navy Yard, Washington; John McDonough and John Sellers, Manuscript Division, Larry Sullivan, Rare Book and Special Collection Division, Library of Congress; William Sherman and Lane Moore, Judicial, Fiscal and Social Branch, Richard von Doenhoff and Barry Zerby, Military Reference Branch, National Archives, Washington; James Owens, Stanley Tozeski, and George Young, National Archives-New England Region, Waltham, MA; Joost Schoklenbrock, Kendall Whaling Museum, Sharon, MA; Mary Jean Blasdale, Old Dartmouth Historical Society, Whaling Museum, New Bedford, MA; Robert Webb, Maine Maritime Museum, Bath, ME; Stephen Rice, Connecticut Historical Society, Hartford, CT; Mark Renovitch, Franklin D. Roosevelt Library, Hyde Park, NY; Earle G. Shettleworth, Jr., Maine Historic Preservation Commission, Augusta; Evelyn Cherpak, Naval Historical Collection, Naval War College, Newport, RI; and Josephine Rafferty, Portsmouth Naval Shipyard Library. I also thank the staffs of the Boston Public Library, the Boston Athenaeum, the New England Historic and Genealogical Library, the Massachusetts Historical Society, and the Massachusetts Archives, Boston; Maine Historical Society, Portland, ME; Sterling and Beinecke Libraries, Yale University, New Haven, CT; Widener, Lamont, Pusey, and Houghton Libraries, Harvard University, Cambridge, MA; Hawthorne-Longfellow Library, Bowdoin College, Brunswick, ME; Frost Library, Amherst College, Amherst, MA; and Sawyer Library, Williams College, Williamstown, MA.

Writers, editors, indexers, compositors, publishers, and historians have contributed much to this book, many of them working unselfishly since this study's inception. Their unstinting help has made this publication possible. Several have as well graciously extended to me the hospitality of their homes during periods of research. I thank Fred Crawford, Lansing, MI; Nancy Hunt, Lyme, NH; Peter Randall, Hampton, NH; Chester Wolford, Harbor Creek, PA; Kathleen Brandes, Spruce Head, ME; Ray Brighton, Ronan Donohue, Mark Lingenfelter, Patricia Mullaney, and David Goodman, Portsmouth, NH; Woodard Openo, Somersworth, NH; Richard E. Winslow, Jr., Rye, NH; and Robert Whitehouse, Rollinsford, NH.

Civil War naval specialists William Marvel, South Conway, NH; Joseph Geden, Stoughton, MA; William Still, Kailua-Kona, HI; and Duane Shaffer, Epping, NH, generously shared their research and ideas about the *Kearsarge-Alabama* sea battle.

Captain Lennis Lammers, Captain Peter Bowman, Rear Admiral Lewis Felton, and Captain Lance Horne, successive Portsmouth Naval Shipyard commanders from 1988 to the present, authorized permission to visit the Yard library and various Civil War-related sites. Constance Barberi, Security Clerk, facilitated my visits to the Yard.

James Dolph, historian of the Portsmouth Naval Shipyard, has worked tirelessly for years in creating a museum. As director of the Portsmouth Naval Shipyard Visitor Center, Jim has shared with me everything he has found—manuscripts, photographs, and artifacts—to the enrichment of this book.

No Portsmouth-area historian can ever forget the late Joseph P. Copley, whose interest in and assistance with various projects were legendary. Joe devoted his life to the collection, organization, and preservation of Portsmouth history. Many times he would call up and say, "Dick, do you have this?" The vast majority of times I had no inkling that such materials existed, for Joe was a master sleuth at ferreting out Portsmouthiana. I would then head over to Joe's New Castle home, where he would already have set out on his living room table his latest discoveries for my use, just for the asking.

I also wish to thank the many people, a few since deceased, who have aided and encouraged my writing career for the last thirty years. In addition to those already mentioned, I extend my appreciation to Phil and Katherine Young, Eric and Nancy Marshall, Betty Brighton, Judy Randall, Clay Sauls, Ken Butler, Robert Wheeler, Robert Dunn, Elizabeth Ihle, Deborah George, Ken Deutsch, Eleanor Hall, Warren Hohwald, Rick Quarton, Bill and Carol Wilson, Gretchen Wolford, William Greenleaf, Bob Gilmore, Hans Heilbronner, David Long, Charles Clark, Bob Dishman, Coddy Hislop, James Morley, Bea Lammers, Warren Hassler, Gerald Eggert, Bob Murray, Bern Oldsey, John Simon, Bob Seager, Charles Roland, Holman Hamilton, Charles and Melba Hay, James Robertson, Mike Birkner, Robin Wagner, John and Greta Vairo, George Franz, Priscilla Clement, Parker Huber, John Tallmadge, Scott Russell Sanders, John Elder, George Russell, Wesley and Esther Roberts, Jim and Elizabeth Mohr, Rob Perkins, Virginia Winslow, and Donald, Ellen, Beth, and Heather Ruhl.

Ronald Spector and Dean Allard, successive directors of the Naval Historical Center, Washington, awarded me a Vice Admiral Edwin B. Hooper postgraduate fellowship to pursue work on this topic. The late Admiral Hooper, a historian in his own right, endowed a fund to sponsor such United States naval history projects.

Finally, I salute the memory of the Civil War participants who appear in this book—-the Port of Portsmouth ship captains and crews, the Portsmouth Navy Yard officers, sailors, and workers, as well as their Confederate opponents. Having vicariously re-lived their careers, I stand thoroughly convinced of their pivotal role and significant impact upon both United States and world naval history.

Preface

I<small>N HIS</small> 1991 <small>BOOK</small>, *An American Iliad: The Story of the Civil War*, historian Charles P. Roland makes an apt comparison of the Greco-Trojan War to an epic conflict in American history. The American Iliad occurred in a nineteenth-century setting during the most momentous and pivotal crisis in United States history.

In 1860, before the advent of the Civil War, the United States government maintained seven navy yards along the Atlantic and Gulf Coasts—Portsmouth, Boston, New York (Brooklyn), Philadelphia, Washington, Norfolk (Gosport), and Pensacola—as well as one on the Pacific Coast, San Francisco (Mare Island). The Norfolk and Pensacola yards fell to the Confederacy in 1861, but both were recaptured by Union forces during the spring of 1862. From then on, the North's eight yards and its control of the sea provided overwhelming naval superiority. "Uncle Sam's web feet," as President Abraham Lincoln referred to the Union navy, extended their nesting and feeding territory. Three years later, in 1865, the Union's eight navy yards, with their ships, officers, sailors, and workers, in concert with the Union army, crushed their Confederate opponent.

This book focuses on one of these yards, the Portsmouth Navy Yard, from 1860 through 1865. The Port of Portsmouth, too, is part of this narrative. A microcosm of the national and international upheaval, Portsmouth, New Hampshire, and surrounding communities, like hundreds of other Union hamlets, towns, and cities, participated in a gigantic military undertaking. Outside events affected Portsmouth, and Portsmouth, in turn, influenced the rest of the world. The USS *Kearsarge*, built at the Yard during 1861 and 1862, fought the CSS *Alabama* off Cherbourg, France, in 1864. The Portsmouth merchant ship *Rockingham,* destroyed by the *Alabama*, became the center of Anglo-American diplomatic negotiations, leading to international treaties a few years later.

Daniel Marcy of Portsmouth, shipowner and wartime congressman from the First (or "Navy Yard") District, and Peter Marcy of New Orleans, shipowner and outfitter of Confederate privateers, literally competed "brother against brother." The House of Marcy, divided against itself during the war years, never fully recovered.

Thousands of unpublished letters, diaries, and documents (the majority never intended for a historian's eye), along with printed letters and reports, have preserved many an anguished voice: a ship captain describing difficulties on the high seas or in faraway ports; Yard commandants reporting problems to Secretary of the Navy Gideon Welles or to bureau chiefs; a New Hampshire senator alleging graft and corruption at the Yard; officers and seamen aboard the USS *Kearsarge* and aboard gunboats on blockading duty detailing combat hazards. Individual agony spread nationwide as the Civil War changed forever, for better or worse, the direction of the United States.

In this book, which I hope captures the tenor of those tumultuous times, I have allowed the participants to speak for themselves through excerpts from their writings, most heretofore unpublished. Supporting details come from articles and editorials published in Portsmouth newspapers, a source virtually untouched by modern historians. I have also consulted the much more readily available *Official Records* (the naval records alone run to thirty-one volumes), standard biographies, and widely used monographs on various aspects of this story. Since excerpts from these sources have appeared in the literature for more than a century, I have often chosen to let new voices tell the familiar tales in slightly different versions.

The exact transcriptions of contemporary accounts retain many misspellings, erratic punctuation, and other grammatical idiosyncrasies. I have inserted typographical additions only in the interest of clarity, without clusters of "sic" to signal the presence of errors. I have provided, within brackets, definitions of obsolete words, unfamiliar nautical terms, or other vagaries I felt worthy of explication. Outside readers have confirmed the accuracy of the quotations. I have italicized the names of all vessels, regardless of how they appeared in the original. These occasional minor adjustments to nineteenth-century language and style are designed to streamline the text for the modern reader. Despite their idiosyncratic approaches to writing, Civil War participants left no doubt about what they meant or where they stood. Their sometimes awkward and ragged composition often articulates their thoughts and viewpoints even more dramatically and effectively than would conventionally polished prose.

It is a humbling and numbing experience to view microfilm boxes, shelf after shelf, row after row, stack after stack, of Civil War materials at the National Archives in Washington, as well as multitudinous letterbooks and Hollinger boxes in many library collections. Government documents pertaining to the Portsmouth Navy Yard during the Civil War number in the tens of thousands. In order to produce a book of tolerable length from such a mountain of materials, I have had to select and condense rigorously.

I have followed the war chronologically from the viewpoint of the Portsmouth Navy Yard—and, to a lesser extent, the Port of Portsmouth. Only when events on land relate to and support this topic have I mentioned such matters as the surrounding forts guarding the Yard and the 1863 and 1865 Portsmouth riots. I have concentrated on presenting a wartime narrative of individuals making and carrying out decisions, and on interpreting the results. This book marks the third time that I have "fought" the Civil War in the role of author: first as a biographer of Union General John Sedgwick; then as an associate editor of *The Cormany Diaries*, a pair of journals kept by a Pennsylvania cavalry officer and his wife; and now as a chronicler of the Portsmouth naval scene. The more I delve into the research, the more compelling the subject becomes. The Portsmouth story further convinces me that the topic will never be exhausted; the Civil War will be endlessly written about, argued, and analyzed. As an epic, it will never lose its fascination.

Herman Melville, a prewar crew member of a merchantman and whalers, and also a sailor aboard the frigate USS *United States* during 1843 and 1844, declared in 1866 that the Civil War was "the great historic tragedy of our time." The Civil War, for both the Portsmouth Navy Yard and the Port of Portsmouth, was, indeed, heroic and grand, but also costly and lamentable. This ordeal was, for the United States, an important rite of passage that changed the national consciousness for succeeding generations of Americans.

Little Harbor
Rye, New Hampshire
February 2, 1994 (Centennial of the wreck of the USS *Kearsarge*)

List of Abbreviations

THE ABBREVIATIONS BELOW appear in illustration captions throughout this book, within the text, as well as in the Notes at the end of the book.

ACAB	*Appletons' Cyclopaedia of American Biography*
CSS	Confederate States Ship
CWNC	*Civil War Naval Chronology, 1861-1865*
DAB	*Dictionary of American Biography*
DANFS	*Dictionary of American Naval Fighting Ships*
HU	Harvard University
LC	Library of Congress
MHS	Maine Historical Society
MsHS	Massachusetts Historical Society
MSM	Mystic Seaport Museum
NA-DC	National Archives-Washington, DC
NA-NER	National Archives-New England Region
NHC	Naval Historical Center
NHDRMA	New Hampshire Division of Records Management and Archives
NHHS	New Hampshire Historical Society
ORN	*Official Records of the Union and Confederate Navies of the War of the Rebellion*
PA	Portsmouth Athenaeum
PC	*Portsmouth Chronicle*
PEM	Peabody Essex Museum
PH	*Portsmouth Herald*
PHS	Portsmouth Historical Society
PJ	*Portsmouth Journal of Literature and Politics*
PNSVC	Portsmouth Naval Shipyard Visitor Center
PPL	Portsmouth Public Library
PT	*Portsmouth Times*
RG	Record Group
SU	*The States and Union*
UNH	University of New Hampshire
USN	United States Navy
USS	United States Ship

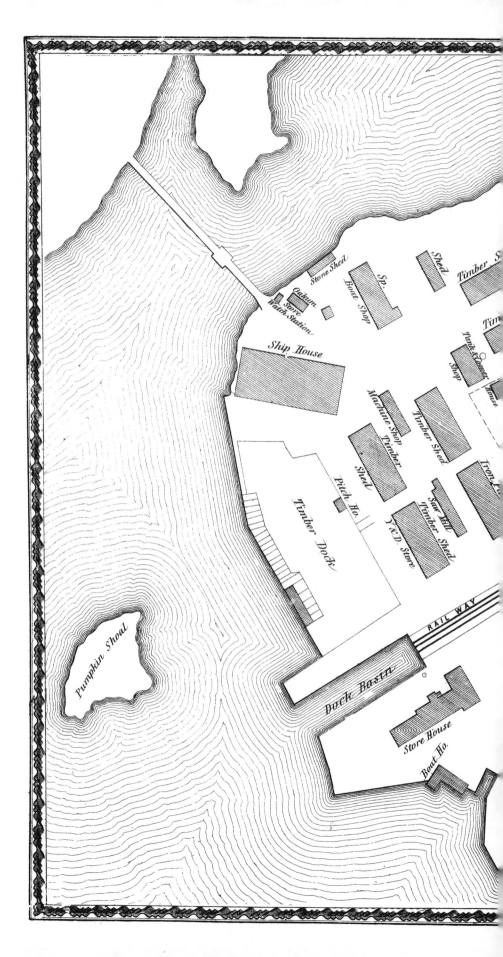

Stone Shed

Sp.

Shed

Timber S

Boat Shop

Oakum
Store
Watch Station

Ship House

Timber

Tank & Cooper's
Shop

House

Machine Shop

Timber
Shed

Timber Shed

Pitch Ho.

Iron Fo

Timber Dock

Saw Mill
Y & D. Store

Timber Shed

RAIL WAY

Dock Basin

Pumpkin Shoal

Store House

Boat Ho.

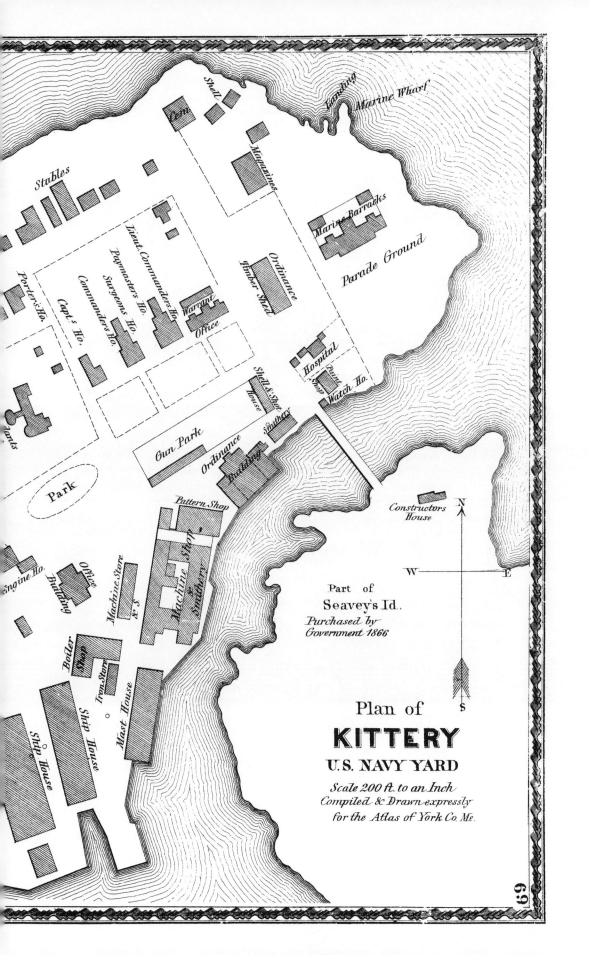

Stables

Shell

Cem

Magazines

Marine Wharf

Landing

Porter's Ho.

Capt's Ho.

Lieut. Commanders Ho.

Paymasters Ho.

Surgeons Ho.

Commanders Ho.

Warrant
Office

Ordnance
Timber Shed

Marine Barracks

Parade Ground

Hospital

Paint
Shop

Watch Ho.

Shell & Shot
House

Smithery

Gun Park

Ordnance Building

Park

Pattern Shop

Constructors
House

N

W   E

S

Part of
Seavey's Id.
Purchased by
Government 1866

Engine Ho.

Office
Building

Machine Store

Machine Shop
Smithery

Boiler

Iron Store

Mast House

Ship House

Ship House

Plan of

KITTERY

U.S. NAVY YARD

Scale 200 ft. to an Inch
Compiled & Drawn expressly
for the Atlas of York Co. Me.

After undergoing repairs at the Portsmouth Navy Yard railway dock, the historic USS Constitution *is readied for launching on May 27, 1858. During the Civil War, the Yard repaired numerous vessels, including the USS* Constellation, *also dating from the 1790s. Although militarily obsolete for wartime action, such older ships served the Union navy in a number of ways, primarily as supply ships. The* Constitution *was employed as a training vessel for midshipmen at the temporarily relocated U.S. Naval Academy in Newport, Rhode Island; in 1862 the* Constellation *sailed from the Yard on a diplomatic mission to the Mediterranean to protect American interests. PA*

(Preceeding page) An 1872 map of the Portsmouth Navy Yard pinpoints the many buildings, docks, shiphouses, and officers' quarters associated with and constructed during the frenetic growth of the Civil War era. Many of these structures, built during the tenure of Yard Civil Engineer Benjamin F. Chandler, are still being used. In the center of Navy Yard Island (top to bottom) is the Commandant's Quarters ("A"), the Park (now the Mall), and the administrative headquarters Office Building ("13"). At upper left, the bridge crosses Back Channel (an arm of the Piscataqua River) to connect the Yard to the village of Kittery, Maine, while the bridge at center right spans Jenkins Gut (a channel now filled in) to Seavey's Island, acquired in 1866. PNSVC

I 1860: The Winds of Peace Shift Toward War

Portsmouth Shipping Around the World

"PORTSMOUTH [NEW HAMPSHIRE] sends out her captains all over the world—and Portsmouth, too, has her enterprising men that are found in every commercial mart in New York, Philadelphia, Boston, North, South, and in the Middle States—almost everywhere you find Portsmouth or Boston boys, or boys grown men," exuded a *Portsmouth Journal* correspondent, writing from San Francisco in 1859. In glowing anticipation ("Well may the spread eagle proud[ly] wave"), this reporter noted just a few of the Piscataqua-built vessels in that California port across the continent: the *Prima Donna*, the *Morning Glory*, the *Orion*, and the *Dashaway*.[1]

Closer to home, Portsmouth family enterprise was vital in New York: "In one of the older neighborhoods on the western side of Fulton Street, is another long-established business that ... of Messrs. Hoyt, Badger & Dillon ... where Portsmouth shipmasters get their watches and chronometers regulated when they arrive in port."[2]

Across the Atlantic, Portsmouth-built vessels, especially the *Liverpool Packet*, received acclaim in England: "The *Packet* has been examined by all the Inspectors here," stated a private 1860 Liverpool letter, "and they pronounce her good. Several ship builders have visited her, all of whom admire her model, and some of them have taken

1

notes. The dock master says she looked nice enough to be placed in the exhibition at London."[3]

Such opinions were widely held. The Port of Portsmouth—its vessels, captains, and crews—had long enjoyed a sound reputation and prestige extending far beyond its home waters. Ever since English explorer Martin Pring sailed up the mouth of the Piscataqua River in 1603, Portsmouth has represented quality in both ships and shipbuilding. Local shipwrights have, for almost 500 years, built, outfitted, and repaired vessels for the Royal, Continental, and American navies, as well as for private interests.

In 1860, Portsmouth was a major North Atlantic port, engaging over the years in the fishing, whaling, mast, West Indies, China, cotton, and California trades. While the Piscataqua formed the watery boundary between Maine (part of Massachusetts until 1820) and New Hampshire, the Port of Portsmouth customs district administratively embraced both sides of the river (the communities of Newington upriver from Portsmouth, and the island village of New Castle below on the New Hampshire side, with Eliot and Kittery across the Piscataqua in Maine).

By 1860, the Port of Portsmouth had enjoyed forty-five years of peace. Not since the War of 1812 ended militarily in 1815, and as the Mexican War posed no restraints to local shipping, had the Portsmouth merchant marine faced interruption in worldwide commerce. With no foreign threat to cloud the horizons that summer, the average Piscataqua mariner strolling along the Portsmouth waterfront doubtlessly quibbled about the slack fishing season and the sluggish maritime trade.[4]

The stagnant economy, moreover, was reflected in Portsmouth's population figures as the decade began. The census of 1860 counted 9,344 inhabitants, a decline from the 9,739 figure recorded ten years earlier. The *Portsmouth Journal* attributed "the deficit" to the floating population present in 1850 "consequent upon the railroad business, employees in our ship-yards, etc., which were not here in 1860." Crippled by the Great Fire of 1813, coupled with War of 1812 privations, the Port of Portsmouth partially rebounded with the brisk California trade in the 1850s, building twenty-eight clippers between 1850 and 1859. The average life of these clippers was approximately twenty years, an exceptional record in an era of far-flung ports of call, piracy in distant ports, storms, and poor charts.[5]

During the spring of 1860, the three leading private shipbuilding firms of Tobey & Littlefield, Marcy & Pettigrew, and that of the late Samuel Badger, carried on by William F. Fernald, hoped to reverse the disturbing trend that had set in, dropping from the average of 11,000 tons during the clipper years of the mid-1850s to only 4,049 tons in 1859. But their optimism was illusory: 1860 brought forth only three ships (2,956 tons), no brigs, one bark (384 tons), three schooners (305 tons), and no sloops—for a total of 3,645 tons. Registered, enrolled, and licensed vessels going to sea held up reasonably well at 34,982 tons for 1860, down from the peak year of 1856 of 40,717 tons, a record for the port.

In his excellent unpublished six-volume history *Early U.S. Customs Records and History, Portsmouth, N.H.*, George A. Nelson, onetime deputy collector of customs, concluded that the Piscataqua shipbuilders, no matter how superbly their vessels might be built, simply could not reverse the economic realities of the time:

> With the find[ing] of gold in California and, a short time later, in Australia, [that circumstance] created the demand for speed in transportation which resulted in the clipper ship. As soon as the urgent demand for goods and personal transportation had been met, speed was no longer at a premium. The clipper ship in 1855 was then forced to enter in competition with the slower vessels with greater cargo-carrying space, resulting in a surplus of vessels.[6]

Apart from statistics and economic trends in a year of peace, Portsmouth vessels struggled against the sea itself. The fishing season of 1860 met with tragedy. On July 14, the *Portsmouth Journal* reported that the "schooner *Nile*, Capt. Batson [commanding] of New Castle, [had] sa[i]led about the middle of April to the [Grand] Banks of Newfoundland. She was in company of two other schooners, and parted from them in a storm. She has not been seen or heard from since, and fears are entertained that she went down with all on board. Her crew was composed of nine persons," all local mariners. Three were married. The grim speculation in time proved true: The *Nile* had disappeared.[7]

At the end of the year, readers of the *Portsmouth Chronicle* saw under "DEATHS" the following notice: "At sea, off Cape Horn, Sept. 30th, were drowned from on board ship *Prima Donna* [sailing from

San Francisco in 1859], MR. CHAS. H. PRAY, aged about 26, and MR. GEORGE P. HACKETT, aged 19 of this city."[8]

Notwithstanding the danger at sea, Piscataqua ship captains relentlessly pursued their risky profession, as they had for centuries. A typical listing in the August 14, 1860, issue of the "MARINE CHRONICLE," a regular column in the *Portsmouth Chronicle,* reveals the importance of shipping to the Portsmouth economy:

PORT OF PORTSMOUTH

SATURDAY, August 11.

Arr   sch *Harriet*, [Captain] Herrick [commanding], Baltimore.

MONDAY, Aug. 13.

Arr   Br[itish] sch *Ann*, Lavache, Pictou, NS [Nova Scotia],—with Coal to Spalding & Parrott.

Br brig *Douglas*, Douglas, Maitland, N.S.

sch *Lizzie M. Stewart*, Stewart, Boston.

Hannah Clarke, Call, Bangor.

Ship *Mary Storer*, Mathes, f[ro]m Cronstadt [Germany], for Bristol [England], ar at Cowes 25th ult.

Ship *Western Empire*, Soule, fm Liverpool, arr at Boston 12th.

Ship *Adelaide Bell*, Robertson, fm Havre [France], ar at New Orleans 10th.

Ship *City of New York*, Salter, from Liverpool, ar at New York 11th.

Ship *Kate Hunter*, Healey, lading at Liverpool July 28th, for Rio [de] Janeiro, via Cardiff [Wales].

Ship *Star of Peace*, Hale, from London for Calcutta, was off Torbay [England] July 27.

Ship *Henrietta Marcy*, Keyser, from Liverpool, for St. Thomas [West Indies], spoken 23d ult, lat 49 08. lon 12 30.[9]

A similar entry for November 17 listed Portsmouth vessels sailing for or arriving at such ports as Whampoa (near Canton), Calcutta, and Manila.[10]

The Portsmouth Navy Yard in Peacetime

The Portsmouth Navy Yard was charged with the responsibility of defending this merchant fleet and of protecting the interests of the United States. This naval facility, established as the first government

In an 1859 photograph, the General Stores Building (foreground) at the Portsmouth Navy Yard fronts on the Piscataqua River, with the Portsmouth skyline on the distant horizon. For many years, Yard workers commuting to and from Portsmouth provided their own transportation— often in unseaworthy rowboats, wherries, and dinghies. They were hampered often by fog, strong tides, and even ice in winter. Alarmed by the risk from inadequate and substandard craft as well as by security concerns, the U.S. Navy in early 1865 inaugurated safe, dependable, and regularly scheduled ferry service aboard the USS Emerald, *using authorized landing sites. PNSVC*

yard in 1800, was located on Navy Yard Island, across the river from Portsmouth. The original deed of William Dennett, Jr., transferring the property to the government for payment of $5,500 and dated June 12, 1800, specifies the extent of the holding:

> ... the whole of a certain island lying in the Piscataqua River in Kittery opposite the town of Portsmouth, and at the distance of about three quarters of a mile therefrom, which island was formerly called Lay Claim Island afterwards Fernald's Island and now called Dennett's and contains fifty acres to the same more or less and is the same I purchased of James Sheafe as by his deed dated 29 Sept'r 1794 more fully appears.

The document was found in the York County, Maine, records, and the deed executed in Rockingham County, New Hampshire, being acknowledged before Jeremiah Smith, a New Hampshire Justice of the Peace. Throughout the history of the Navy Yard, controversy has raged over whether the island lies in Maine or in New Hampshire waters.

On June 13, 1846, the *Portsmouth Journal* sought to define in a local context the hybrid geopolitical status of this federal facility. Almost as if writing a legal brief, its reporter explained:

> The island on which the Navy-Yard is located belongs to the United States, and although on the Maine side of the channel is not taxable anywhere. No mechanics or laborers who work on the Yard are permitted to remain there over night, unless they are connected with the navy or are enrolled on the civil list. No officer, soldier or sailor resident there is taxed, nor is he permitted to exercise the right of suffrage in Maine, unless he chances to be a native of that State. The office of the Navy Agent is always kept in Portsmouth—all letters for the Navy-Yard are sent to the Portsmouth Post-office, and the supplies of the Yard are nearly all obtained from Portsmouth. Portsmouth collection district extends around the island to both sides of the river. The Navy-Yard is indisputedly in Portsmouth Harbor.[11]

During its early years, the Yard struggled for government funds and did not launch its first ship, the USS *Washington,* until 1814. By 1860, only fourteen sailing vessels had been built, among the most important being the *Congress*, a first-class frigate (1841); the *Saratoga*, a sloop of war (1842); and the *Portsmouth*, a twenty-four-gun sloop of war. In 1847, the *Saranac*, a side-wheel steam frigate, the first steamer built at the Yard, signaled the beginning of a more modern era.[12]

At the beginning of 1860, the Yard was in the doldrums, with only 207 civilian employees: "1860 opened with poor prospects for the Yard," wrote Walter Fentress, its first historian. "The appropriations were exhausted, and no work of any importance could be accomplished."[13]

In this atmosphere of little activity and the absence of any foreign threat, security at the Navy Yard Island was nonexistent. "The courtesy of the officers of our Navy Yard is such," the *Journal* reported

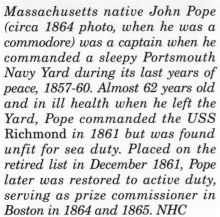

Massachusetts native John Pope (circa 1864 photo, when he was a commodore) was a captain when he commanded a sleepy Portsmouth Navy Yard during its last years of peace, 1857-60. Almost 62 years old and in ill health when he left the Yard, Pope commanded the USS Richmond *in 1861 but was found unfit for sea duty. Placed on the retired list in December 1861, Pope later was restored to active duty, serving as prize commissioner in Boston in 1864 and 1865. NHC*

Relieving Captain John Pope in October 1860, Captain George F. Pearson, an Exeter, New Hampshire, native, remained commandant of the Portsmouth Navy Yard until the fall of 1864, a crucial period of wartime expansion. With 46 years of naval service under his belt in 1861, Pearson was legally retired, being over the age of 62, but he was reinstated in order to serve his country in a time of crisis. Pearson's valuable wartime service culminated in his promotion to rear admiral in 1866. NHC

on September 1, "that no restriction to landing is made during the day, and visitors from the city and country may be seen at all hours visiting the public works. On Saturday morning last several curious strangers had arrived at that part of the Yard where a battery of eighteen pounders faces Portsmouth." One man fired the alarm gun with a tremendous blast. Captain John Pope, commandant of the Yard, hastened from his office for an explanation from the stranger who had set off the gun. The man was incensed, complaining, "Blast your big guns. See how I have ruined my vest."[14]

Pope had been commandant of the Yard since 1858. Sixty-one years old in 1860, he was in failing health. "Mental anxiety, loss of sleep, and indigestion, connected with an affection of the liver, contracted in China [during the 1850s]," Pope wrote a year later, relative to these chronic ailments, "have ... reduced my strength. A surgeon at the time declared that Pope was showing "inertness of mind" and diagnosed him as "suffering from nervous exhaustion."[15]

Whatever Pope's limitations, he was relieved of command on October 1, 1860. His successor was Captain George Frederick Pearson, a native of Exeter, New Hampshire, who had joined the United States Navy as a midshipman in 1815. Sixty-four years old when he took charge of the Yard, Pearson had commanded several ships during his long career and served as a junior officer at the Portsmouth Navy Yard from 1839 to 1841.[16]

Described as "a man of rare and lovable personal qualities," Pearson set to work. He was fortunate to inherit from previous commandants the services of Benjamin F. Chandler, who had been civil engineer at the Yard since 1852. Chandler sought to modernize the Yard's physical plant and to erect new buildings. During 1860, Chandler directed his attention to enlarging its area. East of Navy Yard Island, and separated from it by Jenkins Gut, was Seavey's Island. Upon the recommendation of a Navy Board, the Yard made preliminary plans to acquire this 101-acre island. Chandler executed a map of the island that showed the various owners of the thirty-one lots, as well as their boundaries.[17]

That fall another Chandler project, a new powder magazine, was completed, affording storage for 5,000 barrels. He insisted that Orcutt copper lightning rods be installed on the magazine, which, "if exploded[,] would cause immense destruction."[18]

The "LOG BOOK, U.S. NAVY YARD, KITTERY, MAINE" (hereinafter referred to as the "Log") records an important official visit two days before Pearson was about to assume his duties. (The Log, maintained by the Yard clerk, was a daily record kept under various headings: "State of Weather"; "Total number of Mechanics and others employed this day"; "Temperature of the Air" at various times during the day; "High Water" and "Low Water" (the tides); and the all-important "REMARKS." This last entry included the significant events of each day, visits of important people, commissionings, ship arrivals and departures, accidents, and anything else worthy of record. On quiet days, the clerk often left the REMARKS space blank.)

During the Civil War, the Yard's Franklin Shiphouse was the scene of continuous repair work and launchings. Originally built in 1838, the structure was enlarged in 1854 to facilitate the overhaul of the USS Franklin, *ultimately launched a decade later. Known thereafter as the Franklin Shiphouse, this edifice was one of the largest buildings of its kind in the United States, serving the U.S. Navy for almost a century—until an accidental fire leveled it in 1936. PNSVC*

On September 29, 1860, the REMARKS entry reads, "A Committee of Naval Officers consisting of Commodore Stringham, John Lenthall, Chief of the Bureau of Construction, Sam'l Archibald, Engineer in Chief, B.F. Isherwood, Chief Engineer, and B.F. Delano, Naval Constructor, to examine and determine upon the expediency of converting the sailing vessels of the Navy into steamers, visited the Yard." The Navy Bureau heads from Washington stopped at the Yard during an extended tour of the East Coast Navy Yards.[19]

A few days later, one of the commissioners (not identified) issued a public statement:

At Portsmouth—The old (or new) liner *Alabama* was brought under our notice a short time after our arrival at Kittery, Me.,

Built at the Portsmouth Navy Yard in 1843, the 24-gun sloop-of-war USS Portsmouth *sailed from the Yard in 1859 for a three-year tour of duty in the African Squadron, helping to track and seize slavers off Africa's west coast. Called back to American waters in 1861, the* Portsmouth *ably contributed to the Union naval war effort, pursuing blockade runners off the Gulf Coast and participating in the successful 1862 Mississippi River campaign to capture New Orleans. PNSVC*

(adjoining Portsmouth, N.H.) and we left not a crevice of the craft unexamined. She has been 42 years on the stocks, notwithstanding which we concluded to recommend her being worth converting. She will make a splendid steamer of the first class. The *Franklin* also received due attention from us; and we decided in a very short time to "pass" her. The vessel was once before recommended for conversion; and operations were commenced on her, but were never completed. She is the most "likely" to turn out well of any yet overhauled. The *Cumberland, Dale,* and *Macedonian* were considered as fit to be made steamers of. The *Santee,* a frigate never sent to sea yet, caused some discussion; but will never, I presume, be propelled by steam.[20]

These recommendations were incorporated in the "Report of the Secretary of the Navy" for 1860. Isaac Toucey, the incumbent in that post during President James Buchanan's administration, further stated, "I concur in the measure which they propose, as in the event of war no one of these line-of-battle ships, in present state of steam navigation, could go to sea with a reasonable degree of safety."[21]

The USS Portsmouth and the Slave Trade

The need for a steam-powered navy pressed by Isaac Toucey and the United States Navy high command reflected not only military realities but also the shifting priorities of American defense. In 1860, continuing internal strife threatened to collapse the Union, a house divided against itself. The North clashed with the South over the issue of slavery, which had plagued the nation since its inception.

The United States Navy, along with Britain's Royal Navy, had been committed for years to intercepting slave ships, with the Yard supplying and outfitting vessels for the African Squadron of the U.S. Navy. Since the passage of the Act to Prohibit the Importation of Slaves on March 2, 1807, banning the slave trade, the United States had joined Great Britain and other nations in forbidding their citizens from engaging in such traffic. The Act became effective on January 1, 1808. This law, however, was an idealistic scrap of paper with little enforcement value. Many millions of slaves continued to be transported illegally across the Atlantic. From 1842 to 1861, American vessels on patrol off West Africa intercepted only a fraction of this trade, taking twenty-four slavers and freeing 4,945 blacks—roughly one-tenth of the British record of accomplishment during the same time. With no State Department officials in Africa, United States naval officers in the African Squadron, for all practical purposes, assumed and carried out the responsibilities of American foreign policy in that remote area.[22]

On October 4, 1860, the USS *Marion*, fresh from African Squadron duty, docked at the Yard with sensational news. The *Marion* was carrying as prisoners some of the slaver *Erie*'s officers and crew, the *Erie* having been captured by the Portsmouth-built USS *Mohican* off the coast of Africa. Remaining at its duty station, the

Mohican transferred the prisoners to the *Marion* for passage back to the United States and arraignment for trial. At the Yard on October 5, Thomas Nelson, Samuel Sleeper, Thomas Savage, and John McCafferty were taken from the *Marion*'s brig to appear before Commissioner Webster of the Portsmouth court, "charged with voluntarily serving as seamen on board the ship *Erie*, and being engaged in transporting negroes with the intent to enslave them." The four prisoners pleaded not guilty.[23]

Notwithstanding their plea, their crime was evident. The *Erie*, with 897 (987, according to another source) blacks on board, was captured about fifty miles outside the mouth of the Congo River. The captives were freed and landed at Monrovia, Liberia, an independent black nation on Africa's west coast. The *Erie,* now under the control of the *Mohican*'s crew, was sent to New York, where she was libeled, condemned, and sold for $9,596.62.

After describing the particulars of the capture, the *Portsmouth Chronicle* of October 8 continued:

> Twenty-nine of the poor slaves died, principally of fever and dysentery, caused, it is supposed, by Congo water on the passage, and one fell overboard. Rev. John Seys received the negroes on the 23rd of August, and distributed them amongst the inhabitants of Monrovia, who promised to treat them kindly. They were perfectly naked when taken, and were delighted with the disposition made of them. They clapped hands, sung, shouted, and raised a jolly time generally. The officers and men of the *Mohican*, who escorted the negroes to Monrovia, describe their sufferings during the middle passage as positively revolting. They would not undertake similar duties for any consideration.
>
> The *Erie* is a fine sailer, and looks like anything but a slaver.... Her fitting up was most artistic; she had slave coffers [boxlike compartments], a sufficient quantity of water, vinegar in casks, placed fore and aft, to last 900 people sixty days; and an exceedingly large quantity of rice, pork, beef, farina, bread and peanuts, of which a good portion was given to Mr. Seys at Monrovia.
>
> ... The *Erie* was boarded in the Congo River by the British steamer *Spitfire*, previous to receiving slaves. She was only seventeen hours from the slave wharf when the *Mohican*

seized her. No other craft was ever captured on the African coast with so many negroes.[24]

As early as the late 1840s, slave-trade vessels had become sophisticated in evading the African Squadron: "So expeditiously do the fast sailing vessels employed in the slave trade manage their business, that they will run into some inlet, where four hours suffice for them to take in wood, water, and several hundred slaves."[25]

Two of the chief slave depots were Fernando Po, a small Spanish island off the African coast, and St. Paul de Loando, a Portuguese enclave (now Angola) on the African mainland. Henry Eason, a seaman aboard the *Marion*, sketched these two localities in his journal during his African Squadron service from 1858 to 1860. His drawings look innocent enough—harbor scenes with ships offshore, forts on high ground with flags flying from parapets, government buildings, residences, and churches—until one notices, at water's edge, "barracoons" (holding sheds), human warehouses of the nefarious slave trade.[26]

News of the African Squadron was of prime interest for Portsmouth residents, especially any word on the USS *Portsmouth*, which had sailed from the Yard on May 24, 1859, for three years of duty off the African coast. On December 15, 1860, the *Journal* printed a private letter, dated October 10, written from St. Paul de Loando by a sailor aboard the *Portsmouth*:

> . . . We have only lost two men; one died at Porto Praya in May last, and the other, poor fellow, fell overboard at Cape Palma, shortly after leaving Portsmouth....
>
> Flag-ship *Constellation* sailed from this place yesterday, on a cruise down the coast. She took the American bark *Cora* with 705 slaves on board, near the River Congo, on her last cruise. The *Sumpter* and *Mystic* are now at this place. The *Mohican* and *San Jacinto* are now on a cruise for three months. The *San Jacinto* has taken the brig *Storm King* of New York, with 600 slaves oh [on] board, and the *Mohican* captured a bark [*Erie*] with 987 on board, and we (the ship *Portsmouth*) have sent home two brigs and one bark, on suspicion. So you will see that the slave trade is very active here;—and the English have taken three cargoes and sent them to St. Helena. This coast is lined with vessels;—they

Drawn by sailor Henry Eason of the USS Marion, *assigned to the African Squadron from 1858 to 1860, these two sketches depict Fernando Po (above), a Spanish island off the West African coast, and St. Paul de Loando (below), a town in the Portuguese enclave (now Angola) on the African mainland. Under close scrutiny by patrolling American and Royal Navy ships, these two settlements served as major slave depots, with government buildings, forts, residences, churches, and, at water's edge, "barra-coons," or holding sheds, the human warehouses of the slave trade. Judy Beisler Photos. MSM*

come with the pretence of trading for palm oil, and as they have clear[ance] papers from the New York Custom House, we cannot touch them; so the next we hear of them they have taken their slaves, and with a good wind, in a few hours they are out of all danger of the cruisers. Where one is taken with slaves on board, ten get clear. It is not for want of cruising that we have not taken a full one, for we have not been in port a month at a time since we went into commission; and there is not a place in this part of the coast but we have looked at.

We arrived here on the 4th, and sail again to-morrow for a cruise of three months. We are now very busy taking stores on board from the *Relief....*

We all expect to be ordered home early in the coming Spring; if so, we shall probably arrive in the month of July or August. We shall all be glad enough when the day arrives for us to set sail for the States again; for we can see nothing on this dismal coast. Two years is long enough to be here.[27]

The Politics of Panic

When the *Portsmouth* arrived home in September 1860, her officers and men discovered a rising sense of political chaos among the citizens. The Yard, the city, the state of New Hampshire, and the United States at large grappled with steadily deteriorating domestic conditions. The nation was adrift, a ship blown toward rocks in a storm. Commandant George Pearson geared his energies at the Yard to respond to the emergencies the country was facing.

The presidential election of 1860 brought the crisis to a head. On Tuesday, November 6, with the frenzied atmosphere of the threat of Southern secession crackling in the air, American voters elected Abraham Lincoln of Illinois as the sixteenth president of the United States. The South viewed the election results with fear. Lincoln carried Portsmouth handily, gathering 778 votes, a majority of 219 over the other three candidates. There were also scattered ballots. One voter in Ward One caught the distraught spirit of the hour, throwing away the value of his ballot to vote for John Langdon, William Whipple, Josiah Bartlett, Matthew Thornton, and Peirce Long, Revolutionary War-era patriots long since deceased.[28]

Governor Ichabod Goodwin of New Hampshire was reelected to a second term. Born in Maine in 1794, Goodwin rose from lowly origins to prominence in his adopted state of New Hampshire. Moving to Portsmouth as a young man, Goodwin went to sea, starting as a supercargo (ship's business agent) and eventually becoming a ship's

Ichabod Goodwin
Granite Monthly, *May 1880*

master. After twelve years at sea, he combined those responsibilities, as a Portsmouth merchant and ship investor. In time, he became the owner of two ships and part-owner of twenty-three more. Other Goodwin enterprises included banking, whaling, and railroad interests, as well as a pier company. In short, Goodwin knew the business of ships and shipping as well as any man in New England.[29]

Immediately after Lincoln's victory, several New England editors started a campaign to place Goodwin in the president-elect's administration. "Among the names suggested for Lincoln's Cabinet," declared the *Nashua Gazette*, "is that of Gov. Goodwin of New Hampshire for Secretary of the Navy." The *Concord Standard* stated flatly, "Gov. Goodwin is a sound and solid man—a man of good judgment—and would probably be more acceptable to the people at large than any other man yet named." Such a proposal was echoed by the *Salem* (MA) *Gazette*: "We shall think the end of the world is coming—at some time—if an appointment so obviously fit and proper as this should be made. The usage for many years has been to take for Secretary of the Navy a country lawyer, who has not known a ship from a sloop."[30]

The Salem editor was hardly exaggerating. Secretary Isaac

Toucey of the outgoing Buchanan administration had begun his career as a country lawyer in his native Connecticut and owed his cabinet appointment more to his public service as governor, congressman, and senator in his home state than to a maritime background. Moreover, Toucey was known as a sympathizer of the South, and as the secession crisis deepened, he was accused, perhaps unfairly, of "deliberately sending some of the best vessels of the navy to distant seas to prevent their being used against the Confederates." To compound matters in this difficult time of transition, President-elect Lincoln delayed naming Toucey's successor.[31]

The Readying of the USS Macedonian

It was in this nebulous and shifting atmosphere that Captain George Pearson sought to discharge his duties as Yard commandant during the fall and winter of 1860-61. Perhaps his most important charge was to ready and recommission the USS *Macedonian*, a thirty-six-gun frigate, for sea duty and whatever orders she might receive. This old vessel, launched and placed into service back in 1836, had arrived in July 1860 at the Yard where she was originally dismantled and decommissioned ("put in ordinary").

But the Navy Department changed its mind about the veteran of the seas. Captain George Magruder, chief of the Bureau of Ordnance and Hydrography, wrote to Pearson from Washington in mid-November: "The Department having directed that the Sloop of war *Macedonian* be prepared immediately for service in the Home [eastern Atlantic coast off the United States] Squadron, you will please supply her with the requisite Ordnance equipments and store, & Nautical Instruments, Charts and Library Books. The Charts will be forwarded to you from the U.S. Naval Observatory."[32]

In early December, Pearson received Magruder's circular letter regarding ships' libraries and a printed "TABLE OF ALLOWANCE OF BOOKS for Libraries of Vessels of War and Navy Yards," containing a list of more than fifty books, including the Bible, the United States Constitution, naval laws and tactics, dictionaries, an atlas, various naval technical manuals, and even Washington Irving's *Life of Washington*.[33]

Other Navy Bureau chiefs also sent orders: "You will please direct," wrote Horatio Bridge, chief of the Bureau of Provisions and Clothing, "that requisitions for the stores furnished by this Bureau for the *Macedonian* be made upon the Commandant of the Boston Yard as follows, viz: Provisions for five months. Clothing, the usual quantity of each article...."[34]

Much of the correspondence exchanged between Magruder and Pearson concerned small arms, including "eighty Sharps Rifles and 5000 ball cartridges," as well as "the cartridges and percussion caps for revolvers which Col. [Samuel] Colt was requested to send to the yard for the *Macedonian*." Regarding space requirements, Pearson explained, "In these old ships there is a want of room in the shell rooms & magazines, for all that the Ordnance department requires; and yet there is no room to be spared anywhere else without contracting the store rooms already authorized." Pearson suggested, perhaps facetiously, that "the first exercise at target practice would create all the room required" to relieve the cramped space in the ship's magazine.[35]

Upon receiving the rifles, Pearson was dissatisfied: "I regard the thirty two Rifles of the old pattern ... all of which will go off only half cocked, as unsafe. But shall of course, unless otherwise instructed by the Bureau, put them on board the ship." Magruder relented: "You are authorized to supply the *Macedonian* with Rifle Muskets in place of the 32 Sharps Rifles reported unsafe. Please have these Rifles put in serviceable order for issue to some other vessel when required."[36]

Before the *Macedonian* could go to sea, Pearson waited for the ship's complement of 300 men to be sent from the Boston Navy Yard, with arrival on Christmas Day. On December 26, Pearson informed Captain William L. Hudson, commandant of the Boston Yard:

> That portion of the crew of the *Macedonian* which arrived at the Kittery depot yesterday were in such a state of intoxication that it was very difficult to keep them under control. It appears that a number of the men were drunk before leaving Boston & many of them deserted the [passenger] cars at the several stopping places between Boston & Portsmouth....
>
> The number of men on board the *Macedonian* today is twenty six short of the number sent.[37]

The next day the *Portsmouth Chronicle* picked up the story:

> Orders have been received at our Navy Yard to prepare the sloop-of-war *Macedonian* for sea, and as she is about ready,

will sail immediately under sealed orders. Three hundred sailors arrived at the Yard on Tuesday; a hard looking, jolly crew, requiring the officers considerable trouble in managing them. Notwithstanding all their exertions, however, about fifty of them managed to elude the vigilance of their keepers, and escaped after the cars had been stopped, by jumping out of the car windows, the doors being locked. Several of them have since been recovered.[38]

As Pearson struggled to ready the *Macedonian* for sea, national events did not allow any delay. On December 20, only five days before the drunken deserters fled the railroad cars, by unanimous vote in its state legislature, South Carolina elected to secede from the Union. Within six weeks, six other states of the Lower South followed suit. While Lincoln waited helplessly to assume office on March 4, President Buchanan proved weak and ineffectual during the interregnum crisis.

If Buchanan was plagued with indecisiveness, Secretary of the Navy Toucey followed the example of his commander-in-chief in the administration of his department. Toucey meekly accepted the resignation of United States naval officers from the seceded states, many of whom then switched their allegiance to the Confederacy, already taking shape. By the time of Lincoln's inauguration, sixty-eight naval officers had resigned; eventually the figure would be more than a hundred. While Toucey's policy reflected complete capitulation, many Unionists held that such officers had simply broken their oaths and deserted their country in time of need and should face at least dismissal from the service, if not arrest and court-martial.[39]

Pearson must have wondered who in the Union navy could be trusted when even Captain George Magruder, chief of the Bureau of Ordnance and a Virginian, submitted his resignation, along with those of all his clerks. Magruder wanted it both ways, asking that his resignation be accepted on the ground he would remain neutral. His appeal was later rejected during the Lincoln administration, and Magruder was dismissed.

At the Yard, Commander John S. Missroon, a South Carolina native, stood firm and did not resign. "I feel isolated here [Portsmouth Navy Yard]," he wrote. "It would be easy just now to be made a hero at home by resigning one's commission—a hero of a week's duration—but I have no such ambition."[40]

While Missroon remained, Pearson was still short twenty-six men for the *Macedonian* as late as January 7. (Whether the complement was ever filled apparently was not recorded.) On January 12, she was hauled alongside a wharf, and a quantity of powder and shot was put on board. "Charleston [South Carolina, the seat of the secessionist movement] is her supposed destination," reported the *Chronicle*, "although it is a matter of speculation. She might do good service at the above named place, though would be better if she was a steam craft."[41]

The *Macedonian* finally sailed on Sunday, January 14, 1861, headed not for Charleston (where Fort Sumter was under siege in that harbor), but rather for Pensacola, Florida, to help defend Fort Pickens. One of the few Union forts still holding out in the Lower South, Fort Pickens was considered to be the key to the Gulf of Mexico. Although the Florida and Alabama state militias had seized the Pensacola Navy Yard, Union troops escaped across the bay to Santa Rosa Island and Fort Pickens. This fort, which controlled Pensacola Harbor, remained in Northern hands for the rest of the war, thanks in part to the arrival of the *Macedonian*.[42]

The Marcy Brothers, Builders and Shippers

The growing crisis of 1860 affected not only career United States naval officers but also the citizens these officers had sworn to protect. The American merchant marine was exposed to disaster. For a community such as Portsmouth, whose economy was geared to the sea, an outbreak of war would mean total disruption: cancellation of shipbuilding and shipping contracts, establishment of new shipping lanes to avoid capture on the high seas, and major losses—in financial matters, vessels, cargoes, and captains and crews. When the Civil War finally broke out, the Portsmouth-born Marcy brothers, Peter and Daniel, were divided by the national schism of brother against brother on the high seas.

Peter, the elder of the two, was born in 1806. Apprenticed to a local carpenter in his youth, he left his native town in the fall of 1828, bound for New Orleans as ship's carpenter aboard the *William Badger*. Establishing his home in New Orleans, Peter Marcy built the first dry dock in that city. In time, he became a partner with two other men whose firm specialized in dry docks. With Daniel, whom he saw on his visits back to Portsmouth, he invested in Piscataqua shipping.

Daniel Marcy (1809-93), wealthy Portsmouth shipowner and wartime Democratic "Copperhead" congressman, suffered severe financial, political, and family losses during the war. PA

After acquiring considerable wealth, he entered public life, serving sixteen years in the Louisiana legislature. Peter Marcy became part of the elite of New Orleans business and social circles, living at his plantation, "Waverley," across the Mississippi River from the city itself.[43]

Daniel Marcy, born in Portsmouth in 1809, managed to achieve a similar station in life. Upon the death of his father when Daniel was twelve years old, the youth went to work on a Portsmouth-area farm but soon opted for a seafaring career. He learned his profession well, climbing through the ranks from common seaman, ship captain, and investor to shipowner and shipbuilder. By 1860, with his brother and other partners, Daniel Marcy owned seventeen vessels. With William Pettigrew, he built three ships. Seeking political office, he served in both the New Hampshire legislature and the state senate. Known throughout the Piscataqua area, even to children, as "Honest Captain Daniel," Marcy lived in a mansion on Pleasant Street in Portsmouth as "one of its foremost and best-loved citizens."[44]

What the Marcys read and heard about shipping became increasingly disturbing. In mid-November, rumors were current in the North that the Port of Charleston, South Carolina, was closed. To dispel such talk, Collector William Ferguson Colcock issued a statement: "It is reported that clearances are refused at this office. Contradict it.—The business of the office goes on as usual." After South Carolina seceded, however, the rumor became fact. Charleston papers by late December 1860 were publishing proceedings of Congress and dispatches from the North under the heading of "Foreign News."

Stories about commercial sea travel grew ugly. On September 29, 1860, the *Journal* reported that a Portsmouth gentleman

> was a passenger on board a steamer from New York for Charleston, S.C. On the way, he heard a lady passenger speak openly in the cabin in condemnation of Slavery. A gentleman cautioned her to beware of what she said. A day or two after, the boat arrived in Charleston, and as soon as it touched the wharf, the vigilance committee came on board—went directly to the lady before communicating with any passenger—and forbid her landing. In vain she pleaded her wish to see her Southern relatives—and the next boat found her homeward bound. Our surprised informant afterwards was told, that a telegraphic dispatch had informed the committee of the lady's departure from New York. Such is the surveillance, and such the oppression of the South. Should a single case of this kind occur in New England, should a Southern planter, or Mr. [William L.] Yancey [outspoken Alabama secessionist] or his lady be forbidden to land on the shores of the Piscataqua, the whole South would burst with indignation.[45]

During the last months of peace in late 1860, the Marcys received a devastating blow—not from sectional strife but from nature itself. The *Georgianna*, one of the newest Marcy-built ships, had sailed under the command of Captain James H. Salter in the fall of 1860 from New Orleans, bound for Liverpool. As Daniel Marcy learned in December from Salter's letter sent from Queenstown [now Cóbh], Ireland:

> It is with very painful feeling I have to communicate the total loss of the Ship *Georgianna* in Lat 37.50 Lon 66.40, having

been struck by lightning on the morning of the 20th of November and burnt to the water's edge.

We were picked up by the *Levi Woodbury*. Yesterday spoke the Cork pilot boat, the wind being to the eastward and every appearance of it holding on, with strong westerly current, I made a bargain to take some of us to Cork & to relieve Capt. Young as water & provisions were getting scarce. I have hastily written these few lines only in time for the mail which leaves in an hour.[46]

The survivors related a harrowing tale. The *Georgianna* burned so rapidly that Captain Salter and his crew salvaged very little when forced to take to their boats. They were out all night until their rescue by the *Levi Woodbury*, ironically and providentially another Marcy-built and -owned ship.

This unfortunate whim of nature produced a financial disaster. The *Georgianna*'s cargo consisted of 3,470 bales of cotton and 3,000 staves, the whole valued at $210,000. The ship was valued at an additional $50,000. Having insured the vessel and freight to the amount of $64,000, the Marcys and their partners incurred, owing to insufficient coverage, a loss of $196,000.[47]

As reported in the "MARINE JOURNAL" column, the last great day in Port of Portsmouth shipping occurred in late December 1860, the decade ending with a final spurt. Some twenty-eight Portsmouth ships were at sea or in foreign ports. A sampling of this list indicates the magnitude of this far-flung global empire: the ship *Gulf Ranger* had arrived in Indianola, Texas, the *Sierra Nevada* was en route to San Francisco; the *Frank Pierce* was off Liverpool; the *Charles Hill* had arrived in New York from Calcutta; the *J Montgomery* had cleared New Orleans for Le Havre, France; the *Annie Sise* had arrived at Liverpool from Mobile, Alabama; the *Criterion* had sailed from Melbourne, Australia, for Callao, Peru; the *John Henry* was sailing from Bordeaux, France, bound for Cadiz, Spain; the *Winged Racer* was en route from Foochow, China, for New York; the *Typhoon* had arrived at Singapore from Hong Kong; the *Midnight* had arrived at Adelaide, Australia; the *Sonora* had sailed from Sydney, Australia, for Calcutta, and so on. The captains and crews, the Portsmouth builders, investors, and suppliers, as well as the town's general populace, did not realize it then, but another such day would never dawn again. Future events would forever doom the global extent and volume of Portsmouth shipping.[48]

The year of 1860 thus ended with the catastrophe of the *Georgianna*, the Portsmouth Navy Yard hastily preparing the *Macedonian* for sea, and the United States itself drifting without a set course. A *Boston Courier* correspondent effectively summed up the economic factors underlying the shipbuilding industry in the decade of the 1850s: its early growth, the middle stable years, and its decline toward the end. The growth, he asserted, was created by (1) immigration in great numbers from Europe; (2) the discovery of gold in California and in Australia; (3) the Crimean War; and (4) the demand for guano. By the close of 1860, the gold rushes were winding down and the Crimean War had ended. An outbreak of war would diminish the demand and traffic relating to the other two factors.[49]

As the New Year began, an entry in the Portsmouth Navy Yard Log for January 4, 1861, reflected the somber mood of the times: "This day being set apart by the President of the United States [James Buchanan] as a day of fasting, humiliation, and prayer, no labor was performed at the Yard."[50]

MARINE JOURNAL.

FRIDAY, Dec. 21.
Arr sch Olive Branch, Bartlett, Pembroke.
Coal to E. F. Sise & Co.

SATURDAY, Dec. 22.
Arr sch Ploughboy, Donnell, Lanesville.

Ship Gulf Ranger, Smith, hence, arr Indianola prev to 8th.

Ship Sierra Nevada, Foster, fm New York for San Francisco, spoken Nov 22, lot 8 N, lon 29.

Ship Ida Raynes, Jennings, cld New Orleans 15th for New York.

Ship Mary Washington, Chapman, arr Charleston 16th fm Philadelphia.

Ship Noonday, Henry, arr Baltimore 18th fm Callao, via Hampton Roads.

Ship Frank Pierce, Brooks, off Liverpool Dec 5 fm New Orleans.

Ship Manchester, Trask, ent for ldg at Liverpool 6th for New York.

Sch Lizzie M Stewart, Stewart, cld Boston 22d for this port.

Ship Chas Hill, Small, arr New York 22d fm Calcutta.

Ship Margaret, Arm, arr Savannah 16th from Portsmouth.

Ship J Montgomery, Hamilton, cld New Orleans 17th for Havre.

Ship Annie Sise, Sullivan, arr Liverpool 11th fm Mobile.

Ship Athens, Shields, ent for ldg at Liverpool 11th for New Orleans.

Ship Shooting Star, Hotchkiss, ent for ldg at Liverpool 12th for Boston.

Ship Belle Wood, Bush, ent for ldg at Liverpool 12th for New York, and sailed 15th.

Ship Guiding Star, Hall, arr Melbourne Oct 19 fm Boston

Ship Criterion, Harding, sld fm Melbourne Oct 18 for Callao.

Ship Benj Adams, Chase, arr Liverpool 14th fm New York.

Ship Webster, Lawrence, arr Liverpool 10th fm New York.

Ship Dashaway, Hill, arr London 16th fm New York.

Ship John Henry, Carver, sld fm Bordeaux 3d for Cadiz.

Ship Winged Racer, Trundy, fm Foochow for New York, passed Angier Oct 15.

Ship Typhoon, Salter, arr Singapore Oct 25 fm Hong Kong.

Ship Midnight, Brock, arr Adelaide, N Z, Sept 4 fm Melbourne, and sld Oct 11 for Calcutta

Ship Sonora, Board, sld Sydney, N S W, Sept 25 for Calcutta.

Ship Granite State, Weeks, sld fm Saugor Oct 21 for New York.

Bark Sea Duck, Stanwood, cld New York 24th for Falmouth.

Sch W Freeman, Freeman, arr Boston 25th fm Isugles.

Steel engraving of Vice Admiral David G. Farragut (circa 1863) reveals the wartime demeanor of the officer that President Lincoln considered (according to Gideon Welles's diary) to be his best appointment in either branch, Army or Navy. In a speech before cheering Portsmouth Navy Yard workers in July 1865, Farragut praised the Yard's war effort. PNSVC

II 1861: The Yard and the Port Spring into Action

Ominous News from the South

JANUARY OF 1861 found the United States still at peace. Despite rumors of war, the average Portsmouth mariner, Navy Yard officer, enlisted man, and worker did not believe that hostilities would ever break out to wrench the Union apart. Yet by the end of the year, the Portsmouth waterfront bristled with activity related to fighting a war on every ocean.

In mid-January, the Yard was literally frozen. When the air temperature was deemed so cold that outside work would risk frozen fingers and faces, the Yard hoisted a ball (apparently on top of a building) to signal crews that no labor would be performed that day. On Saturday, January 12, the Yard's Log reads, "It being 'Ball Day'—but few of the Mechanics &C mustered, and only those who worked in Lofts where fires are kept."[1]

As the winter cold brought the Yard to a standstill, news from the South became hotter with each passing day. William Ferguson Colcock, collector of the Port of Charleston, issued papers and clearances in the name of South Carolina that rendered every vessel subject to seizure. The North considered such action "entirely illegal," since such a policy violated the federal revenue laws. A foreboding letter, dated December 17 from a man in Charleston to his brother in Boston, found its way into the *Journal* by mid-January 1861:

I never thought I should witness such times. We are in the midst of a revolution. Every man is enrolled—all kinds of business at a stand[still]—no shipping in port—all Northern communication cut off—Custom House officers resigned their office—no cotton coming in. There are twelve hundred drays in the city—not ten of a day get one load. All the banks stopped—our State notes out of the State not worth one cent. We are in a state of starvation—no meat to be got.

I am in hopes the abolitionists of the North will be paid in their own coin. There will be no compromise—it is out of the question. The Lincoln party will commence as soon as he takes his chair, and we are all prepared for him. It is impossible for him to put us down—ten years' war can't do it.... All the Boston steamers have stopped; the New York steamers all stopped.[2]

Two months later, navigational aids along the southern coast were being systematically destroyed, one by one, to the dismay of Northern ship captains and United States naval officers. The lights on the Pensacola Bar on the Florida coast were turned off on March 8. Four days later, the lights at Mobile Point and Sand Island at the entrance of that Alabama port were extinguished by the Confederate commander at Fort Morgan. In early September, the Confederates blew up the lighthouses at Jupiter Inlet and Cape Florida.[3]

Such Confederate actions quickly precipitated the inevitable: cargo rates soared, those to Europe doubling, thus producing great profits for those shipowners willing to risk their vessels on the sea. Relating the saga of the Maine ship *William Singer*, which had arrived in New Orleans in November 1860, the February 9, 1861, *Journal* recounted:

No broker in New Orleans would procure a freight for her, no factor or planter would ship a bale of cotton in her, and no office in New Orleans would insure a dollar on her cargo. The owner was not frightened, but sent word to the captain to haul her up and wait for more peaceful times. A few days ago, after every ship in port was taken up, her captain put her into the market, and obtained a full cargo of cotton for Liverpool, at the highest rate which has ever been paid at any time since the cotton trade became a regular business.[4]

The USS Dale *Sinks and Survives*

As the United States slid closer to chaos with every passing day, the *Chronicle* on January 28, 1861, published "Munitions of War at the Navy Yard." This document, probably released by naval authorities, listed the Yard's vessels and munitions of war that, in its words, "may be made available, should the occasion require."

The five ships at the Portsmouth station were listed:

> Steam Frigate *Franklin*—Now on the stocks, about 4000 tons, and pierced for about 90 guns. Could not be put in readiness for sea in less than a year. Engines not yet built, and no appropriations made for them.
> *Alabama*—74 [guns]. On the stocks; commenced in 1819. This ship will probably never be launched in her present condition....
> Frigate *Santee*—44 [guns]. In good condition to receive an armament. Could be fitted for sea in two months. This ship was commenced in 1821. In President Pierce's administration [1853-57] she was greatly improved by being lengthened out at each end, and otherwise modernized, and would prove an efficient vessel.
> Sloops of War *Marion* and *Dale*—Each of these vessels are third class sloops, in ordinary [decommissioned]. Both of them have been attached two years to the African Squadron, and are not probably in a safe condition for service.

With regard to naval preparedness, the report concluded, "The *Santee* ... is the only vessel at this station that could be readily prepared for active service."[5]

The quantities and kinds of ordnance, arms, and ammunition detailed in the report seemed to indicate that the Yard could have successfully defended itself against a potential attack. A gun park, to which Civil Engineer Benjamin F. Chandler had devoted considerable time, had been recently completed with "Shot Beds," with a total of 351 guns and carronades. The armory was stocked with carbines, muskets, Sharps' rifles, pistols, and revolvers. Powder and shot, some 65,000 pounds, were stored in the magazine. In a letter to Commandant Pearson, however, Chandler was still thinking in terms of a peacetime budget, referring to "a surplus balance," "expenditure

Built in the 1840s and sited near the Back Channel, safely away from major buildings, the Magazine House (Building 31) was used to store explosives during the Civil War era. When a warship carrying live ammunition arrived at the Yard, the explosives were unloaded immediately as a precaution against shipboard accidents until the vessel was ready for departure. PNSVC

[which] will not embarrass any work now authorized," and "mechanics [that] can be obtained at reduced rates."[6]

To prepare for any emergency, Pearson instructed Commander John Missroon, the loyal South Carolinian and executive officer, to inspect the Yard's equipment and facilities. On February 4, Missroon reported back: "I have examined the Fire Engines[,] Hoses[,] and all the Apparatus belonging to the Fire Department of the Yard[,] including the Fire Buckets &c. and find them in serviceable condition...."[7]

This inspection was most timely. Less than a week later, on February 7, at 9:45 A.M., the USS *Dale* began sinking at her moorings at the Navy Yard wharf. The next day, Pearson reported to Secretary of the Navy Toucey in Washington:

The *Dale* was found to be leaking fast, and I therefore hauled her into shoal water and got the pumps & two fire engines with buckets to work as soon as practicable. The leak increased as she settled below her late line of flotation, and at 6:30 P.M. we had gained only 8 1/2 inches, when the weather became so excessively cold, that the men were unable to continue work in a situation so exposed. The thermometer this morning is at 20° below zero.

My impression is that the ice & snow may have depressed her an inch or two below her usual line of flotation she being an old condemned ship.

By February 14, Pearson reported on the salvage of the *Dale:* "Having cleared her of water and removed her to her old position, I am now caulking the seams immediately above her present water-line."[8]

The local press made much of the incident. The *Chronicle* observed that the ship had been raised "by means of placing empty casks under her.... The *Dale* has once been razeed [the cutting away of the upper deck of a wooden ship]; and when examined, recently, it was recommended that $50,000 be appropriated to repair and improve her." Countering rumors of sabotage, the *Journal* asserted that no holes had been bored through the hull, but that "some of the upper planks were removed, and when replaced, of course would not be water-tight, without caulking." Leakage through these two new seams and two years' exposure to the elements, it was believed, had caused the sinking. The *Chronicle* dismissed the notion of any plot to scuttle the *Dale* "so that she could not proceed to Pensacola!"[9]

A few days later, on February 14, Pearson advised John Lenthall, chief of the Bureau of Construction and Repair, in Washington: "As the *Dale* is a condemned ship, very much in the way, and the keeping of her is necessarily attended with more or less expense, I would respectfully suggest whether it would not be advisable to break her up or dispose of her by sale."[10]

In less troubled times, Pearson's evaluation would have been perfectly valid. But in the spring of 1861, the United States Navy sought to press into service virtually every available vessel afloat, regardless of condition.

On April 20, work crews began to repair the *Dale* in dry dock. They were still at it on Sunday, May 5, "on account of pressure of labor," thus inaugurating the practice at the Yard of a Sunday work shift, a custom that continued through the rest of the war. Soon the *Dale* emerged, in the words of the *Chronicle*, as "one of the best vessels of her class in the Navy." She was outfitted with sixteen guns and was furnished as well with spiritual ammunition in the form of twenty-five Bibles and fifty pocket Testaments from the American Bible Society of New York, courtesy of the Reverend Nicholas Medbury, Portsmouth City Missionary. Recommissioned on June 30, the *Dale* sailed seventeen days later to join the South Atlantic Squadron.[11]

The Specter of Jefferson Davis

The crisis that had gripped the nation for months created tension and fear among the citizens of Portsmouth that proved difficult to dispel. Wild rumors abounded, even to the extent that Confederate forces might destroy the Yard. Who was loyal to the Union? Who was a secret Confederate sympathizer? Commandant Pearson had to address the loyalty issue before building or repairing a single vessel.

On March 28, New Hampshire Governor Ichabod Goodwin issued "A Proclamation for a Day of Public Fasting and Prayer" for Thursday, April 11, asking "the people to assemble on that day, in their respective places of public worship, for the purpose of offering to Almighty God their humble supplications." Goodwin fully recognized the stakes involved: "Never in our national history has there been greater occasion for humility, penitence and prayer."[12]

But the prayers did not work. On March 3, as President-elect Lincoln prepared to take office the following day, he offered the post of Secretary of the Navy not to Goodwin, but rather to Gideon Welles of Connecticut, as New England's contribution to the cabinet. Welles accepted, bringing to his post a background in journalism and political appointments from previous administrations. Welles was sworn in on March 5. From the outset, he supported Lincoln's determination to relieve Fort Sumter, the island fortress off Charleston, South Carolina. As days passed, both sides stiffened their resolve: the North to retain control of the fort, the South to reduce and capture it.[13]

The uneasy standoff over Fort Sumter inadvertently affected the voyage of the schooner *Rhoda H. Shannon* of the Port of Boston, en route with a cargo of ice to Savannah. On April 3, the *Shannon*, encountering bad weather, was forced to beat toward Charleston Harbor to ride out the storm, only to be fired on from batteries on

Gideon Welles, secretary of the navy from 1861 to 1869, performed the herculean task of transforming the tiny Union navy of 1861 into a superb naval force approaching that of Great Britain by 1865. Welles personally inspected the Portsmouth Navy Yard in 1863. NHC

Morris Island. The captain of the *Shannon* managed to anchor near a bar to escape the brunt of the storm, and then seized the first opportunity to head for open sea rather than face "the land pirates" again.[14]

The entire entry in the Yard Log for Thursday, April 11, 1861, states: "'Fast Day' in Maine and New Hampshire. No Labor performed on the Yard." The citizens of Portsmouth quietly observed the spirit of Governor Goodwin's proclamation. "The weather was splendid," observed the *Chronicle*. "Meetings were held in the North and Middle Street churches.... A large club of base-ball players amused themselves at playing ball on Pierce's [Peirce's] Island, in the afternoon, and a cricket club were [sic] enjoying themselves on the large playground at the Plains." The next day, a total of 80 "Mechanics and others" reported to work at the Yard.[15]

That same morning, Confederate batteries, including those that had fired upon the *Shannon* only nine days earlier, shelled Fort

Sumter, resulting in its surrender thirty-four hours later.

The shelling of Fort Sumter signaled the beginning of the Civil War. The date of this pivotal, cataclysmic event, April 12, 1861, marks a momentous day in American history. Many historians have called the war the "Second American Revolution." From that fateful April day onward, the United States was forever changed socially, militarily, politically, constitutionally, and in virtually every other aspect. The conflict affected every American, every community, every ship, and every Navy Yard.

Portsmouth reacted at once to the emergency created by the Fort Sumter crisis. Commandant Pearson immediately sought to secure the Yard. On April 18, he wrote to the Bureau of Yards and Docks in Washington:

> In view of the present state of affairs and the unprotected condition of this Yard, I would respectfully suggest that a battery of 8 inch guns be placed upon Seavey's Island and one hundred men shipped or otherwise employed to be exercised at them daily, to be in readiness day & night.
>
> I mention this as a precautionary measure, not that I have the least reason for supporting an immediate attack.[16]

Pearson's optimism was not shared by the local populace. Wild stories were rampant. "When the last train reached Durham [a village ten miles inland] Tuesday evening [April 23]," a *Chronicle* reporter wrote, "it was at once surrounded by an alarmed and excited crowd, who supposed that Portsmouth had been alarmed by the rebels, and that they were rapidly marching upon Durham. They were quieted by the passengers, who assured them that so far as they knew, Portsmouth was safe, and they had heard no news of any invaders being on our coast." Another *Chronicle* article on April 29 reflected such fear: "A heavy firing was heard in the direction of Portsmouth.... The rumor that the Charleston Floating Battery had come down and was attacking the Navy Yard and Fort, which was current in some of the adjacent towns[,] has not been confirmed."[17]

Rumors continued, among them the story that Confederate President Jefferson Davis had been a spy lurking around Portsmouth only a year earlier. The local press explained: "JEFFERSON DAVIS, the President of the Traitors, visited Portsmouth last year, made no disclosure of his name, but was recognized by one who had a previous

JEFFERSON DAVIS A SPY IN PORTSMOUTH.

We have heard from a source which leaves no doubt, that JEFFERSON DAVIS, the President of the Traitors, visited Portsmouth last year, made no disclosure of his name, but was recognized by one who had a previous acquaintance with him. He visited our Navy Yard, Forts, &c. and was industrious in taking minutes of what he saw, and heard from those who exhibited to him the public works in this vicinity. There is little doubt that the dissolution was then in his mind, and we are called upon to exercise a greater vigilance from the circumstances of that secret visit.

PJ, April 27, 1861

acquaintance with him. He visited our Navy Yard, Ports, &c. and was industrious in taking minutes of what he saw, and heard from [those] who exhibited to him the public works in this vicinity." In May 1861, a guard at Fort Constitution, at the entrance of Portsmouth Harbor, further elaborated: "The notorious Jeff. Davis visited the fort last summer, and took accurate drawings of it, together with the harbor, Navy Yard lights, and surroundings. He was also very intimate with the best pilot of the harbor during his stay here.... About two weeks ago the pilot mysteriously disappeared, and many fear he has gone out to repay Jeff.'s visit."[18]

Such imagination concerning Davis's spying around Portsmouth has no historical basis. To combat such dark musings, the *Chronicle* on June 4 printed the story of a member of the New Hampshire Seventh Regiment. The soldier related an anecdote about General Winfield Scott, the aging Union army commander-in-chief. When asked what he intended to do with Davis, Scott merely put up his open hand and gradually closed his fingers, until his fist clenched.[19]

With Jefferson Davis hundreds of miles away at the Confederate capital of Montgomery, Alabama (moved to Richmond, Virginia, on May 29), Pearson was more immediately concerned with loyalty to the Union within the Navy Yard itself. Virgil D. Parris, the naval storekeeper, was an avowed Southern sympathizer. A Democrat, Parris was no ordinary naval storekeeper, having had a long career in public life, including two terms in Congress and a stint as Maine's acting governor. The previous October, Parris purportedly had written a controversial letter that was later published in the *Charleston* (SC) *Mercury*. The letter defamed Hannibal Hamlin of Maine, Lincoln's running-mate on the presidential ticket. Later reprinted in the *Journal* on March 16, 1861, this prejudicial statement had incurred the wrath of many Piscataqua citizens.

On Saturday evening, April 21, a mob gathered outside Parris's Portsmouth home. He was not there, thus evading being tarred and feathered. After fleeing across the river to Kittery to hide in various houses for temporary refuge, Parris left town permanently on April 23 for his native village in central Maine. Making it official, Pearson on the same day notified Welles that he had granted "Storekeeper V.D. Parris [a] leave of absence for seven days." To replace Parris, Pearson appointed Dr. Mark F. Wentworth of Kittery. Although ill at the time, Wentworth vowed to rise from his bed to assume his duties as the new naval storekeeper as well as the captain of the Kittery Artillery.[20]

Pearson reacted officially to dispel the atmosphere of hysteria around the Yard. On May 20, he administered the new Oath of Allegiance to the United States to all commissioned, warrant, and civil officers at the Yard. Two days later, Pearson stood before the Yard's work force, now numbering about 1,100 men. "The clerks, master workmen, mechanics, laborers, marines, and all others not mentioned," states the Yard Log, "had the oath of allegiance to the United States administered to them by Capt. G.F. Pearson, Comdt., and all accepted it with the exception of a blacksmith and a cooper."[21]

A *Chronicle* article, however, vindicates the reputations of the ones who refused. Originally three objected, but one of them, upon reconsidering, took the oath, leaving only two for discharge under the rule. "These three men were by no means traitors, or unfaithful in any way. On the contrary, they were honest, worthy men, and good mechanics.—They are Advent brethren, and deemed the taking of oaths to be a breach of a biblical prohibition."[22]

Perhaps the rule was stretched (evidence is lacking) so that with the scarcity of good mechanics, the two religiously conscientious workmen were allowed to continue their labors for the Union cause.

The Defense of Portsmouth Harbor

If Pearson needed time and patience to organize the Yard, Secretary of the Navy Gideon Welles and New Hampshire Governor Ichabod Goodwin likewise struggled to prepare the navy, its ships, its yards, and its personnel to win the war.

In Washington, Welles had inherited a department rife with red tape and inefficiency. Its full strength in early 1861 numbered seventy-four draftsmen, clerks, and messengers. The pitifully small Union navy at the beginning of the war consisted of forty-two commissioned vessels, twelve of which were assigned to duty with the Home Squadron along the Atlantic coast.[23]

Welles had chosen excellent men to provide advice in naval matters. His most important subordinate proved to be Gustavus Vasa Fox, appointed chief clerk of the Navy Department in early May 1861 and elevated to the post of Assistant Secretary of the Navy, a newly created position, on August 1. "He [Fox] is a man greatly superior to the person under whom he immediately serves," commented the *Boston Transcript*. "Everybody is pleased with the selection of Capt. Fox." He brought to his position an ideal blend of civilian and military experience. A Massachusetts man, Fox had served fifteen years in the navy. After his resignation in 1855, he became a successful businessman, acting manager of the Bay State Woolen Company's mill in Lawrence, Massachusetts.

Fox's association with Portsmouth was long-standing. On October 29, 1855, at St. John's Church, he married Virginia L. Woodbury of Portsmouth, daughter of the late Levi Woodbury. Fox's marriage connected him with a prominent and influential family, for Levi Woodbury had been among New Hampshire's most noted public figures, serving as senator, governor, and Supreme Court justice. Fox frequently visited Portsmouth during the war years, attending to professional matters at the Yard and strengthening ties with his wife's family. Fox was a favorite of President Lincoln's social circle, so Portsmouth ties to the White House were strong during the war.[24]

Governor Goodwin coordinated his efforts with Fox, Welles, and Pearson to bring the state onto a war footing. Although Goodwin's second term as governor was due to expire on June 5, that impending date did not stifle his energies during the spring of 1861 to safeguard New Hampshire's borders and improve military security. Since the state legislature was not in session and would not convene except under special call until June, Goodwin secured $680,000 in loans from banks and citizens to meet the state's military obligations, raising two army regiments to defend the Yard. A flurry of correspondence, telegrams, and requisition orders among Goodwin, Fox, Welles, and Pearson during the spring achieved that objective.[25]

On April 23, Pearson wrote Welles:

> As there are a number of Forts & Breastworks about this harbor which have few if any serviceable guns, and as the security of this Navy Yard, of Portsmouth and Kittery, may depend upon heavy guns in all these forts & breastworks, I ... request authority ... to loan to either or both of those places, such guns on this Yard as would not be needed here or in ships to be fitted for immediate service—taking proper receipts and security for the return of the same.[26]

On April 27, Pearson instructed Lt. Colonel William Dulany of the Yard marine detachment:

> Until further orders, the sentinels on post will be provided with loaded muskets, ball cartridges.... You will also ... inform me of the number of officers & privates of your command, which you could at any moment, day or night, have drawn up ready for immediate action. The sentinels are not to fire upon persons unless they are endeavoring to force their way into the Yard and then only after hailing them three times and giving ample warning to depart.[27]

Such prompt action brought results. By April 29, Pearson notified Welles, "I have loaned the authorities of Kittery, Maine, four long 32 pounder guns and twenty charges of powder & shot, to be mounted at Fort McClary for the preservation of that town and of the Navy Yard in case of any sudden attempt to enter the harbor, which ... was quite unprotected...."[28]

Time was pressing. "As it will delay us very much," Pearson informed Captain William Hudson of the Boston Navy Yard that same day, "to wait the water conveyance for the ordnance stores required of the Boston Yard, you will oblige me by sending all of them, save the powder, shell and shot, by rail as early as possible."[29]

Pearson and Goodwin could not afford the luxury of waiting for approval of all the legal technicalities of effecting the Yard's defense.

As a key part of the ring of forts guarding Portsmouth Harbor and the Navy Yard, Fort Constitution, at the mouth of the Piscataqua River, hummed with heavy construction during the war years. Note the narrow-gauge railway, hand-pump cars, and the guy lines used for raising granite blocks. PA

On April 25, a detachment of twenty-five men under an army captain proceeded to New Castle Island and Fort Constitution (called Camp Constitution in the early stages of the war), the strategic, Gibraltar-like key to the entrance to Portsmouth Harbor first fortified during the 1630s. This unit began to ready the fort for defense—work that was authorized by Governor Goodwin without orders from the War Department. Four days later, 150 men of the "Home Guard" and the Portsmouth Volunteer Corps assembled at Market Square in the center of Portsmouth and marched to Fort Constitution to join the defending force. As part of their daily training, these civilian volunteers were instructed in the operation of the guns.

On May 1, Welles ordered Pearson, "For the purpose of manning Fort Constitution and McCleary [McClary], and erecting a battery on Seavey's Island, you will, upon requisition of the Governor, furnish the necessary guns and munitions." By mid-May, a forty-two-pounder gun was mounted on a circular track in the southwest embrasure at Fort Constitution to join the twenty-four-pounders already in place.[30]

Duty at Fort Constitution quickly followed a printed "Order of the Day": reveille at 5:00 A.M., morning roll at 6:00 A.M., training, drill, work details, three meals, the relief guard at 8:00 P.M., and "Tattoo" at 9:00 P.M., "when the lights are to be extinguished, and quarters kept quiet until morning." Officers "will encourage their men in all reasonable and proper recreation or amusement, while off duty; but will strictly prohibit, and put [a] stop to, smoking, gambling, or other dangerous and vicious practices, in quarters."[31]

To provide the nutritious requirements of their forces, the Union government issued vast quantities of provisions. According to the *Chronicle* on May 18, the troops at Fort Constitution consumed for their daily rations "8 barrels of beef, 3 of pork and hams, 1 of beans, 300 loaves of white bread, and 125 of brown, besides other articles." Three days later, the *Chronicle* printed the weekly "Bill of Fare," which, in addition, included salt fish hash, eggs, rice, molasses, cabbage, greens, potatoes, pickles, butter, cheese, and coffee. At the Yard during 1861, the marines received their rations, with each man granted "a pound and a quarter of fresh beef or three quarters of a pound of pork, and eighteen ounces of bread, *per diem*, with an allowance to each one hundred rations of ten pounds of coffee, fifteen pounds of sugar, eight quarts of beans, four quarts of vinegar, two quarts of salt...." On paper, these diets appeared to be adequate. As the war

CAMP CONSTITUTION,

PORTSMOUTH, MAY 5, 1861.

GENERAL ORDER,
No. 2.

Order of the Day.

THE REVEILLE—will be beat at 6 o'clock, A. M. by the drums of the company on guard, and is the signal for the men to rise, and to put themselves and their equipments and quarters in order for the day.

PEAS-UPON-A-TRENCHER—at 7 o'clock A.M. is the signal for breakfast. Companies will march or send details to the kitchen for rations, in the order of their quarters in the barracks. Those occupying quarters nearest the kitchen, taking precedence in successive order, and those occupying the lower floor taking precedence over those occupying the upper floor. As rations are served out, the companies or detachments will move off with them as rapidly as possible, so as to make room for others. The same order will be observed for all meals. Detachments will be sent by commanders of each company, to return dishes and utensils to the kitchen, immediately after meals.

THE TROOP—will be beat at 8 o'clock A. M. for roll call and for the purpose of assembling the men for duty and inspection at guard mounting. The guard will then be relieved, by detail drawn from such company or companies as the Officer of the day may direct.

Reports are to be presented or sent to Head Quarters at 9 o'clock A. M.

At 9 1-2 o'clock A.M. detachments of Companies without arms will march to different Churches designated to the commanders to attend morning Divine Service,

ROAST BEEF—the signal for dinner, will be beat at 1 o'clock, P.M.

THE ASSEMBLY—at 4 o'clock P. M. The Companies will then be marched, without arms, to the Temple, to attend Special Divine Service.

THE RETREAT—at 7 o'clock P. M. Roll call and Supper.

Relief Guard, by details from companies, at 8 o'clock, P. M.

THE TATTOO—at 9 o'clock P. M.—when the lights are to be extinguished, and quarters kept quiet until morning.

Platoon officers are charged with the duty of immediate supervision of the police of their respective divisions. They will encourage their men in all reasonable and proper recreation or amusement, while off duty; but will strictly prohibit, and put stop to, smoking, gambling, or other dangerous and vicious practices, in quarters.

As the practice of carrying pistols, knives or other small arms while in this camp, is an unnecessary exposure to accident, Captains of companies are hereby directed to collect all such small arms in the possession of their men, and to deposit them for safe keeping in the Arsenal near the camp, until otherwise ordered.

Lieut. THOMAS SNOW is hereby appointed Officer of the Day, and is to be respected and obeyed accordingly.

By command of BRIGADIER GENERAL GEORGE STARK.

O. W. LULL, Aid-de-camp.

NHDRMA, May 6, 1861

progressed, however, bad or poorly prepared food became the chief bane of Northern soldiers and sailors. "The Lord sends meat," went one adage frequently quoted during the conflict, "but the Devil sends cooks." Once when a field chaplain was reciting the Lord's Prayer with the line, "Give us this day our daily bread," a soldier added in a loud voice, "Fresh."[32]

In mid-June, a new flag was raised at Fort Constitution to replace the tattered one first raised by Major Robert Anderson, who had been stationed at the fort in years past. (Anderson had been the heroic Union defender at Fort Sumter during the bombardment two months earlier.) The elevation of the new flag, together with the booming of cannon, brought cheers from the fort's personnel.[33]

At nearby Fort McClary, overlooking Portsmouth Harbor, the Kittery Artillery, hearing the noise, appeared on the parapet and also gave three cheers. Posted at Fort McClary since late April, this unit was composed of about fifty volunteers, some more than eighty years old and none younger than forty-five. One patriot had lost a leg aboard "Old Ironsides," while another also was a veteran of the War of 1812. All the men in the unit had enrolled their names for the Union to form a "Coast Guard" in service to the governor of Maine.

Commandant Pearson authorized on behalf of the "Coast Guard" the donation of as many guns as necessary to fortify the high ground behind Fort McClary. "The Guns are not wanted," Pearson informed Welles, "for any ship or for any purpose in the Yard." Accordingly, on a Saturday in late April, about fifty yoke of oxen, drawing carriages adorned with flags and banners, proceeded to the Yard to pick up four cannon. By Sunday morning, the guns were mounted, in the words of the *Chronicle*, "in a position that can rake the harbor, and from their brazen throats send fire and death to whatever dares approach our harbor with hostile intent." In mid-August, the Kittery Artillery was withdrawn, since most of its members were ship carpenters whose services were greatly needed at the Yard. The unit was replaced by a Biddeford (Maine) company.[34]

Personnel at Forts Constitution and McClary exercised the utmost vigilance. As early as May 2, when a schooner bearing no flag was about to sail past Fort Constitution, a gun crew at the fort fired a warning shot. The schooner at first hesitated, then stopped, hoisted the Stars and Stripes, and sent a boat, as ordered, to the fort to establish her design and purpose. The schooner turned out to be a friendly vessel out of Portland, bringing oil to the Yard.

The steamer *Nelly Baker* of Boston, conveying seamen from that city to the Yard, passed by the fort on two occasions. The first, during early July, occurred at night. With 150 seamen on board, the *Nelly Baker* came within sight of Fort Constitution. "What boat is that?" hailed a sentry at the fort. "*Nelly Baker*," came the response, which to the sentry's ear sounded like "Will ye take 'er?" The sentry ordered the boat to stop or be fired upon.

After a hasty council of war aboard the *Nelly Baker*, a civilian passenger seized a trumpet and, standing near the wheelhouse, bellowed out her name and purpose in distinct tones. The guard responded, "All right—pass *Nelly Baker*," whereupon all concerned breathed more easily.

The next time the *Nelly Baker* steamed by the fort's parapet in early September, her sighting elicited a much more hospitable reception. She passed by en route to the Yard with a draft of 400 men. A discharge of guns from the fort signaled a welcome from the gunners, with cheers and applause from about 200 ladies and gentlemen standing on the parapet, waving handkerchiefs as part of the noisy festivities.[35]

Within the first few weeks of the war, Secretary of the Navy Welles was leery about—but ultimately discounted—wild rumors about the Yard's vulnerability, including a story that an attempt would be made to burn the ship *Franklin* on the stocks. On May 2, responding to Pearson's request for additional men and guns, Welles counseled, "The Department does not apprehend an attack on the Navy Yard at present, if at all, and thinks the carrying out of the measure suggested [providing more men and guns] would involve an unnecessary expense."[36]

Welles's assessment proved sound. The Yard was never attacked during the Civil War, and no enemy vessel ever slipped by—or even attempted to pass under—the guns of Fort Constitution.

Beefing Up the Union Navy

When Fort Sumter was fired upon, the Union navy totaled 7,600 men, a woefully inadequate number to man the ships, Navy Yards, shore stations, and other facilities. Secretary of the Navy Welles struggled to circumvent an 1813 law that specified that "citizens of the United States, or persons of color [blacks] and natives of the United States [Indians]" could legally serve aboard the United States naval vessels only on the basis of a three-year enlistment. A three-year tour of duty was much too long to attract volunteers. Welles realized that this policy had to be changed. He later wrote:

> When it became necessary to enlarge the navy, numerous recruiting rendezvous were opened on the Atlantic coast and on the [Great] lakes for the enlistment of seamen, ordinary seamen, and landsmen. In order to procure the necessary crews at the earliest possible moment, and with a view also to induce those engaged in the fisheries and the coastwise trade to enter the naval service, the term of enlistment was abridged from three years to one year.[37]

Regarding the role of blacks in the navy, Welles was initially hampered by federal policy and tradition, inherited from previous administrations. On December 24, the *Chronicle* caught—although somewhat inaccurately—the spirit of a lingering prejudicial practice:

> In answer to some inquiries about negro sailors in the United States Navy, we state the fact that there used to be more or less of such sailors in the crew of any large ship of war; and they were commonly good sailors. They were found there from the time when our navy was begun, and remained till about five and twenty years ago, when there was *a true* complaint made, that some officers from the South had slaves on board our national ships, as servants, and that the masters drew their pay! This complaint raised a small storm in Congress, which was finally calmed by a *compromise*, so arranged that no negroes should be in our navy! This was a piece of meanness, to thrust out the free sailors, because the bondsman's [slave's] master could not draw pay for his slaves; but so it was.[38]

The slender historical record—documents relating to blacks in the navy before the Civil War are meager—belies this statement, but the section regarding their restricted service is factual. Blacks had served in the navy continuously from the Revolutionary War onward, especially during the War of 1812. From 1839 until the outbreak of the Civil War, however, the Navy Department allowed enlistment of freed blacks (slaves being excluded), restricting the total to no more than five percent of the total number of whites. Such blacks at sea inevitably served as firemen, coal heavers, cooks, and stewards, with no opportunity to advance in grade to chief petty officer and commissioned officer.

The realities of the Civil War immediately changed the generally adhered-to five-percent quota, as the undermanned Union navy eased racial barriers to fill crews. Black refugees flocked to Union lines and ships for the protection of the American flag. As early as July 1861, these refugees (called contrabands) sought haven aboard the USS *Minnesota* and served on gun crews. As the initial trickle swelled to a floodtide of contrabands during the summer, Welles issued a regulation in September to permit ex-slaves to serve in the navy (the Union army did not admit blacks until the latter part of 1862) with a pay allowance of "$10 per month and one ration a day." By the end of the war, blacks composed from—estimates vary—eight to twenty-five percent of naval personnel, some serving aboard Portsmouth-built ships.[39]

In its drive to enlist sufficient recruits, the navy similarly bypassed citizenship requirements to allow foreign immigrants, many of whom knew little or nothing of seamanship, to swarm the ranks. After a month of this open policy, and facing complaints that many newly recruited sailors were inexperienced, Welles was forced to tighten his standards to exclude those of insufficient caliber. Throughout this year of adjustment, Commandant Pearson sought to reconcile Navy Department regulations and directives with everyday realities to attract recruits both for the navy and for the Yard's civilian labor force.

In an initial surge of patriotism after the fall of Fort Sumter, northerners flocked to recruiting stations ("rendezvous," in naval parlance), wrote letters to governors offering their services, and otherwise made themselves available to the Union cause. New Hampshire zeal was strong. In a typical letter to Governor Goodwin, one G.B. Russell, a student at Phillips Exeter Academy, explained:

The Students of Phillips Academy have formed a company for the purpose of drill & perfecting ourselves in the use of fire arms, in view of preparing ourselves for active service in [on] behalf of our country, if necessary. We desire to obtain arms, suitable for drilling, & inquire of you, if such can be obtained from the state, & if so[,] on what conditions.[40]

Phillips Exeter Academy
Apr 27th 1861

To His Excellency Gov. Goodwin
Dear Sir

The Students of Phillips Academy have formed a company for the purpose of drill & perfecting ourselves in the use of fire arms, in view of preparing ourselves for active service in behalf of our Country, if necessary.

We desire to obtain arms, suitable for drilling; & inquire of you, if such can be obtained from this State, & if so on what conditions.

Yours &c.
G.B.Russell.

NHDRMA

During the spring of 1861, the U.S. Navy, the Marine Corps, and the U.S. Army placed recruitment notices in the Portsmouth newspapers. The naval announcement, initially featuring an American flag, switched to an eagle a few days later:

Rendezvous Open at the Navy Yard.
        PORTSMOUTH, N.H.
For ABLE SEAMEN, ORDINARY SEAMEN,
LANDSMEN AND BOYS,
        For the NAVAL SERVICE OF THE UNITED
        STATES—for the term of one year, or three
        years.

Apply to COMMANDER E. PECK
U.S. Navy Recruiting Officer.

If the prospect of seasickness appeared disconcerting, one could join the Marine Corps:

Wanted—for the Marine Corps
    50 Healthy, able-bodied young Americans,
between the ages of 21 and 35, to whom
will be given the best of Rations, Clothing, and
medical attention.
    Pay, $11 per month. Term of enlistment, 4
years, unless sooner discharged. None taken under 5 feet 5 inches in height.
    Apply between the hours of 8 A.M. and 3 P.M.
    at the Marine Barracks, Navy Yard, Port[s]mouth,
N.H.   WM DULANY
        Bet. Lt. Col. U.S.M.C.
        Comm'dg Post.

Those who preferred army duty could respond to this notice:

Troops Wanted Immediately
TO GARRISON FORT CONSTITUTION, at the
    mouth of this harbor. Apply to
    JOSIAH G. HADLEY,
    Commanding Officer.[41]

Pearson's ardent commitment to recruiting went beyond public newspaper announcements. Writing to William Hathaway, acting master at Nantucket, Pearson urged:

Should there now be any young Seamen or Ordinary Seamen in Nantucket who are desirous of shipping from the Naval ser-vice for *three* years, unless sooner discharged, you will remain there one week after the receipt of this communication and enlist them—that is to say, all healthy men between the ages of 21 and fifty—none under or over. Landsmen & boys are *not* to be shipped at all. You must ship these men on the following conditions, namely—That when you deliver them on board the

Rendezvous Open at the Navy Yard,
PORTSMOUTH, N. H.,

For ABLE SEAMEN, ORDINARY SEAMEN, LANDSMEN and BOYS,

For the NAVAL SERVICE OF THE UNITED STATES—for the the term of one year, or three years.

Apply to **COMMANDER E. PECK,**

may2   **U. S. Navy Recruiting Officer,**

PC, May 9, 1861

U.S. Recg [Receiving] ship at Charlestown [Massachusetts], they are to pass the rigid examination of the medical officer and if found by him fit for the service, then their shipment holds good, otherwise null and void.

The passages of these men to Boston will be paid by the Navy Agent on my approval of the bill, which you can arrange with the Agent who furnishes the transportation, so that his bill can be paid in this manner and not at the time you convey the men to Boston.

Let me hear from you at once.

The pay of Seamen in the Navy is $18, and of Ordinary Seamen $14, per month.[42]

Notwithstanding his strenuous efforts to recruit, Pearson in July heeded the warning of Secretary Welles:

Be careful not to enlist again the following described parties, who have been discharged in disgrace:

James Sweeny, O.S. [Ordinary Seaman]—Age 28 yrs. Shipped at Warrington, Fla., Sep. 8, 1860—Height 5 ft 5 3/4 in—Gray eyes—Dark hair—Brown complexion—Born in Ireland;

Edwd [Edward] Neill, O.S.—Age 28 yrs.—Shipp[e]d at Warrington, Fla.—Height 5 ft 7 in—Gray eyes—Dark brown hair—Dark complexion—Born in Ireland.[43]

Such instances of dishonor within the navy appear to have been negligible during 1861. Patriotism—officially and unofficially—was the order of the day. To administer the Oath of Allegiance to the crew, Commandant Pearson in October visited the USS *Constellation*, then undergoing light repair at the Yard. On October 8, the *Chronicle* reported:

> The oath was read, and those who declined taking it were told to step to one side, and those who wished to take it hold up their hands. While Capt. Pearson was explaining the oath, and before he had fairly got through, every arm was upstretched, and nine cheers for the Union were given spontaneously by all on board. Three cheers were given for Capt. Pearson. The men would have cheered until he left the ship, had not the first lieutenant stopped them.[44]

George C. Abbott underwent a protracted ordeal to offer his services to the Union navy. Forwarding Abbott's application for the appointment of acting boatswain on November 1 to Secretary Welles, Pearson related unusual circumstances:

> I was not acquainted with an incident, which I believe the Department will be pleased to consider favorably when acting upon his request.
> He [Abbott] was in Texas when she seceded. He left Texas in July, and finally was enabled to reach New Orleans.
> Determined to reach one of our ships, he then took a skiff with two men & pulled toward the *Brooklyn*. When the two men found that Abbott was going to the *Brooklyn*, they refused to pull him there, until he forced them to do so, under the influence of a revolver. When on board, Abbott & the two men were deemed suspicious and put in confinement, but Abbott was known to be a true man by some person in the *Niagara*, and was therefore released.
> He seems to be an excellent man.[45]

William G. Saltonstall, a prominent maritime figure in nearby

Salem, Massachusetts, also discovered that joining the navy involved much red tape. In his "Autobiography and Reminiscences," Saltonstall recalled:

> Tempted by curiosity to see something of it [the war], and quite willing to lend a hand if opportunity offered, I obtained a passage to Fortress Monroe [Virginia] the latter part of May, 1861, in the steamer *Cambridge*, bound there from Boston with troops and munitions of war. Major-General Benjamin F. Butler was then in command of the fortress and district, and ascertaining from a mutual friend that I had had considerable nautical experience in the merchant service, proposed my going to Washington with a letter from him to the Secretary of the Navy, Hon Gideon Welles, asking an appointment in the Navy with permission to serve under his (Butler's) orders, in command of one of two steam vessels he had been sent to purchase, which he proposed arming on their arrival at the fort and using in conjunction with the Army. With an excess of zeal (for I had better have waited to see the vessels before shipping), I at once went to Washington and made my application. The Secretary [Gideon Welles] smiled at the idea of thus amalgamating the two branches of the service, but granted the unusual request by conferring upon me the appointment of "Acting Master in the United States Navy without pay, with permission to serve under Major-General Butler at Fortress Monroe." No pay could be allowed, as, from the nature of the appointment, my name could not well be on the rolls of either an Army or Navy paymaster.
>
> My patriotism far exceeded my cupidity. I accepted this document and returned to my commander, who desired me to select the vessel I preferred of the two which had arrived during my absence, and proceed, with his assistance, of course, to convert her into a gunboat. To my chagrin I soon found myself relieved of the latter responsibility, for one of the vessels was the smallest tug-boat I ever saw, filled up on deck with bitts and houses to an extent which prevented the mounting of the smallest piece of ordnance, and with accommodations only for a captain, engineer, and one deck-hand. The other, a canal boat for the conveyance of fruit and vegetables through some canal, of the lightest possible build, with boiler and engine on deck

and a very small propeller out behind. The discharge of a 24-pounder on deck would have shaken her to pieces, and she had no accommodations whatever. Where these vessels had come from, or by whom bought, I never learned; but there had evidently been a job somewhere. The General, upon examination, agreed with me that they were entirely unsuited for such service as he had proposed, and the object[ive] abandoned. My high hopes and ambitions received a heavy blow, and I was naturally, for the time being, very sorry I had shipped.[46]

A circuitous route in obtaining a naval commission was not uncommon. John F. Tasker, a Manchester, New Hampshire, resident, faced a similar ordeal. Receiving a congressional appointment to the United States Naval Academy at Annapolis, Tasker, as it turned out, was compelled to report elsewhere. Since the academy was in an area subject to Confederate attack, Union officials decided in April to move it to Newport, Rhode Island, for the duration of the war. Upon reporting to Newport in the fall for an examination by the Board of Officers, Tasker received his commission as acting midshipman in the United States Navy.[47]

On December 23, Welles announced the opening of recruiting offices during the year in Portsmouth, Boston, New Bedford, New York, Philadelphia, Baltimore, and Washington. The travel expenses of recruits from their residences to the rendezvous were charged to the government, and each man was furnished with an outfit (clothes and equipment) valued at $31.27. Seamen received three months' pay in advance, with landsmen being allowed two months' advance.[48]

Assistant Secretary of the Navy Gustavus V. Fox strove to enlist every potential recruit. To the editor of the *Boston Journal* in early December, Fox declared:

> Attention has been called to an article in a recent number of your paper stating that there are "between five and six thousand brave, hardy fishermen at the present time out of employment" and that they "are full of patriotism and are willing to bestow all their energies in the service of the country."
>
> No where, it seems to us, can they be so usefully employed as on board our Naval vessels, and we hope they may be induced to enter that branch of Government service. The entire number named will unquestionably be required and we

shall be glad to learn that the Navy can confidently count on a large addition to its force of brave seamen from the source you have indicated. Rendezvous for enlistment are now open in Boston, New Bedford and Portsmouth.[49]

Such recruiting zeal strengthened the Union navy. By the end of 1861, the aggregate number of naval personnel—only 7,600 the previous March—had increased to 22,000.[50]

African Squadron Ships Return to the Yard

Along with increasing the number of Union naval personnel, Secretary Welles in 1861 also needed every available vessel to defend home waters. In late April, he called back ships serving at foreign stations. Only three vessels remained at distant stations, where they were badly needed, and during the course of the war, a few others joined them; these exceptions were primarily in the Mediterranean to protect American merchant vessels from potential attack by Confederate warships. The entire African Squadron was ordered back, something of an irony since the slave trade was among the contributing causes of the war. Portsmouth and other Union government yards awaited the return of these vessels.[51]

Piscataqua citizens eagerly welcomed any scrap of news about or from the African Squadron. As early as February 1861, the *Chronicle* printed a letter from William Fernald Laighton, a local master carpenter aboard the USS *San Jacinto* off the coast of Africa. Writing from St. Paul de Loando (now Angola) on December 16, 1860, Laighton reported, "We found at anchor in Loando harbor, the flag ship *Constellation*, U.S. ship *Portsmouth*, and U.S. steamer *Mohican*. The officers and crews of the squadron are all well."[52]

By fall, all three of these warships returned to the United States, the first two to the Yard and the other to Boston.

Sensational news arrived in June about two Portsmouth vessels: the U.S. frigate *Saratoga* and the slaver *Nightingale*, both built in Portsmouth Harbor. The *Saratoga* was built and commissioned at the Yard in 1843; eight years later, the clipper *Nightingale* was launched up the Piscataqua at the Hanscom boatyard in Eliot. On April 23, 1861, the vessels met, by chance, halfway around the world. "CAPTURE OF A SLAVER," announced the June 18 *Chronicle* headline:

The *Nightingale* was captured April 23, off Kabenda [now Angola] on the Western coast of Africa, by the U.S. sloop-of-war *Saratoga*, having on board 950 negroes. She was taken into Monrovia [Liberia], where the cargo was put on shore. The slave cargo which was landed consisted of 272 men, 97 women, and 340 boys and 92 girls—160 having died on the passage from Kabenda. A prize crew was put on board the vessel, and the ship brought to New York.[53]

The night before the *Nightingale*'s capture, Francis Bowen, her captain, escaped with his cabin servants, leaving three mates in charge of the slaver. These captured men were sent home in the ship and delivered to federal authorities.

While New Hampshire awaited the return of the USS *Portsmouth* during the summer of 1861, the *Chronicle* reported the death of an individual who, in his limited way, symbolized the chaos in which the nation was currently embroiled and underscored the original need for the African Squadron. On July 5, Colonel Shadrach F. Slatter died at Mobile, Alabama. A notorious slave trader, he was the model for Simon Legree in Harriet Beecher Stowe's *Uncle Tom's Cabin*. "He had died in the midst of a war against the Union," editorialized the *Chronicle*, "waged by the 'peculiar institution' [slavery] of which he was a poculiar [*sic*] ornament."[54]

The *Portsmouth* sailed home to bolster the Union in undermining the institution Slatter had personified. On September 24, after a passage of forty-six days from St. Paul de Loando, she arrived at the Lower Harbor and docked the next day at the Navy Yard. Her record was impressive. Having left the Yard on May 23, 1859, for twenty-eight months of African Squadron duty, she had captured three prizes and sailed 50,000 miles by log. During her return voyage, the *Portsmouth* on September 15 boarded the American schooner *Ann Hinks*, eight days from Boston, bound for the Caribbean. Finding no illegal cargo, she released the vessel.[55]

A few weeks after the *Portsmouth* returned, the *Journal* published an informative account, "Two Years on the African Station," evidently written by one of her officers:

The Naval Store-houses are situated at St. Paul de Loanda [*sic*] ..., and at this place the Squadron have [*sic*] been in the habit of touching for the purpose of refitting and obtaining their supplies....

About 400 miles further South, is another little settlement called "Fish Bay," which affords a very good stopping place, and is much resorted to by the men-of-war and whaling ships in order to procure supplies of fresh beef and vegetables, which are always much needed by their crews, especially after several months of feasting on "salt junk," and wormy biscuit. Indeed few places can boast of finer cattle and Irish potatoes, than Fish Bay, or in greater abundance.

... Fernando Po is usually visited at the close of each month, by some vessels of war, of the several nations for the purpose of obtaining their mails, which come out by the way of England, and the arrival of which is always anxiously looked for, as "news from home" of whatever description or however old, is ever a welcome occurrance [sic]. Coal depots are here established by the several Squadrons for supplying the steamers, but the settlement itself affords little else that is required, and is considered very unhealthy.

With respect to the healthiness of the climate, it may be observed that in the rivers and near the coast, where the malaria prevails, fevers, and other diseases are common, and ... in most cases prove fatal to the whites. During the time, however, that the Squadron was on the coast (30 months) the crews of the several vessels enjoyed excellent health, and fewer deaths occurred than is generally the case on Stations having a healthier reputation.

On the 21st of April, 1861, a treaty was made by Commander [John] Colhoun [of the *Portsmouth*] at the native village of Ambuzette [Ambrizette, Angola] with the Queen of that place, and on the 9th of August the welcome cry of "all hands up-anchor for home" resounded through the ship, and we took a final farewell of Africa.[56]

Once home, the officers and men of the *Portsmouth* waged their battle to be paid. After arrival at the Yard, the crew waited for weeks, finally writing a public letter to seek redress:

The citizens of this city must be aware of the arrival of the U.S. ship *Portsmouth*, and the detention of the crew in this city on account of non-payment, as yet, of their wages:—twenty-one days having passed since her arrival. The crew think they have done their duty like men, and see no reason why they should be detained so long from their friends, many of them having no money in order to get home with, their expenses having been large since they have been ashore.[57]

It turned out that no officer had the requisite authority to disburse the money, the paymaster of the ship having become ill in Africa and been sent home earlier. The assistant paymaster claimed he had no power to make disbursements. The question was finally submitted to and resolved by the U.S. Attorney General in Washington, who ordered the men to be paid. Payday at last arrived at 10:30 A.M. on October 23, a month after the *Portsmouth*'s return.[58]

The matter resolved, Commandant Pearson accelerated the repairs schedule to ready the *Portsmouth* for sea, loaded coal, and replenished her "kitchen." After refitting, the *Portsmouth* sailed on December 11. Her new captain was Commander Samuel Swartwout, previously with the New York recruiting rendezvous. Swartwout's orders were to sail to the Gulf of Mexico for duty with the Gulf Blockading Squadron.[59]

On Saturday, September 28, the USS *Constellation*, then the oldest United States warship afloat and flagship of the African Squadron, docked at the Yard. She proudly waved the ensign of Flag Officer William Inman, since the old ship had performed admirably during her two years of duty off the African coast. The *Constellation* had been 406 days at sea and had logged almost 43,000 miles. Under Inman's command, the squadron had captured and sent home thirteen slavers. Some 3,594 slaves were taken from five of the ships and delivered to the agent of the United States at Monrovia, Liberia. The *Constellation*, for her part, had seized the slave brig *Triton* at the mouth of the Congo River on May 21, 1861.

But putting past glory aside, the Navy Department deemed the sixty-four-year-old warship, launched in 1797, too antiquated to continue. On October 1, the *Constellation* went out of commission, and her crew was discharged. After examination, however, the *Constellation* was found to require no major repairs. In a time of need, the *Constellation* received a new lease on her nautical life. She was recommissioned and overhauled, and in February 1862, Navy Secretary Welles authorized a crew from the Boston Rendezvous.[60]

The navy took pains to prevent a repetition of the *Macedonian* escapade of drunken sailors deserting from railroad cars. On February 21, under the supervision of eight acting masters, a draft of 205 men for the *Constellation* arrived by railroad at Portsmouth from the Charlestown Navy Yard. All reported without incident.

Only nature herself seemed to conspire against the *Constellation*. In late February, a severe gale struck northern New England, knocking down chimneys in the Portsmouth Navy Yard. The *Constellation* twice broke her mooring cables, but alert watchmen brought the ship to anchor.

On March 11, the recommissioned *Constellation* sailed, defying the odds against her ever being readied for sea again. Her destination was the Mediterranean, where she would protect American commerce. Her assignment was due in part to a request from a deputation of Boston merchants to Washington to safeguard their interests in that area.[61]

The *Mohican* was the third vessel of the African Squadron slated to report back to the United States. In June 1861, speculation held that the *Mohican* would probably head back to the Yard. She had been built there in 1858, sailing the following year for Africa on her first cruise. A 994-ton screw sloop, she was considered "the fastest vessel in the Navy, next to the *Iroquois*." As it turned out, however, the *Mohican* sailed for Boston, docking on September 27. The vessel and engines proved to be in good condition. After taking on coal and provisions, she left less than a month later to join the South Atlantic Blockading Squadron.[62]

The African Squadron thus passed into history, no longer off the coast of Africa but still fighting slavery in its new role off the Confederate shoreline. The Anglo-American Treaty of 1862 drastically reduced the activity of slavers, giving the Royal Navy authority to stop and search all suspicious ships, including American vessels. Except for isolated incidents, this treaty effectively put the slavers out of business. Between 1859 and 1861, some 170 slavers deposited their cargoes: 117 of these were American, including 74 from New York. During 1862, not a single slaver sailed out of New York. The decision of the Union government to summon the African Squadron home placed the *Portsmouth* and the *Mohican* in position to intercept such slavers as well as Confederate vessels at their port of origin. The blockade had simply shifted from one continent to another.[63]

The Blockade Begins

The primary goal of the Union navy during the Civil War was the implementation of a blockade—a process of strangulation (General Winfield Scott's "Anaconda Plan") that, given sufficient time, would slowly squeeze the economic and military life out of the Confederacy. Ultimately, it was the closing of her ports that starved the South.

The Union high command immediately grasped the critical importance of a blockade, a strategy used against the United States with great effect by the British during the War of 1812. The concept of "freedom of the seas," a traditional United States policy, was temporarily abandoned. The Union pressed into service all U.S. Navy warships, purchased merchant marine vessels—everything from ocean liners to ferryboats—to take up blockade stations or to serve as supply ships, and rushed to completion all warships under construction. The blockade required time for results (1861 was marked by lapses and inefficiency), but it grew stronger with each passing year.

President Lincoln wasted no time in executing the plan. On April 19, only six days after the fall of Fort Sumter, he issued a proclamation declaring the Confederacy blockaded from South Carolina to Texas; on April 27, he extended this to include North Carolina and Virginia. This ambitious plan covered 3,549 miles of Confederate coastline, an undertaking without precedent in naval history. Although Southerners and Northern newspaper editors initially scoffed at such a "paper blockade" (with only three ships on duty in April), the Union navy in time gradually created a strong and effective blockade force. With an ever-expanding number of Union blockading ships hovering offshore from Fortress Monroe, Virginia, to the Rio Grande and the Mexican border, the federal fleet assigned to this duty was soon subdivided into four squadrons—North Atlantic, South Atlantic, East Gulf, and West Gulf—each with its own sphere of authority and responsibility.[64]

To establish identification and ensure secrecy within its naval force, the Northern command employed a special system. Each Union ship was designated by a private number known only to the commanders of the vessels and to the Navy Department in Washington. These ships of war bore no painted name or number by which they could be distinguished, differing from the practice accorded to merchant ships. Navy numbers were arranged by private signals.

During the peacetime Buchanan administration, such private

signals and numbers were listed in the *Navy Register*. In February 1861, for example, the ship *Allegheny* was No. 48. When signaled at sea, she would display this number and would be recognized immediately as the *Allegheny*. In the early days of the war, Confederate vessels and shore batteries availed themselves of these registers and signaled Union ships lying off the coast. Welles and the Navy Department quickly prepared a new set of signals and numbers for the navy to protect itself against enemy trickery.[65]

Disguises with false colors and dummy ships had been employed as ruses long before the Civil War. As early as 480 B.C., in the Battle of Salamis, the outnumbered Greeks feigned withdrawal in order to lure Xerxes's Persian fleet into a trap and achieve victory. Both Union and Confederate naval captains kept flagmakers busy in case of a need for deception. Less than a month after the Civil War broke out, the Northern merchant marine, subject to increasing insurance rates because of the danger of assault by Confederate vessels, hoisted a British flag instead of the Stars and Stripes. Many Northern shipowners simply effected a transfer of registry with British consuls to safeguard their ships.

At the Portsmouth Navy Yard, Pearson supplied U.S. Navy vessels with an abundance and variety of flags as standard equipment. "We have made for the *Kearsarge*," Pearson informed John Lenthall, Bureau Chief of Construction and Repair, in September 1861, "English, French, Spanish, Mexican & New Granada [Colombia] flags.—In the scarcity of bunting will not these be sufficient for her?"[66]

The Portsmouth Navy Yard and the other government yards simply could not outfit enough vessels for official use in 1861. Welles was forced to solicit help from private yards in an attempt to bolster naval strength. In June, the Navy Department issued a circular to each of the 200 bidders for building gunboats, proposing to give $56,000 for a gunboat constructed in seventy days, $54,000 for one ready in ninety days, and $52,000 for one completed in 105 days—a total of twenty-five boats to be built. If the offers exceeded this number, they were "to draw lots, or otherwise decide to whom the contracts should be awarded."

During the summer of 1861, Assistant Secretary Fox toured the various Navy Yards, as well as private shipyards where chartered and purchased vessels were being fitted out. On August 8, Fox visited the Portsmouth Yard and received a gun salute. He and Pearson then talked ships.[67]

On September 19, in a letter marked "Confidential," Pearson reported to Fox:

> Three schooners belonging to Rockland, ME [Maine], will prob-
> ably answer for carrying the guns named in your confidential
> communication, save that they will *all* probably draw more
> than 6 feet of water.... Will you please inform me by telegraph
> "Yes," if you think these vessels will answer, and if situated as
> they are, they will be in time for you; and "no" if otherwise. I
> am still on the look out for other vessels."[68]

One of the vessels Welles and Fox obtained for eventual use in
the blockade was the *Augusta*, a side-wheel steamer built by William
H. Webb in 1852. The Navy Department purchased the vessel on
August 1, 1861; nine days later, Welles issued orders for Commander
Enoch Greenleafe Parrott to take "command of the U.S. Steamer
Augusta." Parrott was a career naval officer from a distinguished
Portsmouth family. Unmarried, he had devoted his life to the navy. On
June 3, 1861, while commanding the *Perry*, Parrott captured the
Confederate privateer schooner *Savannah* sixty miles off Charleston.
For this first prize of a Southern privateer, Welles officially commend-
ed Parrott. Then he transferred Parrott to the command of the
Augusta.[69]

In a private letter, dated October 1, Parrott vented his frustrations to "Susan," evidently a cousin back in Portsmouth, regarding his
attempts to ready the *Augusta* in New York:

> There are so many vessels fitting out at the same time that it
> is hard to get the wants of any particular vessels attended to
> and it is necessary to fight the [Brooklyn Navy] yard officers
> for every item. I generally go to bed early and tired. To-day we
> have left the yard and come down off the [military] battery [at
> the southern tip of Manhattan] to take in our powder and
> await orders. How long we will remain here I cannot say[;] may
> be for only a day or two or it may be for a longer time. The
> *Augusta* is a handsome and comfortable steamer, but I am not
> satisfied about her battery. A sort of ordnance board here made
> a great mistake in deciding that she was not to have a Parrott
> pivot gun as had been previously determined and gave her in
> place a small rifled howitzer. I got this decision reversed and

NAVY DEPARTMENT,

10 August 1861

Sir:

Proceed to New York

and report to Comm. Breese

for the command of the U.S. Steamer

Augusta.

I am, respectfully,

Your obedient servant,

William Welles

Commander

E. G. Parrott,

U. S. Navy,

Reported Aug 21st 1861.   Washington

Saml L Breese   D. C.

Comm.

an order from Washington to give me the gun if it would not detain the ship. The same obstinate stupids decided that it would detain the ship but since then more time has already passed than they said they required to prepare the gun carriage &c. Keeping this gun away has, in my opinion, reduced the efficiency of the battery one half—I have never been so annoyed and disgusted at any thing that has happened to me since I have been in the service. There is a sort of half promise or intimation of sending this gun to me after I leave, but I fear that when I leave it will be the last of it. Tell Mrs. [Montgomery] Blair, my friend, of my sorrows[;] perhaps she may help me to get back my gun. I want it to fight the secesh [Northern slang for Southern secessionists]....

I visited Robert Parrott at Cold Spring [New York]....

To-morrow I am to have a grand and single combat with the Commodore[,] the object of which is to make that functionary give me a new suit of sails—mine being rotten—

That functionary gives nothing on a verbal request but when you write to him he comes down[,] cause why—cause he is afraid of having the communication inclosed [sic] to the "Honorable Secretary of the Navy."[70]

Commander Parrott's private feelings formed his preferences in naval gunnery. Parrott guns, it so happened, were manufactured at Cold Spring, New York, a few miles up the Hudson River, by the commander's cousin, Robert Parker Parrott, a Portsmouth-area native, inventor, and ordnance expert. ("An effective Parrott rifle," commented Rear Admiral Louis M. Goldsborough, commander of the North Atlantic Blockading Squadron, during 1864, is "by far the best for naval purposes that has been produced.") Despite delays, the *Augusta*, whether with or without Parrott guns, sailed to join Goldsborough's squadron the following month, remaining on blockade duty for the rest of the war.[71]

Such grumblings about the Navy Department bureaucracy was common in 1861. Furthermore, the Confederacy regularly mocked the Union blockade as little more than a token fraud that would never materialize. "A vessel arrived here to-day from Savannah with a cergo [cargo] of rice," read a letter from Havana, dated August 3 and received in Boston, "which will pay a great profit. So much for your blockade, which we don't think much of." On this point, the *Boston Transcript* editorialized: "By the telegraph dispatches ... it will be seen there is now a universal impression in Washington that the Navy department is inefficient. Out of Washington the impression has been current for months."

On August 12, the *Chronicle* commented further:

We do not know whether the inefficiency is supposed to exist in the Secretary, or in the heads or clerks of the several Bureaus... .

It seems strange that we sometimes have Secretaries of the Navy, who know nothing about a ship—though there are men like Robert B. Forbes, of Boston, Ichabod Goodwin of Portsmouth, and scores of such men in New York, who know how a ship should be built, manned, provisioned, armed and sailed. If a change is to be made, by all means let us have a practical man, yea, practical men, to provide and order the navy, as well as the army.[72]

Such criticism was inevitable as Welles struggled to bring efficiency and honesty to his department while fighting political favoritism and corruption. The two men mentioned by the *Chronicle* were, by their own volition, unavailable for the post. Robert Bennet Forbes preferred to remain in Boston and preside over his vast shipping and business interests; he demonstrated no inclination for public office. Ichabod Goodwin was also preoccupied with his own private affairs. After completing his tenure as New Hampshire governor in early June 1861, Goodwin returned to Portsmouth and his many business interests. Speculation about these men was only that, while the Navy Department went about setting up a blockade that required years, not weeks or months, to tighten its deadly grip.[73]

Blockade duty by its very nature was monotonous, with constant grumbling by sailors about the daily routine, food, hot weather, and homesickness. Notwithstanding its onerous nature, the blockade in its preliminary stages during 1861 set the pattern for the future. Union forces burned the Norfolk Navy Yard (located in Portsmouth, Virginia) on April 20 to prevent its ships and facilities from falling into Confederate hands. Managing to escape capture, the USS *Cumberland* took up blockade duty in Hampton Roads, a watery bulge of the James River near the Chesapeake Bay, just off the gutted yard now under Confederate control. A Portsmouth, New Hampshire, sailor aboard the *Cumberland* was one of the detachment that had torched the Norfolk Navy Yard. During late April, he wrote home, describing his blockading duties:

> We stop every vessel that comes in here, and search them. Yesterday we took the schooner *Louisa Weed* as a prize; she was from Annapolis, bound to Richmond with supplies for the Southern army. She was loaded with artillery pieces, small arms of all sorts, and soldiers' clothing; so we sent her to Washington with a prize crew.
>
> Then the harbor masters of Norfolk and Richmond came down to our ship to see the Commodore [Hiram Paulding], and wanted him to explain why he would not let the

vessels come up [the James River] unmolested; and we took them prisoners for allowing the harbors to be blockaded [by Confederates]. They came down in a tow-boat; and our Commodore just took the tow-boat, captain and all, for aiding in a blockade against Government vessels.[74]

The sailing frigate USS *Santee*, another Portsmouth Navy Yard ship, also left the stocks to assume blockade duty. She was laid down at the Yard in 1820, but shortage of funds left the vessel uncompleted. In 1855, the *Santee* was overhauled, remodeled (her prow was made sharper), and then launched. But since the navy did not need the ship at that time, she remained moored at one of the Yard's wharves until the crisis of 1861. In May 1861, 500 men went to work on her. "The large gang of workmen at the Navy Yard here," reported the *Chronicle* on May 6, "were employed on Sunday. War knows no Sabbaths." On June 8, the *Santee* was finally commissioned, some forty years after her keel was laid. The long delay actually helped her final design: her lines improved with the progress of naval architecture.

The *Santee* was well prepared for blockade duty, with 470 men on board. She carried forty-eight guns (including two pivot guns, each weighing 12,000 pounds), with 34,000 pounds of powder. "The destination of the *Santee* is not made public," reported the *Chronicle*, "but will probably be for the South Carolina blockade. When the name of *Santee* was given forty years ago, it was little thought that her first cruise would be to blockade the rivers of the State whence that name was derived."[75]

By mid-June, the *Santee* was ready for sea, but on June 18, an unexpected alarm jolted the officers and crew of the vessel, the Yard, and the city of Portsmouth. Captain Henry Eagle of the *Santee* explained:

About 7:30 P.M., smoke was seen to issue from the main hold as if there was fire. We beat to quarters, rang the fire bell, broke out the main hold, sail rooms, and had all the shells got on the gun deck in readiness to throw overboard, also those ready to drown the magazine. After a while it was discovered that the alarm was caused by a lamp which had been used in the armory for upwards of an hour.... The Gunner extinguished the light.[76]

An alarm of fire (three guns) sounded from the Yard. Word passed from house to house in Portsmouth that the *Santee* was ablaze. The Fire Engine Company of Portsmouth rushed to the scene. Many citizens crossed the river in boats to view the event, and regimental volunteers ran to the main part of town "with bayonets fixed and guns grasped with an unyielding clasp, as if they fully expected to rush upon an opposing foe. There were a thousand and one rumors on the street ... in regard to the matter."

Damage to the *Santee* proved to be inconsequential (only a small part of a timber burned) and caused no delay in her departure. Pearson immediately wrote Welles about the fire, enclosing Captain Eagle's report. Referring to himself in the third person in "A CARD" he had inserted in the *Chronicle* Pearson praised the efforts of "the Fire Engine Companies of Portsmouth, and to the citizens and soldiers of Portsmouth and Kittery ... He [Pearson] will not fail to represent to the Government that in time of need the loyal people of New Hampshire and Maine are not only ready to build her ships, but at a moment's notice to protect them against fire and sword."[77]

Two days after the fire, the *Santee* sailed, fully provisioned and carrying 48,000 gallons of water. Her first stop was Fortress Monroe (on a peninsula separating Hampton Roads from the Chesapeake Bay), where she loaded ammunition. Contrary to earlier rumor, the *Santee* eventually reported for blockade duty, not off South Carolina but, as it turned out, off the Gulf coast. By autumn, the *Santee* lay off Galveston, Texas.

A newspaper correspondent vividly described a daring night raid outside that port:

> On Nov. 7th a boat expedition, consisting of two launches carrying howitzers under the command of Lieut. [James E.] Jouett, left the *Santee* at moonset, 11:30 P.M., and pulled five miles towards Galveston, with the intention of capturing the steamer *General Rush.*—On passing up the bay they were hailed by the [Confederate] schooner *Royal Yacht*, on coast guard duty, but were allowed to pass as they were supposed to be rebel boats.
>
> They then kept along until abreast of the fort, when they observed the rebels passing to and fro with torches. Supposing that they were discovered and having wind and tide against them, they again stood out and approached the

schooner. The gunner in charge of the first launch pulled the lock string, but the piece missed fire [misfired]. The gun was reprimed and fired, the shell entering below the water mark and lodging in the schooner's hold. It quickly exploded, causing consternation amongst the rebel crew. The gunner and one man gallantly leaped aboard from the bow of the boat, while the launch by the force of their spring rebounded and left them "alone in their glory."—Five of the rebels retreated into the forecastle, followed by the gunner who held them at bay and compelled them to deliver up their arms.

During the interval (but a moment transpiring) the officers and men of both launches were aboard. They met with a manful resistance, but the rebels were soon subdued and surrendered. At this time the forts opened fire upon the schooner, and a steamer was seen firing up, which caused the prisoners to be hurried into the boats, lest she might bear down upon them.

The schooner was now rapidly filling by reason of the hole which the shot had made, and it was thus rendered impossible to tow her out. The mattresses, bedding and other combustible articles were fired, and she was soon in flames, lighting up the sombre darkness of night and throwing a lurid light upon the surrounding waters, rendering the retreating boats painfully but distinctly visible to the astonished Galvestonians. The loss of the rebel crew was two killed and several wounded: the number that jumped overboard is unknown. Thirteen were taken prisoners, among them the celebrated Capt. [Thomas] Chubb of Boston negro stealing notoriety. His phizograph [picture] would be a valuable addition to the *rogues' gallery*. He was owner and captain of the schooner. Our loss was two killed and two wounded.[78]

The brave gunner was identified as William Carter, the same man who had extinguished the smoldering fire aboard the *Santee* earlier that June.

As an adjunct to the blockade, the "Stone Fleet" (otherwise known as the "Rat-Hole Squadron") went into action amid great fanfare during the fall of 1861. This entailed the sinking of stone-laden vessels as obstructions to Southern harbors and channels. It seemed logical enough; once the Stone Fleet was at the bottom of a mouth of a river, presenting an obstacle to the deep-draft Southern ships, the Confederate navy and merchant marine would be bottled up in their own harbors. (The "Government Sinking Fund" was the *Chronicle*'s term for the Stone Fleet.) Buying up old whaling vessels, Assistant Secretary Gustavus Fox promoted this plan a his pet project.

Purchasing twenty-five barks and ships for the first Stone Fleet, Fox later acquired twenty-one more as a second lot. None of these were Portsmouth vessels, but of the latter group, the *Jubilee*, the *Marcia*, and the *Peri* were from nearby Portland. Two Portsmouth naval officers, Commander John S. Missroon off Savannah and Commander Enoch G. Parrott off Charleston, struggled amid storms and other difficulties to execute the plan.

The Stone Fleet plan ultimately failed; such obstructions were unable to oppose the powerful forces of nature. The vessels sank into the shifting sands at the bottom of Charleston Harbor and disappeared forever. Winds and tides scoured out new channels that the Confederate vessels could use. The final stanza of Herman Melville's poem "The Stone Fleet" ridicules the costly fiasco:

> And all for naught, the waters pass—
> Currents will have their way;
> Nature is nobody's ally; tis well;
> The harbor is bettered—will stay.
> A failure and complete,
> Was your Old Stone Fleet.[79]

As 1861 drew to a close, the blockade off the Southern coast became more formidable with each passing day. Reports of its effectiveness drifted to the North. "From various sources we learn," observed the *Chronicle* the day before Christmas,

> that the affairs of the confederates are not rose colored just now. The blockade of their ports has produced the severest effects.—Many staple articles of living are so scarce that they command ruinous prices. Salt is extremely dear; tea costs four dollars per pound, butter seventy-five cents, and cotton thread is twenty-five cents a spool, and sewing silk cannot be had. So pressing are the wants of the people in Virginia for articles of prime necessity that the news from England respecting the capture of Mason and Slidell [two Confederate diplomats taken prisoner] was received with spasmodic joy.[80]

The Port of Portsmouth Rides Out the Storm

If, during 1861, the Southern economy was suffering, the Northern merchant marine was also experiencing hard times. The Union war effort demanded every available Northern vessel, shipwright, and sailor, leaving a negligible labor pool for private shipowners, captains, and yards. Along with the traditional dangers of storms, mutinies, and other disasters at sea, Portsmouth commercial shipping now faced new enemies—Confederate privateers and warships, darkened lighthouses, shore batteries, and unsympathetic foreign governments. Many historians believe that the Civil War dealt a blow to the American merchant marine from which it has never recovered.

The business world, North and South, recognized the situation immediately: War meant financial losses. Even before the fall of Fort Sumter, English insurance companies and private underwriters introduced the following clause, posted at Lloyds: "Warranted free from all loss, claim or damage, arising from seizure, detention, or any other hostile act of the government or people of any revolting or seceding States of the Union, generally known as the United States."

By summer the resolve of the insurance companies had stiffened even more as evidenced by a story, datelined Calcutta, that was printed on September 1, 1861, in the *Journal*:

> The employment of American vessels for the present is about stopped, from the impossibility of shippers obtaining insurance, as most of the insurance companies have received orders from home to avoid them altogether until further orders, while the few that will insure are so limited as to extent and directions as to preclude any business of importance being done.[81]

James Neal Tarlton of Portsmouth experienced the dilemma facing many New England businessmen during the nation's crisis. Born into an old New Castle family, Tarlton was first associated with his father in the fishing trade in that island community. Later he moved to Portsmouth, going into business as a ship chandler. James Tarlton also was an investor in shipping enterprises, becoming a close associate of Daniel Marcy.

At the outbreak of the Civil War, Tarlton, age forty-nine, assessed his future. Severing most of his ties with the shipping industry, he established a grain and flour business in town to ride out such troubled times. Remaining, however, as a confidante of Marcy, he wrote many business letters on behalf of "Captain Daniel." (Marcy, hampered by limited education, was only marginally literate.) Among Tarlton's regular correspondents was Captain Richard Hawley Tucker, the Wiscasset, Maine, shipping king. In a May 13 letter to Tucker, Tarlton lamented, in his somewhat erratic writing style:

> It is too bad that this country should be brought to this state of things, just for the few d——d loafers that want to get into power[;] this is the whole story, about one hundred in the South and as many [in the] North [should] have been hunted up and the hemp put to their necks and hung square up six months ago[; then] we should have sailed along smooth and had a good business for our ships.
>
> He [Daniel Marcy] has been to Boston for two weeks repairing the *Eloise* from Manila, has coppered [the vessel's bottom]. She is chartered from Calcutta.... Marcy talks of going to Europe to sell some of his ships. He will have five or six of them there. There are a great many heavy failures in NY and Boston and more expected[;] the cause is the Southern merchants refusing to pay their honest debts. I tell you it is hard times for most all of us, there are a few that will make money out of this war business. We are all as dead as a door nail here.[82]

Reflecting this slump, Piscataqua shipping as a whole soon encountered wartime restrictions and regulations, sapping its energy even further. In August 1861, the Portsmouth ship *Frank Pierce* returned to her home port for repairs but soon left for Boston. She could not be repaired locally because almost all the mechanics and shipwrights were at the Yard. Some men were brought down from Portland for the express purpose of working on the *Frank Pierce*, but they, too, were diverted to employment at the Yard.[83]

Cargoes were subjected to increased scrutiny. Portsmouth ship captains learned that clearance for vessels at Matamoros, Mexico, just across the Rio Grande from Brownsville, Texas, was being halted. By Secretary of the Treasury Salmon Chase's order, any shipment of cargoes to that port amounted to giving aid and comfort to the Confederacy. Such cargoes were simply transshipped across the river to Southern hands.

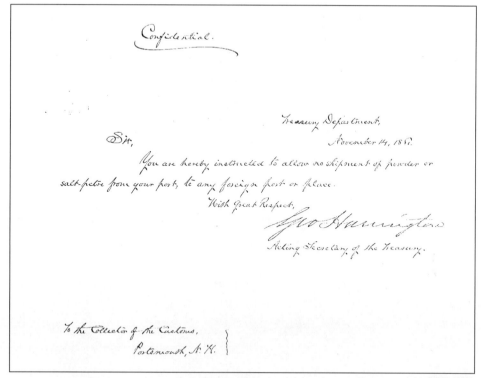

NA-DC

In like manner, a Treasury Department communication, dated November 14, 1861, and marked "Confidential," arrived at the Port of Portsmouth office: "You are hereby instructed to allow no shipment of powder or salt-petre from your port, to any foreign port or place."[84]

Confederate attitudes also hardened. Concerning the only admissible basis for peace, a *Mobile Mercury* article (reprinted by the *Journal* on July 27) stated:

We must dictate the terms of peace, the first article of which should be an acknowledgment of the right of secession. This is a fundamental principle. The next article should be that she [the Union] pay, to the uttermost farthing, the expenses of this war. The third is that she pay for the destruction of all property, both public and private, which she appropriates to her own use. The fourth is, that, as an evidence of her sincerity, she impeach and remove from office Abe Lincoln, indict and hang him for treason and other crimes.

Adding to this hysterical outburst, the *New Orleans Delta* published "a full and accurate description of the new gunboat fleet built and building at the government Navy Yards and private ship yards [in the] North. The names, tonnage, number, and calibre of guns" were "given in full."

When a schooner arrived at a Portsmouth wharf in early October with a cargo of corn and flour, she was found the next morning to have several feet of water in her hold, with much damage to the freight. This singular case gave rise "to rumors of secessionists['] scuttling, and the like."[85]

The Trent *Affair*

More serious than loose talk and rumors was the distinct possibility in late 1861 of war with Great Britain—a circumstance that, given the powerful Royal Navy, would have almost certainly swept the Northern merchant marine from the seas. The implications arising from the "*Trent* Affair" temporarily affected American shipping worldwide.

On November 8, Captain Charles Wilkes of the USS *San Jacinto*, one of the ships that had been on African Squadron duty, stopped the British mail steamer *Trent* in the Caribbean. Aboard the *Trent* were two Confederate diplomats, James M. Mason and John Slidell, who, having slipped through the Union blockade and reached Havana, were en route to their respective posts in London and Paris. After seizing and transferring them to the *San Jacinto*, Wilkes sent Mason and Slidell to Fort Warren, Boston Harbor, for imprisonment.

"Why are Mason and Slidell like the Apostle Paul?" asked a New Hampshire minister, who also provided the answer: "Because they are ambassadors in Bonds," a rough paraphrase from Ephesians 4:20. Although Wilkes was lionized throughout the North for his exploit, President Lincoln and Secretary of State William Seward quickly realized that this brazen impressment might precipitate war with Great Britain. As these Union leaders realized, British support for the Confederacy, especially among the upper classes, was widespread. The English landed gentry believed the South represented an aristocratic society, while merchants and manufacturers, knowing that the South had virtually no factories of her own, reasoned that the Confederacy would be expected to purchase freely from Great Britain.

The South, in championing its own cause, anticipated a strong bargaining position in establishing close commercial ties. British cotton factories were dependent upon this Southern staple. To obtain the essential cotton and to ensure the flow of other goods, both the Confederacy and Great Britain envisioned that the Northern blockade would, by economic necessity, eventually be broken. Hence, the Northern diplomatic posture with regard to Great Britain was extremely delicate and precarious. If the *Trent* crisis had erupted into war between the Union and Great Britain, Southern prospects for independence would have been greatly enhanced. Aware of the international ramifications at stake, Lincoln and Seward in turn acted wisely. The prisoners were released, the crisis died down, and war was averted.

Northern newspapers, in the wake of this crisis, commented on the situation. The *Boston Post* asserted:

> Such a war will bring starvation to [British] doors. We have been their best customers; we have furnished them with bread, and we have bought their goods. The first hostile gun fired, and the doors of Commerce will be slammed in the face of insolent Britannia. Not a bushel of grain—not a yard of cloth—shall cross the ocean.[86]

Journal readers on December 7 received a telling report from George Francis Train, a Bostonian then living in London. A strong Unionist, Train was abroad seeking capital for American railroads. In a letter home, he shrewdly gauged the prevailing English mood:

> "The whole dress circle" in England is [supporting] secession, viz: the Army, the Navy, the Church, the Parliament, the Aristocracy, the Banker; while, on the other hand, "the pit and the gallery" is sound, and "goes for the Union to the last." .... The English steamships (Cunard line excepted) leave port constantly under English colors, with every sort of contraband to aid the rebellion. The reply of Lord Palmerston [British Prime Minister] to Mr. [Charles Francis] Adams [U.S. ambassador to Great Britain] is, "We know it; catch them if you can."[87]

Trying to "catch them," in all the manifestations of that phrase, would dominate the fortunes of Portsmouth and American shipping for the next four years.

Marcy Ships Fly Opposing Flags

The Civil War engulfed not only diplomats, foreign steamship lines, and the international business world, but also individual families. The fraternal bonds that linked Daniel and Peter Marcy were torn asunder throughout the conflict. Flying different flags—Union for Daniel and Confederate for Peter—on the high seas, the House of Marcy was at war against itself.

In his many letters (written in a clumsy hand with erratic spelling and punctuation) to Daniel just before and during the war years, Peter Marcy was blunt in his zeal for the Confederate cause. "The Southern market will be Efected[,] time alone Can tell," Peter wrote on February 14, 1861. "If the Blacks [Black Republicans, pejorative term for Lincoln's party]. attempt to Blocklead [blockade?] our Ports[,] we shall have war[?] for It Self Is tantamount to a declaration of one—northern Commerce would be Swept from the ocean by Letters of Mark [privateering licenses]." A week later, Peter declared, "Shiping Business has Been so dull for the Last 4 years you can Find a few willing to Engage In It. If war Ensue we had better sell them [the Marcy vessels] all To Some European Subject. If the Blacks Should Attempt to Bloackhead our Ports you know what such Insane [fools?] they are. The South is Preparing for the Worst."[88]

On April 22, Peter Marcy backed up his words; along with others, he applied for and received the first Confederate Letter of Marque. She was the 400-ton *Joseph Landis*, with two large-caliber guns and one hundred men.[89]

In their bid to gain Southern independence, Peter Marcy and other Confederate maritime figures had resorted to privateering. Dating from the 1200s, this type of nautical warfare was used by nations with weak navies to fight stronger opponents. By granting a privateering license (or letters of marque and reprisal), the state authorized such privateers to prey on the enemy's commerce. If a privateer were successful in overtaking an enemy ship, its captain and crew were entitled to a percentage of the sale of the "prize," the captured vessel and its cargo. The Declaration of Paris in 1856 abolished privateering, but the United States was not a signatory to that international agreement.

When Confederate President Jefferson Davis issued a proclamation on privateering on April 17, 1861, panic initially spread through Northern shipping circles. Five days later, Lincoln countered by threatening that Southern privateers (the term applying, as well, to the individuals sailing such ships) would be regarded as pirates, with orders issued to that effect to Union vessels on patrol. The *New York Commercial* urged "That the contumacious be immediately hung from the yard-arm and the crew and more penitent officers placed in irons to await their trial as ocean brigands."[90]

The Confederacy, in turn, issued its own ultimatum that if any Southern privateers were hanged, a corresponding number of captured Union officers would suffer the same fate. Northern alarm over Confederate privateering, however, was short-lived. By the summer of 1861, Southern privateering forays were virtually over; their captains were experiencing increasing difficulty taking their prizes through the tightening blockade to friendly ports.

Before the practice died out—the last incident occurred in February 1863—one of the Marcy ships, the *Sarah E. Pettigrew*, flying the Union flag, was seized by a Confederate privateer. Like so many Northern ships during the early stages of the war—some returning from distant ports—the *Pettigrew* had no advance warning of the recent outbreak of hostilities when approaching New Orleans. "It appears by our latest advices from New Orleans," reported the *Journal* on July 27, 1861, "that Northern ships are daily arriving there, in utter ignorance of the existing war, and that they are seized at the bar by armed vessels, prize crews put on board, and then sent up to the city. There are many valuable vessels now bound to New Orleans without any knowledge of the danger incurred."[91]

The *Sarah E. Pettigrew* was built in Portsmouth in 1857, 1,192 tons burthen, and originally cost $83,000. Repaired and coppered in 1861, she was owned by the Marcys—one-fourth by Peter and three-fourths by Daniel and his Portsmouth partners. In late May 1861, en route from Liverpool, the vessel was approaching Pass l'Outre (now Pass a Loutre), off the mouth of the Mississippi River, with a cargo of salt worth $17,000. The Marcys thus had a major investment in this venture.

In a letter dated "Off Pass l'Outre, mouth of the Mississippi, May 21," an unidentified crew member of the Confederate steamer privateer *Ivy* describes the capture of the *Pettigrew*:

Last Friday [May 17] I left New Orleans for this place and boat for a little privateering—to assist in annoying the enemy's commerce; but the enemy's commerce has ceased almost to spread its wings in this latitude.—On board the *Ivy* are guns and men enough to accomplish great destruction, were we called on to open with our cannon. Our human fighting material is constituted of good bone, sinew and pluck, and some of the crew have entered the privateer service with only one intent—*commendable revenge on the North*.

To-day we succeeded in sighting a vessel of the largest dimensions and full rigged, which proved to be the *Sarah Pettigrew*, but, to our sorrow, was without a cargo, there being in her hold only two or three thousand sacks of salt from Liverpool. We soon had a prize crew on her decks, greatly to the muddled surprise of her officers and crew.

After the formality of taking possession, your correspondent being among the boarders ... overhauled the flag-bag, and soon had bunting in plenty for a pretty Southern Confederacy flag, which was immediately sent aloft to flutter defiance to all who don't like us. The *Ivy*'s capacity enables her to do her own towing, and after she cruised around in the Gulf for two or three hours to overhaul other sails, she returned to us, and we turned our prows towards Pass l'Outre near where the *Pettigrew* now lies, waiting to be towed to your city [New Orleans]. The privateer *Calhoun* gave chase to the same vessel, but the *Ivy* was too fast for her. We lie in or near the river every night, *but start out after midnight*, and keep a sharp outlook for any speck on the horizon, and when the cry of "Sail-ho" is heard, the *Ivy*'s "tendrils" *don revolvers, swords, knives and rifles, with great excitement and good nature.* We have exceeding good times and "duff" [a pudding served to crew on Sunday], but I fear all will be closed with the appearance of the blockading force.[92]

War continued to plague the Marcys' maritime ventures. Sandbars at the mouth of the Mississippi temporarily blocked Peter Marcy's vessels from entering the open sea. Then, in June, the *Alice Ball*, a Marcy ship owned by Peter and Daniel and his partners (75 percent) "was spoken" at sea (communicated to by another vessel) as she sailed from New Orleans to Liverpool. She was displaying the flag of the Southern Confederacy. In early September, a special dispatch from Eastport, Maine, reported the capture of the *Alice Ball* by the revenue cutter (of the U.S. Coast Guard) *Arago*. Boarding the *Alice*

Ball near St. Stephen, New Brunswick, the Union officials discovered that the captured vessel had no register or other papers except a Liverpool clearance. A few days earlier, the *Arago* had seized another Marcy ship, the *Orozimbo*. "*Express* [should be *Alice Ball*] and *Orozimbo* are seized by the federal government," read a terse telegraph sent to Daniel Marcy. The *Chronicle* summarized:

> The brothers Marcy, one residing in Portsmouth, and the other in New Orleans, owned jointly four ships. The Southern brother hoisted the secession flag on two, and the old stars and stripes floated over two. The fortunes of war have so turned that the two secession crafts have been seized by the United States authorities, while the Confederates have captured the two belonging to the loyal Northerner.[93]

The impoundment of Daniel's vessels was brief. "Ships *A. Ball* and *Orozimbo* have been released," reported James Tarlton on September 23. Secretary of the Treasury Salmon P. Chase, a New Hampshire native, ordered their release, perhaps on the legal technicality that both were seized in Canadian waters, coupled with the Marcys' political influence.[94]

The *Trent* affair played havoc with Marcy shipping, resulting in delays, uncertainty, and expense. On November 14, 1861, in his letter to Tucker, James Tarlton noted:

> There is a report here by telegraph today that Mason and Slidell [have] been taken from a British steamer [the *Trent*] and are now prisoners at Fortress Monroe [Virginia]. I hope it will not make any trouble with England by so doing. Some say that there is a question in regard to this, in [taking] these people from a British steamer.[95]

Tarlton's fears were soon realized. Less than a month later, Captain Charles H. Brooks wrote from Havre de Grace (now Le Havre), France, to his employer, Daniel Marcy, then in Liverpool, England:

> At present things look rather *Squally* so far as our Government is concerned and I suppose that a war with England depends entirely on the answer of the Government at Washington with regard to the Slidell and Mason affair[;] any-

thing like business appears to be completely done for our Ships at present. There is [*sic*] now about seventy-five American ships here all with Grain[.] Some are laying up untill [*sic*] they can learn the decision of [the] Government[.] Others are going as soon as ready[.]⁹⁶

The Tribulations of Portsmouth Ship Captains

The turmoil caused by blockades, ship seizures, and diplomatic crises was only a portion of the larger conflict that had been waged against Portsmouth captains, who also battled storms, shipwrecks, mutinies, men's loyalties, and tropical fevers. These problems caused casualties, wrecked vessels, and lost cargoes, as they would have even if the Civil War had not broken out. Capricious winds continued, indifferent to either Union or Confederate whims.

In the spring of 1861, Portsmouth citizens learned that the Northern steamer *Daniel Webster* had narrowly escaped capture. Bound for New Orleans with passengers and cargo, the *Webster* encountered the Confederate privateer steamer *William H. Webb* at a sandbar outside that city. With two thirty-two-pounders and a crew of seventy-five men, the *Webb* was poised to take the Northern vessel as a prize. Without landing her passengers and freight, the *Webster* made good her escape, arriving at Havana in late April. The Confederate commander of the *Webb* was Captain Joseph Leach, a native of Portsmouth.⁹⁷

Another Portsmouth native, Captain Henry Libbey, master of the ship *Orion*, faced a member of his crew in a close brush with death. On May 22, aboard the *Orion* at Whampoa, China, a trading station near Canton, Captain Libbey shot and killed Joseph Parks, a knife-wielding cook "in liquor." In an apparent case of self-defense, Libbey was placed under arrest at the house of the American vice-consul.

In a time of extraterritoriality, although the murder took place within Chinese jurisdiction, American authorities, not the Chinese officials, deliberated the case. Following a coroner's inquest, coupled with the testimony of the officers and men of the *Orion*, the decision was accordingly rendered:

> I, Oliver H. Perry, U.S. Consul at Canton, after having careful-
> ly examined and weighed the part, both of the United States
> and the prisoner Henry Libbey, Captain of the American ship

Orion, charged before the U.S. Consular Court of Canton with the murder of Joseph Parks, late cook of the said ship *Orion*, do find the prisoner, Henry Libbey, "not guilty," of the offence charged.

Below appeared an official seal with Perry's signature. Another document, in much the same language, attested, "We, the undersigned Jurors, called by order of Oliver H. Perry to try the case jointly with him, of the United States v. Henry Libbey do honorably acquit him of the said charge," followed by their six signatures.[98]

Aside from violence in faraway places, catastrophe on occasion occurred within sight of Portsmouth Harbor. On March 21, 1861, the *Chronicle* reported that the schooner *Sarah Ann* of Rockland, Maine, "became leaky, and her cargo of lime took fire, destroying the vessel. Two people perished by drowning: viz. the captain, whose body has not been found; and a boy sixteen years old, whose body was recovered and forwarded to his friends by railroad from this city [Portsmouth]. The remaining two of the crew were saved."[99]

A *Chronicle* item on December 28 was terse:

Sch. *Peru*, from this port from Thomaston [Maine], Dec. 18th, lost a man overboard off Whale's Back [a ledge in Portsmouth's Outer Harbor]—name unknown here.—of dark complexion, and about 25 years old. The captain is desirous of recovering the body, and will gladly pay all charges for the same. Refer to M. Fisher & Co. or J. Eldredge & Son, Portsmouth.[100]

Sometimes maritime accidents resulted from human carelessness. On June 17, the Portsmouth ship *Eagle Speed*, bound for England, was underway from the rice-trading town of Bassein, Burma, on the Bassein River, a navigable delta-branch of the Irrawaddy. With a careless pilot at the helm, the *Eagle Speed*, laden with rice, never reached the open sea. She struck Orestes Shoal at the mouth of the Bassein, becoming a total wreck. The crew was saved and the salvage was sold for 1500 rupees. A court of inquiry suspended the pilot.[101]

The forces of nature and cruel winds probably sank or disabled more Portsmouth vessels in the remaining four years of war than all the Confederate privateers and warships combined.

This officer and muster-room building (now Building 13), constructed in 1859, served as the headquarters of the Portsmouth Navy Yard during the Civil War. The building faced a park (now the Mall), which was the site of Civil War musters, oath-of-allegiance and change-of-command ceremonies, and general assemblies. PNSVC

The Yard Expands

While the malevolent whims of nature could not be controlled, Commandant George F. Pearson at the Portsmouth Navy Yard strove to eliminate accidents and delays in order to make his facility as productive as possible. Exchanges of official correspondence to and from Washington and within the Yard itself—voluminous and all-encompassing—attest to its massive expansion throughout 1861, and continuing without letup until the end of the war.

Pearson closely oversaw the rapid increment of Yard workers. In May, the Yard employed nearly 1,100 men. By August, the figure rose to about 1,500, a portion of them employed on Sundays. In late September, the *Chronicle* reported, "The muster roll now includes about 1700 men—and the monthly pay roll amounts to about $35,000; the total outlay per month being from $100,000 to $115,000." For November, the clerk of the Yard reported that the monthly payroll contained 2,134 names, some duplicates since a few men were listed in two classifications. The diversity of the Yard's work force was reflected in many job categories: Eight men were masters in the skills of smith, joiner, caulker, mast-maker, painter, cooper, machinist, and mason. The rolls included "622 carpenters, 42 gun-carriage makers, 31 sawyers, 166 borers, 414 laborers, 94 smiths, 149 joiners, 118 caulkers and reamers, 27 night watchmen, 29 sail-makers, 23 mast-makers, 70 riggers, 50 masters' men, 47 painters, 35 boat-builders, 9 coopers, 102 machinists, 90 gunners' men, 6 masons, 10 writers, 16 teamsters, and 16 watchmen."[102]

Pearson hired with discretion. "By direction of the Hon. Secretary of the Navy," he wrote on May 5 to Benjamin F. Martin, "you are appointed Master Mast & Block Maker at this Yard. The Secretary of the Navy desires it be understood that this appointment is made upon probation, to be revoked, if after a fair trial, the appointee shall prove unworthy or not fitted for his position."[103]

Passing the probationary requirement, Martin remained on the job throughout the war, and his spar-making department underwent a rapid build-up. During April, this group of employees worked a total of sixty-two man-days, for an accumulated $145.72 in wages. With Martin himself appointed as "master workman" to head the department in mid-May, the workload increased steadily; for December, these figures inflated to a monthly total of 693 1/2 man-days, for $1,519.83 in wages.[104]

In addition to the construction and repair of ships, a less publicized responsibility of the state of New Hampshire and of the Yard was the acquisition of guns and manufacture of gun carriages. On April 24, Samuel Colt of the famous "Colt's Patent Fire Arms Manufacturing Co." (according to his stationery) in Hartford, Connecticut, wrote to Governor Goodwin with regard to the state's arms requirements: "We will at once Extend our works for the production in large numbers of the government regulation rifle latest model and Springfield pattern. The price of these rifles with bayonet will be twenty dollars each."

Ironically, the real inventor of the Colt pistol was a New Hampshire native, Otis W. Whittier of Enfield, who secured his patent in 1837. Following a fire that destroyed his manufacturing facility, he

The Mast Building (now Building 7) was equipped with a loading/unloading dock; the bowsprit of an unidentified ship is at right. In addition to the regular arrivals and departures of U.S. naval vessels, contracted civilian ships docked almost daily at the Yard to deliver such essential raw materials as lumber, oil, coal, and naval stores for construction and maintenance. Tight wartime security provided by the U.S. Marine detachment greatly reduced theft and sabotage of government property. PNSVC

renewed the patent in 1851, selling it the same year for $2,000 to two Hartford men, who in turn sold the rights to Samuel Colt. Colt weapons were used by the Yard watchmen, the marines, and those aboard ship.[105]

The Gun Carriage Department of the Yard, a new branch of government work, played a crucial role during the fall of 1861. Andrew A. Harwood, Chief of the Ordnance Bureau in Washington, and his assistant, Henry A. Wise, endeavored to supply guns to Major General John C. Fremont in St. Louis. In the struggle for control of Missouri, Union forces under General Nathaniel Lyon had suffered defeat at the Battle of Wilson's Creek in mid-August, and Lyon was killed during the fighting. The federal cause in the border state was thrown into jeopardy.

On September 5, Assistant Chief Wise telegraphed orders to Pearson: "Forward with the Utmost possible expedition to Major Gen. Fremont, St. Louis, Mo. The Sixteen IXin gun carriages that are ready *immediate* ... 5th Sept. 11 P.M."[106]

The next morning at 10:15 A.M., Harwood telegraphed Pearson:

> Send a Competent person with the gun carriages, and order him to use every means, by day and night, to get the Carriages through in the shortest possible time to St. Louis.
>
> Inform the transportation agents, all along the line, that every exertion must be made to push the Carriages forward.
>
> Let the person you send telegraph the Bureau, if any delay occurs on the road.[107]

Continuing to press, Harwood on September 7 inquired of Pearson, "Have the carriages gone to St. Louis? Answer by telegraph[.]" At the bottom of the slip, the Portsmouth and American Telegraph Company clerk noted, "Capt. Pearson paid 25¢ for the above—charged—"[108]

The gun carriages arrived on schedule, thus bolstering Union military strength in Missouri. Both Harwood and Gustavus V. Fox sent letters of commendation. Signing as "Act[ing] Sec'y Navy," Fox notified Pearson, "The Department takes this occasion to commend the general promptness and energy displayed at the Portsmouth Navy Yard."[109]

Pearson routinely attended to minute details. On May 25, in a letter to Commodore Joseph Smith, chief of the Bureau of Yards and Docks, Pearson wrote, "Owing to the great amount of work now in progress at this Yard, the services of another yoke of oxen are needed[;] I therefore respectfully request authority to purchase them."

That did not end the matter. On July 18, Pearson informed Smith, "One of the Yard oxen has, in consequence of lameness, become unfit for service, I recommend that he and his mate be sold in the usual manner [at public auction], and another yoke of oxen be purchased in their stead."[110]

Another administrative responsibility involved recordkeeping relative to the constant arrival and departure of vessels of all categories, including gundalows (a bargelike craft utilizing the strong Piscataqua tide), to transport raw materials, machinery, men and supplies to the Yard. On Saturday, July 27, a typical entry in the Yard Log noted: "Ard [Arrived] Gondola [gundalow] from Dover with Timber[,] also a Gondola from Dover with Powder[.] Ard Sch. *Elizabeth English* from Phila with coal[.]"[111]

In the fall of 1861, John Greenleaf Whittier, the Quaker poet, provided a telling comment about the flow of materials arriving at the Yard. Whittier and a friend named Moses, also a Quaker, were traveling together by train to the White Mountains. Moses told Whittier that he was on his way to contract for a lot of oak timber, which he knew would be used for building gunboats at the Yard.

"Is it exactly in consistence with the peace doctrine of the Quaker denomination?" Moses asked.

"Moses," Whittier responded, "if thee does furnish any of the oak timber thee spoke of, *be sure that the timber is all sound*."[112]

Along with the highest quality of materials and the best workers he could bring to the Yard, Pearson was also committed to observing sound and efficient business practices. In accordance with official Navy Department policy to make every cent count, Gideon Welles in a September 20 letter articulated his expectations to Pearson:

> Under the present exigencies of the service, the large purchases and repairs of vessels and other expenditures, great power is delegated to you, [and] with it great responsibility. In exercising the authority with which you are necessarily invested, and especially in all that involves expenditure of money, I feel it is a duty to enjoin upon you a strict regard to economy.
>
> Let me also urge upon you the importance of promptness in preparing and equipping the vessels, and that you devote your whole time and attention to the completion and discharge of the duties with which you are invested. We are in the midst of a formidable rebellion, and every man is required to use his best efforts in behalf of his country.
>
> Promptitude, vigilance and economy are urged upon you. Scrutinize closely all bills that you approve, for you will be held to a close accountability, not only for dispatch but [also] for expenditures.[113]

As the Yard expanded throughout 1861, its primary mission was to supply ships to tighten the blockade. On August 24, the *Journal* effectively summarized the Yard's and Navy's goal:

> The blockade has not so far been effectual, for want of suitable vessels. They are now being rapidly supplied, so as to close every inlet from the Chesapeake to the Rio Grande. From 100 to 150 steamers and other suitable merchant craft have been purchased or chartered, and are now arming and every day departing. In addition, twenty gun boats, as they are called, are building—several of which are already launched, and all, by contract, are to be ready for service on the 1st of September. These *boats* are schooner rigged ships of 1000 or more tons, with propellers to take them fifteen miles an hour on a chance, while they draw but nine feet of water, and so can penetrate shallow inlets. They carry twelve 32-pounders, with a pivot columbiad [heavy, long-chambered muzzle-loaded gun],—and the complement of two hundred men.[114]

Building the USS Kearsarge

From the outbreak of the war, the Yard hummed with ship construction and refitting. Yard workers who lived in Portsmouth crossed the Piscataqua every day in more than sixty boats—in wherries, ferries, and rowboats—to commute to their jobs. So many men had moved into Portsmouth and Kittery from surrounding communities that tenements were full; by September 1861, housing became scarce. These naval employees worked on twelve vessels during the latter half of the year. "The activity at this Navy Yard is unabated," commented the *Chronicle*.[115]

During the late spring, Yard shipwrights had begun construction on a steam-screw sloop of war that was destined to become, like the *Monitor*, a renowned Union vessel of the Civil War. This ship was the USS *Kearsarge*. Her naming and construction history were relegated to relative obscurity until three years later, when the *Kearsarge* was thrust into the spotlight as a result of her celebrated sea battle with the CSS (Confederate States Ship) *Alabama*.[116]

At first this vessel had no name. "Sawyers[,] 9[,] on the New Steam Sloop," reads the Yard Log for May 25, 1861, the initial reference to the as-yet-unnamed *Kearsarge*, with the number of workers assigned to her work detail for that day. Even official Washington spelled the new name indifferently during her early days. John Lenthall, chief of the Bureau of Construction and Repair, wrote to Pearson:

> The Department directs the Steam Screw Propeller ship "Kearsage" [variant spelling] shall be fitted with a stationary Propeller ....
>
> It is further directed that for the present emergency the vessel be masted and rigged as a three masted schooner. As a contract has been made for the machinery of this vessel to be completed in 4 months, you will press on the Vessel with the utmost dispatch, giving the work on it precedence over that of the *Ossipee*.[117]

The name for the ship originated from a mountain in New Hampshire called "Kearsage" (an early variant) or "Kearsarge" (the modern spelling), but confusion remains to this day about which landmark was intended. The claimants advanced for this honor have been either the peak near Warner, Merrimack County, or the one near North Conway, Carroll County.

After the 1864 sea battle had been fought, memorializing the *Kearsarge* name, various partisans submitted evidence, documents, old maps, and hearsay to verify that it was *their* mountain that had lent its name to the Union ship. In 1915, the controversy even reached the United States Senate and the United States Geographic Board.

Support for the North Conway mountain was derived from the suggestion of Mrs. Gustavus V. Fox in the spring of 1861. Having summered near the more northerly Kearsarge, she mentioned the mountain's name to her husband for the proposed ship, who in turn passed it on to Gideon Welles. The busy secretary of the navy knew only that the word identified a New Hampshire mountain, little realizing that two summits had the same name.

Henry McFarland, one of the publishers of Concord's *New Hampshire Statesman*, sought to honor the other mountain. On June 8, 1861, his paper ran an article entitled, "Sloops of War":

> Of the new steam sloops of war ordered to be built at Portsmouth, one will be named *Ossipee* and the other *Kearsarge*. These are Indian words, but, unlike many of that

dialect, pass easily over the tongue. *Kearsarge* was suggested to the Navy Department by one of the publishers of this paper. He wrote that as the *Merrimack* was burned at Norfolk, it would be gratifying to New Hampshire folks to be again remembered in this matter of names of national vessels; and in presenting Kearsarge said it was an isolated and imposing eminence in the centre of the State, in the midst of a loyal people, and that young Ladd, who fell at Baltimore, crying, "All hail to the stars and stripes," was buried almost within its shadow at Alexandria [New Hampshire].[118]

Apparently without knowledge of Mrs. Fox's proposal, McFarland was boosting the southerly Mount Kearsarge in Warner, a few miles northwest of Concord. Luther C. Ladd, the soldier mentioned in McFarland's article, was New Hampshire's first fatality in the Civil War. He was only seventeen years old, an enlisted man in the Sixth Massachusetts Regiment. A native of Alexandria, New Hampshire, a few townships north of Warner, Ladd was killed in April when an armed mob attacked his unit on its march through the streets of Baltimore.

On June 10, the *Chronicle* reprinted McFarland's article, which further publicized McFarland's proposal. (Later in September, his wife sponsored the launching of the *Kearsarge* at the Yard.) Advocates for both mountains, with legitimate evidence on each side, still argue to the present day.[119]

Pearson, in accordance with Lenthall's orders, made every effort "to press on" with the building of the *Kearsarge*. Yard shipwrights had already determined the lines of the new vessel. The *Journal* announced on June 15:

> The *Kearsarge* (named from a mountain in New Hampshire) is of the size and built from the model of the *Mohican*, sent from this station two years ago. The new ship will carry two eleven-inch pivot guns, and four thirty-two pounders of 42 cwt. each. It is highly creditable to Constructor W[illiam] L. Hanscom [at the Charlestown, Massachusetts, Navy Yard in 1861] that the *Mohican* is to be duplicated in form; and our [Portsmouth Navy Yard] Constructor, Isaiah Hanscom [William's brother] will equal her in workmanship. The *Mohican* has proved herself one of the best ships in the service. The *Kearsarge* will be built

Commandant's Office,
Navy Yard, Portsmouth, N.H.
5. Oct. 1861.

Sir,

I have the honor to report that the "Kearsarge" built up on the railway of the Dock, has this day been put afloat.

I am most respectfully your obt. servt.

T. T. Hardon
Comdt.

Hon. Gideon Welles,
Secretary of the Navy
Washington,
D.C.

NA-NER

on the [marine] railway and launched through the Floating Dock in October.[120]

Pearson bettered that projected schedule. In late August, the *Kearsarge* was planked and put on the Floating Dock. On Wednesday, September 11, "the steamer *Kearsarge*," reads the Yard Log, "was taken into the Dry Dock this day from the ways on which she was built. The work of taking her out was commenced at about 10:00 A.M.

and [she] was got into the Dock at about 6 P.M." The operation was conducted in a steady rain. Workmen then coppered the hull of the *Kearsarge*.[121]

On Saturday, October 5, Pearson proudly informed Welles, "I have the honor to report that the *Kearsarge*[,] built up on the railway of the Dock, has this day been put afloat." (The *Ossipee* would be launched more than a month later.) The next day, the schooner *G.T. Hubbard* sailed from Hartford with machinery for the *Kearsarge*—two engines of 400 horsepower, built by Woodruff & Beach of that city, by contract, for $104,000. During the fall, the machinery was installed, and on Sunday, December 1, "the *Kearsa[r]ge*," according to the Yard Log, "was 'fired' for the first time, for the purpose of testing the machinery."[122]

To command the *Kearsarge*, the navy appropriately ordered a Granite State officer, Commander Charles W. Pickering, to the Yard. A native of Portsmouth, Pickering had been stationed at Key West, Florida—in Union hands throughout the war—with the Light House Board.[123]

A Year of Accomplishment at the Yard

The *Kearsarge*, only a naval architectural plan a few months earlier, heralded the emergence of the new Union navy. In his annual report, Secretary of the Navy Welles noted that in March 1861, at the beginning of the Lincoln administration, there were only forty-two vessels in commission. By year's end, this figure reached 264 vessels, including the old navy, purchased and leased vessels, and new ships completed or under construction. Guns and tonnage increased proportionately.[124]

The Portsmouth Navy Yard contributed its share to this herculean buildup of naval strength. On December 6, the *Chronicle* summarized these accomplishments:

> Since about the first of May, more work has been done on the Yard than during any four years preceding. Since then, the *Santee, Marion* and *Dale*, vessels of war, have been almost rebuilt, fitted for sea, and sent off to join the squadrons; the *Sabine* refitted and sent off; the *Portsmouth* and *Constellation* ordered here, refitted and ready for sea; the sloop *Kearsarge* built, launched and ready for her trial trip; the *Ossipee* built,

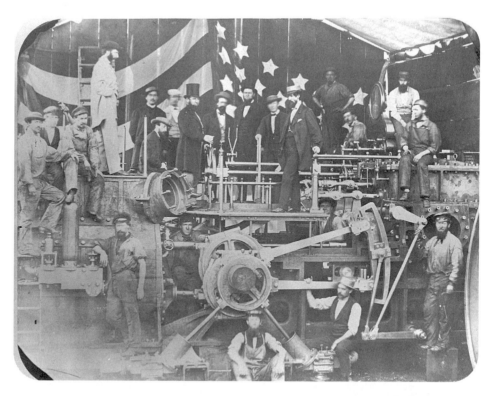

Company officials and workmen of Woodruff & Beach Company, Hartford, Connecticut, pose with a newly completed marine engine in 1861. In the fall of that year, two of these 400-horsepower engines were transported by the schooner G.T. Hubbard to the Portsmouth Navy Yard for installation in the USS Kearsarge, then under construction. On December 1, 1861, the machinery was successfully "fired" for the first time. Courtesy Connecticut Historical Society, Hartford.

launched, and approaching completion; the *Sebago* built and launched; the *Mahaska* built, and about ready to launch; three more vessels already commenced, and a great deal of miscellaneous work in the ship-building line dispatched. Besides this, Mr. [Joseph] Williams has made thirty or 40 pivot gun-carriages, and a large number of the smaller kind; and in the machinists', smiths', boat-builders' and joiners' departments, a quantity of work has been turned out which would astonish the beholder.[125]

The naval record of the frigate *Sabine*, with her officers and crew, encapsulates the sequence of events during 1861. On July 4, the *Sabine* arrived in Portsmouth Harbor and provided a "handsome national salute from her guns at noon." The officers and men aboard were happy to celebrate the national holiday in New England. Since January, the *Sabine* had been at Pensacola to reinforce Fort Pickens and remained on the blockade there until sailing for Portsmouth on June 15. Just before the ship left on her cruise north, a sailor described life aboard the *Sabine*:

> We arrived here [Pensacola, Florida] about four months ago. This is the only ship that never lost sight of Fort Pickens during that time, and although we came very near being driven on a lee shore, still our noble old captain [Henry A. Adams] held his position, from which he could reinforce the fort in a short time with two hundred sailors, who were ready to land at the signal from the fort.
>
> We have been short of provisions and water, living on half rations, and that of the worst kind, for some time, scurvy breaking out among the crew, and since the fort was first reinforced, the men have been at work day and night discharging transports, and yet there is but one wish expressed among the men and that is for the ball [hostilities] to open soon, so that they may have a fair chance at the secessionists.[126]

Upon arrival at the Portsmouth Navy Yard, the *Sabine* carried a complement of 465 sailors and marines, who had the choice of discharge or remaining in the service. On Friday, July 10, they were paid off, and many visited Portsmouth. Welles congratulated Captain Adams of the *Sabine*: "The cruise has been arduous and tedious on a debilitating station. The service in which she has been most of the time engaged, has been of the highest importance."

On July 6, the Yard work force began stripping the *Sabine*, and the navy decommissioned her six days later, preparatory to repairs.

Shore liberty with pockets full of money proved too much to handle for some of the *Sabine* sailors. On July 17, the *Chronicle* reported:

> Between one and two hundred of the crew of the frigate *Sabine*, passed through Boston, Saturday evening [July 13], most of them en route to New York. Some of the men-of-wars-men have been on a long cruise and received from $400 to

$600. Two of them, who together had about $1000 in gold in their pockets, were taken care of by some of the Police, Saturday afternoon, they being intoxicated, and surrounded by several suspicious characters. A well disposed shipmate promising to look after them, they were allowed to depart in the last train to New York.[127]

By August 30, the *Sabine* had been overhauled and was recommissioned, with Captain Cadwalader Ringgold as her new commander. Officers reported to duty, and a marine guard of forty-seven men from Brooklyn, New York, arrived by rail. A portion of the original complement reenlisted, and the remainder, a draft of about three hundred men, arrived aboard the steamer *Nelly Baker* from Boston.

The *Sabine* set sail from the Yard on Sunday afternoon, September 15, gliding through the harbor under the control of a pilot. "She is now one of the staunchest vessels in the Navy," commented the *Chronicle*. "finely manned and officered; and is altogether admirably fitted to stand a winter cruise on the coast." The *Sabine*'s destination was Fortress Monroe, for assignment to blockade duty.[128]

The pride of the Yard workers was also reflected in soliciting money for the Union cause. In November, "the Officers, Writers, Master Workmen, Mechanics, Labourers and Watchmen employed at the Navy Yard, Portsmouth, NH." raised a subscription fund of $3,441.49 to supply some of the immediate wants of the army and navy volunteers from Maine and New Hampshire. A letter from the Yard paymaster to New Hampshire Governor Nathaniel Berry, who had succeeded Ichabod Goodwin on June 4, 1861, asserted that "many of the Workmen [were] giving no small proportion of wages due them on the Roll."[129]

As the year was ending, Donald McKay, the eminent Boston clipper shipbuilder, advocated that the emerging new Union navy should be built with iron, the old wooden navy becoming an outmoded relic of the past. Such thinking also circulated in the United States Navy. As early as August, Congress had authorized Gideon Welles to appoint a three-officer Ironclad Board. The next month, the board reported back to Welles, recommending three ironclads. These ships, when built, would revolutionize naval warfare. John Lenthall, the conservative chief of the Bureau of Construction and Repair, and the designer of the best wooden naval vessels up to this time, had the foresight to defer to Gustavus Fox and others who wanted to proceed with the construction of light-draft monitors and iron gunboats.

McKay's plan for 1862, printed in the *Chronicle* on New Year's Day, strove to modernize the Union navy: "Cut down all our line of battle-ships one or two decks, plate them with iron, arm them heavily, and moor them across the entrance of our harbors. Plate our heavy frigates with shell-proof iron."[130]

The frigate USS Cumberland, *docked next to the General Stores Building, was overhauled at the Yard during 1859 and 1860. She was then recommissioned and sailed in November 1860. The* Cumberland, *sunk in a heroic battle with the CSS* Virginia *at Hampton Roads in 1862, was later memorialized in poems by Henry Wadsworth Longfellow and Herman Melville. PNSVC*

III 1862: The Yard's Ironclad, Inventions, and Reforms Aid the Union Navy

A Tragic Explosion

As the Civil War entered its second year, Navy Secretary Gideon Welles endeavored to implement shipbuilder Donald McKay's vision of converting the Union's naval construction from wood to iron. A spirit of reform and charity brought needed benefits for Northern naval officers and sailors. During 1862, the Portsmouth Navy Yard experienced occasional difficulties—two strikes, industrial accidents, and desertions. Despite these problems, however, Commandant George Pearson oversaw the construction, completion, or repair of numerous vessels, including the ironclad *Agamenticus*.

The Yard became more active throughout the year. "Business is tolerably brisk," noted the *Chronicle* on October 17, "at the Portsmouth Navy Yard." Two weeks later, the *Chronicle* observed, "The Portsmouth Navy Yard presents a lively scene of labor just now."[1]

Early in 1862, disaster struck. On Monday, January 6, via United States Military Telegraph, Pearson notified Welles, "This morning while getting up steam at the Ordnance building an explosion occurred which demolished the boiler room & a portion of the gun carriage shop[.] The engineer [Martin] Bridges was killed & a boy slightly hurt[.]"[2]

That morning, a few minutes before the seven o'clock roll call, "a loud noise, resembling the discharge of a heavy cannon," reported the *Journal*, on January 11, "was heard in all parts of the city." The cause of the explosion was unknown. The brick boiler room and its chimney were entirely demolished. The eastern end of the gun carriage shop was shattered, requiring $10,000 to $15,000 for temporary repairs so that the shop could resume work. The accident caused a delay of two weeks.

Martin Bridges, the engineer who died in the blast, was about forty years old, with experience on railroads and in machine shops before his employment at the Yard. He left a widow, whom he had married on Christmas Day, less than two weeks earlier. The tragedy might have been much greater. "It has been the custom of many of the workmen on the Yard," noted the *Journal*, "to visit this Engine house on arriving in the morning, to place their dinner kettles where they will be kept warm. Had the explosion taken place fifteen minutes later, the lives of fifty men at least, would have been endangered."[3]

Strikes at the Yard Collapse

The explosion shut down the Gun Carriage Department for only two weeks, but controversy over wages and hours brewing during the same period threatened to close down the entire Yard. In the absence of labor unions, coupled with the government's urgency to prosecute the war, the demands of the Yard workers received only limited sympathy from Washington and Commandant Pearson.

The dispute originated in an Act of Congress on December 21, 1861, scheduled to take effect on January 1, 1862: "An Act to Promote the Efficiency of the Navy," in its eighth section (reprinted in the *Chronicle* on January 16, 1862), prescribed that the pay and hours of labor in the Union Navy Yards should conform to those prevailing in private shipyards. The comparable or adjusted wages were "to be determined by the commandant of the navy yard."[4]

Even before the legislation went into effect, Portsmouth Navy Yard workers organized. Faced with the prospect of commencing work at sunrise each morning with their wages cut by twenty-five cents per day for all grades, they met on December 31, 1861, at Jefferson Hall in Portsmouth. Vowing to fight the order, more than a thousand attended, elected officers, formed committees, and sent a delegation to Washington. However, they agreed to report for work on New Year's Day "under protest."

Tensions grew. The wages of the "laborers" were originally cut from $1.50 and $1.25 to $1.25 and $1.00. Most minors, eighteen years or younger, were slated for discharge. The pay of the mechanics was not reduced, but they objected to going to work earlier. Pearson referred their grievances to a committee, probably the first committee of its type in the Yard's history.

Within two weeks, a compromise offer was presented, listing a few changes. The new plan would reduce the mechanics' pay twenty-five cents. Laborers would receive a cut of twelve and a half cents per day, an improvement from the twenty-five cents originally proposed. Minors would be retained. Those over nineteen would receive $1 per day; those under nineteen, seventy-five cents. The new proposal would go into effect on January 14.

Yard workers were unimpressed with these concessions. The Yard Log entry for Tuesday, January 14, reads, "The gun carriage makers, smiths, and the boat builders refused to work this morning and at noon the carpenters, [hole] borers, laborers, sawyers, ca[u]lkers, and part of the sailmakers also refused."[5]

Out of a total work force of about 1,100 men, some 900 engaged in the strike. Those reporting for work included the machinists, joiners, boatbuilders, painters, and block and spar makers.

On January 15, another meeting of Navy Yard workmen was held. According to the *Chronicle*, "milder counsels prevailed.—This morning the men will return to work, and will endeavor by petition to obtain their former wages, etc." The next day, the workmen returned to their jobs, again "under protest." When news of the strike reached Washington, a telegram was immediately sent to the Yard, directing that, as the *Chronicle* reported, "if the strike was general[,] the work at the Yard might be at once suspended." The Navy Department ordered the discharge of three or four of the principal strike organizers, who were not to be reinstated at the Yard without special permission from Secretary Welles or his department. "It is said," the *Journal* on January 18 editorialized "that some men of Southern sympathies, who are not employed on the Yard, have exerted no little influence in stirring up the strike."[6]

In his letters and telegrams to Commander Joseph Smith, Bureau Chief of Yards and Docks, Commandant Pearson sought to downplay the effects of the strike. During mid-January, Pearson sent daily reports on his attempts to restore normal activity. Responding to Smith's directive for a regional hours-and-pay survey, Pearson wrote on January 14: "I addressed letters requesting to be informed as to the hours of labor and rates of pay of the several classes of workmen in the respective places, to shipbuilders, machine shops, and others, in Boston, Salem, Newburyport, Portsmouth, Concord, South New Market [South Newmarket, now Newfields], Kennebunk, and Portland." With reference to the strike, he commented, "Some of the absentees are sick and several of them, as usual, are probably absent for the day." In his subsequent letter of January 15, Pearson noted, "Of the out-door workmen, but few are present; and owing to a snow-storm now prevailing, this would have been the case, had not the difficulty of yesterday [the strike] occurred. If the weather had been favorable this morning, I believe a large number of carpenters & others would have appeared at Muster."

On January 16, Pearson reported the end of the strike, explaining that the various categories of workers had "mustered, and are at work. Indeed, I am informed that all the workmen save only those whom I have excluded, will cheerfully return to their work. This most of them would have done yesterday, but for the storm."[7]

Responses from private yards to Pearson's query pertaining to hours and wages soon reached his desk. These letters attested that, in general, the hours worked and the wages paid by the Navy Department compared favorably, if not better in most cases, to those in effect elsewhere. The replies of two private Portsmouth yards, and one each from Boston, Newburyport, Kennebunk, and South Newmarket, unanimously concurred on a ten-hour day or a sunrise-to-sunset schedule during the winter. The wages at the City Point Works, Boston, offered a slightly higher wage scale, with a foreman in the patternmaker, machinist, boilermaker, and blacksmith categories making $3.50 to $5.00 a day, and "Helpers" at $1.00 a day. Responding from a private Newburyport shipyard, John Currier explained, "Shipbuilding as you are well aware is very dull here at present. All the carpenters I have employed are at work by the job, so that I cannot name any sum as the average rate of wages. I have only a few Irishmen and chip-pilers at work by the day."[8]

Pearson provided the results of his survey to Smith, thus collecting data for future negotiations. But the intense excitement generated by the one-day strike had lessened. On January 31, after an absence of two weeks, the two representatives of the Committee for the Navy Yard who had traveled to Washington on behalf of the strikers returned home—empty handed. "They bring no definite report from headquarters," reported the *Chronicle*.[9]

By an Act approved on July 16, 1862, the Lincoln administration "amended" the December law, but in effect simply restated it with virtually the same phraseology. The new Act asserted that the hours and wages in the government Navy Yards should conform, "as nearly as consistent with the public interest, with those of private establishments in the vicinity of the respective navy-yards," and going beyond the December law, "subject to the revision of the Secretary of the Navy." Thus, in the event of future disputes, Gideon Welles and his successors were legally bound to enter such negotiations to uphold the interests of the government in a much more powerful role.[10]

The last wartime gasp of the weakened Portsmouth Navy Yard labor movement occurred three months later. On October 21, the Yard riggers struck for higher wages. A new wage rate for the Yard had been approved, with most departments receiving increases. The riggers' wage, however, remained at $1.75 per day. They wanted $2.00. Two days later, a crowd of striking riggers seized John Fisher, second-class Yard rigger and strikebreaker, when he arrived at Union Wharf. "A rope was thrown over his head," reported the *Chronicle* on October 25, "and drawn tightly around his waist and he was threatened with suspension from the yard arm of a schooner hard by." The gang suggested to Fisher that he would be wise to suspend his labors at the Yard until his fellow riggers resumed work. After the strikers convinced Fisher of his proper course of action, he was allowed to depart.[11]

The riggers' strike died quietly—so inconspicuously, in fact, that neither the Portsmouth press nor the Navy Yard Log mentioned it. While the question of hours and wages came up frequently until the end of the conflict, changes and adjustments prevented any work stoppages. The Yard had experienced its last wartime strike.

The USS Kearsarge *Sails for Spain*

After the one-day strike of January 14, 1862, work on the USS *Kearsarge* resumed without letup. Engines arrived for installation, guns were mounted, bunkers were filled with coal, and crew complements reported for duty. Her lines took shape: length overall, 214 1/4

☞ The following is a correct list of the officers of the U. U. S. steamer Kearsarge, which will probably sail from the Portsmouth Navy Yard on Thursday :

C. W. Pickering, Commander.
T. C. Harris, Lieutenant.
John M. Browne, Surgeon.
Jos. A. Smith, Ass't Paymaster.
E. M. Stoddard, Acting Master.
James R. Wheeler,   "
J. H. Somner,   "
Ed. E. Preble, Acting Midshipman.
F. A. Graham, Acting Gunner.
James C. Walton, Boatswain.
Chas. H. Danforth, Master's Mate.
Ezra Bartlett,   "
W. H. Cushman, Chief Engineer,
James W. Whittaker, 1st Ass't Engineer.
W. H. Badlam,   2d   "   "
Fred'k L. Miller,   3d   "   "
Henry McConnell,   3d   "   "
Sidney L. Smith,   3d   "   "
Charles O. Muzzey, Commander's Clerk.
Geo. A. Tittle, Surgeon's Steward.
Dan'l B. Sargent, Paymaster's Steward.

PC, Jan. 28, 1862

feet; length on the waterline, 198 1/2 feet; beam, 33 feet; depth, 16 feet; displacement, 1,550 tons. Her two engines generated 400 horsepower, which, according to one naval officer, could deliver a speed of thirteen knots. For armament, the *Kearsarge* carried two eleven-inch smooth-bore Dahlgrens, one 30-pounder Parrott rifle, and four 32-pounders. Her crew numbered 162 men. The vessel cost $286,918.05. The *Journal* on February 1 declared that the *Kearsarge* "is one of the finest vessels ever built at this station."[12]

After the *Kearsarge* was commissioned on January 24, Commandant Pearson paid special attention to final details. "I have to report," he notified Construction Chief John Lenthall on February 4, "that the Engines of the *Kearsarge* have been tried for seventy two consecutive hours, and they are found to perform satisfactorily for new engines. They will be ready for trial at sea to-day at 12 meridian." The next day, Pearson wrote Gideon Welles, "I have the honor to report, that the U.S. Steamer *Kearsarge* departed from this Yard on her cruise, this day at 11 1/2 o'clock A.M."[13]

Secretary Welles in his written orders of January 18, 1862, to Commander Pickering was most explicit: "You will proceed with the *Kearsarge* with all possible despatch to Cadiz in Spain, in search of the Piratical Steamer *Sumter*, which vessel is reported to have arrived recently at that place." According to public speculation, reasonably accurate in this instance, the *Kearsarge*'s destination was the island of Fayal in the Azores, halfway across the Atlantic, to load coal. "It is generally understood," explained the *Chronicle*, "that she is to go in pursuit of [Confederate] privateers. Should she fortunately fall in with any of the craft, it is doubtful, from the well known character of the *Kearsarge*'s officers, if they would be able to give her the slip."[14]

For Portsmouth and the Union, anticipation of sea battles and taking of Confederate ships constituted the greatest excitement of the war at that moment. The war on land was stalled while Union General George B. McClellan hesitated to launch an offensive toward Richmond. While awaiting news from the *Kearsarge* and other Portsmouth ships, *Chronicle* readers were provided anti-McClellan jokes:

> The Washington wags have got up a new "plan," which they dub "McClellan's." It is somewhat as follows: That McClellan is waiting for the Chinese population of California to increase to such a vast number that they will be able to cross the Rocky Mountains and bring up the right wing, by which time the Russian Possessions [Alaska] and Greenland will have a redundant population, which can be drafted down to the support of the grand left wing of the Union army—and that when those great events take place, the war will commence in earnest. This is the hotel joke now, and even McClellan listened to it the other day with good natured laughter.[15]

In his voyage across the Atlantic, *Kearsarge* Commander Charles W. Pickering felt similar frustrations in his bid for glory. The vessel experienced a very stormy passage. On the third day out, a gale picked up and continued for three days. The captain's dinghy was washed overboard. From the island of Madeira on February 22, Pickering reported to Lenthall:

> I found my cabin and stateroom flooded. In moderate weather I have been obliged to walk around the cabin on gratings, and in rough weather in India rubber boots. Notwithstanding the constant bailing of water from the cabin day and night, it found its way into the wardroom and endangered the magazines [powder storage room] from the passage of which, in moderate weather, the water was bailed out before it overflowed the risings at magazine doors.[16]

These difficulties notwithstanding, the *Chronicle* on April 1 printed a private letter reporting that the *Kearsarge* proved "to be a very fast and staunch vessel. With reefed topsails and screw dragging, she run [ran] 11 knots, with about a merchantman's top-gallant breeze; and several days she made 200 to 230 miles. She's bound to make a name for speed."[17]

The *Kearsarge*'s prime objective was to track down and capture the CSS *Sumter*, reputedly in the vicinity of the Azores and command-ed by Confederate Captain Raphael Semmes. Since the three-day storm had driven the *Kearsarge* past the Azores to the island of Madeira, close to Europe and Africa, Pickering decided to proceed to Cadiz, Spain. "We learned," wrote William H. Badlam, the second assistant engineer of the *Kearsarge*, "that the ... *Sumter* was anchored under the guns of Gibraltar, guarded by the United States steamer *Tuscarora* [under Commander Titus Augustus Craven, a Portsmouth native], which was lying at anchor in the port of Algesiras [Algeciras], a Spanish town across the bay from Gibraltar." By March 20, the *Kearsarge* had joined the *Tuscarora* in the blockade of "the pirate *Sumter*," as the Northern press named her.[18]

The rest of 1862 was a monotonous ordeal for the *Kearsarge*. Upon relieving the *Tuscarora*, she kept a sharp watch on the *Sumter*. The *Chronicle* on February 11 had accused "the pirate [Raphael] Semmes," the ship's commander, "of sending his family to Cincinnati for safety, where they are now living unprovided for by him and dependent upon the charity of loyal connections living in the North."[19]

On Sunday, July 13, the *Kearsarge* suffered its first casualty. While most of her officers were ashore attending a bullfight in Algeciras, the sailors went to the bay for a swim. "While the crew of the *Kearsarge* were taking their customary bath," reported the *Chronicle* on August 15, "a huge ground-shark appeared among them, and attacking one named Edward H. Tibbetts, caught him immediate-ly under the armpit on one side and dragged him to the bottom. It is the only instance of the kind known in that vicinity."

On July 14, the day after the accident, Commander Pickering submitted his report of the fatality, with related enclosures, to Secretary Welles. Tibbetts was nineteen years old, a native of Brunswick, Maine, who had entered naval service on New Year's Day of 1862. "His death," stated *Kearsarge* Naval Surgeon John M. Browne, "did not 'originate in the line of duty.'"[20]

Life aboard the *Kearsarge* during the summer became an exer-cise in tedium. "We have been lying here for 3 months," wrote a crew-man on September 7, "watching the *Sumter*, who is dangerous in spite of her best teeth having been extracted, but we hope soon to be relieved by the *Tuscarora* so that we can take a more active part in the war."[21]

This protracted wait ended abruptly. The Confederate government decided to sell the *Sumter* at her Gibraltar moorings. Semmes, with his officers and crew, escaped to England. In time, they went to the Azores to pick up a new English ship purchased for them by Confederate authorities. After arming his new vessel and naming her the *Alabama*, Semmes resumed his plunder of Northern commerce. Pickering and the *Kearsarge* headed for the Azores, but he was unable to track down the wily Semmes and "the British pirate *Alabama*," as the Northern press immediately dubbed the ship.[22]

In the fall of 1862, the *Kearsarge*, temporarily suspending her patrolling and blockading duties, proceeded to Cadiz, Spain. "The winter of 1862-1863," explained Engineer Badlam, "was spent at La Carraca [Caraca], Spain, at the Spanish Navy Yard [six miles from Cadiz], repairing our stern bearing, which had worn down to such an extent that it was not safe to continue cruising under steam. It took from the 1st of December, 1862, until the middle of March, 1863, to have the work finished, a job that ought not to have taken more than three weeks at the longest, had it been done in the United States."[23]

In its "NAVAL" column of December 9, 1862, the *Chronicle* reported, "Capt. John A. Winslow, formerly of the Mississippi flotilla, has been ordered to the command of the screw-sloop *Kearsarge* [seven guns], vice Captain Pickering detached and ordered home. Lieut. Commander [James S.] Thornton has been ordered to *Kearsarge*, vice Lieut. Commander Thos. C. Harris, ordered home."[24]

The CCS Virginia Destroys the Cumberland and the Congress

Across the Atlantic, in the vicinity of Norfolk, Virginia, seaman Nicholas Garginlo, wardroom steward aboard the USS *Cumberland* also experienced the uncertainty of waiting. A native of Naples, Italy, and from a family in comfortable circumstances, Garginlo had entered the United States Navy there with the help of purser John Bates. In his adopted hometown of Portsmouth, Garginlo was well known and esteemed.

His assignment aboard the *Cumberland* placed Garginlo in waters strategically important to the Union Navy. Together with the USS *Congress*, built at the Yard in 1841, and other warships, the *Cumberland* was part of the naval squadron blockading Chesapeake

Bay and the mouth of the James River in southern tidewater Virginia. The Union controlled the northern shore of this wide and vital waterway, with Fortress Monroe guarding Old Point Comfort and Camp Butler protecting the town of Newport News. Across the James, the Confederacy controlled Norfolk—protected, in turn, by the Gosport Navy Yard at nearby Portsmouth, Virginia. Separating the opposing navies was the wide bulge of the James River known as Hampton Roads.

During the fall of 1861, the *Cumberland* and other Union ships slipped away to Hatteras Inlet to bombard Forts Hatteras and Clark, to secure a foothold on the North Carolina coast. This Union naval victory sealed off Pamlico Sound, ending the threat of Confederate raiding and blockade running in that area. From Newport News, Virginia, in an undated letter during the winter of 1861-62 to a Portsmouth, New Hampshire, friend, Garginlo proudly described the recent action:

> We had, at Hatteras, a two days' [September 28-29, 1861] engagement, which was terrible, from beginning to the end, the *Cumberland* using her Dahlgren and pivot guns in such a manner as to compel the enemy to succumb to our stars and stripes.
>
> We have had, since, some little skirmishes, and the *Cumberland* came out victorious. May she never do less. At present we are lying here at Newport News. The rebels have raised up the frigate *Merrimac*, and are threatening to come and take us.
>
> We are looking for them every day—and if they should come, you may depend that we will give them a good reception, so much so as to satisfy them that the *Cumberland* still lives. Friend, never fear for our ship; when she shall be taken by the rebels, it will merely smoke, and we will go down with our glorious stars and stripes."[25]

Even as a ship steward, Garginlo knew what was common knowledge throughout the Union naval officer corps—that the Confederates were constructing an ironclad in hopes of breaking the Union blockade. William G. Saltonstall had an opportunity to observe the scene closely:

As an Acting Master, [I] was ordered to the frigate *Minnesota*, then lying in Hampton Roads, where I served as Flag Lieutenant on the staffs of Rear Admirals [Louis M.] Goldsborough and [Samuel P.] Lee.... [The *Merrimac*] had been a sister ship to the *Minnesota* and had fallen into the hands of the Confederates when they seized the Norfolk [Gosport] Navy Yard. It was well known that they had razeed [cut the ship down to a lower size by reducing her decks] and were plating her with iron, with a view of attacking our vessels in the Roads and doing whatever damage she could.

...The *Congress* and *Cumberland* frigates ... were guarding the entrance to the James River and kept a sharp lookout for anything approaching them at night. One evening, after dark, I was ordered to take the steamer *Philadelphia* and carry some dispatches to the commander of the *Congress*. It seems that the quartermaster on watch had reported us as coming out of Norfolk; and although we had our signals set, they decided we were a Rebel vessel trying to get up the James, and prepared to stop us. On we went, unsuspecting danger, until nearly up to the *Congress*, when fortunately the bell was rung to stop, and simultaneously a hail came from the ship, ordering us to stop. Our boat was lowered and I proceeded on board, well aware from appearances that something unusual was up. I found all hands at quarters, and being invited into the cabin was informed by the captain that had we not stopped as we did, a broadside would the next instant have been poured into us, the belief was so strong that we were a Confederate steamer trying to run the blockade.[26]

The jittery anticipation of the Union officers and men soon became a reality. On Saturday, March 8, 1862, the rebuilt ironclad CSS *Virginia* (formerly the *Merrimac*) ventured out.[27] "At 12:40 P.M., the *Merrimack* [sic]," reported Lieutenant Austin Pendergrast of the *Congress*, "with three small gunboats were seen steaming down from Norfolk. When they had turned into the James River channel and had approached near enough to discover their characters, we cleared the ship for action."[28]

Bypassing the *Congress*, the *Virginia* headed for the *Cumberland*, anchored at the time and exceedingly vulnerable. Lieutenant George U. Morris, executive officer of the *Cumberland*, saw the *Virginia* bearing down. "We opened fire on her," Morris wrote. "She stood on and struck us under the starboard fore channels; she delivered her fire at the same time; the destruction was great."[29]

From a vessel near Fortress Monroe, Union sailor J.P. Morse saw the great naval battle. On red, white, and blue patriotic stationery, showing a Union flag with the caption, "FAST COLORS, 1776 [to] 1862. WARRANTED NOT TO RUN," and dated, "Fort Munrow, March 13," Morse, in semiliterate orthography but vivid language, rendered a graphic account to someone named Will:

> The *Merymack* came up and pord [poured] a brod side in to the *Congress* and part on to the *Comberland* [*sic*] and ran in to hur sarbour [starboard] bows and pord a brod side through and through her receiving deth in every direction. We were laying so near at the time that they took a horser [hawser] to us from the *Cumberland* when they found that they were sinking, but they let us go again and we went in under the shore and we went up to the camp and helped to work the guns on the batrey, but the shells were flying in every direction. But about the *Merymack*: she looks like a large house sunk down to the roof. You can not see anyone on board of hur. She is a devil's machine in the hands of his imps. The *Congress* ran on shore and struck her colors and hoisted the white flag as she was on fire. She burnt all nite. It was the greatest fire works that I ever beheld. Her guns were going off at allmost as regular as tho they were fired by hur guners. At a bout twelve o'clock magaxine blew up. It was the greatest site that I ever beheld."[30]

While the battle was being waged, the "Ericsson iron-clad battery *Monitor*" approached during the late afternoon. A pilot-boat captain in the vicinity of Fortress Monroe informed the *Monitor*'s officers and men about the naval clash. "We did not credit it at first," wrote *Monitor* Lieutenant Samuel Dana Greene in a letter to his mother, dated March 14, 1862, from Hampton Roads, Virginia, "but as we approached Hampton Roads, we could see the fine old *Congress* burning brightly, and we knew that it must be so.... Our hearts were very full and we vowed vengence [vengeance] to the *Merrimac* if it should ever be our lot to fall in with her....[31]

On Sunday, March 9, the *Monitor* had fulfilled Greene's pledge.

The *Monitor* and the *Virginia* (ex-*Merrimac*) fought a fierce four-hour battle, generally considered to be the first combat between ironclads in history. The result was a stalemate. From his vantage point, sailor J.P. Morse observed, "It was sport to see them go rite up to each other and pore brodsides in to each other." During an interlude in the battle between the ironclads, the *Virginia* inflicted severe damage on the wooden-hulled USS *Minnesota*, demonstrating the obsolescence of wooden vessels. Captain John A. Dahlgren of the Union navy instantly recognized the significance: "Now comes the reign of iron," he explained, "and cased sloops are to take the place of wooden ships."[32]

The immediate result of the drawn battle was also clear. The Union blockade of Chesapeake Bay remained intact; the Confederacy had control of Norfolk and the Gosport Navy Yard (until Union recapture on May 10-11, 1862) and the upper James River. Assistant Secretary of the Navy Gustavus Fox, an eyewitness to the battle, saw for himself the dawn of a new age in naval technology. From aboard the grounded *Minnesota*, which the *Monitor* was ordered to protect, Fox greeted Lieutenant Samuel Dana Greene, who, at age twenty-two, had assumed command of the *Monitor* when Captain John L. Worden was temporarily blinded during the shelling. "As we ran alongside the *Minnesota*," Greene wrote, "Sec'y Fox hailed us, and told us we had fought the greatest naval battle on record and behaved as gallantly as men could. He saw the whole fight."[33]

William G. Saltonstall provided an excellent military analysis of the naval battle at Hampton Roads: "Our debt of obligation to the *Monitor* and her officers is incalculable. I do not think the *Merrimack* would have ventured outside the capes [Capes Charles and Henry], but she would have held undisputed possession of the Roads, Ches[a]peake Bay, Baltimore, the Potomac and Washington[,] could she have reached them. The day ... was ... momentous with the fate of the Union."[34]

The citizens of Portsmouth and the officers, sailors, and workmen of the Yard followed the news of the two-day battle with pride, relief, and sadness. The heavy casualty lists of the *Congress* and the *Cumberland*—more than a hundred for each ship—included several local naval personnel. In March, the *Chronicle* reported:

> Six of these gallant defenders of the *Cumberland* were natives of Portsmouth and vicinity, viz:
> Wm. M. Laighton, carpenter, injured, but doing well.

Eugene Mack, gunner.
Nicholas Garginlo, ward room steward, drowned.
——Webber, of Kittery, coxswain, legs shot off, and drowned.
——Pierce, seaman.
Thomas Moore, ward room boy, slightly wounded in the face.
Walter Gray and Frederick Willey, boys.[35]

A few weeks later, Asa Beals, age 32, of Newmarket, New Hampshire, was added to the list as "one of the lost." He had entered the navy at Portsmouth in 1859, and "when the *Cumberland* went down, he was at his post."[36]

Heroic actions of Portsmouth sailors characterized the last moments of the *Cumberland* before she sank. William M. Laighton, a ship's carpenter, stayed with the ship until the last. "The order went out for 'every man to look out for himself,'" reported the *Journal* on March 22. Men were dying from cannon balls, rifle shots, and rising waters. "After the order for self preservation was given," the *Journal* continued, "and nothing could be done, Mr. Laighton went below to his ward room, when the water there was up to his knees. On coming up, he took a position under the rigging. The vessel righting before going down, he was thrown under water. He swam to a floating cask, and afterward to some other floating article and, after being in the water for about twenty minutes, was taken up in a boat and carried to Newport News."[37]

Nicholas Garginlo was less fortunate. Headlining its story "A SAD MEMORIAL OF A NOBLE SAILOR," the *Chronicle* on March 18 recounted Garginlo's death: "He was ward-room steward of the ship, and in the battle was engaged in passing powder. His station was in the ward-room; he did not leave it, but was overtaken by the water as it poured in." The *Chronicle* also printed Garginlo's letter about his premonition of going down with the ship, "making us feel how sad a thing is war."[38]

Northern poets quickly set to verse the *Cumberland*'s dramatic sinking. The *Chronicle* printed Edith Hall's "The Sinking of the *Cumberland*," and Henry Wadsworth Longfellow's "The *Cumberland*," after both poems had appeared in other publications. After the war, interest continued. Herman Melville included his poetic elegy, "The *Cumberland*," in *Battle-Pieces and Aspects of the War* (1866). Immortalizing the sacrifice of Garginlo and his shipmates, Melville wrote:

Long as hearts shall share the flame
Which burned in that brave crew,
Her flame shall live—outlive the victor's name;
For this is due.
Your flag and flag-staff shall in story stand—
Cumberland![39]

The Building of the Ironclad Agamenticus

The *Monitor-Virginia* clash of ironclads underscored a trend already underway in the Union navy—the development and acceptance of new inventions and techniques. In 1862, the Portsmouth Navy Yard readily adopted such changes and originated a few contributions of its own.

The ironclad was not a new war vessel. As early as 1861, France and England had separately developed ironclad warships, with the *Glorie* and the *Warrior* already afloat. But once the Civil War had started, the Union navy quickly displayed its capacity, tested by battle conditions, for adopting existing ideas and developing new ones. By war's end in 1865, the United States Navy was perhaps the world's most technologically advanced maritime force. Following the success of the *Monitor*'s design and its revolving turret, the Navy Department ordered construction of more ironclads of the basic *Monitor* class or slight modifications of it.[40]

Senator John Parker Hale of Dover, chairman of the Senate Naval Committee, represented New Hampshire in Washington to push for a strong commitment to build ironclads. On March 14, 1862, he introduced a bill authorizing a steam ironclad ram and twenty steam ironclad gunboats, with an appropriation of $1 million for the ram and $13 million for the gunboats. Eight days later, the *Journal* enthusiastically informed its readers:

The United States have the following iron-clad vessels already built, contracted for, and proposed:

The *Monitor*	1
The *Galena*, built at Mystic [Connecticut]	1
The powerful vessel at Philadelphia	1
The *Adirondack*	1
The Stevens battery	1
The *Naugatuck*, built by Stevens	1

Iron clad gunboats ordered by Congress	20
Iron clad frigates recommended by	
Senate Naval Committee	20
The iron ram, do [ditto]	1
Gunboats ordered by Massachusetts	2
Total	49

New York State will probably add one or two more, thus making a naval force of fifty iron clad gunboats—greatly exceeding the combined iron-plated vessels of all Europe, and able to whip the navies of the world.[41]

During the fall of 1862, the Navy Yard began construction on its first ironclad, the USS *Agamenticus*. The town of York, Maine, a few miles north of the Yard, was originally known by the early settlers as Agamenticus, an Indian word meaning "small tidal river beyond." Also in the immediate area were the Agamenticus (now York) River and Mount Agamenticus. This 692-foot monadnock, rising abruptly about nine miles northwest of the Yard, had already earned its niche in maritime history. Its summit had served as a conspicuous landmark for early explorers and later for ship captains as they sailed along the New England coast.[42]

A member of the Monadnock class of Monitors, the *Agamenticus* was begun in the fall of 1862, when her keel was laid. "A large temporary wooden workshop has been erected at the Navy Yard," reported the *Chronicle* on September 29, "to be used in getting the iron work on the new iron-plated steamer to be built there. Immense lathes and other machinery for working the iron, are already in position. The machine shop is to be lengthened out forty feet to make room for machinery and workmen in this branch of ship building."[43]

The *Agamenticus* was larger than her prototype, being 250 feet long (compared to 179 for the *Monitor*) and 1,564 tons (987 for the *Monitor*). In addition, the *Agamenticus* carried two turrets (the *Monitor* had only one), each furnished with two guns weighing twenty-five tons each. "The *Agamenticus*," observed the *Chronicle* on October 17, "is being built on a [marine] railway, and is progressing favorably. She will be a queer looking craft when finished, with her rail but twenty inches above water, when in fighting trim."[44]

Work proceeded slowly on her construction. Pearson first needed to obtain construction plans from Rear Admiral Francis H. Gregory of

The double-turreted USS Agamenticus, *her wooden hull sheathed with iron plating, was the only ironclad constructed at the Portsmouth Navy Yard during the Civil War. Requiring three years of work, she was commissioned in May 1865, after the conflict was over. Four months later, however, with the downsizing of the navy, she was decommissioned. PNSVC*

New York. Admiral Gregory had been recalled from retirement, a frequent circumstance in the Union navy during the Civil War. Seventy-one years old when the war started, Gregory was ordered in July 1861 to superintend the construction of all vessels of war outside government Navy Yards. "Agreeably to the instruction of the Bureau of Construction, &c," wrote Commandant Pearson to Gregory on October 30, 1862, "I request you will furnish me with a plan of turrets and turning apparatus connected therewith, for the iron-clad steamer *Agamenticus* building at this Yard, so that the wood work may be prepared accordingly."

Also contributing to the *Agamenticus*'s construction delays was the necessary work to be completed at the Yard itself. A temporary building to protect the *Agamenticus* from snow and ice had to be completed, causing partial suspension of work on the vessel.[45]

Also competing for time and labor on the Yard's first ironclad was the side-wheeler *Sassacus.* "The *Agamenticus,*" reported the *Chronicle* on December 19, "does not progress very fast, owing to the fact that all the force of carpenters that could be employed has been thrown upon the *Sassacus* in order to get her off."[46]

The *Agamenticus* was launched the following spring.

Innovation and Testing at the Yard

A spirit of innovation increasingly energized the Yard during 1862. Gone were the last lingering effects of the labor strife experienced earlier that year as the Yard began to assume its full burden of responsibility. An attitude of improvisation and inventiveness designed to end the war as quickly as possible became the new, unofficial order of the day. Besides work on an ironclad, the Yard spent much time developing and testing new concepts.

Commodore Joseph Smith, Bureau Chief of Yards and Docks as well as an Ironclad Board member, called upon the Yard personnel to test a new shell. On January 30, 1862, he wrote to Pearson: "Mr. Geo[rge] C. Jones desires to have his patent Missile projectile tested by a Board of Officers. You are authorized to allow him to make a shell at the yard under your command himself. Also to prepare the Crib work on some Island or safe place to test its effects, and when ready, inform the Bureau of Ordnance, who will designate a Board to witness the test and report to the Ordnance the result."[47]

The tests were conducted in March 1862. The improved bomb shell was successful. According to the March 15 *Chronicle*:

> Mr. George C. Jones ... patented an improvement in the shell, by which it is made capable of discharging, through perforations, with or without exploding, a large number of musket balls in every direction horizontally. The experiments ordered by the Secretary of the Navy were made at the Portsmouth Navy Yard last week. An eight-inch shell, weighing 60 lbs., charged with 20 ounces of powder and 112 musket balls, was placed in a box of four-inch plank, seven feet square. Marks of every ball were found in the sides of the box, some of them passing through the plank. Sixteen pieces of the shell were found, which weighed only 34 lbs., leaving 26 lbs. scattered out of reach. The experiment was, we understand, satisfactory, and

the shell would probably be introduced into the service.[48]

Another concern of the Union naval command was to develop a color scheme to camouflage its vessels. Before the war, all United States warships were painted black. Since black profiles were easily sighted on the water at night, innovative Confederate blockade runners, seeking to slip by Union vessels on station, soon painted their hulls with various neutral colors to escape detection.

Preempting this improvision from the enemy, the U.S. Navy Bureau of Construction and Repair, under Captain John Lenthall's supervision, quickly conducted experiments with different colors. The tint that proved to be the least conspicuous under the greatest variety of conditions was bluish gray, called "Union color," today's battleship gray. A formula for its preparation, along with the necessary materials, was immediately distributed to the government Navy Yards and the blockading fleets.[49]

"Herewith enclosed," wrote Captain Lenthall to Commandant Pearson on July 31, "you will find a Sample Card of the Color which the Department directs shall be used in painting the outside of Iron vessels and also vessels in the Blockading Squadron, whenever they require repainting, including the inside of Port Shutters, heads of Masts, and all parts exposed to distant observation."[50]

On Tuesday, September 10, the U.S. steam transport *R.R. Cuyler* arrived at the Yard for overall repairs. "The transport *R.R. Cuyler*," reported the *Chronicle* on September 27, "is receiving a new coat of paint inside and out, and a thorough cleansing of all parts of the vessel is going on." Less than a month after her arrival, the *R.R. Cuyler* left her mooring on October 7 to return to blockade duty in her old cruising grounds off the Southern coast, "thoroughly cleansed and re-fitted in a very short time." In "A Change Of Color," the *Chronicle* on September 27 summarized the effectiveness of the newly painted hull in revolutionizing naval camouflage:

The deep black, which our war ships have been painted, has proved to be a very prominent mark to shoot at, in consequence of which, a change has been made to a grayish drab. The steamers *R.R. Cuyler*, and *Ossipee*, now at the Portsmouth Navy Yard, have both been painted this shade, which makes them much more "invisible," so that one standing on this side of the [Piscataqua] river can hardly distinguish the vessels from the wharf or water, whereas a small black boat and a schooner in the immediate vicinity stand out in bold relief.[51]

Later that fall, Commandant Pearson received a request from Rear Admiral Andrew H. Foote, Chief of the Bureau of Equipment and Recruiting. A well-known and beloved officer, Foote was the hero of Fort Henry and Fort Donelson. Commanding a gunboat flotilla on the Tennessee River during General Ulysses S. Grant's February 1862 campaign, he had coordinated the naval efforts to capture these forts. Wounded during the fighting and in poor health, Foote was compelled to take a less strenuous desk job as a Navy Bureau chief. In this capacity, on November 20, 1862, he wrote Pearson a three-page letter soliciting ideas for developing new galley equipment:

> The principal cooking in Ships of war is boiling, and heat is conducted laterally through liquids. Baking and roasting have not hitherto been considered to be essential, but if they can be combined to a greater extent than heretofore, it would add very much to the health and comfort of the crew....
>
> The Bureau would be glad to have your cooperation and requests your views on the subject with any suggestions that in your opinion will be beneficial; and if you have a plan, drawing, or model you will be good enough to send them....[52]

In response to Foote's hopes of devising a wrought-iron galley heated with anthracite coal, Pearson answered on December 16:

> I herewith forward plans of a galley (accompanied by a statement from the Master Machinist at this Yard in relation to the same)—which I believe will answer a better purpose than any galley I have yet seen.
>
> It is adapted for the burning of coal, or wood when coal cannot be obtained. I hope you will allow Mr. Prescott, Master Machinist, to construct one here under his own supervision, in order that it may be tried.
>
> With regard to ovens for baking bread for the crew, I believe that this galley will answer that desirable purpose in part, and without taking up much room. Our ships, generally speaking, cannot have large ovens separate from the galley

Fresh Beef & Vegetables for the Navy.

NAVY DEPARTMENT,
Bureau of Provisions and Clothing,
WASHINGTON, May 8, 1862.

Sealed proposals will be received at this office until THURSDAY, the fifth day of June, 1862, at noon, for the supply of such quantities of Fresh Beef and Vegetables as may be required on the Portsmouth, N. H., station, during the fiscal year commencing on the 1st day of July next, and ending on the 30th June, 1863.

The Beef and Vegetables must be of good quality, and the best the market affords; and each article must be offered for by the pound.

Bond with approved security will be required in one half the estimated amount of the contract, and twenty per centum in addition will be withheld from the amount of each payment to be made, as collateral security for the performance of the contract, which will on no account be paid until it is fully complied with. Payment to be made in certificates of indebtedness, or in Treasury Notes, at the option of the government.

Every offer made must be accompanied (as directed in the act of Congress making appropriation for the naval service for 1846-'7, approved 10th August, 1846,) by a written guaranty, signed by one or more responsible persons, to the effect that he or they undertake that the bidder or bidders will, if his or their bid be accepted, enter into an obligation, within five days, with good and sufficient sureties, to furnish the articles proposed.

No proposal will be considered unless accompanied by such guaranty. may6 ev Tues 4w

PC, May 6, 1862

without discommoding the crew in their limited accommodations.[53]

On December 18, Foote responded enthusiastically: "Your letter … covering drawings of a Galley, which appears to possess great merit, has been received. You will please have a Tin-Model made at your earliest convenience, and send it to the Bureau."[54]

Considerable time was required to prepare a satisfactory model. Finally, in early 1864, the Portsmouth galley was nearing completion, evidently approved for general use throughout the United States Navy. (Precise documentation is lacking.) On February 2, 1864, Commander Albert N. Smith, Foote's successor as Navy Bureau chief (Foote had died in June 1863), wrote to Pearson: "As soon as the

Galley now under construction at the Yard under your command is completed, you will please have it shipped to Boston, to be shipped to Washington."[55]

During the last year of war, the officers and crews aboard Union warships were able to enjoy better meals, courtesy of the Portsmouth galley.

The Navy Acquires Seavey's Island

The massive construction and larger labor force at the Portsmouth Navy Yard during the Civil War required more space. The 58-acre Navy Yard Island was inadequate for increased wartime demands. In 1862, the United States Navy, in an effort to ease overcrowding, sought to acquire at least part of adjacent Seavey's Island.[56]

Seavey's Island lay immediately south and east of Navy Yard Island, the two separated by a narrow channel, Jenkins Gut. Containing 105 acres, Seavey's Island was the larger of the two. Some twenty-eight people owned these 105 acres, parceled into thirty-one lots of various sizes on Seavey's Island, administratively part of the village of Kittery. Most were farmers.

As early as 1860, following the recommendation of a Navy Board, Civil Engineer of the Yard Benjamin F. Chandler made a map of Seavey's Island in anticipation of expansion. The Yard needed to build a hospital, and nearby Seavey's Island provided a logical site.[57]

In January 1862, a statement of estimates, presented by Mark F. Wentworth, the naval storekeeper at the Yard, and prepared by Commodore Joseph Smith, Bureau Chief of Yards and Docks, projected the amount of money required for anticipated construction and completion of works, and for repairs at the Yard for the fiscal year ending June 30, 1863:

For machine shop and smithery	$88,900
Fitting and furnishing ditto	34,826
Reservoir, &c	9,000
Capstan for sheers	5,359
Quay wall near landing	12,200
Futtock saw mill	10,000
Extension of store house No. 11, 50 ft.	10,000
Repairs of all kinds	34,750
	$205,035

Also, for hospital	20,000
for a west wing to ordnance building	36,491

$261,526[58]

Commandant Pearson and other Yard officials decided to acquire only the most desirable portion of Seavey's Island to avoid engaging in a protracted battle with the twenty-eight owners for the whole island. The navy needed an appropriation from the United States Congress for the purchase, and the congressman from the First ("Navy Yard") District, Gilman Marston, secured the necessary amendments to the Navy Appropriation bill, which were adopted in turn by the House of Representatives in Washington on February 15, 1862: "For the purchase of 27 355/1000 [twenty-seven and roughly a third] acres of land on Seavey's Island, for fitting up the buildings thereon for a hospital, buildings, coal wharf and shed and fencing the ground—$20,000."[59]

By the time the U.S. House of Representatives passed the bill in May, the funds for the futtock saw mill had been deleted. The House appropriated $55,000 for the purchase of the portion of Seavey's Island and $10,000 for the erection of the hospital, "*Provided* that no building shall be erected or extended until complete plans, specifications, or estimates of cost in detail, shall be furnished to and approved by the Secretary of the Navy, and contracts, therefor shall be made upon due and public advertisement."[60]

The owners of the lots in question on the island rejected the original offer as too low. At a meeting in mid-May 1862, they agreed to sell their rights to the island for about $60,000.[61]

Commandant Pearson quickly discovered that all the various owners were reluctant to sell, most holding out for higher compensation. He opted instead to deal directly with Mr. and Mrs. Horatio Bridge, the owners of the most strategic and sought-after acreage, in order to acquire land quickly. On August 25, in a three-page letter to recently promoted Rear Admiral Joseph Smith, chief of the Bureau of Yards and Docks, Pearson detailed his difficulties in conducting the negotiations:

As yet I have not been able to obtain the sum now charged for land by Mrs. [Horatio] Bridge [who apparently held the legal title], but presume it will be the $13,000 previously decided upon by Mr. Bridge.... [Not only was Horatio Bridge Seavey's Island's largest landowner, with lots #1 and #2 bordering on Jenkins Gut, but he also was the chief of the U.S. Navy Bureau of Provisions and Clothing.]

The road is a town road, and it is not considered in the number of acres.—the land given by the proprietors and the town of Kittery.

If the whole Island is purchased, the road and the school house will of course belong to the Government. Otherwise the road and the school house must be retained for the use of the proprietors who remain upon the island, as well as for the use of the Government.

Mr. D[aniel] Trefethen demands a large price apparently for his lots 19 & 20 and will not sell one without the other. He is averse to selling at all, and will only do so on his terms even to the kind of money. He is an elderly person and so very deaf as to prevent any constant employment beyond his home. Here he can obtain a certain maintenance.—here he has brought up his family, and here he has buried his dead! Under the circumstances one cannot but appreciate his feeling—his determination not to relinquish a good home without being sufficiently paid for it.

Citing case after case, Pearson noted individual objections to the government's offer. Compounding the problem was Pearson's realization that the navy, for military security, had to acquire not only a few strategic lots, but the entire island. "It would undoubtedly be advisable to purchase the whole of Seavey's Island," Pearson continued, "but for the security of this Navy Yard at night, I look upon it as all-important that the Government should own all the shore from A to B [reference points on Chandler's map]—the long narrow, and in some places very shallow passage between the Navy Yard and that shore, leaving the Navy Yard ... exposed to evil-designed persons."

With respect to the hastily erected fort on Seavey's Island at the outbreak of the war, Pearson concluded, "The fort is merely an earthwork, but its position is very commanding, and therefore it should belong to the Government and a strong fort be built upon its site."[62]

Pearson and the Navy Department were, nevertheless, realistic in their land acquisition aims, initially satisfied to obtain the most critical portion of the island in 1862 and leaving the rest for the future. On September 1, Pearson again wrote to Rear Admiral Smith:

> I herewith return to the Bureau the plan of Seavey's Island,
> and have thereon inserted a red line which with the shore from
> A to B embraces the 27 355/1000 acres [Horatio Bridge's lots],
> which I deem the best for naval purposes.
>
> I have notified the inhabitants of Seavey's Island that in
> case [the] Government should purchase their lands for the pur-
> pose of erecting navy improvements, the ground so purchased
> would be walled in, and the Bridge [connecting the two islands]
> appropriated exclusively to Government use.

Concluding that the navy could only obtain Horatio Bridge's
twenty-seven "continuous acres" at the price the navy was then offering, Pearson added, "I perceive that on the plan the sum of $14,500
has been set opposite the name of Mr. [Horatio] Bridge by the Bureau,
as the price of his lands."[63]

Thus, in 1862, the Yard acquired Horatio Bridge's two lots
(twenty-seven-plus acres) on Seavey's Island for a hospital site. It was
not until 1866 that the navy obtained possession of the entire island for
$105,000 from twenty-eight other owners. "The owners of this island,"
wrote Rear Admiral George Henry Preble in his history of the Yard,
"undoubtedly took advantage of the necessities of the Government in
fixing a price upon their land." Lawyers also profited. "The necessary
papers for its [Seavey's Island's] transfer," reported the *Journal* on
June 16, 1866, "are being drawn up by Francis Bacon, Esq., who will
search the records at Alfred, ME [seat of York County in which Kittery
is located], to substantiate the validity of the present titles."[64]

Obtaining Seavey's Island took years, but Pearson made other
land improvements around the Yard in 1862. In September, on Navy
Yard Island, workmen excavated eighteen feet of solid ledge for a
reservoir with a holding capacity of 140,000 gallons. Construction of
the new hospital on the island began that fall.[65]

"The British Pirate Alabama*"*
Antagonizes Portsmouth

All the various activities at the Yard were focused on a single goal:
the defeat of the enemy, personified on land by Confederate President

Jefferson Davis and at sea by Captain Raphael Semmes, commander of the CSS *Alabama*. Constantly harping about "that pirate Semmes," the Portsmouth press quickly found an emotional outlet for its readers in the person responsible for the loss of thousands of dollars worth of Piscataqua shipping. "His [Semmes's] whole appearance," commented the *Journal* on October 25, 1862, "is that of a corsair, and the transformation appears to be complete from Commander Raphael Semmes, United States Navy, to a combination of [Jean] Lafitte, [Captain William] Kidd and [Charles] Gibbs, the three most notorious pirates the world has ever known." Linking Semmes to these individuals cast him in the most contemptible company. In addition to recognizing the well-known names of Lafitte and Kidd, most older *Portsmouth Journal* readers would easily recall the heinous Charles Gibbs. Born in Rhode Island about 1794, Gibbs supposedly had served aboard American privateers during the War of 1812. Turning pirate in 1821 and becoming the bane of the United States Navy, Gibbs and his men allegedly murdered 400 mariners during their cruises along the North and South Atlantic coasts. Captured in 1830, Gibbs was hanged the following year at Ellis Island in New York Harbor. In associating Semmes with this American pirate, the *Journal* doubtlessly hoped that the detested *Alabama* captain might soon share Gibbs's inglorious fate.[66]

The primary goal of the Union navy was rightly blockade duty to immobilize the South, but Northern civilian alarm and hysteria influenced the Lincoln administration to spend an inordinate amount of time chasing Semmes and a handful of other Southern raiders. Since the British supplied excellent warships to the Confederacy and many English citizens supported the Southern cause, Portsmouth responded with undisguised ire. Such bitter feelings increased in 1862, when Semmes, aboard the British-built *Alabama*, began his two-year cruise of destruction against Northern (including Portsmouth) shipping.[67]

On October 25, 1862, the *Journal* described Semmes's strategy in detail:

> The plan that Semmes has adopted to bring fish to his net is as follows: It will be seen at a glance that the position he was last reported in was in the track of many vessels bound to and from Europe. This is the position he has chosen to do the greatest possible amount of destruction and he certainly has been most

successful. Whenever he captured [captures] a ship, after taking from her all that he and his officers want, he lays by her until dark and then sets her on fire. The light of the burning ship can be seen many miles, and every other ship within seeing distance stands toward the light, thinking to rescue a number of poor fellows from destruction. The pirate keeps in the immediate vicinity, awaiting the prey that is sure to come, and the next morning the poor fellows, who have, to serve the cause of humanity, gone many miles out of their course, find themselves under the guns of the *Alabama*, with the certainty that before another twenty-four hours they will share the fate of the ship they came to serve.

This plan will enable him to destroy an immense amount of property without much cruising. He can lay in one position and gather the ships around him during the night, ready for operations on the coming day, for weeks to come; for it will be a long time before his depredations can be made known, so that our unsuspecting merchantmen will be on the look-out for him.

Again, he will be enabled to cruise for an indefinite length of time; for he uses no coal, depending upon his canvas entirely, which, it seems, is all sufficient for his purpose. He carries stores for eight months, and can always replenish from the prizes he may take. He will be here to-day, there to-morrow, and will be certain to be found where no one is looking for him. Looking for him will be like "looking for a needle in a hay stack," and with the majority of vessels we have cruising at the present time, should one of them be fortunate enough to see him, all we shall benefit thereby will be a look, and so it will continue to be until we have ships of greater speed than we now possess or expect soon to have.[68]

On October 3, 1862, the officers and crew of the Portsmouth clipper *Emily Farnum*, under Captain Nathan Parker Simes, experienced for themselves Semmes's "hospitality" at sea. Bound from New York to Liverpool, England, with an assigned cargo, the *Emily Farnum* sailed in company with the *Brilliant* out of New York. At sea about 300 miles southeast of Newfoundland, the *Emily Farnum* saw a steamer to the westward under sail. The distant vessel displayed St. George's cross, the British flag. Not long afterward, the "British" steamer fired a shot across the bow of the *Emily Farnum* and quickly ran up Confederate colors. A Southern officer and armed sailors soon boarded the Portsmouth ship from a longboat. While this was happening, the *Alabama* chased down and captured the *Brilliant* as well.

Captain Simes of the *Emily Farnum* was soon taken aboard the *Alabama*. Carrying his ship's papers, he was ushered to Semmes's cabin. Captain Simes's private log and subsequent memories record his reception:

> [Semmes] was enjoying his cigar and wine, but unmindful of the forms of hospitality to his visitor. He took Capt. Simes' papers, and asked many questions about the ship, her cargo, owners, &c., and her value, where the cargo was owned, &c. Among the papers attached to a bill of lading was a certificate of the British consul in New York, showing that the goods on board were the property of John B. Spence, of Liverpool. When this was shown, he declared it to be "bogus," and that it was "prepared by the owners for the purpose of saving their vessel."
>
> The rebel commander then asked the Yankee many questions about the armies and their movements, how many vessels were being added to the navy, their whereabouts, and sought information of this character with much apparent interest.[69]

The meeting continued in this vein for some time. Finally Semmes offered to parole the *Emily Farnum*, provided she take aboard all the prisoners he had taken from his previous captures, the whaling barks *Virginia* and *Elisha Dunbar*, both of New Bedford, Massachusetts, together with those from the *Brilliant*. Given this chance to save his vessel and rescue compatriots, Captain Simes accepted the offer. Semmes's apparent clemency reflected his realistic options. Carrying more prisoners than he could adequately house and feed, as well as wanting to avoid any offense with Great Britain regarding a neutral cargo, Semmes chose to release the *Emily Farnum*. The next day, October 4, the paroled Portsmouth vessel received on board seventy-eight of Semmes's prisoners. As the *Emily Farnum* got underway for Liverpool, Captain Simes, his officers, his crew, and his added passengers saw flames from the *Brilliant* rise in the distance. Before torching her, the *Alabama* had stripped her of freight, cargo, and ship's stores and equipment worth $80,000.[70]

The burning of the *Brilliant* produced much comment. Captain Hagar of the *Brilliant*, along with the captains of the two whaling vessels, published a card expressing gratitude to Simes and the *Emily Farnum* "for the kind and generous treatment received by them while on board his vessel."

A published account of Hagar's brief captivity in irons while a prisoner aboard the *Alabama* revealed the enmity of the opposing sides. Confederate Lieutenant Richard F. Armstrong, Semmes's junior officer, told Hagar: "We are nothing to each other as countrymen. The North and the South are now distant races, with no feelings or interests in common. The people of the South are the only true representatives of the American race. You of the North have intermarried so much with the lower classes of Europeans that you have, in great measure, if not altogether, lost your nationality, and are not worthy to be considered of the same people as ourselves."[71]

On October 17, Thomas P. Salter, an agent of Daniel Marcy in New York, wrote his employer, "Our village [New York City] is much excited,—the news of the destruction of the *Brilliant* & other vessels creates great indignation. She was loaded wholly with cargo on *British accounts*—there are no doubt others which have shared a similar fate."[72]

On November 15, the readers of the *Journal* finally learned from the "MARINE JOURNAL" column that "Ship *Emily Farnum*, [Captain Nathan Parker] Simes, [commanding,] f[ro]m New York arr[ived] Liverpool Oct. 21st,—with upwards of 80 seamen captured by the pirate *Alabama*." On October 25, Captain Simes, on behalf of himself and the owners of the *Emily Farnum*, had submitted a claim to the United States government for reimbursement of his unexpected expenses:

To board & lodging [lodge] 70 Distressed Amn [American] Seamen
from Oct. 3rd to Oct. 24th 21 days at 1/6 [one shilling, six pence] each per day   £110,5,0
'[Ditto mark] 8 distressed Seamen Oct 3 to Oct. 6
3 days at 1/6 per day each   1, 16, 0

Received Payment   £112, 1, 0

In addition to the claim and the receipt, an affidavit, sworn and subscribed before Thomas H. Dudley, United States consul at Liverpool, on October 31, 1862, attested that Simes deposed that "the above bill is for expenses of Seamen placed on the *Emily Farnum* by the Confederate Steamer *Alabama*, that the number of seamen placed on my ship was 78, eight of whom I placed in the brig *Golden Lead* and 70 I brought to Liverpool ... and that the above bill is correct in all things[.]"[73]

The ship *Manchester*, another Portsmouth-built vessel, also was captured by the *Alabama*—on October 11, 1862. Built in 1840, the *Manchester* was owned and registered in New York. On October 3, she had sailed from New York to Liverpool, with a cargo of "45,141 bushels wheat, and 14,666 bushels corn." In this instance, Semmes was not lenient—he burned the *Manchester*.[74]

Concurring with prevalent Northern public opinion, Portsmouth citizens always insisted that the *Alabama* was, in truth, a British warship. "This vessel has never been in American waters," commented the *Journal* on October 25, "but only in British waters or upon the high seas. This fact may lead to reclamations by our government upon that of Great Britain for acts of a vessel that has no stamp of nationality other than British." The *New York Express* was more outspoken in its condemnation of the *Alabama*, or "No. 290," its original designation: "The origin of the name of this famous, or rather infamous ship, is not generally known. The ship was bought by a subscription made by 290 British merchants, from that honorable class of whom [Edmund] Burke [British orator and statesman] said the counting house was their temple, the ledger their Bible, and gold their God. One of these days a settlement of this will be made."[75]

The Portsmouth press regularly provided its readers with anti-British commentary and jokes. "Earl Russell [the British minister of foreign affairs who was actually pro-Union], though supposed to be a very dry subject," reported the *Chronicle* on December 31, "is something of a wag, for he tells Englishmen whose property has been destroyed by the *Alabama*, that they can claim compensation in a Confederate Court! He must have laughed at the joke as he penned it. They might as well try to get a pat of butter out of a black dog's mouth."[76]

"Are there any reasons in the History of England," went another story, "why that country should be cautious about making war upon us? Yes, 1776 reasons in one place and 1812 reasons in another." A third commentary noted, "The British lion threatens to lick us. Well, he licked us once before—licked our feet!"[77]

From the British point of view, animosity toward the North was mutual. This attitude flourished in certain circles of British government, commerce, and society. British textile manufacturers, in particular, facing what they called the "Cotton Famine" of the 1860s, needed this Southern raw material to keep their mills running. Other English industrialists feared and resented the federal Union, which they feared as a competing commercial and industrial colossus across the Atlantic. After the Union split, their reasoning went, British business would profit from the opening of a vast Southern free-trade market. Thus, as a trading nation, Great Britain, at least in theory, stood to gain economically from the establishment of an independent Confederacy. With the hindsight of two months' residence in Liverpool, a Portsmouth, New Hampshire, woman described the British anti-Union feelings in a letter home in the fall of 1862:

> As to the dress, the appearance, and the language of those we meet, we might think ourselves in the United States. There is so much intercourse between New York and Liverpool, that there is said to be more resemblance here to whatever is American than anywhere else in England. But while all are personally attentive and courteous, they are so intensely Southern in their feelings, that we cannot convince them that the North is not thoroughly beaten.... all say openly that they are the friends of the South. Englishmen, both high and low, favor the South, and espouse Southern interests as warmly as the Southerners themselves. We hear more of the war here than at home; and in my opinion, if the South needs the aid of England in this contest, it will be given without hesitation.[78]

American Merchant Marine Strategies

Since "King Cotton" was the lifeblood of the Confederacy, and since Great Britain was the major importer of Southern cotton, the Union Navy sought to intercept such trade. Portsmouth citizens followed closely the calculated actions of the Union government in its precarious policy of curtailing Confederate maritime commerce while avoiding offense to Great Britain. One *Trent* affair was enough.

The port of Nassau in the British colony of the Bahamas illustrates the Union's difficulties in attempting to deal with an ostensibly neutral port. A sleepy Caribbean fishing harbor off the coast of Florida prior to 1861, Nassau was suddenly transformed by the war into a commercial boomtown. Confederate blockade runners as well as British vessels laden with war supplies for the Confederacy constantly clogged Nassau Harbor.[79]

On January 30, 1862, one T.E. Wood wrote from Nassau to the editor of the *Chronicle* a perceptive letter that "might interest some of my friends in Portsmouth." Along with an excellent analysis of the geography, people, economy, and climate of the Bahamas, Wood addressed the dilemma the Union faced in enforcing the blockade:

> The white inhabitants are mostly from England or of English descent (except for a few Americans here on business or for their health) and they are almost all of them in sympathy with the Southern rebellion and secessionists, and while in years past the South has had a great dislike for Nassau because of its being a place of refuge for slaves, yet this is now made a regular rendezvous for Southern vessels engaged in running the blockade; and vessels carrying the rebel flag or sailing under British colors are allowed to come and go at pleasure, either landing their cargoes or transferring them from one vessel to another under the protection of the English men-of-war.
>
> One large steamer, the *Gladiator*, brought a valuable cargo from Europe—said to be valued at $300,000, of arms, ammunition, boots and shoes, &c. She lay for several days in the harbor, and in the absence of the U.S. steamer *Flambeau*, which sailed on a cruise to Key West while the vessel was in port, she steamed up and sailed for the South port of the island and there discharged her cargo, as it is said, into small vessels, which can more easily run the blockade. Just previous to this, another large steamer, formerly the *Isabel*, which ran between Charleston and Havana, left port and succeeded in running the blockade at Charleston, as it is said.
>
> On Monday last [January 13, 1862] the U.S. steamer again returned to port, and on Saturday [January 18] another Southern steamer, called the *Carolina*, carrying the Confederate flag, came into port and passed the American steamer, and some said she saluted the U.S. steamer by dipping the flag—and I have heard it stated by two gentlemen

from the state of Maine, a captain and his mate, that the captain of the American steamer said in their presence and before the U.S. Consul, that if he had been on board of his vessel at the time and had seen the flag dipped, he should have returned the compliment to him. If this be true[,] such officers are unworthy of their calling, and it is not strange that so many vessels succeed in running the blockade.

The U.S. Government has shipped several cargoes of coal to this place for their own steamers, but this Government would not allow them to coal their steamers here or make this a coal depot. Some of the vessels[,] therefore, have had to depart for some other place with their cargoes.[80]

The situation in the Bahamas reflected unofficial British policy. Although Great Britain remained officially neutral throughout the war, English businessmen, expecting large profits from shipbuilding for blockade runners and the cotton trade, enthusiastically embraced this newfound enterprise. Encouraged by Confederate agents in England, British-fronted blockade-running operations became, as one contemporary termed them, "bold and gambling ventures."

Navy Secretary Gideon Welles was not fooled by the pretext of British neutrality. Blockade running had become, he noted in his diary, "systematized into a business and the ingenuity and skill of the Englishmen and the resources of English capital are exhausted in assisting the Rebels."[81]

If Confederate and English businessmen, merchants, and shipbuilders operated through deception and evasion, their Portsmouth counterparts showed that they could play the crooked game equally well. In order to avoid capture on the high seas by British-built Confederate raiders, exemplified by the *Alabama*, many Portsmouth shipowners sold their vessels outright to the British. In 1862, at least two Portsmouth vessels were transferred under this wartime plan. In March, the ship *Isaac H. Boardman*, built in Portsmouth in 1855, was sold in London for $42,000 by her Newburyport, Massachusetts, and Seabrook, New Hampshire, owners. The ship was renamed, somewhat ironically, the *Commander-in-Chief*, one of President Lincoln's *ex officio* titles. Two months later, in May, the New York Shipping List announced "the sale of ... new ship *City of Montreal*, built at Portsmouth, N.H., in 1861, at $60,000, bought by Thomas Dunham and Stephen W. Cary, to go in Dunham's London Line."[82]

Freight Wanted for New York.

SCHOONER SARAH, HASKELL
Master, — now discharging at the
Portsmouth Navy Yard. For freight
apply to

L. COTTON,
Railway Wharf.

decl 3t

PC, Dec. 1, 1862

With so many changes of ownership, transfers of title, switching of flags, and other ruses of war, the United States acted to protect its own interests. In notices to all Collectors of Customs, in September 1862, Secretary of the Treasury Salmon Chase detailed instructions for enforcing a new congressional law that required "all shipmasters, whenever they clear, whether foreign or coasters, to take an oath of allegiance to the United States."[83]

The United States Navy was compelled to adopt a clandestine approach for security reasons. On April 22, Secretary of the Navy Gideon Welles issued a "GENERAL ORDER":

Officers of the Navy, and all other persons in the employment of the Naval branch of the public service, are hereby forbidden to give publicity to any hydrographical knowledge obtained during their service afloat.

Intelligence respecting any contemplated Naval or Military operations; descriptions of Naval vessels or armaments; their destination, or the names of such as are under repair, or fitting for sea, and any other information whatsoever that can be used to the injury of the Government by the public enemy, are also prohibited.[84]

The Marcy Brothers Suffer Losses

The vortex of war quickly engulfed Daniel Marcy in Portsmouth and his brother Peter in New Orleans. Ship captures, financial losses, and a battle-related death of one of the Marcy nephews were among a series of disasters. In the fall of 1862, Daniel Marcy decided to run for Congress, undoubtedly hoping that, if elected, he might be able to help end the ordeal he and the nation were experiencing.

On January 25, 1862, Daniel Marcy probably first learned from the columns of the *Journal* about the capture of Peter's Confederate schooner. Writing from Ship Island in Mississippi Sound off Biloxi on December 29, 1861, an unnamed Northern correspondent provided a graphic account:

> The *New London* has been harassing the rebels again the past week—this time with some profit.... On Friday night [December 27, 1861], intelligence was received that the U.S. gunboat *Wisschicken* [*Wissahickon*] was ashore at the east end of Horn Island. The *New London* got under weigh at 11 o'clock and went to her assistance. She succeeded in getting her off the following day. While thus engaged, a schooner was seen running about Mississippi Sound, apparently watching the movements of the steamers, and about noon the *New London* started in pursuit and approached within a half mile of her, at a point ten miles northeast of Horn Island. The *N.L.* fired at "secesh," which caused considerable commotion on board. Boats were got out and the schooner was abandoned by those on board, who attempted to prevent her falling into the hands of the enemy by setting her on fire. Two boats started from the *New London*, one in pursuit of the fugitives, and the other to board the schooner, which proved to be the yacht *Gipsey* of New Orleans—a vessel of considerable notoriety in Southern waters. She was loaded with 150 bales of cotton, with which she was attempting to run the blockade. When boarded, the flames were bursting up the for[e]castle, the hold and the cabin, and the fore and main-sails were already on fire. The flames were extinguished and the vessel and cargo saved....
>
> The boat which went to overtake the fugitives failed to overtake them, but several musket shots were fired and one man was seen to *lie down* suddenly in the boat.
>
> The prize was taken in tow and brought into this harbor [Ship Island] in charge of "Commodore" Johnson of Mattapoisett, Mass., Acting Master of *New London*, who has been appointed prize master, and will proceed North in charge of the cargoes which have been taken. She [the *Gipsey*] is a beautiful yacht, of remarkable sailing qualities, and was formerly owned by Mr. Robinson of Biloxi.... She has been taken four times by United States cruisers, and each time released, having been under British colors. At the time of the late action she was owned by Peter Marcy, a wealthy merchant of New

Orleans, having exchanged hands for $5000. Vessel and cargo were valued at $10,000. This is the first cargo of cotton which is known to have been captured by U.S. vessels.[85]

Found aboard were several letters (reprinted in the *Journal* article), including one from Samuel Marcy to his uncle Peter, describing his strategy for running the blockade: watching for a signal on the point—"red if dangerous, and white if the channel is clear." This would help him evade Union blockading ships, which Samuel referred to as "the Hessians," or "the Lincolnites."[86]

The loss of a blockade runner was only the beginning of Peter Marcy's troubles as the war continued. During 1862, the stakes mounted, costing Marcy his home. During April 1862, Vice Admiral David G. Farragut, the Union commander of the West Gulf Blockading Squadron, assembled seventeen ships at the mouth of the Mississippi to undertake a campaign to capture New Orleans, about one hundred miles upriver. On April 24, Farragut's fleet ran past Fort Jackson and Fort St. Philip, destroying Confederate warships on the way. The next day, Farragut's fleet anchored before New Orleans, Peter Marcy's home. Farragut's victory thus placed the South's largest and wealthiest city in Union hands.

The USS *Portsmouth*, commanded by Samuel Swartwout, was one Portsmouth-built ship that participated in the crucial river battle of April 24, sealing the fate of New Orleans. In a letter dated June 15, 1862, written aboard the *Portsmouth* off Carrollton, Louisiana, and printed in the *Journal* on July 12, a New Hampshire sailor recalled,

When the signal was given to the fleet to get underweigh, we were towed to our position under a most galling fire from Forts Jackson and St. Philip, and from a masked battery within 200 yards of us. We there let go our anchor and ran a hawser ashore to the bank, so as to bring our broadside to bear on the forts. We then gave them three broadsides. It now being daylight, they could see us distinctly, and we were getting good range when our hawser was shot away, and the ship swung down stream so that we could not get a gun to bear on them. Immediately a solid shot, weighing 64 pounds, came on board, raking range, killing one man and tearing up some eight planks in our deck, then lodged in a beam. Their shot was cutting up our rigging and we could not get a steamer to come to our assistance. We slipped our anchor with thirty fathoms of cable, and dropped down the river. A sailing ship can do no more than that. Sailing ships are about played out. I will venture to say, no one ship in the fleet was under such galling fire as the old *Portsmouth*. The shot and shell were falling around us as thick as peas, but the men stood their ground like all noble tars fighting for their country.[87]

One of the shots fired in the battle for New Orleans struck Samuel Marcy, nephew of Peter and Daniel. As one of Daniel Marcy's agents in New York, Thomas P. Salter reported to his chief, "Your nephew Sam was badly wounded across the breast by a shot from one of our [Union] Gun Boats during the engagement at New Orleans[,] so a man told me who came in recently."[88]

Salter's initial report proved to be not as alarming as first feared. Private Samuel Marcy, a member of the Confederate Guards of the Louisiana Militia, recovered from his serious wounds and survived the war.[89]

Back in Portsmouth, Daniel Marcy sought to shore up his battered shipping empire. Speaking for Marcy, James N. Tarlton often conveyed his employer's sentiments to Captain Richard H. Tucker at Wiscasset. In a letter dated April 29, 1862, Tarlton expressed hopes that Farragut's victory might result in the reopening of the cotton ports to Northern shipping:

> I think the surrender of New Orleans must be a death blow to the rebil [sic] leaders....
> *Alice Ball* [the ship released at Eastport, Maine, in 1861] had a long and hard passage [eighty-eight days at sea from Le Havre, France, to New York], pretty well shook up. Marcy is on [down?] there looking after her.... Let all this [the extensive repairs] in regard to the *A[lice] B[all]*, be *confidential*, to speak plain about it, she is the dambdest [damnedest] thing in the shape of a five year old ship that I ever saw. I dont want any thing said about this a/c of insurance, will tell you all when I see you, please distroy [sic] this part of the letter.[90]

During the rest of the year, Tarlton kept Tucker (who, nevertheless, saved such outspoken letters) intimately informed about ship repairs, the Portsmouth Navy Yard, and local politics, coupled with a grousing commentary on the war itself. On August 28, 1862, Tarlton noted: "They [the United States government] have employed at our navy yard for most of the time since this war began all our mechanics and such a sett [sic] of loafers you never saw, the ship carpenters in particuler [sic], T & L [Tobey & Littlefield, a private Portsmouth shipbuilding firm that had constructed a number of ships for Daniel Marcy] complain of them very much, say they are worse than ever. Their Bark is hung up waiting for the bottom plank."[91]

On September 8, an official at the Tobey & Littlefield firm similarly lamented the demise of local commercial shipbuilding: "We did not use our Southern frame for the Bark, but have it on hand now.... If no more ships are ever wanted, rotten timber will be about as valuable as anything.... Mr. Fernald is building a Small Schnr at Mr. Raynes Yard, and Mr. Badger is building one at Capt. Marcy's, aside from this there is nothing doing except at the Navy Yard, and it has been quiet still there."[92]

In a September 13 letter to Tucker, Tarlton reflected on Daniel Marcy's interest in public office. A lifelong Democrat, Marcy had run unsuccessfully for a congressional seat in the elections of 1858 and 1860. Tarlton recalled:

> Capt. Marcy was one of the deligates [sic] at Charleston [South Carolina, site of the April 1860 Democratic Party presidential nominating convention]. I have repeatedly heard him say that [Stephen A.] Douglass [sic] and his clique was the cause of this trouble and he says he told Mr. [John] Slidell [delegate from Louisiana] at that convention if they broke up and went without making a nomination the country would be ruined. He says with these difficulties and the few Black republicans at [in] the north ware [were] the main cause of this unholy war. I am fully satisfied of this my self....
>
> Supposing at the bombardment of Fort Sumpter [sic] that a part of the North had joined these rebels which was their calculation, they counted on fifty thousand from New York City to assist them for god sake what would have been our condition now. For one I should as lives [lief] be in hell if there is such a place than that thing should take place.[93]

Determined to make an active effort to rectify the wrongs

Tarlton had elaborated, Daniel Marcy in the fall of 1862 decided to seek election to the Thirty-Eighth Congress, which would convene in Washington the following spring. As a Democrat with Southern sympathies in a strong Republican state, Marcy had a difficult political posture for many First District voters. However, in championing a quick resolution of the war to recoup his shipping losses, Marcy embraced the outlook of many voters who also were enduring economic hardships as the war dragged on. Marcy's name was synonymous with Portsmouth maritime issues, a strong point of his candidacy. His wealth, moreover, allowed him to wage a well-financed campaign.

In late October 1862, the Democratic Party of New Hampshire unanimously nominated Marcy as its candidate for the First District. "Hon. DANIEL MARCY," commented the *Dover Enquirer*, ". . . will no doubt call out the full vote of his party, if not more than that. He is one of our self-made men, and would well 'represent' the commercial and industrial interests of the District, the State and the country; and it would be for the advantage of the citizens of Portsmouth and vicinity especially, if we had in Congress, a practical merchant, ship-builder and business man who would look after Portsmouth Navy Yard as assiduously and intelligently as would Capt. Marcy."[94]

The Black "Contraband" Sailors of the Minnesota

One growing concern for those seeking election to the Thirty-Eighth Congress, as well as for the United States Navy and the Lincoln administration itself, was the status of blacks within Union lines and waters. In the fall of 1862, some twenty-five black sailors, or "contrabands," arrived at the Portsmouth Navy Yard as part of the crew of the USS *Minnesota*. When the *Minnesota* sailed five weeks later, these blacks stayed ashore at the Yard. As part of the Union military forces, they were entitled to—and received—rations, pay, medical care, and educational opportunities.

The black sailors had a special legal status within the Union and the navy. If slavery was "the peculiar institution," the Union resolution of the legal status of slaves during the war represented a peculiar—and successful—adaptation to the law. When Union General Benjamin F. Butler, a lawyer prior to the conflict, set a precedent in 1861 by declaring runaway slaves reaching the Union lines as "contraband of war," he put them to work as laborers for the Northern army. (The term *contraband* stuck throughout the war. Others included in this overall category were black slaves who had been smuggled behind Union lines or who had remained behind in territory captured by the Union army.) Avoiding the legal and political question of emancipation, Butler knew that these slaves were still technically bound to their masters and, by law, should have been returned to them. However, his position was supported by Northern public opinion, and the Lincoln administration did not overrule him. Thus, in practical terms, the blacks aboard the *Minnesota* were working sailors in the Union navy.[95]

"I have the honor to report the arrival here to-day of the U.S. Steam Frigate *Minnesota* from Boston," reported Commandant Pearson to Gideon Welles on October 30, 1862, "and shall proceed without delay to lighten & dock her. After completing the repairs [the bottom of the *Minnesota* had been badly damaged in the Hampton Roads clash with the CSS *Virginia* in March], I shall send her to the Boston Yard. In the meantime, I shall grant leave for ten days to the crew, and such leave to the officers as can be consistently granted."[96]

The "contraband" sailors came ashore. "Ex-Gov. [Ichabod] Goodwin," reported the *Chronicle* on November 7, "at their request, recommended suitable boarding houses to them. We learn that some of the young ladies of this city are exerting themselves in their behalf, and are teaching several of them to read.—They are represented to be, generally, intelligent and anxious to learn."[97]

The cordial Portsmouth reception continued. On Sunday, November 9, despite unfavorable weather, "the Contrabands," reported the *Chronicle*, "drew a large audience to the Temple," a local auditorium. About twenty-five black sailors appeared on stage, stating their "opinion of slavery, and of 'secesh' in general." The occasion ended with a "singing of some of their sacred songs."[98]

Since colonial times, Portsmouth had been a familiar port to black sailors. For many years, a small black population had resided in town, and itinerant lecturers had frequently spoken in Portsmouth on race-related issues. On Saturday, March 15, 1862, Frederick Douglass, the internationally known black orator, had appeared at the Temple to deliver his lecture, "The Black Man's Future in the Southern States." On October 19, William Wells Brown, the noted black reformer and writer, appeared at the Temple. The newspaper notice of his appearance included, "Collection taken for his expenses." Brown's topic was timely: "The President's Proclamations, and its effects on the Blacks of the South and the Laborers of the North." In an editorial entitled

"THE CONTRABANDS," published on November 24, the *Chronicle* declared, "We have had no more civil, well-behaved, and orderly men here for a long time, than the five and twenty colored sailors who have been in this city for two weeks past, on leave from a U.S. armed ship at the Navy Yard."[99]

Repaired and recommissioned, the USS *Minnesota* sailed on November 27 from the Yard to Boston. The black sailors, however, remained behind, assigned to defense duty on Seavey's Island and given an opportunity to advance their education.[100]

Prize Money Deprives Jefferson Davis of His Tea

A more efficient and effective Northern blockade during 1862 further weakened the Confederacy. "Since the war broke out," the *Chronicle* noted on June 21, 1862, "our blockading fleet has captured 167 vessels, viz., 14 steamers, 9 ships, 10 barques, 18 brigs, 110 schooners, and 11 sloops." Aiding the patriotic zeal of Union naval officers and crews to seize Confederate vessels was the incentive of prize money. A story current in the North contended that the scarcities resulting from the capture of many Confederate ships had ignominiously deprived Confederate President Jefferson Davis of his breakfast tea. "It seems to be confirmed," related the *Chronicle*, "that Jeff. Davis drinks [a] sassafras decoction in the morning, for want of a decent article of Bohea or Souchong."[101]

To ensure that Davis would have to reconcile himself to such substitutes, the Union government revived the maritime legal machinery dating from the Revolutionary War and the War of 1812 Admiralty Courts to award prize money to victorious Union crews. During the Civil War, Congress enacted at least five prize-case laws to implement the judicial process. The net proceeds from all prize cases eventually accrued to more than $24 million, parceled out to the captors, the government, and the naval pension fund for crews. In May 1862, a *New York Evening Post* correspondent provided a brief and relatively simple explanation of the complex system:

> With some vessels it has been a perfect harvest time for seamen in the way of prize money, as the records of prize courts will show. Seamen share in the proceeds of every vessel taken and condemned, for attempting either to run in or out of a blockaded port, or captured at sea with goods contraband of

war on board. Let me give you a single instance. The storeship *Supply*, not long since, captured with, among other things, ten thousand [English-manufactured] Enfield rifles on board, which have been sold at the appr[a]isal—twenty dollars apiece—making the aggregate two hundred thousand dollars. [It was undoubtedly the CSS *Stephen Hart*, which the *Supply* captured south of Sarasota, Florida, on January 29, 1862, with a cargo of arms and munitions.] Of this amount one half goes to the United States, leaving one hundred thousand dollars to be divided between the officers and crew. The seamen, ordinary seamen, landsmen, &c., get seven-tenths, or thirty five thousand dollars, and as they number but seventy-two, the share of each one is within a small fraction of five hundred dollars. Add the vessel and the remainder of the cargo, and each seaman must receive over five hundred dollars as his share of the prize money. This is not an solitary case, and is not the most favorable one that could be presented.[102]

One Portsmouth native avidly interested in prizes and quick wealth was Thomas Aston Harris. Born in 1824, since his youth Harris had followed the sea for his livelihood. On his second voyage, he reached California aboard the ship *Mary and Susan* in February 1848, "when the gold fever had turned the attention of the world to the new El Dorado." Harris was a member of "the famous gold bear class of California pioneers." In 1850, he hired on with the Pacific Mail Steamship Company. When the Civil War broke out, he offered his services to Secretary of the Navy Welles, and on May 27, 1861, he was commissioned Acting Master.[103]

In early 1862, Harris was assigned to the USS *Penguin*, which had been purchased a year earlier by the navy for immediate service. Assigned to the South Atlantic Blockading Squadron, the *Penguin*, along with the USS *Henry Andrews*, another private steamer acquired by the navy, patrolled the Florida coast. Both these vessels were of light draft, especially agile in navigating the shallow rivers and sounds of the coast to stop blockade runners and to gather intelligence.[104]

Aboard the *Penguin* off St. Augustine, Florida, on March 16, 1862, Harris penned a letter in his ungainly scrawl to Albert R. Hatch, a friend in Portsmouth. Both men were Democrats, and Hatch was a prominent Portsmouth lawyer as well as clerk of the Rockingham County District Court. To Hatch, Harris confided:

Yours of the 20th of Feby I gladly received yesterday—we were then at St. Marys [Florida], but the conveyance of your letter brought an order to come here on the blockade and the Relief.... We have been every where from the North boundary of [illegible word] to this [place] and on all sorts of duty and I begin to think we shall not end until we get to Galveston. I could talk a week and write a year but have not the time....

. . . We have certainly fallen upon evil times and for myself I feel I am making great sacrifices: the poetry of war is well enough, but the reality is exactly what I thought it to be before I left—and for what good, and to what end are we suffering all this to gratify the machinations of a few rabid fanatics [the Lincoln administration and the abolitionists].... Our Country, Our Country we now can see all the inconveniences of this unnatural quarrel, but for myself I can see no adequate benefit. I wish the Nigger was where it is warmer [that is, hell].[105]

Only six days later, Harris was aboard the *Henry Andrews* during a naval clash in a war he deplored. On March 22, the *Mosquito* and the *Henry Andrews* went on a reconnaissance mission up Mosquito Inlet, encountering fire from Confederate batteries and musketry. In addition to submitting official reports to his naval superiors, Harris provided Hatch a more unguarded account of his recent naval activities in a letter headlined, "U.S.S. *H[enry] Andrews*, New Smyrna, Fla[.], March [30?] 1862":

We have been having stirring times.

On the return of a Boat expedition with fifty men from this ship and the *Penguin* up Mosquito inlet on the 22nd having been up some twelve miles, when within one mile of this vessel [we] were attacked from a thick growth on the banks of the narrow stream by three companies of the Rebels[,] about 200 men. We lost 7 men including both Captain [Acting Lieutenant Thomas A.] Budd [of the *Penguin*] & [Acting Master S.W.] Mather [of the *Henry Andrews*], four severely wounded and three prisoners. I have communicated with the enemy since. They are under the command of Senior Capt[ain] Bird and he says our men were gallant but would not inform me [of] his loss—neither would I [inform] him.... [Commander Samuel F.] Dupont [Du Pont] came down the same day in the *Wabash*. Confirmed me in this Command [to replace Mather]. On the 24th I took possession of a large quantity of live oak—some 21,000 sticks, about 50,000 feet[;] also about 2000 feet of Red Cedar—in Halifax River and the Commodore will send immediately down some six schooners to transfer it North. A prize more than equal to all the Cotton thus has been taken and now much needed by the Government. Give it a favourable notice in the newspaper, for I think it [is] pretty well the second day of command—and some have thought I was a sympathizer....

I am very desirous of getting North and hope to soon—and wish that this horrid, unnatural strife [could be] at an end—and Wendell Brooks [well-known Boston abolitionist, Episcopal minister, and orator] hung [hanged].

It is very warm here now and the duty arduous, but I appear to stand it well.[106]

Another more immediate matter that irked Harris was the lack of readiness of the USS *Henry Andrews*, his new command. He requested from Du Pont a 12-pound rifle howitzer for mounting on the stern of his vessel in case of attack. Another deficiency involved the lack of coppering on the *Henry Andrews*, since worms are very destructive to unprotected hulls in Florida's warm waters.[107]

Farther up the coast, soon to join the North Atlantic Blockading Squadron in search of prizes, was the Portsmouth-built USS *Mahaska*. A wooden double-ended side-wheel steamer, the *Mahaska* engaged in her sea trials on May 9, 1862. A *Portsmouth Chronicle* reporter on board, ignoring the news blackout on naval matters, observed:

> The trial trip of the gunboat *Mahaska* ... was a delightful pleasure excursion indeed, for the selected company of ladies and gentlemen who (of the larger number of invited guests) were able to comply with the naval regulations of the occasion.
>
> We left the wharf at 7 o'clock, and ran out along Cape Ann [Massachusetts], passing Rockport, &c, so as to get a fine view of Gloucester—about forty miles—returning about six o'clock....

Off Cape Ann, a shot from the 100-pound rifled Parrott gun, at the bow, was fired, striking the water at some three or four miles distance; and immediately after, several of the schooners in the vicinity ran up the stars and stripes at their peaks. The *Mahaska* also carries a 10-inch Dahlgren smooth-bore, at the stern, and four 24-lb. boat-howitzers amidships.

The *Mahaska* is a match-boat, in model and build, with the *Sebago* [another Portsmouth-built vessel of the same class]—and we think will prove the more favorite craft. She gave complete satisfaction on her trial—running very smoothly and steadily. With about nineteen revolutions of her engine per minute, her log told 11 knots; and under most favorable circumstances, it is thought she can show 13 or 14 knots. Her run of from 80 to 100 miles, was made in eleven hours, including various stoppages for the adjustment of the new machinery, &c.

The officers of the *Mahaska* ... are a fine set of young men, and we venture to say will make good account of themselves when opportunity offers.... The crew numbers about 100 men, and are a staunch and lively lot of blue jackets.[108]

The sea trials and the social excursion over, the *Mahaska* then turned to the more serious business of engaging the enemy. On May 15, 1862, she sailed from the Yard, and, "after a pleasant passage of five days," arrived at Fortress Monroe, Virginia, where she joined the North Atlantic Blockading Squadron. Commander Foxhall A. Parker soon reported as the warship's new captain.

On October 11, while on blockade duty with the USS *Maratanza*, the *Mahaska*'s baptism of fire occurred off Cape Fear, North Carolina. A shore-based Confederate battery with field pieces opened fire, hitting the *Maratanza*. Shells killed a master's mate and a sailor and wounded five men, two mortally. The *Mahaska* immediately returned the fire. Although out of range of the ship's guns, the Confederate gunners soon retreated. On her voyage back to Fortress Monroe, the *Mahaska* "experienced very heavy weather, and lost one man overboard while securing an anchor."[109]

Not long afterward, the *Mahaska* engaged in two significant actions. On November 1, Commander Parker navigated his vessel up the York River (Virginia) and destroyed enemy entrenchments. Heartened by this success, the Union command assigned Parker to

Supporting the Union Army of the Potomac's withdrawal after the unsuccessful Peninsula Campaign, gunboats USS Galena (left) and Portsmouth-built USS Mahaska (right) shell Confederate positions at Harrison's Landing, Virginia, on July 1, 1862. Such naval coordination enabled the army to maintain its supply lines and safeguard its flanks during the evacuation. NHC

lead a joint army-navy expedition to Mathews Court House, Virginia, north of Fortress Monroe on Chesapeake Bay. The objective of this combined operation was to cripple the local Confederate salt industry. Although readily available in the North, salt in the wartime South soon became the scarcest of all commodities, not only for seasoning but also, and more importantly, as a meat preservative. Parker's expedition, conducted on November 22 through 24, was a complete success, destroying seventy-three large cast-iron boiling vessels at nine establishments and more than 1,000 bushels of salt.

In one of his official reports, dated November 27, 1862, Parker admitted he was uncertain about the amount of smuggling going on in tidewater Virginia:

> Large canoes, I find, are now principally used in running the blockade of the rivers flowing into the Chesapeake. I was informed, too, by a man who has given me much reliable information of late, that contraband trade is carried on to some considerable extent between North and Back rivers. "How can this be?" said I to my informant. "Back River is wholly within our

lines." "I know that very well," was the reply, "and the supplies are furnished by the sutlers of your army." I have, of course, made this known to the commanding general at Yorktown.

I have been up the river to-day and captured five boats with over a hundred bushels of oysters intended for the Richmond market.[110]

Writing from aboard the *Mahaska* off Yorktown, Virginia, on December 6, 1862, an officer or sailor identifying himself only as "G.C." vividly described the recent forays:

Our first expedition [on November 1] was made under our zealous Captain [Commander Foxhall A. Parker], who is always on the move to execute the laws. We proceeded as far as West Point [on the York River, Virginia] in a cautious manner, our object being to discover whether any new batteries had been built or old ones occupied. We saw no rebel forces, however, and returned. The next day, we again proceeded to the place, determined to accomplish something if possible. So we landed a couple of boats' crews, armed with picks and spades and guarded by a few marine[s]. The rebels had formerly built a small earthwork [field fortification] and mounted a few guns at this place, but it was evacuated by them on the advance of our forces after the successful issue before Yorktown [on May 4, 1862]. The neighborhood is almost deserted by the male portion of its inhabitants, most of them being in the rebel army, or hucksters for them. We dug away part of the earthworks and blew up the magazine, and then started on our return. When within about 8 or 10 miles of our anchorage, we discovered a huge pile of wood, and soon after we loaded two canal boats for the use of the army at Yorktown. On the same evening the rebels set fire to the wood, and consumed the whole pile, containing from 200 to 300 cords.

Another expedition captured the notorious rebel, Peter Smith, who is supposed to be concerned in the burning of the ship *Alleghany* [*Allegheny*] in Chesapeake Bay. Two or three boats loaded with calico, medicines and other articles,—quite necessary to the rebels, have been taken. Hardly a day passes but some illegal offender is arrested, and his boat and cargo confiscated to our use.

The most important undertaking yet attempted was successfully carried out not long since [November 22, 1862]. We, in company with our two tenders, *May Queen* and *Gen. Putnam*, together with several companies of soldiers, made a visit to the East River, where we discovered a small salt work. The troops and sailors landed, with a force of about 300 men, without opposition, and proceeded to the work, which was capable of making 10 or more bushels a day. They tore down the whole concern, and smashed 30 or 40 salt pans [used to evaporate sea water], some of them belonging to individuals engaged in making salt in a small way. Every one who has an old kettle goes into the business: excepting the slaves, who are not permitted to.

In the meantime, some of the boats' crews proceeded in different directions, destroying every craft which might be used for running the blockade. Some 30 small boats, pecul[i]ar to this section, and 3 schooners were burned. Several of the crew, guided by a contraband, discovered a boat load of salt and a barrel of whiskey; the salt was demolished,—but the whiskey demolished some of them, and they were unable to return to the steamer without help. One of them [landsman Patrick Madden] got dead drunk, dropped out of the lines, and was captured; and with the two soldiers, also lost, were heard of on the road to a Richmond [probably Libby] prison.

Quite a number of the inhabitants are of Northern birth, but of Southern principles. We stopped at this place about 36 hours.

Several other expeditions have followed, in all of which schooners and boats were destroyed. No doubt, we have caused some uneasiness to the enemy. Even as I write, two schooners, valued at $1000 and $400 respectively, are coming down the river, a prize to our energetic officers and crew.[111]

The cumulative effect of the blockade's numerous prizes was damaging to the South. Referring to the Anaconda Plan's constriction of the enemy's territory, a waggish commentator in 1862 listed the names of the Union army and naval leaders applying pressure to an ever shrinking map: "The Southern Confederacy may be bounded as follows: on the north by [Major-General George B.] McClellan and [Major-General Henry W.] Halleck; on the east by [Major-General

Ambrose E.] Burnside and [Major-General David] Hunter; on the south by Fort Pickens and the Gulf Squadron; on the west by Gen. [Benjamin F.] Butler, Commodore [David G.] Farragut and Captain [David D.] Porter."[112]

The Union Navy Institutes Reforms

While the paramount objective of the United States Navy was to squeeze the boundaries of the Confederacy, Secretary of the Navy Welles, the Navy Bureau chiefs, and the officers on ship and shore continued to advocate and implement reform throughout the service. In 1862, the issues included mailing privileges, religious observances, the rights of aliens, and temperance.

Postmaster General Montgomery Blair in early 1862 increased mailing privileges for Union sailors. Postmasters were instructed by Blair's department "to mail without pre-payment all letters written by sailors or marines in active service, and properly certified—thus extending to them the same privileges as had already been extended to the soldiers." (Commissioned officers, however still paid for postal service. Letters addressed to sailors and marines also required pre-payment.) The Act of Congress, which was approved on January 21, 1862, and became a Post Office regulation by February 8, specified the official procedure for each piece of sailor's mail: "The envelope must bear the certificate 'Naval Letter,' signed by the commanding officer or lieutenant on board the vessel, with the name of the vessel.... All such certified letters must be rated with postage at the mailing office, to be collected at the office of delivery."[113]

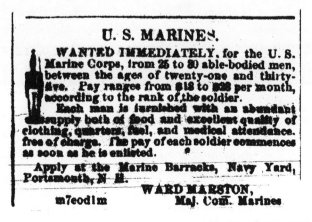

PC, March 17, 1862

General Order.

NAVY DEPARTMENT, DECEMBER 23, 1861.

THE NAVY DEPARTMENT has a rendezvous for shipping men at each of the following places :

Portsmouth, New Hampshire.
Boston and New Bedford, Massachusetts.
New York.
Philadelphia and Erie, Pennsylvania.
Baltimore, Maryland; and
Washington, District of Columbia.

Seamen, ordinary seamen, and landsmen, who can pass the usual surgeon's examination, by presenting themselves at the rendezvous nearest their residence, with an official certificate from the city or town clerk signifying that they are residents and have expressed a desire to leave to enter the navy, will be received on the following terms:

1st. An Allowance of three cents a mile for travelling expenses.

2d. An advance of *three* months to seamen and ordinary seamen, and of *two* months to landsmen.

3d. Permission to leave an allotment of half-pay to their families, to commence the date of their enlistment.

4th, To go on board ship in their ordinary clothes, where an outfit will be furnished and charged as per list, being the present prices, viz:

One pea-jacket	$11 00
One pair blue cloth trowsers	3 89
One blue flannel overshirt	1 60
Two under flannel shirts	2 82
Two pairs woollen drawers	2 16
One mattress	4 90
Two blankets	3 90
One seamless cap	1 00
One black silk handkerchief	1 00
	$31 27

The pay of petty officers averages $20 to $25 per month.

Do.	Seamen	18	do.
Do.	ordinary seamen	14	do.
Do.	landsmen	12	do.

And food found.

No landsman will be allowed to take the benefit of this regulation who has not been four months at sea or on the lakes or rivers.   GIDEON WELLES,

Dec. 24—6t   Secretary of the Navy.

PJ, Jan. 11, 1862

The question of church attendance within the navy and the Union military forces as a whole prompted much discussion during the Civil War. A letter to the editor of the *Boston Pilot* in February 1862 charged that every Marine assigned to the Portsmouth Navy Yard was compelled to attend chapel or meet the displeasure of his immediate commanding officer. This accusation reached the office of Navy Secretary Welles, who sought an explanation from Commandant Pearson. On February 27, Pearson responded:

I herewith forward the explanation from Major [Ward] Marston, Com[manding] the Marines, himself. This statement[,] now made in writing, corresponds precisely with the verbal information given to me by Major Marston before the receipt of your communication:—viz.—that he wished them to attend church, unless restrained from doing so by conscientious motives.

Neither Major Marston or any other person in this Yard, constrains any one whatever to attend church.[114]

Marston's letter of the same date to Pearson was submitted as an enclosure:

The first Sunday after I [Ward Marston] assumed command of this Post, I had the Marines paraded, and informed that all Roman Catholics who had objections from conscientious motives to attend a Protestant church to step one step to the front, and then said to the balance, had they any conscientious scruples to attend an Episcopal church to step two paces to the front, and out of some ninety men, all stepped forward except about twenty five; the twenty five attended church—the others did not.

The next Sunday the same process was gone through when there was only eleven attended out of the same number. I then addressed them, and said, while I would compel no one to attend who had conscientious motives from doing so, yet as the Government had appointed a [navy] Chaplain [Reverend Henry Wood] to perform divine service and who came over every Sunday to do so, it would be pleasing to me to have as many attend as were disposed to do so.

The last two Sundays there have been from ten to seventeen attend, and no one compelled.

On the 22nd of inst [of February] under your information that the Chaplain at the usual hour would read Washington's Farewell Address ordered the whole Command to attend except those on duty or otherwise excused, and about fifty did so, but this I did not consider a religious exercise.[115]

It must be noted in fairness to Marston that Washington's Birthday was a major holiday observance in nineteenth-century America, especially in the North during the Civil War. By proclamation, Lincoln urged that citizens assemble to honor Washington. All work was suspended at the Yard for that day, a Saturday, in 1862. Officers at the station, with their families, assembled at the chapel at 10:30 A.M. to hear the reading of Washington's Farewell Address by Chaplain Wood. A grand salute of 100 guns was fired at noon.[116]

The role of religious activities within the Union military forces eventually commanded the attention of the Lincoln administration. On November 13, 1862, a delegation of clergymen called upon the president and the military department heads at the White House. Taking their advice, Lincoln acted promptly. Two days later, the announcement came that the president, as commander-in-chief, "desires and enjoins the orderly observance of the Sabbath by the officers and men in the military and naval service." Lincoln quoted a similar proclamation that General George Washington had issued in 1776, and the president's executive order went into effect immediately.[117]

Although the matter of religious and patriotic concerns was legally resolved, guaranteeing civil liberties required attention. Such American patriotism brought under review the status of alien residents living in the North. The protection of their rights, within the confines of a nation at war, posed a ticklish problem.

In August 1862, the Lincoln administration, to preserve the nation's internal security, tightened its requirements for federal service. As reported on August 4 by the *Chronicle*: "Henceforth no unnaturalized alien is to be employed in any Navy Yard in the Union. All persons seeking employment, must, before they are accepted, produce certificates of naturalization, properly authenticated. This order will result in the discharge of 6000 men at the various stations. The reason assigned for the adoption of this last order, is that unnaturalized foreigners obtain employment from the Government and then threaten to demand British protection if they are required to render military service."[118]

The situation of James Brooks, a British subject living in New Hampshire, reflected the complexity of the times. In his semiliterate letter, mailed from Manchester, New Hampshire, on July 29, 1862, Brooks appealed to "the British Consul in Portsmouth": "I am a British subject born in Canada[.] left there about 15 years since have been to sea a few years & and the rest of the time have been in different states am now living in Newbury but working in Manchester. & in Newbury i have bn involved in the state militia altho i told them I was a forenor [foreigner] Now i beg of your honor to inform me if I can have British protection papers from you if so will my presents [presence] be required there & how much will they cost. I have no wish to serve a foren nation. pleas answer this by the man who delivers this to your honor."[119]

James Brooks's rights were quickly clarified and upheld. Writing from Portsmouth on August 1, George H. Starr, British vice consul in Portland, Maine, wrote directly to Joseph M. Edmonds, Portsmouth Custom House deputy collector: "I would say to him [James Brooks] that if he is a British subject, can prove himself to be such, and has never taken out papers for naturalization in this country he cannot legally be required to serve in the state militia. The proof of his nationality would have to be some certified document of his birth.... P.S. After Mr. Brooks obtains the necessary document proving his nationality[,] let him keep it in his possession, and if he should meet with any trouble[,] let him either come to Portland or report the case to the consul there."[120]

In addition to protecting civil rights of aliens, the United States government pursued reforms within its armed forces. Since finding and fighting the enemy demanded clear heads and open eyes, the Union navy in 1862 forbade the consumption of liquor aboard ship. Rear Admiral Andrew H. Foote, chief of the Bureau of Equipment and Recruiting, had been among the earliest proponents of abolishing the spirit ration. Between 1849 and 1851, as commander of the USS *Cumberland* in the Mediterranean Squadron, Foote formed a temperance society aboard ship. Doing away with the grog-tub, Foote's vessel became the first temperance (alcohol-free) ship in the United States Navy. The rest of the navy soon followed. Officially promulgating Section 4 of a new law concerning the navy in late August 1862, Secretary Welles announced:

> And be it further enacted, that from and after the first day of September 1862, the spirit ration in the navy of the United States shall forever cease, and thereafter no distilled spiritous liquors shall be admitted on board of vessels of war except as medical stores, and upon the order and under the control of the medical officers of such vessels, and to be used only for medical purposes. From and after the said first day of September next there shall be allowed and paid to each person in the navy now entitled to the spirit ration five cents per day in commutation and lieu thereof, which shall be in addition to the present pay.

Navy Department.

September 16, 1862.

Sir:

    The 4th section of the act of July 14, 1862, which directs that, after the 1st of September instant, "no distilled spirituous liquors shall be admitted on board of vessels-of-war, except as medical stores, and upon the order and under the control of the medical officers of such vessels, and to be used only for medical purposes," is considered as applying to all such liquors on board of vessels of the Navy, whether in the possession of commissioned or warrant officers, or any other persons on board. It will be, therefore, the duty of every commanding officer to send out of the vessel any such liquors found in the possession of any person on board which have not been provided by the government as medical stores.

    The law does not include ale, beer, wine, or other liquors not distilled.

    I am, &c.,

GIDEON WELLES,
Secretary of the Navy.

NA-NER

In a printed circular order dated September 16, 1862, and distributed throughout the navy, Secretary Welles proclaimed: "It will be, therefore, the duty of every commanding officer to send out of the vessel any such liquors found in the possession of any person on board which have not been provided by the government as medical stores. The law does not include ale, beer, wine, or other liquors not distilled."[121]

Despite initial rumors that Union sailors were dissatisfied with this reform and had even threatened to refuse boarding their ships again unless the ration were restored, the measure proved successful. Officers and sailors respected both the letter and the spirit of the law. In October 1862, Admiral Samuel P. Du Pont reported that when he received the official navy announcement, he and his officers offloaded all their wines, with no further complaints. The reactions were the same in the other naval squadrons. "The grace with which Jack [nickname for an American sailor] has conformed himself to this regulation surprises everybody," reported the Washington correspondent of the *New York Tribune*. "The necessity of its enforcement is apparent from the fact that since the rebellion broke out not less than three hundred and seventy officers have been dismissed for drunkenness."[122]

In a lengthy article, "Moral Character Of Our Navy," the *Journal* on December 6 commented on this new attitude—engendered, no doubt, by the sobering responsibility of fighting a war. An interview with Reverend Charles E. Stewart, the senior naval chaplain, elicited these conclusions:

> He [Stewart] has been an intelligent observer of the moral condition of the service, and gives the results of his observations for thirty years. Thirty years ago, he says, gross and profane language was common with the officers on the quarter-deck; now it is the exception; he has hardly heard in ten years an oath from such officers. Thirty years ago ardent spirits were generally used by officers, and intoxication would not be disgracefull [sic]. Then an avowedly religious officer was seldom met; now it is not unusual for half of the ward-room mess and large numbers of the crews to be professedly religious and church members. Then, religious service was unknown in the ship, except on Sunday; now, daily prayer meetings are not uncommon on shipboard.[123]

Charity Begins at the Yard

The Union spirit was manifested not only in reform but also in benevolence. The Yard stood firmly in the forefront in donating money and clothes for Union soldiers. Charity was as helpful as government appropriations in prosecuting the war.

As early as November 1861, the "Navy Yard fund" was established to raise money for the benefit of Maine and New Hampshire volunteers in the field or otherwise in government service. Contributions from Yard officers, sailors, and employees were administered by a committee headed by the governors of Maine and New Hampshire, as well as other officials. Each contributor authorized one day's pay from the monthly payroll to be retained by the paymaster of the Yard. Such monies were then used to purchase articles needed by those fighting the war.

The success of the Navy Yard fund is evident in a report from Lieutenant Colonel Frank S. Fiske of the Second New Hampshire, assigned to Hooker's Division in northern Virginia: "I wish to acknowledge ... the receipt of 284 knit woolen shirts, 175 prs. drawers, 228 mittens & 879 woolen socks from the workmen at the Portsmouth Navy Yard.... The present was most seasonable, appropriate, and generous, and contributed very much to the health and comfort of the men."

By June 30, 1862, a statement of receipts and expenditures indicated that the Navy Yard fund had collected $3,441.59, which went for clothing, including some 4,793 pairs of woolen socks and 1,003 pairs of woolen mittens. Flannel was made into 1,500 sets of undershirts and drawers. The fund also paid the freight charges for delivering these articles to the various Maine and New Hampshire infantry, artillery, and sharpshooter regiments in the field. Commandant Pearson made facilities available at the Yard for packing and storing the various articles.[124]

Charity also alleviated the needs of individuals within the Yard. On May 6, 1862, a young apprentice was seriously injured at the Yard while working on the U.S. steamer *Mahaska*. Cleaning machinery, the man had caught his hand in its workings, severing the hand at the wrist. He was quickly conveyed to the Yard hospital, after which the officers of the *Mahaska* contributed $40 to him.[125]

On Christmas Day 1862, Nathan F. Mathes and John Stokell, two Portsmouth contractors, continued their custom of providing a Christmas dinner for the garrison of men at the marine barracks. "Things were got up in regular home style," reported the *Chronicle* on December 27, "plenty of turkeys, mince pies, and other fixin's."[126]

Nor was charity limited to the Yard workers. For instance, one old lady from Chester, New Hampshire, sent a package containing this note: "These socks were spun and knit by Mrs. Zeruah Clapp, 96 years old, whose hands in youth were engaged in moulding bullets in the Revolutionary War. *Keep the toes of these socks toward the rebels.*"[127]

The Steamer R.R. Cuyler *Fights Jinxes*

Although the navy was imbued with a spirit of reform, charity, and personal sacrifice for the war effort, incidents of theft and desertion occasionally occurred.

During 1862, the U.S. steamer *R.R. Cuyler* was plagued by bad luck. Commander Francis Winslow, a career naval officer from Dunbarton, New Hampshire, was the ship's captain. During the summer of 1862, he received orders to proceed from Boston to Nassau to ascertain the status of the *Oreto*, then under the British flag but rumored to be soon transferred to the Confederate navy. (Northern intelligence proved correct; the *Oreto* later became the CSS *Florida*.)

While conducting this investigation in Caribbean waters, several officers and men aboard the *R.R. Cuyler* fell victim to the ravages of yellow fever, and a few were dangerously ill for several days, but all except one ultimately recovered. The exception, Commander Winslow, died at sea on August 26, and Acting Master Simeon N. Freeman assumed command of the vessel. The *R.R. Cuyler* headed north, and stopped briefly in New York to allow Winslow's remains to be interred temporarily at the Quarantine burial ground at Staten Island. On September 9, the vessel arrived for repairs at the Portsmouth Navy Yard.[128]

The misfortunes of the *R.R. Cuyler* continued. Commandant Pearson was notified about several disturbing situations concerning the recently arrived warship. On September 16, writing from aboard ship, Acting Master Freeman informed Pearson:

> Charles Hilger was enlisted as landsman 5th July 1862 at Boston, on the 21st of same month he was rated as Officers Steward by the late Commander Winslow....
>
> On the 26th of August whilst Commr. Francis Winslow was dying, he surreptitiously took his rings from his fingers and put them in his pocket.
>
> He also took Commander Winslow's purse in the same manner, the contents were unknown, beyond the fact, that Commd Winslow was known to have had a Five dollar bill in paper, some Gold and silver....

After numerous other incidents of theft and Hilger's "loud and insolent tone," he "was then placed in Double irons to await further orders."[129]

No further documentation of this case appears to have survived, but it seems clear that Hilger subsequently was incarcerated in a military prison or otherwise given a dishonorable discharge.

Nor was this the only controversy surrounding the *R.R. Cuyler*. Complaints from her officers concerning the vessel's alleged unreadiness reached Pearson's office. In response, he ordered Thomas Williamson, the Yard's chief naval engineer, to inspect the vessel. On September 20, Williamson reported to Pearson: "We have held a strict and careful survey of the Engines, Boilers, and appurtenances of the U.S. Steamer *R.R. Cuyler*. We find nothing more than the ordinary derangements consequence upon the wear and tear of all Marine Machinery, and such as is within the pretense and means of the [engineering] force onboard the ship to repair. We would most respectfully state that the greater part of the truth lies in the carelessness of those in charge."[130]

To respond to charges that the ship's water supply was unhealthy, Pearson relied on the Yard naval surgeon, M.G. Delany, for a professional opinion. After conducting his investigation, Dr. Delany assured Pearson: "I have carefully examined the Hold of the U.S. Steamer *R.R. Cuyler*, and find her clean, and sweet, without any odour of Bilge Water. I report her to you as being, in my Opinion, in a healthful condition, not having any Sick on board, and fit to return to her station."[131]

The erratic pattern of the *R.R. Cuyler*'s affairs persisted. Eight of her sailors deserted from the vessel, but Portsmouth policeman Frank Johnson tracked down and apprehended seven of them.

Finally, on October 7, to the undoubted relief of Commandant Pearson, the repaired and troublesome *R.R. Cuyler*, camouflaged with Union gray paint, steamed away to rejoin the blockade.[132]

Sometimes problems originated within the Yard itself. On April 22, 1862, at 11 P.M., employee John H. Ferguson, a twenty-six-year-old resident of nearby Eliot, Maine, attempted to enter the Yard. As he began walking over the bridge, the sentry on duty heard the footsteps and issued a challenge:

"It's me," answered Ferguson.

The sentry challenged again.

"You'll know when I get there."

From Kittery, a wooden bridge (now the Gate 1 steel bridge) spans the Back Channel to Navy Yard Island. In this circa 1865 photo, the huge Franklin Shiphouse (far right) faces the Piscataqua River. A "watch station" shed (center) at the Navy Yard end of the bridge sheltered armed security guards. Each day, as dusk approached, a short section of the bridge was temporarily removed to prevent unauthorized access. PNSVC

The draw of the bridge was up for the night, with a bar placed across the end of the walk to prevent people from falling into the river. Ferguson either stooped down to go under the bar or climbed over it, fell into the water, and was swept away. On an extremely dark night, it was impossible to save him. Six weeks later, Ferguson's body was recovered near Badger's Island, a short distance from where he fell in.[133]

Desertion also affected those stationed within the Yard. The U.S. marine force saw its ranks occasionally lessened by unauthorized leaves of absence. Ironically, such desertions tended to follow recruiting drives. On August 7, 1862, Lieutenant Colonel Ward Marston placed a public notice in the *Chronicle* for "able-bodied MEN, between twenty-one and thirty-five. Pay ranges from $13 to $17 a month.... The pay of each soldier commences as soon as he is enlisted, and he

U. S. Marines.

WANTED IMMEDIATELY, for the U S Marine Corps, able bodied men between twenty-one and thirty-five. Pay ranges from $13 to $17 a month, according to the rank of the soldier.— Each man is furnished with an abundant supply both of food and clothing of excellent quality.— Quarters, fuel and medical attendance free of charge. The pay of each soldier commences as soon as he is enlisted, and he will receive a bounty of One Hundred Dollars, in addition to his pay, at the end of his term of service.

Any person furnishing recruits, will receive Two Dollars for each one that shall be accepted.

Apply at the MARINE BARRACKS, Navy Yard, Portsmouth, N. H.   au6 3taw

PC, Sept. 6, 1862

will receive a bounty of One Hundred Dollars, in addition to his pay at the end of his term of service." In the same issue, immediately below the recruitment notice, Marston submitted another "Notice":

"FIFTEEN DOLLARS will be paid for the apprehension and return of each of the following persons to the Marine Barracks, Navy Yard, Portsmouth, N.H., who are supposed to have joined the Volunteers somewhere in the vicinity of Portsmouth, and who are respectively described as follows, viz: WARREN S. COOPER ... STEPHEN FLYNN[,] WILLIAM H.[enry] SARGENT," each name followed by the marine's rank, age, physical description, and occupation.[134]

With the capable Portsmouth policeman Frank B. Johnson on the job, the three marines did not remain at large very long. On September 3, Johnson found William Henry Sargent. Sargent had gone to Pittsfield, New Hampshire, where he had joined a company of volunteers, thus securing an enlistment bonus. This group had in turn gone on to Concord to become part of the Eleventh Regiment. Just as Sargent's company was marching to its designated camping ground in Concord, Johnson managed to apprehend him. Stephen Flynn was the next to be captured. Finally, on September 17, Johnson nabbed the last of the marine deserters. At New Hampton, New Hampshire, in the central part of the state, he arrested Warren Cooper, a recent enlistee in the Twelfth Regiment, stationed at Concord. Having received a $300 enlistment bounty, Cooper was on a two-day furlough when he was arrested. Two hundred dollars of the money was recovered.[135]

Notice.

FIFTEEN DOLLARS will be paid for the apprehension and return of each of the following persons to the Marine Barracks, Navy Yard, Portsmouth, N. H.. who are supposed to have joined the Volunteers somewhere in the vicinity of Portsmouth, and who are respectively described as follows, viz:

WARREN S. COOPER, a Corporal, born in U. S., State of N. H., County of Belknap, Town of Alton, enlisted 16th April, 1861, at Boston, for four years by Maj. Reynolds, aged 21 years, 5 feet 9 1-4 inches high, grey eyes, light brown hair, light complexion, and by trade or occupation a Shoemaker.

STEPHEN FLYNN, a Private, born in Ireland, County of Cavan, Town of Enniskillen, enlisted 24th March, 1859, at Portsmouth, for four years, by Capt. Garland, aged 28 years, 5 feet 7 1-4 inches high, grey eyes, light brown hair, sandy complexion, and by trade or occupation a Laborer.

WILLIAM H. SARGENT, a Private, born in U. S., State of N. H., town of Chichester, enlisted 16th Feb. 1859, at Portsmouth for four years, by Capt. Garland; aged 21 years, 5 feet 6 1-2 inches high, hazel eyes, black hair, dark complexion, and by trade or occupation a Farmer.
WARD MARSTON,
Aug. 9.   3w   Lt. Col. Com'g Marines.

PC, Aug. 9, 1862

The Constellation *in the Mediterranean*

The officers and men of the Portsmouth-outfitted *Constellation* compiled a brighter record for the Union during 1862. The citizens of Portsmouth closely followed the activities of the *Constellation* as she cruised the Mediterranean to protect American interests. The fact that President Lincoln and Secretary Welles were able to dispatch this vessel to an area far from the coastline of the Confederacy reveals the growing strength of the Union navy.

Commander Henry Knox Thatcher, grandson of General Henry Knox of Revolutionary War fame, was assigned to undertake this important mission. After repairs, provisioning, and taking on crew, the *Constellation* set sail from the Yard on March 11, 1862.[136]

The *Constellation*'s transatlantic passage was tempestuous. On March 16, an able seaman, a Scot named Campbell, went overboard in a squall. The crew of the *Constellation* recovered his body, which was later interred with appropriate services. When the *Constellation* arrived off Fayal, the Azores, a week later, Commander Thatcher had a boat lowered to visit the U.S. consul on the island, but heavy seas forced abandonment of his visit. By evening, the wind had increased to a heavy gale, and the *Constellation* had to head for the open seas, in the direction of Portugal. She arrived in Lisbon on March 31.[137]

As the *Constellation* approached the Levant (the lands of the Eastern Mediterranean then controlled by the Ottoman Turks), the delicacy of Thatcher's diplomatic and military mission became more evident. (Perhaps in recognition of the importance of the mission, the United States Navy, on July 16, promoted Thatcher to the rank of commodore, with no intervening commission as captain.) Since 1860, civil war had raged between the Maronite and Druze factions in the Ottoman province of Syria (which at that time also included present-day Lebanon). Muslims had massacred Christians—more than 6,000 in Damascus alone. In this turmoil, the lives of American missionaries throughout the Ottoman Empire were jeopardized.

On August 22, the *Constellation* lay off Smyrna (now Izmir), Turkey, as Thatcher met with Mehmet Reschid Pasha, the Turkish governor-general, and other officials. Aboard his vessel, Thatcher received the pasha and his entourage, including Captain Huseyin Bey, commander of the Turkish ship of war *Scheriff Numa*. When the pasha left the *Constellation*, Thatcher honored him with a nineteen-gun salute. After a ten-day "good will" visit in Smyrna, the *Constellation* set sail on August 29 to continue her cruise, venturing eastward toward the war-torn regions.[138]

The relatively tranquil atmosphere of the cruise was shattered when the *Constellation* anchored off Adana (in modern-day Turkey). Thatcher received information from the American consul in Beirut that the Reverend Jackson Coffing, an American missionary, had been ambushed and killed in nearby Alexandretta (now Iskenderun) in April. (In July, another American missionary, William W. Meriam of the Bulgarian mission, had been shot and killed by brigands.)

The American consul's letter also reported the sultan's *firman* (decree) that Coffing's murderers would be executed immediately upon their apprehension. Within a month, in October, the Ottoman government carried out its promise, decapitating the murderers in the presence of a large crowd.

The prompt execution of Coffing's assassins succeeded in restoring the confidence to the other missionaries, fifty or more, in that section of the country. The *Constellation*'s presence also demonstrated America's military commitment in the Eastern Mediterranean and prevented a withdrawal of American missionaries from Turkey. After additional negotiations with the Turkish officials, Commodore

Thatcher continued his cruise along the Syrian coast and other locales before landing at Messina, Italy, on October 18.

Thatcher's efforts were successful, and no more American missionaries were slain. "The *Constellation*, under her admirable commander, Commodore Thacher [*sic*]," summed up the *Chronicle* on January 19, 1863, "had been most actively employed in visiting commercial and other ports, and had convinced the Pashas and the people of Syria that Christian Missionaries were not to be murdered with impunity."[139]

Requesting additional ships for the Mediterranean station, Commodore Thatcher wrote on November 3, 1862, to Assistant Secretary Fox:

> I feel a considerable degree of national pride in wishing our force here to be increased for the prevailing opinion here, evidently is, that our country is not sufficiently strong to admit of withdrawing another vessel from the blockade. But the paramount object is that of the efficient protection of our commerce and citizens who are engaged in commercial pursuits and to be prepared, should any rebel cruisers venture into the Mediterranean.[140]

In the late fall of 1862, the *Constellation* arrived in Genoa, Italy, to spend the winter in port. Not long afterward, on November 23, sailor William Wallace Clark was killed in a rigging accident. Young Clark was a Portsmouth native, the son of Captain John Clark, and once an employee at the *Chronicle* office. About eighteen years old at the time of his death, Clark had enlisted in the navy at the Portsmouth rendezvous the previous February.[141]

Referring to Clark's funeral service, attended by Commodore Thatcher, the rest of the officers, and part of the crew, an officer of the *Constellation* wrote to Pearson: "A purse was made up by the officers and crew, to send to his sister, and to give him Christian burial; and no officer was ever buried with more solemnity or respect. A handsome stone had been prepared, of marble, and about $40 paid the priests for the privilege of putting it up."[142]

A New Spirit

For the Union navy and the Portsmouth Navy Yard, 1862 had meant many successes and a few failures. At year's end, much of the uncertainty and inexperience—and even the bungling characteristic of the Union navy in its early months—was gone. Union naval fortunes had risen significantly. New Orleans was in Union hands, and the recaptured Norfolk and Pensacola Navy Yards were once again servicing Union warships. An ironclad fleet was under construction. The North's control of the seas, challenged only by a few pesky Confederate raiders, prevented the South from receiving diplomatic recognition from the European nations. By the end of 1862 (despite the floundering and loss of the USS *Monitor* on December 31, off Cape Hatteras, North Carolina), the Union navy, engendered with a new spirit, was clearly on the ascendancy.[143]

When Navy Secretary Welles prepared his annual report of the Navy Department for 1862 for President Lincoln, he articulated this new-found optimism and pride. The report, released to the public in early December 1862, revealed that the Union navy was increasing its numerical edge in the battle of statistics. Welles wrote:

> When I became Secretary of the Navy, only 42 vessels were in commission, and out of 7,000 seamen only 207 were at hand on March 10, 1861, to aid us against the rebels. We now have, including those building, 104 steam vessels and 323 sailing vessels, in all 427, of 440,036 tons, carrying 3,268 guns....
>
> Last year's report gave the number of prizes to the blockading squadrons as 153. Since that time 390 more have been taken, in all 543....
>
> The navy employs about 28,000 men on board ships, and about 12,000 mechanics and laborers at the navy yards and stations....[144]

The Portsmouth Navy Yard's activities had contributed to the navy's growth. The Yard's work and industry did not go unnoticed when Assistant Secretary of the Navy Gustavus Fox made a personal inspection of the Yard in August. During the year, Yard workmen built, launched, and repaired about a dozen vessels. In addition to those previously mentioned, there were three side-wheelers, the *Sebago*, the *Sonoma*, and the *Conemaugh*; the screw steamer *Sacramento*; the steam sloop *Ossipee*; and others. Approximately 1,800 men were on the November 1862 payroll.[145]

Secretary Welles and Commandant Pearson realized, however,

that building and outfitting war vessels formed only part of their responsibility; the navy also needed trained and qualified officers to command them.

On July 16, 1862, the navy introduced the grades of rear admiral, commodore, lieutenant commander, and ensign. The requirements for these grades differed in regard to age and previous experience; merchant marine captains were especially favored. The Navy Department specified that, "Before entering the Navy, Acting Ensigns and Acting Master's Mates will be required to furnish to the Navy Department proof of their age, sea service, sobriety and professional knowledge. Letters of recommendation should come from Captains with whom they have sailed, owners for whom they have sailed, and insurance officers acquainted with their professional character and sobriety." New annual pay rates for volunteer officers of the line at sea were established as of July 16, 1862: Acting Lieutenants, $1,875; Acting Masters, $1,500; Acting Ensigns, $1,200; and Master's Mates, $480. Each grade also received one ration (an allowance for food).[146]

For those who were unqualified, a Captain Thompson offered a quick cram course in Boston to attain certification. With "high commendations from Edward Everett, Caleb Curtis, and a host of merchants and shipmasters, and naval officers of Boston," Thompson placed an ad in the *Journal* on August 9, less than a month after the new naval regulations went into effect:

Navigation
PRACTICALLY TAUGHT BY Capt. E. THOMPSON
At French's Nautical College
94 Tremont Street————Boston

"CAPT. THOMPSON is the only experienced Shipmaster teaching in Boston, and is specially appointed to qualify Masters and Mates for the Navy and Revenue Marine Service [forerunner of the United States Coast Guard]...."[147]

The officers and men of the hard-luck vessel *R.R. Cuyler* reflected this growing professional pride. In a lengthy letter, headlined "BLOCKADING OFF MOBILE, Dec. 20, 1862," one "T.S.G." noted a sense of purpose:

> We are now lying at Pensacola, to which place we have come from Mobile to coal ship. Having been employed in the monotonous duty of blockading the latter port for the last two

months, everything in this portion of "Secessia" remains "In status quo." But how long it will remain so it is impossible for me to say; for Admiral Farragut is not in the habit of inviting the crews of the different ships to dine with him, and explaining his instructions from the Navy Department. The Sloops-of-war *Brooklyn*, *Oneida*, and *R.R. Cuyler*. with the gunboats *Pocahontas*, *Kennebec*, *Wyoming*, *Aroostook*, with others occasionally, effectually blockade Mobile Bay, and smart indeed must be the craft that eludes the united vigilance of this squadron....

Sometimes a Confederate paper finds its way to us, and it is highly amusing to read their prophecies of what is about to be done, and the result thereof. Heretofore they have proved themselves false prophets, and will no doubt do so to the end. Although the previous operations of the [Union] navy have been somewhat slow, they have certainly been sure, as the rebels know to their cost; but there is no one so blind as they who will not see, and rebeldom seems determined to remain in the dark, notwithstanding all our attempts to force the light on them.[148]

A Mascot for the Union Navy

The acquisition and commissioning of the yacht *America* provided a mascot for the rest of the fleet. This famous racing schooner had been launched as a private vessel a decade earlier in New York. On August 22, 1851, the *America* handily won a challenge race around the Isle of Wight, England, leaving seventeen English competitors in her wake. As the *America* breezed to the finish line, she had completely outsailed her opposition, winning the coveted trophy that became known as the America's Cup. An apocryphal exchange relating to this circumstance had been part of the *America*'s legend ever since:

"Signal Master," asked Queen Victoria, "are the yachts in sight?"
"Yes, may it please your Majesty."
"Which is first?"
"The *America*."
"Which is second?"
"Ah, Your Majesty, there is no second."[149]

Purchased by a British nobleman who renamed her the *Camilla*, the schooner-yacht later became a blockade runner. In that role, she shipped out of England, loaded with supplies, and in 1861 made a successful run to the Confederate port of Jacksonville, Florida. Falling into Confederate hands, the famous yacht was again renamed—this time as the CSS *Memphis*. Chased up the St. Johns River by a Union gunboat, the vessel was scuttled by her Southern crew. In March 1862, Union warships found the yacht, her masts rising out of the water and her bottom full of auger holes. The Union commander in charge of the expedition reported that "it was generally believed she was bought by the rebels for the purpose of carrying Slidell and Mason to England"—another myth, but often held to be true.[150]

Raised and taken by Union ships to Port Royal, South Carolina, for repairs and refitting, the vessel later sailed to the Brooklyn Navy Yard for conversion to military uses. According to the November 18 issue of the *Chronicle*, workmen equipped her with a "formidable rifle gun." On December 24, 1862, the United States Navy put the USS *America* into commission, restoring her original name. On December 29, the *Chronicle* reported, "She sails immediately." As the New Year approached, the *America*, in her new role, was now playing in a game with much higher stakes.[151]

LIST OF

UNITED STATES VESSELS

SOLD AND

TRANSFERRED TO BRITISH SUBJECTS

IN THE

YEAR 1863.

Name of Ship.	Tonnage	Name and Address of Owner.	Particulars of Mortgage.
JEWESS—(no foreign name given.)	476	John A. Willard, of New Castle, New Brunswick, merchant's clerk.	Mortgage, dated October 29, 1863, for $10,000 and interest at 6 per cent., to Charles Watson, of Boston, United States of America.
SYDENHAM—(and her foreign name is "Windermere.")	1,236	George F. Lovitt, of St. John, New Brunswick, merch't.	Mortgage, dated November 21, 1863, for $40,000 and interest at 6 per cent., to Hartley Lord, of Boston, in the U. S. of America, merchant.
CATHEDRAL—(and her foreign name is "Gulf Stream.")	1,046	George F. Lovitt, of St. John, New Brunswick, merch't.	Mortgage, dated November 21, 1863, for $38,000 and interest at 6 per cent., to Hartley Lord, of Boston, in the U. S. of America, merchant.
MONTEBELLO—(and her foreign name is the same as she now bears.)	1,089	Raymond Leeman Gilchrist, of Liverpool, county of Lancaster, ship owner.	Mortgage, dated September 8, 1863, for an account and interest at 5 per cent. to Dunbar Henderson, of Thomaston, Maine, United States of America, merchant.
W. E. ALEXANDER—(no foreign name is given.)	190	Edward Lyster, of Yarmouth, Nova Scotia, now of New York, U. S. A., stevedore.	Mortgage, dated June 10, 1863, for $7,000 and interest at 5 per cent., to Nathaniel G. Tucker, of Harrington, Maine, United States of America, master marines.
KENILWORTH—(and her foreign name is "Volant.")	987	William Miller McLean, of St. John, New Brunswick, merchant.	Mortgage, dated August 11, 1863, for $35,000 and interest at 6 per cent., to Francis Custis and Samuel Endicott Peabody, of Boston, U. States of America, merchants, joint mortgagees.

Pages from A List of United States Vessels which have been Sold and Transferred to British subjects in 1863, and which have been Mortgaged by the Registered Owners to Persons Residing in the United States. *Rare Confederate pamphlet. LC*

IV 1863: The Portsmouth Draft Riot Fails to Impede the War Effort

Clashes of Senator Hale

THE PROTRACTION OF THE CIVIL WAR had begun to test civilian resolve by the beginning of 1863. Gone was the early enthusiasm of 1861, when Northern citizens had expected the war to be over within months. Now, as they began to weigh the human and financial costs of defeating the South, many became embittered. The Emancipation Proclamation, the institution of a draft, and increased political activities of the "Copperheads" (Northerners who either openly or secretly supported the South) aroused the passions of the Portsmouth populace, culminating in the Portsmouth draft riot of June 1863. That year, victory seemed very distant.

The year of 1863 began inauspiciously for the Yard with the continuing feud between New Hampshire Senator John P. Hale, chairman of the Senate Naval Affairs Committee, and Gideon Welles, secretary of the Navy. The two men repeatedly clashed throughout their years in the Lincoln administration. Hale, who deemed Welles incompetent and corrupt, attacked him on the Senate floor. Welles regarded Hale as self-serving, seeking patronage for contracts at the Yard. The antagonism between the two worked to the detriment of the Yard itself.[1]

161

On January 10, 1863, the *Portsmouth Journal* reported the status of the government appropriation to purchase a portion of Seavey's Island and to erect a hospital there. Hale had written to Welles on December 29, 1862, to complain that the secretary was failing to release the appropriated money. On the same day, Hale wrote to Charles W. Brewster, editor of the *Journal*, to request that the newspaper publish his long letter to Welles. Brewster wrote in an editorial that the delay was surprising and that "the best policy would be to purchase the whole island and place it under the control of the Government."[2]

Hale's letter reveals him in his best fighting mood. Addressing objections of Captain Joseph Smith, chief of the Bureau of Yards and Docks, whose recommendations Welles was following, Hale blasted the contentions that the land was not feasible for the hospital and that keeping the road on Seavey's Island open for a public right-of-way would constitute a security risk. Hale concluded:

> The citizens of Maine and New Hampshire ... feel indignant that the benevolent purposes of Congress in providing necessary and comfortable quarters for sick and wounded sailors, who had been enfeebled and disabled in vindicating the national life and honor, who have borne aloft in triumph the National Flag, though they have been stricken down should be thwarted and delayed because the wisdom of the act for their benefit was not precisely coincident with the opinion of the Chief of the Bureau of Yards and Docks.[3]

Eventually the hospital was built, but such squabbles only delayed the process and besmirched the reputations of the Yard and the navy.

Fire and Ice Exact a Toll

Fire, cold weather, and explosions during 1863 hampered the Yard and its ships, even though the Yard administration took every precaution to prepare for such emergencies. On January 2, 1863, a new steam fire engine arrived from the Amoskeag Machine Works in Manchester. Appropriately named "Union," the engine "cost Uncle Sam about $3000." The *Chronicle* reported its trial run eight days later: "A stream of water was brought to bear on the Franklin Ship

House, and with 100 pounds pressure of steam, she threw a stream over the building, which is seven stories in height. Her boilers are capable of sustaining 160 pounds pressure of steam."[4]

On Wednesday, February 4, the "Union" was rushed into action in an actual crisis. Conditions could not have been worse. At 5:30 A.M., the house in the Navy Yard occupied by Edward N. Anderson, porter of the Yard, erupted into flames, apparently from a defective chimney. The temperature was about -14°F, a heavy northwest wind was blowing, and the Piscataqua River was shrouded in "sea smoke." The house was a total loss; Anderson, his wife, and several children barely escaped with their lives. Since Anderson had no insurance, he was devastated. However, unlike the two hand engines, which had frozen water in their pumps, the new steam fire engine performed admirably. The furnace's heat kept the "Union's" pumps from freezing up, and the "Union" was able to direct two heavy streams of water onto the flames.[5]

His colleagues and fellow Portsmouth citizens rallied to Anderson's support. In a card published on March 16, 1863, Edward N. Anderson gratefully acknowledged the donations of food, needed articles, and money, including:

From marine officers and privates, through Col. Ward Marston, commanding, the sum of	$ 57.25
Officers of the Yard and workmen,	173.00
Citizens of Portsmouth,	150.00
	[$]380.25[6]

On the evening of March 11, 1863, the weight of snow on the roof caused the collapse of the wooden shed erected over the *Agamenticus*, the ironclad under construction. About three-fourths of the building fell with a crash that was heard across the Piscataqua in the village of New Castle.[7]

Nor were disasters occurring only at the Yard. On April 27, 1863, the Yard-built USS *Preble*, serving as a guard and store ship off Pensacola, Florida, burned at sea. The *Preble*, a sailing sloop carrying sixteen guns and a complement of 300, had joined the Gulf Blockading Squadron at the outbreak of the Civil War. Carelessness caused the accident; the captain of the hold carried an open lamp (a candle, according to another account) into the storeroom, where the flame quickly ignited a cask of oil. After burning fiercely, the *Preble* finally exploded, sending her three masts high into the air. Fortunately, all hands were saved.[8]

Shortly thereafter, an unidentified officer of the *Preble* described the loss of his ship:

> Those on the lower deck had barely time to escape with their lives, some of them being quite severely burned.... In fifteen minutes the ship was untenable, and the order was given to leave. It was impossible for many of the men to reach the gangway, and they were obliged to throw themselves overboard, to be picked up by the boats.
>
> In less than an hour after the fire broke out the magazine exploded, and all that remained of the *Preble* was in mid air. It was the most sublime and fearful sight I ever witnessed. The flames seemed to shoot upwards for nearly a mile, and writhed and wriggled like so many fiery serpents, and near the top of the flames a second explosion took place, caused by a shell or a large box of ammunition. The three masts were still standing when the explosion took place, and up they went into the air, whole, with the guard flag still flying at the fore.[9]

The Lure of Prize Money

Perhaps even surpassing the motivation of patriotism, the incentive of prize money stimulated Union naval officers and crews to defeat the enemy. In governmental policies, newspaper articles, and Union naval officers' and sailors' private letters, the topic of prize money commanded universal attention. Such a monetary incentive helped win the war at sea.

Fully recognizing the morale-building effect of prize money, the Union government endorsed its special status within the Union navy. An act passed by Congress in early 1863 changed the method of distributing prize money in the navy, placing the money in the hands and the pockets of the victorious Union crews more efficiently. "The act provides that the share adjudged to each officer, seamen [seaman] or marine," reported the *Chronicle* on April 21, "shall be paid [by] the Navy Department and credited by it in the account of the person to whom it belongs, so that it may be paid to him as his wages or salary is paid, by the purser of the ship or paymaster of the yard to which he may be attached."[10]

U. S. Ship St. Lawrence.

THE CREW of the United States ship ST.
LAWRENCE will be paid off at the Paymaster's
Office off the Navy Yard, on TUESDAY the 2d of
June, at 12 o'clock noon.

WASHINGTON IRVING,
Paymaster, U. S. Navy.

PC, June 1, 1863

The Northern press regularly covered the continuing flow of news pertaining to prize money. "Running the blockade," editorialized the *Chronicle* on April 21, "seems to be a paying business to the British and the rebels—and taking prizes seems to be a paying business to the [Union navy] blockaders."[11]

The powerfully armed Portsmouth-built sloop of war *Sacramento*, commanded by Captain Charles S. Boggs, received her 200-man crew complement on January 7, 1863, and was commissioned the same day. She left the Yard on February 10, rumored to be headed for Fortress Monroe, Virginia. "Should she fall in with the pirate *Alabama*," the *Chronicle* predicted, "there will be straightway [immediately] a fight which means capture for the pirate."[12]

Some time later, Captain Boggs, on his blockading station off Beaufort, North Carolina, below Cape Hatteras, summoned the men of the *Sacramento* to receive a characteristic incentive: "To the man who reports a sail, and we take her as a prize, I will agree to give one-tenth of my prize money, and will enter into a written obligation to that effect."[13]

On May 2, 1863, the *Sacramento* seized the British blockade runner *Wanderer* off the North Carolina coast with a cargo of salt and herring. This prize, however, turned out to be Boggs's last. Exhausted by overwork and exposure, he sought shore duty and spent the rest of the war years in New York, building and outfitting ships for the navy.[14]

Closer to home, in operations in and around Chesapeake Bay, the men of the USS *Mahaska* also sought to profit from prizes and the booty of war. Lieutenant Elliott C.V. Blake, the *Mahaska*'s new commander, continued the aggressive forays for which the ship was noted. On February 20, 1863, the *Mahaska* and the USS *Crusader* approached the Confederate schooner *General Taylor*. The *Crusader* was in front and captured the blockade runner. Four days later, cutters sent out from the *Mahaska* destroyed the sloop *Mary Jane* and the barge *Ben Blue* on Back Creek, York River, Virginia.[15]

Adding to the formal official military accounts of these naval actions, one "B.J." (either an officer or a sailor aboard the *Mahaska*) provided an unauthorized rendering of what he felt had actually happened—and furthermore expected—in an undated letter, published in the February 28 issue of the *Chronicle*:

> We have left Yorktown for a while, but shall probably return thither to-night. We have some of the Generals and other officers on board, with their wives; so you see that we are up to the same old trade, viz. running pleasure excursions. I don't know but it will do about as much toward putting down the rebellion, as anything we have done lately. The officers are all good Democrats, and this war will last as long as they can draw their pay and do nothing, in my opinion.
>
> The *Crusader* took a prize valued at $80,000, and as we were close by we shall share with them. After they had taken it, the crew told us that another schooner [actually the sloop *Mary Jane*] had run the blockade, and gone up East [probably the York] River. We run [sic] up as far as we could with the gun boat and launched two small boats and sent them up. When they got where the schooner was, it was aground and had been unloaded. We then had to return and leave the fair sex, and when we got back[,] the rebels had burned the schooner. So you see by going back with the ladies, we lost from $6000 to $10,000. This is rather poor encouragement for us out here.[16]

"Copperhead" Congressman Daniel Marcy

The disgruntled "B.J." aboard the *Mahaska* had properly gauged the national mood. Wild-eyed chauvinism had not won the war for the Union, and with the conflict dragging on, many in the North looked toward the ballot box as a means to wind down and end the fighting. Democrat Daniel Marcy continued to loathe the war. In March 1863, as his shipping empire continued to slip away, Marcy ran for Congress. He wanted to save the Union, his economic stake, and his family.

Marcy's well-known ties to his brother Peter were a political liability in New Hampshire's First District. Immediately branded a

"Copperhead," Daniel was suspected of disloyalty to the Union during the war, even of aiding the South directly. Peter Marcy's inflammatory private letters, which Daniel regularly received and saved, may have affected Daniel's spirits on this issue. "If the war continues many years longer," Peter lamented on January 15, 1863, in his idiosyncratic spelling and punctuation, "paper promises to pay will not be worth much. all Must admit their is a dark gloom Hanging over the financial affairs off this Country, through which the ablest off financiers can not perceive a ray off light. Ship owners must I think Soon feel the Efects off the war, unless the capture off their [word omitted] Is prevented." Again on February 21, 1863, Peter railed at length, telling his brother:

> [You] speak off the Condition of the Country. It is indeed in a deplorable State. the yankees are blamed for the [w]hole of it. you have no idea of the bitter hatred which prevails in the South towords the Newingland States. fifty years will not Sufice to alay It.... I know that you have done all you Could to prevent It and further that you have at this Time nothing to reproach your Self with. you And all the others at the north have got to make up your mind, for a Separation off the Country, and the longer you are fighting the the [sic] longer that Separation will be.[17]

Three days later, on February 24, Peter Marcy's son William Henry Marcy, who had just turned eighteen, enlisted in the Confederate army as a private in Company A, Crescent Regiment, Louisiana Volunteers. Since New Orleans was then under Union military occupation, William evidently slipped through the lines to enlist at Confederate-held Mobile, Alabama.[18]

The rift within his family did not deter Daniel Marcy as he continued his campaign, but repeated charges of being a Copperhead blighted his candidacy. "Remember the election of Ira A. Eastman for governor, and Daniel Marcy, John H. George and William Burns for Congress," editorialized the *Journal* on February 23, "will cause rejoicing in the Rebeldom, as did the election of [Horatio] Seymour, Fernando Wood and Co., in New York, over which Charleston was illuminated in rejoicing." Although the Republican *Journal* considered all Democrats more or less Copperheads, Daniel Marcy had an advantage in the forthcoming election. The popular Republican Congressman Gilman Marston of Exeter had relinquished his seat to become a general in the Union army, and Judge Joel Eastman of Conway, from upstate in Carroll County, Marcy's Republican opponent for the seat, lacked Marston's appeal and popularity.[19]

The results of the March 10 election were extremely close, with the outcome in doubt for some days. Finally Marcy pulled ahead by fewer than 100 votes to win his seat in the Thirty-Eighth Congress. The Portsmouth Democratic newspaper, *The States and Union*, exclaimed on March 13, "New England's Abolition Chain Broken! 'Copperhead' Triumph! The Charcoals and Paperheads Squelched in the First Congressional District[,] HON. DANIEL MARCY ELECTED to represent the First N.H. District in Congress."[20]

When Daniel Marcy became a member of the Thirty-Eighth Congress, a family crisis immediately required all his political skills. Samuel Marcy, his nephew and the son of Samuel Marcy, Sr., was captured aboard an English vessel on April 14, 1863, and detained on charges of violating the blockade. At the time of his detention, young Marcy was twenty-nine years old. Seeking to obtain his nephew's release, Congressman Marcy took the matter directly to Secretary of War Edwin M. Stanton. Writing Stanton from Portsmouth on July 7, 1863, Marcy stated, "A nephew of Mine Samuel Marcy was taken on board the English Schooner *Clyde* bound from Laguna Mexico to Havannah [Havana, Cuba]. he was a passenger. Captured on the 14th April 1863—has been sent to Fort Lafayette [New York] & subsequently to Fort Warren [on an island in Boston Harbor], his sister & myself wishes to have a interview with him, if not Incompatible with Public Interest[.] will you grant the above request[?]"[21]

Whether or not the prison interview was granted is not documented, but two Fort Warren letters, from Samuel Marcy to his Uncle Daniel, describe his plight. In the first, dated July 30, 1863, Samuel states:

> On or about the 29th of March I engaged a passage on board the English Schooner *Clyde* belonging to Belize Honduras bound for Havana.... On the 14th we were boarded by a boat from the USS *Sonoma*, and after two hours detention the vessel was seized as a prize and ordered to Key West.
>
> I was there taken before the U.S. Prize Commissioner, examined as a witness in the case of the Sch. and released[.] Two days afterwards and just as I was about leaving for

Havana I was again arrested. I asked what I was arrested for. He replied he was ordered to arrest me as a Prisoner of war. I was immediately sent to Fort Taylor [Florida], where I remained for four weeks. Thence transferred to Fort La Fayette [Lafayette, New York], finally to this place. During the whole of this time I have had no examination, and am totally ignorant of the charges existing against me[.] The vessel was released at Key West.

Now as I was simply a Passenger on board, Under the British flag, proceeding on a Legal voyage between Neutral Ports, and at least 500 miles from blockaded waters, it is plainly evident that my detention is illegal. These facts can be easily established, and my reasons for sending them to you is that you may be able to adopt the proper course to procure my release ... congratulating you upon your election to Congress[.][22]

Samuel's second letter, August 12, concludes with a plea "to procure my release[.] Trusting you may succeed."[23]

The United States Navy's official records present a different version of the incident. "On Tuesday, [April] 14th," wrote *Sonoma* Commander Thomas H. Stevens of the episode six days later, "the *Sonoma* captured a vessel loaded with cotton and resin, having on board 156 bales of the former and 16 barrels of the latter. The *Clyde* was under English colors, and was bound from Laguna to Havana. Her papers were generally correct, but, as the cargo came out of a Confederate vessel to the *Clyde*, and as she had the officers and crew of a Confederate on board, with nothing to show a transfer of property, I took possession of the vessel and cargo and sent them into Key West for adjudication. The officers and crew of the Confederate schooner are on board the *Sonoma*."[24]

The British government elected not to make a second *Trent* affair of the seizure. Samuel Marcy was eventually released and eventually returned to New Orleans.

Transfer of Registry or Sale of Portsmouth Ships

In order to salvage their investments in the changing maritime scene, Daniel Marcy and other Northern shipowners devised plans to circumvent the obstacles created by the Civil War. Roundabout methods quickly evolved. Owners either transferred their ships from United States to foreign registry, with American captains often becoming citizens of the appropriate countries, or they sold their vessels directly to Canadian, English, or European interests. These legal actions reduced the chance of seizure by Confederate raiders.

Reasonably complete documentation traces the process by which Marcy's ship *Orozimbo*, with an American captain and crew, became the *Morena*, flying the flag of the City of Hamburg, out of that North Sea port. In the fall of 1863, Marcy, his agents, foreign speculators, and Captain Joshua W. Hickey of the *Orozimbo* engaged in extensive correspondence—a bizarre blend of business, banking, insurance matters, and international law—to effect the transfer of ownership. From Hamburg, then an independent port city within a loose German confederation, Hickey on September 21 wrote to Marcy in his semiliterate scrawl: "I have made every enquiry about becoming a Citizen of Hamburg[.] they have made a few American Citizens but now they have stopped for they feel that they only become Citizens from Necesstys and are not willing to take any for the Present."[25]

Ultimately abandoning this strategy, Hickey on November 11 notified Supply Thwing, Marcy's business partner, about the deal he was able to strike: "I have obtained a sale for the Hamburgh Ship *Morena* for the sum of ten thousand nine hundred pounds Sterling. I have obtained your price. I shall leave, I hope, in the boat from here on Saturday for N. York. The Purchasers take the Charter and all bills that I have paid. She has been sold to a Bremen House."[26]

The metamorphosis of the *Orozimbo* into the *Morena* involved a legal ruse used by hundreds, if not thousands, of Union merchant marine owners and masters during the Civil War. During these uncertain times, Daniel Marcy understood how to play the game as skillfully as anyone else: Sell, lease, transfer to foreign registry, and undertake whatever was necessary to cut losses.

During 1863, a number of Portsmouth-built ships were involved in "the flight from the flag," as American maritime historians later termed this course of action. Many Portsmouth ships were sold in London: "*Barbara*, 602 tons, built in 1851, for £4500; *Neptune's Car*, built in 1853, for £8000; *Jumna*, 782 tons, built in 1856, for £4500; and the *Sierra Nevada*, 1942 tons, built in 1854, for £10,750." In another transaction, Daniel Marcy sold the ship

Henrietta Marcy, to an English firm in the summer of 1863. The ship was renamed the *St. Albans*.[27]

The Confederate government, however, was not fooled with such transfer-of-registry trickery, being fully aware of the paper shenanigans to which the Northern shipowners were resorting. A Confederate publication, *List of United States Vessels Sold and Transferred to British Subjects in the Year 1863*, documents such activity. Southern officials, in fact, knew the exact particulars of Daniel Marcy's vessel. In the *List*, under "NAME OF SHIP," appears "ST. ALBANS—(and her foreign name is *Henrietta Marcy*;)." The second category, "Tonnage," is "1,266 [tons]"; the third column, "Name and Address of Owner," lists "William Miller McLean, of St. John, New Brunswick, merchant." The fourth and last heading, "Particulars of Mortgage," supplies the information, "Mortgage, dated August 28, 1863, for $55,000 and interest at 6 per cent, to Francis Curtis and Samuel Endicott Peabody of Boston, U. States of America, joint mortgagees, merchants."[28]

Portsmouth Captains and Crews Perish

While sales and transfers of Portsmouth ships to foreign registry were conducted in relative secrecy, tragedy at sea resulting from natural disasters or human motives quickly became public knowledge and commanded as much attention in the local press as the Civil War itself. Probably more Portsmouth lives were lost aboard Port of Portsmouth or otherwise locally related merchant ships than in naval line of duty.

On Monday, February 2, 1863, the barque *Annie E. Sherwood* of New York with a crew of eight men left Kennebunk, Maine, northward bound for Portland. A furious gale soon intervened, blowing the vessel off course to the south. Driven by winds toward Portsmouth Harbor the following afternoon, the ship anchored to wait out the storm. The buffeted vessel lost both anchors and chains, with the crew suffering intensely in the severe cold. It was not until Friday morning, February 6, that the *Annie E. Sherwood* limped into Portsmouth. After presumably undergoing emergency repairs and replacing lost equipment, the vessel again sailed for Portland, this time arriving safely. Her ordeal, however, was not yet over. The barque sailed on March 4 from Portland for Montevideo, Uruguay. Outside Portland Harbor, a seaman stabbed the mate, B.E. Sloan of Kennebunk. "It is the old story of a rebellious crew," commented the *Chronicle*, "who had taken whiskey as part of their outfit, and refused to 'turn to.' His [Sloan's] case is dangerous.—The seaman is in custody, and the barque has returned to port."[29]

A far more serious disaster occurred during the night of February 14-15, 1863, off Whale's Back Ledge, off Portsmouth Harbor. "SHIPWRECK AND LOSS OF LIFE," headlined the *Journal*'s account:

> The British Schooner *Rouser*, Capt. Crafts [commanding], from St. John, N.B. [New Brunswick], for Boston, was totally lost with every person on board, on Whale's Back Ledge, about two miles outside this harbor, on Saturday night last [February] 14th inst. On Sunday morning [February 15, 1863] about 5 o'clock, the keeper of the Light House, looking out of the window, thought he discovered something on the rocks near the Light House, and on opening the door, was shocked to behold, about 20 feet distant from the basement, a piece of a wreck and on it three living men—one of whom cried out "throw us a bowline." The request was complied with as soon as possible, and repeated a number of times, but they seemed incapable of making an effort to save themselves, and the sea being high and beating violently, he could offer no other assistance, and was compelled to see them disappear one after another until all three had gone. Portions of cargo, consisting of pickled fish, shingles, old junk and old iron—have been saved, together with the vessel's chains[,] anchors, and a small portion of the rigging....
>
> Two bodies have been picked up.... The bodies are to be deposited in the tomb by order of the British Consular agent, so that they may be identified.[30]

As days went by, additional details of the shipwreck became known when Deputy Collector Joseph M. Edmonds received letters from St. John. The vessel was owned by Thomas McLeod of that city and was not covered by insurance. Seven—the captain, three crewmen, and three passengers—died in the tragedy. Edmonds communicated the sad news of loss of life to authorities in St. John. On June 14, the last body was picked up from the water, and the remains were interred in Portsmouth's Harmony Grove Cemetery.[31]

In the aftermath of the shipwreck, Portsmouth and federal authorities acted promptly to prevent a recurrence of such accidents. On August 1, 1863, the *Chronicle* announced:

A fog-bell, struck by machinery, has been established at Whale's Back Light-House Station, and will be kept in operation from and after August 1st. The bell tower is a frame structure 25 feet high, whitewashed, standing upon the Light-House pier, and attached to the southerly side of the Light-House tower.

The signal is a steel bell, which will be struck four times per minute, at regular intervals, during the prevalence of fogs, snow storms and thick weather, and should be heard a distance of one-quarter to four miles, according to the circumstances of surf, weather, wind, &c. The bell stands at an elevation of fifty-five feet above mean low water.[32]

The United States Navy and the secretary of the Treasury combined efforts to provide safety measures for the merchant marine. In mid-July 1863, the Navy Department detailed five vessels for permanent service on the East Coast during the fishing season. In the event of an emergency, the department would order other vessels to protect the commerce and fisheries in that quarter. At about the same time, Secretary of the Treasury Salmon Chase tightened restrictions, ordering, "that hereafter, upon the deck of every Revenue Cutter in commission, there must be on duty at all times, whether day or night, at least one commissioned officer and one third of the crew."[33]

Despite these reforms, no foghorn, United States naval vessel, or revenue cutter could have saved the life of Captain John B. Ashby of Salem, Massachusetts, about thirty years old, who was married to a Portsmouth woman. During her husband's distant voyages, Mrs. Ashby lived at the Portsmouth home of her father, Joshua Staples. In mid-July 1863, the woman received news (via telegraph from San Francisco) of her husband's murder at sea.[34]

The Department of State in Washington issued a curt official announcement on July 28. A letter dated May 22, 1863, from Horace N. Congar, the United States Consul in Hong Kong, to Ashby's widow in Portsmouth, captures the poignancy of the death of a "capable, successful, and highly-respected Ship Master." Ashby's many friends in Portsmouth were shocked by the news in Congar's letter, published on

July 23 in the *Chronicle*:

> I am pained beyond measure to communicate to you the death of your husband, Capt. John B. Ashby, which occurred in the China Sea on the 18th of May....
>
> On Monday, May 11th, the second mate of the *Hamlet* had an altercation with one of the seamen, a young and almost boyish person, during which the latter bit the thumb of the second mate badly. He was subsequently called aft by Capt. Ashby and properly rebuked, having been punished by the second mate. Nothing of importance occurred for two or three days. The carpenter observed him sharpening a knife, but did not think that he harbored any purpose of revenge.
>
> On Friday, May 15th, about six o'clock in the morning, Capt. Ashby and the second mate were on deck and this same seaman again used some impudent language, and the captain ordered him below. As he turned to go down into the cabin, he moved slowly and the second mate ordered him on. In a moment or two after, the captain went below and found that the refractory seaman had gone into the back cabin. He ordered him out and went in himself behind him, the second mate being in the middle cabin. At this time, the seaman pulled out his sheath-knife and inflicted two wounds upon Capt. Ashby, one of which was mortal. The knife penetrated under the ribs on both sides. The seaman was immediately seized and ironed, and every attention was paid to Capt. Ashby, who had fallen to the floor. At first Capt. Ashby appeared to consider the wound mortal, and he gave the mate some instructions. Subsequently the hemorrhage was somewhat allayed and he appeared to feel more confident of his recovery. Every attention was paid him by the officers and crew, but in a day or so he became anxious to reach Hong Kong, which desire was participated in by the officers. No change took place of a particular character until early on Monday morning, May 18th, when it was evident that he was sinking rapidly. He soon lost his senses and about 8 o'clock expired. During the last few hours the officers of the vessel were by him, and you have the consolation of knowing that nothing was omitted to render him as comfortable as possible.[35]

A month later, on August 26, *Chronicle* readers received more

> OFFICIAL.
>
> DEPARTMENT OF STATE,
> Washington, July 28, 1863.
>
> INFORMATION has been received at this Depart-
> ment from Mr. H. N. Congar, the Consul of the
> United States at Hong Kong, of the death, on the 22d
> of May, near Hong Kong, of JOHN B. ASHBY, of
> Portsmouth, Master of the American ship Hamlet, of
> Boston, from the effects of a wound inflicted by a sea-
> man on board the vessel.   3 is

PJ, August 1, 1863

sad news: "Capt. John McKinnon, of Rockland Me., commander of the Bark *Emily Banning*, was shot at Shanghai, China, on the 24th of May, by a secession sympathizer named Buckley. He lived but a few hours." [36]

Plots, Hijacked Ships, and Escaped Prisoners

A number of bizarre incidents during 1863 seemed to justify the consternation that gripped the anxious minds of Daniel Marcy, the Northern shipowners, Commandant George F. Pearson at the Portsmouth Navy Yard, and the average Portsmouth citizen. With Confederate plots, Southern prisoners on the loose, the Union ships being hijacked in Northern waters, rumors often became realities. Confederate vessels occasionally even operated off the New England coast on raids, creating a general alarm. Confederate daring in the area had brought the war home to New Hampshire.

Confederate agent James Bulloch had been in Paris since the spring of 1863. Formerly an officer in the United States Navy, Bulloch remained loyal to his native Georgia when the Civil War began and accepted from Confederate Secretary of the Navy Stephen R. Mallory the critical post of agent for the Confederate navy abroad. During 1861 and 1862, Bulloch sought to buy or build naval vessels in England. (He especially favored ironclads.) After successful negotiations to arrange for the building of the ships that ultimately became the *Florida* and the *Alabama* (originally "No. 290"), Bulloch became increasingly frustrated with the waning British support and enthusiasm for the Southern war effort. By 1863, the reality of Union military victories in the field, the patient diplomacy of American Minister to Great Britain Charles Francis Adams, and the crude and blustering resolutions and public speeches of the chief Confederate sympathizers in Parliament had combined to cool any chance for English recognition of the Confederacy. In light of these developments, the Confederacy in the summer of 1863 shifted its efforts to concentrate on courting French support. In Paris, after intimations that French authorities would be more lenient toward building ironclads for transfer to the Confederate navy, Bulloch submitted plans to Mallory on July 8 pertaining "to our two ironclad vessels, which in future reports I will allude to as Nos. 294 and 295."[37]

The next day, Bulloch wrote a letter to Mallory that was kept secret until the end of the war. In the missive, Bulloch confided to Mallory the details of one of their missions:

> Portsmouth, NH, is a city given over to hatred of our cause and country. It is wealthy in itself and opposite the town is an important dock and building yard [Portsmouth Navy Yard]. The whole lies invitingly open to attack and destruction. Suppose our two ironclads [not yet built] should steam unannounced into that harbor on some fine October morning, and while one proceeded at once to demolish the navy yard and all it contained the other should send a flag of truce to the mayor [Jonathan Dearborn] to say that if $10,000,000 in gold and $50,000,000 in greenbacks [paper money] were not sent on board in four hours the city would be destroyed after the manner of Jacksonville [Florida] and Bluffton [South Carolina; both southern towns had recently been destroyed by Union forces]. Portsmouth could well afford to pay that sum for its existence.[38]

Fortunately for Portsmouth and the Yard, this plan was never carried out. The two ironclads, the *Cheops* (never commissioned as a Confederate warship) and the *Sphinx* (later the CSS *Stonewall*) were eventually completed by a French naval contractor, but not in time to take an active part in the war.

The meteoric career of the CSS *Tacony* during June 1863 represented a different matter, creating havoc with Union shipping along the eastern seaboard from Virginia to Maine. Off Cape Henry, Virginia, on June 12, 1863, the captain of the Northern bark *Tacony* noticed a brigantine with the U.S. flag flying upside down, and he responded to this signal of distress. However, this was a ruse perpetrated by Lieutenant Charles W. Read and his Confederate crew aboard the CSS *Clarence*, and the *Tacony* was captured. Realizing that the *Tacony* was a better sailor than his own ship, Read transferred his armament, crew, and prisoners from the *Clarence*, which he torched, to the *Tacony*, which he renamed the CSS *Florida No. 2*. Northerners, however, still referred to her as the *Tacony*. During the next twelve days, Read took fifteen prizes with his expropriated ship. His exploits made *Tacony* synonymous with capture and destruction in the North, and the Union navy redoubled efforts to capture the *Tacony* as she proceeded on her northerly raid. Arriving off the Maine coast, Read sensed his ship was becoming too well known, so he repeated the same devious tactics. After capturing the *Archer* off the coast of Maine, he again switched ships, transferring his crew to his new prize. He then burned the *Tacony*.[39]

Read's most notable exploit was yet to come. As he approached Portland during the evening of June 26, he persuaded two local fishermen to come aboard to help him pilot the *Archer* (which the fishermen believed was a pleasure yacht) into Portland Harbor. Sailing in at sunset, Read and his crew boarded the Revenue Cutter *Caleb Cushing* at 1:30 the next morning and undertook a dash for the open sea and escape.[40]

Two Union ships, the steamer *Forest City* and the passenger steamer *Chesapeake* followed in pursuit. William F. Laighton of Portsmouth, a United States naval inspector who happened to be in Portland overseeing gunboat construction, assumed overall command of the *Chesapeake*. His son, Albert S. Laighton, took the helm, and Henry Ham, another Portsmouth citizen, came aboard to volunteer his efforts. By late morning, despite his five-hour lead, Read was bedeviled with a light breeze and an incoming tide. A Portland *Argus* reporter graphically described the ending of this sea saga:

> The cutter [Read's new prize, *Caleb Cushing*] was about two miles distant. She displayed no colors. The brass fieldpiece on her bow gleamed in the sunlight. Her deck seemed covered with armed men.
>
> But the pirates, always so brave in attacking unarmed fishermen and defenceless merchantmen, feared the coming blow. They fired the cutter, took to the boats, and fled. The small boat containing the cutter's crew ... rowed towards the *Chesapeake*. Presently smoke was seen curling up from the cutter amidships, and there was a shout—"they have set her

on fire,—sink the devils!" But no, for Mr. L[aighton] saw a white handkerchief raised in the boat, and said—"hold! the first man that fires shall be shot; I am not a pirate to fire on a flag of truce!" The boat came alongside, Lieut. [Dudley] Davenport [the Union officer in command of the *Caleb Cushing* and Read's prisoner of war] was among them, and was violently agitated as the men helped pull him on board. He turned and said—"It is hard, after a man has been taken a prisoner, ironed, and his life threatened by pirates, to be shot by his own friends!" [Davenport's accusation during the confusion of the moment is inaccurate; the *Chesapeake* never fired upon the *Caleb Cushing*.]—The men, one by one, (nineteen in all) came up the side, some of them with the irons on their wrists.[41]

Lieutenant William F. Laighton emerged as the hero of the hour. It was soon ascertained, according to the *Portland Press*, that Laighton "had a narrow escape in the recent contest with the pirates in Portland harbor. It has been discovered that the steamer *Chesapeake* was hit, two minie [Minié] balls having passed through the blind and window of the Captain's room on the upper deck.... It was supposed they were fired for the purpose of picking off Capt. Laighton, who was in a prominent position on the deck." For its part, the City Council of Portland on July 6 passed a resolution of thanks to Laighton and several others for their distinguished service.[42]

The embarrassment created by the destruction of the *Caleb Cushing* was not lost on the Lincoln administration. In the wake of Confederate guerrilla raids at sea, Washington implemented immediate measures to tighten security. In a "NOTICE," issued at the Customs House on July 4, 1863 (and published on July 8 in the *Chronicle*), Portsmouth Collector of the Port Joseph B. Upham declared:

"By direction of the Secretary of the Treasury [Salmon P. Chase], notice is hereby given that no Vessel, other than Steamers and Packets known to be engaged on regular lines, or in the employ of the army or navy, will be allowed to leave this port between the hours of Sunset and Sunrise, until further orders."[43]

Notwithstanding Washington's order to curtail the activities of such Confederate captains as Charles W. Read, his swashbuckling reputation continued during the summer of 1863. After their capture, Read and his crew expected to be exchanged for their Union counterparts in Southern prison camps, but their hopes were dashed. Confined briefly at Fort Preble, South Portland, Maine, the Confederates were soon transferred to Fort Warren, on George's Island, in Boston Harbor. Known as the "Gibraltar of the North," Fort Warren was considered escape-proof—the home of more than 1,000 Confederate prisoners during the war. The facility was commanded by Colonel Justin T. Dimick, a Portsmouth career soldier.

On the evening of August 18, 1863, Read and five other Confederate prisoners of war squeezed through a hole in a basement wall. Their escape, however, was only half-completed; they still faced the difficulty of leaving the island. Two went into the water and were never seen again. Captain Read and one other were captured at daylight. But Lieutenant Joseph W. Alexander of the CSS *Atlanta* and James Thurston, a Confederate Marine Corps lieutenant stationed on the *Atlanta*, managed to swim to a nearby island and stole a small boat. It was broad daylight when Alexander and Thurston, seeing that Read and his companion were not at their prearranged hiding place, headed out of Boston Harbor and toward the open sea. They hoped to reach St. John, New Brunswick, the nearest neutral Canadian port.[44]

After sailing all day, the fugitives approached Rye Beach, New Hampshire, just south of Portsmouth. Alexander's narrative of his escape, published thirty-one years later, describes his ordeal:

> Towards night we ran close in shore to see if we could get something to eat. We had no clothes except our hats and shirts, and we were very hungry and thirsty. Just about dark we were close in to the beach. Near the shore we saw a house and a man [John Batchelder] standing in front of it. We hailed him and asked him to come off, which he proceeded to do in a small boat. He looked at us very suspiciously, but listened to our tale calmly. We told him we had sailed out from Portsmouth for a lark, and had gone in bathing, and that while in the water our clothes had blown overboard, and asked him to get us some clothes if he could, and bring us some water and something to eat. He went on shore, and soon returned with some old clothes, a good supply of plain food, some tobacco, and a small bottle of cherry brandy. I am satisfied he knew what we were, but we said nothing, except to thank him for his kindness, telling him we would remain where we were till next day; but as soon as he was out of sight, we hoisted our sail and stood on

up the coast towards Eastport [Maine], intending to land in New Brunswick.[45]

Batchelder was not fooled by his unexpected visitors. He noted that Alexander "had money—bills and silver." The next morning, August 19, after his suspicious guests had disappeared, Batchelder drove over to Portsmouth to inform the authorities.

The hunt was on. "Some of our police," reported the *Journal*, "went over to Hampton, starting about 11 o'clock,—one party by land and another by water. Officers Bailey and Johnson went by water in the yacht *Florence*, Capt. Leach [commanding], accompanied by a squad of soldiers from Fort Constitution; but a head tide and light wind prevented their continuing the pursuits beyond the [Isles of] Shoals. They returned to this city on Thursday noon. They [the escaped Confederate prisoners] reported to have been seen, at 4 A.M., Thursday, four miles east of Duck Island [northernmost of the Isles of Shoals]. Vessels from the Portsmouth Navy Yard and from Boston, and the revenue cutter [*J.C. Dobbin*] from Portland, were in pursuit of them."[46]

At the Yard on August 24, 1863, Commandant George F. Pearson notified the secretary of the navy of his course of action: "I immediately dispatched two boats to look for this vessel along the coast. The officers in these boats soon found that they were on the right track, but before they could reach the vessel, it was ascertained that the Revenue Cutter from Portland had captured her.

"Acting Master [E.D.] March of this Yard & Acting Ensign Wm. H. Thomas of the U.S. Bark *Fernandina* were sent in these boats."[47]

On Thursday morning, August 20, two Portsmouth law officers had gone in the fast-sailing yacht *Viking*, which was also closing in to capture "the pirates," as the Portsmouth press referred to Alexander and Thurston, but the revenue cutter *J.C. Dobbin* was first to intercept them. "As our [Portsmouth police] officers," commented the *Chronicle*, "were devoting their time and expending their money with little expectation of receiving remuneration from anybody, but acted simply from a desire to do their duty, they seem to be entitled, at least, to the thanks of the Department."[48]

At about 1:30 P.M. on August 20, some four miles northeast of Boon Island, off the coast of York, Maine, the game was up. As the *Dobbin* pulled alongside their boat, Alexander and Thurston said they were Eastport fishermen heading home after leaving Boston. The cutter's crew almost let the two men go when someone suggested a search of the two "fishermen." One man was discovered to have a large amount of Confederate money secreted around his waist. They were summarily returned to Fort Warren. Lieutenant Alexander and other Confederate naval officers, including Lieutenant Charles W. Read, were released in the fall of 1864 at City Point, Virginia, in a prisoner exchange for an equal number of Union officers.[49]

Quelling the Portsmouth Draft Riot

Ugly rumors, hijacked ships, speculation about "Copperheads" and their aims, Confederate prisoners at Fort Warren, the Enrollment Act of March 3, 1863—all led to an increasingly charged situation that finally exploded in Portsmouth. From July 14 to 16, 1863, the Portsmouth draft riot brought complete chaos to the city. Shots were fired. The clash pitted the "mob" against the Portsmouth police, the provost marshal's office, volunteers from Fort Constitution, and the United States marines from the Portsmouth Navy Yard. This incident was one of the most crucial events in New Hampshire during the Civil War.

The Portsmouth draft riot was not a locally isolated occurrence. Almost spontaneously, similar disturbances reverberated throughout the North. The well-publicized New York City riot resulted in the killing or wounding of more than a thousand people and property damage of $1.5 million. A riot in Boston left at least eight dead. Minor riots occurred in Rutland, Vermont, and Wooster, Ohio.[50]

For a few days, the Lincoln administration wrestled against potential anarchy. Chaotic conditions in the riot-torn areas completely halted local war efforts. The marines at the Portsmouth Navy Yard were diverted from their main purpose to quell a virtual civil war within Portsmouth's own ranks. Throughout the North, the riots were crushed, but at severe cost to home-front morale.

One man in particular, Joshua L. Foster, emerges as a major figure during these troubled times. Born in Canterbury, New Hampshire, in 1824, Foster worked as a farmer, carpenter, builder, and architect before turning to journalism. Beginning his editorial career with the *Dover Gazette* in 1858, Foster moved to Portsmouth three years later. On January 2, 1863, the day after Lincoln issued the Emancipation Proclamation, Foster published the first edition of *The States and Union*, a weekly Democratic newspaper. The offices and plant of Foster's paper were located on the second floor of a building at the corner of Penhallow and Daniel Streets in downtown Portsmouth. Outspoken, fearless, racist, and inflammatory, Foster projected a vehement pro-Southern, antiwar stance, railing against Lincoln, Republicans ("abolitionists"), and blacks ("niggers"). Hammering away against the administration in every editorial, Foster referred to "Ibrahim Linkum" as a dictator, residing in "Sodom" (Washington).[51]

There was great enmity between the various political and ethnic groups in Portsmouth, and indeed throughout New Hampshire. In early March 1863, President Lincoln signed the Enrollment or Conscription Act as a legal means of drafting able-bodied males. The act also provided for a method of avoiding service by hiring a substitute for $300. To many in New Hampshire, this loophole smacked of despotism, prompting the slogan, "Rich man's war, poor man's fight."[52]

To implement this legislation, the Provost Marshal's Bureau in Washington established an office in Portsmouth, under the direction of Captain John S. Godfrey. Provost Marshal Godfrey opened his office on May 11, 1863, a week after the disastrous defeat of the Union Army of the Potomac at the Battle of Chancellorsville in Virginia. "The whole district contains 82 towns," summarized the *Journal* in late 1865, "each of which was made a sub-district, and enrolling officers appointed thereof. These officers, twenty-four in number, were appointed on the 26th of May 1863, and the enrollment was completed on the 7th of July, 1863. The number of classes in the District reported as liable to military duty was about 14,500."[53]

During that three-month interval, tensions grew. Joseph A. Gilmore had become the new governor of New Hampshire in an election so close that the legislature had to make the final choice. Gilmore, a Republican railroad executive, lacked the necessary political experience to deal with such a complex and sensitive issue as implementation of the draft. Furthermore, should civil unrest break out, Gilmore, from the governor's office in Concord, would be ill-placed to restore order in distant places, especially Portsmouth, the state's hotbed of Copperheadism.[54]

In May, with the Battle of Chancellorsville raging, the schooner *Union Flag* arrived at the Yard with a load of lumber. The schooner's crew was suspected of Confederate sympathies, so during the discharge of cargo, the captain and crew were not allowed in the Yard. "Some one of the crew remarked," reported the *Chronicle*, "that he hoped [Robert E.] Lee would succeed in whipping Joe Hooker's army so completely that he [Hooker] never would rally.... The rest of the crew expressed similar sentiments, which warranted the officers of the Yard in prohibiting the traitors from polluting the soil of the Navy Yard. Accordingly, two watchmen are stationed on the wharf to execute the order." A few days later, the captain of the *Union Flag* went to the *Chronicle* offices to clear his name. "He asserts," stated the *Chronicle* on May 18, "that he is now and has always been a truly Union man; he has long been employed by the U.S. authorities, and never before have any imputations been cast upon him for lack of loyalty to the government, under whose flag he sails.... He admits that some one of the men did make some objectionable remarks; just what they were he is unable to state, as the remarks were made while he was away from his vessel."[55]

Nervousness about the Yard's security was understandable. As the Union continued to wrestle for control of the Mississippi Valley, the Yard served as a transshipment point in supplying powder for that theater of war. Such ammunition was undoubtedly destined for use in the campaign to capture Vicksburg, the key Confederate stronghold on the Mississippi. "Large quantities of gunpowder are being sent from the Portsmouth Navy Yard to Cairo [Illinois, a riverport]," reported the *Chronicle* on June 23, "the same freight cars going clear through by railroad. It is brought by packet to the new wharf, and loaded in battened box cars. Both vessels and [railroad] cars mount the warning red flag all the while. Several hundred tons are to have been sent within a few days."[56]

This vital shipment was made only weeks before the long-smoldering conditions in Portsmouth were about to erupt. The forthcoming draft—with the lottery scheduled to begin at 10 A.M. on Tuesday, July 14, 1863, at Provost Marshal Godfrey's office—generated tremendous local excitement.

Despite the Union victories at Gettysburg and Vicksburg in early July, the Union needed still more men. Reports were already reaching Portsmouth about the bloody New York City draft riots. The air was charged with tension as the draft day approached. On Saturday afternoon, July 11, the Portsmouth Board of Aldermen received and rejected a municipal referendum on the subject of the draft and banned public meetings. Defying the order, many Portsmouth citizens, mostly Democrats, met that evening at the South Church to adopt antiwar and antidraft resolutions. Among the speakers were Joshua L. Foster, secretary of the committee for the gathering, and Daniel Marcy.[57]

Within a day or so, anonymous handbills were posted all around the city, urging, "Citizens of Portsmouth, Awake! Awake!" and calling for a second meeting at the Temple on Monday evening, July 13, the day before the draft would go into effect. An overflow crowd attended the meeting, heard the same speakers as on July 11, and adopted the same resolutions. For his part, Secretary Joshua L. Foster wrote to Governor Gilmore from Portsmouth on July 14: "In pursuance of a vote of instructions, I herewithin transmit a copy of resolutions unanimously adopted at a very large meeting of the citizens of Portsmouth without distinction of party holders on the evening of the 13th inst. and would respectfully invite your attention to the same as expressions of the sentiments of what is believed to be the majority of our people at the present time, upon the subject matters to which they relate."[58]

Foster enclosed a handbill containing the resolutions, which called the draft unconstitutional and declared "That we are in favor of an immediate cessation of hostilities, by an armistice, and the assembling of a National Convention" to negotiate a peace.[59]

Another person who attended both meetings also contacted the governor on July 14, his messages probably unbeknownst to Foster. Charles Robinson, a Democrat and Portsmouth flour merchant, likewise delivered speeches at the meetings, but his attendance evidently served another purpose. Writing Governor Gilmore, Robinson confided: "The Copperheads in this city have held two meetings for the purpose of causing trouble & resisting the Draft.... judging from the spirit manifested of the remarks made at those meetings I should think it might be necessary to send to this city a regiment of men in the place thereof."[60]

Three days later, Robinson wrote Governor Gilmore a second and stronger letter regarding the situation in Portsmouth:

"Yours of yesterday [July 16, 1863] in reply to my letter of 14th & enquiring [sic] as to the meeting that passed the resolutions sent you by J.L. Foster came to hand this A.M. I attended that meeting—remarks were made by an Irish Lawyer named [J. Downing] Murphy & Daniel Marcy (both copperheads); I think the [second] meeting was designed to make trouble but the Leaders, such as [Joshua L.] Foster[, J.R.] Redding [Reding,] & others were foiled in the main[.]"[61]

Whereas, The attempt is to be made to enforce what is known as the Conscript Act, passed by the last Congress, and, by virtue of its provisions, compel still further sacrifices of the lives of our friends and fellow-citizens in the present war, therefore,

Resolved, That inasmuch as many distinguished jurists have pronounced the said Conscript Act unconstitutional, the citizen is entitled to the benefit of the doubt of its constitutionality, and that, therefore, it is the duty of the Governor of this State to take such measures as may be necessary, to prevent our citizens from being ruthlessly torn from their families and homes, until it has been passed upon by the Supreme Court, and we call upon the Governor to exercise this duty.

Resolved, That the right of petition is too sacred and dear to be infringed or disputed; and that it is the plain duty of our public servants, acting in whatsoever official capacity, to heed the voice of the people when it may be expressed by petition or otherwise in a legal and respectful manner; and that, therefore, we call upon our city Administration to take immediate and favorable action upon the petition presented to the Board of Mayor and Aldermen, on the 10th inst., requesting them to call a public meeting of the citizens of Portsmouth, for the purpose of a public expression in regard to the propriety of appropriating from the City Treasury, sufficient monies to pay the commutation fees of all those who may be drafted from our city. And we earnestly request that such meeting may be duly called, and that the action of our city authorities be influenced in this important matter, by the action of said meeting.

Resolved, That we are decidedly in favor of a sufficient appropriation from the City Treasury to pay the exemption fee of every man who may be drafted from the city of Portsmouth, and that we earnestly hope the City Council will immediately make the necessary appropriation.

Resolved—That in case the city authorities fail to comply with the reasonable requests of the foregoing resolutions, that we urge upon the people to voluntarily contribute sufficient sums of money to exempt all who may be conscripted from our city.

Resolved—That we have always exercised the right of discussing and criticising, without stint, public men and measures, and that it is a right which we will never permit to be questioned, and any attempt to thwart it, no matter upon what pretext, will be met on our part, by summary vindication.

Resolved—That we are in favor of an immediate cessation of hostilities, by an armistice, and the assembling of a National Convention to adjust all matters in controversy and restore the Union by compromise upon the basis of equal and exact justice to all the States and all the people.

NHDRMA

July 14—the anniversary of the storming of the Bastille during the French Revolution in 1789—arrived with the drafting officers at their headquarters in the Old Customs House. A marine company from the Yard was stationed inside the building. Just before 10 A.M., the guards opened the doors and local citizens filled the room. At precisely 10 o'clock, the requisition was read, evidently by Captain Godfrey, for 1,968 men from the First Congressional District. Then, anticlimactically and melodramatically, Godfrey or his assistant read a second order, postponing the draft until 2 P.M. the next day. Governor Gilmore was cooperating with orders from the War Department to change the rules. The crisis was apparently defused, at least until the following day.[62]

From this point on, the events, intentions, and interpretations surrounding the Portsmouth draft crisis become murky, embroiled in partisan controversy and newspaper rivalries. Rumors heightened tension. That Tuesday evening, according to the *Chronicle*, "a large crowd of the rowdies, stated as high as two hundred, went to Fort Constitution and attempted to enter the Fort, with the intention of capturing a light field battery there!" A sergeant in command ordered a charge and dispersed them, taking one prisoner. The

Journal branded the story a "CANARD," and "wholly without foundation." Joshua L. Foster's *States and Union* judged the story "a figment of its [the *Chronicle*'s] own disordered brain.... It is a story made up to add fuel to the flames of falsehood circulated by the Abolition leaders."[63]

The crisis appeared to be lessening by the afternoon of July 15. At the provost marshal's office at the appointed time, the announcement came that the draft would be postponed until Thursday afternoon. Posters appearing around town announced that the draft had been put off for an indefinite time, perhaps a week or longer. The marines and other military units continued their guard, inside and outside the building, and the subdued crowds kept their distance.

That evening, however, the situation turned ugly. Under cover of darkness, rocks began to fly. "An assault was made by the mob on the Provost's Marshal's Office," reported the *Journal*, "the windows broken, and a soldier struck on the head by a stone. Some shots were fired by the soldiers, and by the mob, but no one was much injured." The *Chronicle* concurred in its version that "one rowdy threw a stone, and struck a soldier in the head, and that the soldier fired a ball or two, but unfortunately missed the villain."[64]

The standoff continued on July 16, with most of the crowd gone by morning. That evening, however, brought an unexpected turn of events. As biased as the *Chronicle* may have been, its account appears reasonably accurate and complete, the most detailed of all the sources, in depicting a night of bloodshed:

> The following is as correct an account of the doings of the lawless crowd as we have been able to obtain in the excitement of the night. A large extra police force had been detailed, and, with the usual watchmen and the day police, instructed to prevent the congregation of any large crowd near the headquarters of the Provost Marshal, Thursday night, the City Authorities being determined that the outrages of the night previous should not be re-enacted. Several well-disposed citizens, whom curiosity had drawn thither, appreciated the wisdom of the regulation, when it was suggested to them, and quietly withdrew. The first opposition was made by an Irishman, and as he absolutely refused to move, he was placed in the lock-up. Soon another person, an American, was arrested, and as he was being taken off appealed to his "friends" for assis-

tance. A rush was made to rescue him, the police resisted, one or two of the mob were seized, and a pistol was wrested from the hands of Sampson L. Russell, who has been a prominent agitator and fomenter of discord during the past few days. The men who had been seized were taken to the police station and confined. This happened between 8 and 9 o'clock.

About half-past 9, a mob of about 100 men, headed by this Russell, Richard Walden, and others, came to the police station and demanded the pistol. They had come up from Water street and vicinity, and made this their first demand. Their characters were well known to the police, their real object well understood. Their demand was refused. Then they entered upon the foul work they had conspired to do, and made an assault upon the police. Walden selected one of the extra police, Mr. Geo. Fretson, and made a cowardly and brutal attack on him with a long, square iron bolt. Mr. Fretson, who had nobly done his duty during the evening, received a severe and painful wound in the right wrist and arm in warding off a blow aimed at his head. A few moments after, Walden gave the order to his fellow ruffians to "fire!" Report followed report in rapid succession, of pistols.

Meanwhile Marshal Bragdon had sent word to Mayor Dearborn, who was in attendance at a meeting of the Board of Aldermen, that his presence was needed. He was promptly on the spot. Energetic measures were at once taken; the active members of the Board, as well as the Mayor, were equal to the emergency; the garrison at Fort Constitution, and the Marines at the Navy Yard, were notified by signals that their assistance was required; a request was sent to Lieut. Welles, in command of the guard at the Provost Marshal's headquarters, for immediate aid. Everyone appealed to, promptly responded. Many prominent and influential citizens united in the good work.

The Mayor reached the spot just as the pistols were discharged. Several shots were fired by the mob and by the police. Russell's revolver did good execution in the right hands. The leaders of the mob had had a taste of cold lead. Their deluded followers faltered and fell back. Presently Sergt. Gray, with a small squad of soldiers from the headquarters of the P. Marshal, appeared; the faint gleam of their bayonets was seen in the dim light; they charged upon the mob, and it ran like sheep, taking their wounded with them. The mob was crushed. It was not long before a strong force of Marines, under command of Col. [Ward] Marston, arrived from the Navy Yard; and another of soldiers from the fort, under Lt. Wainwright.

The only officer injured was Mr. Fretson, as stated above. Officer [Frank] Johnson had a narrow escape, a pistol ball passing through his glazed cap, within an inch of his head—entering in front and passing out at the top. Of the rioters, Walden was wounded in the forehead, in the side, and in the wrist; his wounds are thought to be dangerous. Russell received a severe wound in the head, inflicted, apparently, with a watchman's hook. The following are also reported to be wounded:—Aug[ustus] Walden in the leg, Geo. Watkins in the throat, and an Irishman, name unknown, in the thigh.

The mob were seen no more during the night. All honor to the Police for their energetic action, and to the Military for their active co-operation.[65]

Charles Robinson concluded in his letter of July 17 to Governor Gilmore, "We have reason to thank God first of all & Mayor [Jonathan] Dearborn & the Police next that several of the leaders of the mob received their just reward for their doings last night. One of the leading ruffians [Richard Walden] probably rec[eive]d last evening his death wounds & the rest seem to be well alarmed. If not[,] the foot soldiers & marines with the mayor and police have strength enough to keep it all right[.]"[66]

The Portsmouth draft riot was over, the draft postponed. After three days of turmoil, the city returned to relative calm, and the law acted quickly to dispense justice. That same week, Sampson L. Russell, Richard Walden (according to one account), Walden's brother Augustus, and Richard Smart, charged with inciting a riot, were bound over, at $1,000 bail each, for appearance at the October Grand Jury of Rockingham County Court. (All eventually recovered from their wounds.) Their lawyers, Albert R. Hatch and John Frink, managed to prevent their clients from coming to trial. One suit, *George Fretson v. Richard Walden*, was ultimately resolved at the Exeter court in April 1865. The charge that Walden assaulted police officer Fretson resulted in a decision substantially favorable to Walden, with the verdict calling for $2.50 in damages and $2.50 court costs for settlement. Thus, the legal aftermath of the Portsmouth draft riot was

Local.

CITY OF PORTSMOUTH.

MAYOR'S OFFICE, July 21, 1863.

The Mayor congratulates the inhabitants of the City, upon the suppression of the riotous demonstrations of last week. This was due not only to the determination and untiring activity of the Marshal and his Assistants, but to the active co-operation of many citizens, who assisted and encouraged him in the performance of his duty, and to whom he returns his heartiest thanks. He was also greatly indebted to Col Marston of the U. S. Marines and the officers and men under him, and to the officers and men of the company at Fort Constitution, for the promptness with which they answered his calls, by day and by night, and for their very efficient services in protecting the government property here, and in preserving the peace of the city. These all deserve and should receive the warmest thanks of every loyal citizen.

By order of the Mayor.

MARCELLUS BUFFORD, City Clerk.

PC, July 23, 1863

settled.[67]

Local newspapers filled their columns with partisan editorials for days after the riot. The *Chronicle* blamed the "secesh sympathizers" and the "mob spirit" for the violence. Expressing relief that the Copperhead leaders were not then holding local city offices, the *Journal* commented, "It is easy to perceive that, on a smaller scale, the bloody and desolating scenes of Boston and New York would have here been re-enacted." *The States and Union* faulted the Republican city fathers: "In our judgment, the blame of the violence and bloodshed, lies at the doors of those whose especial duty was to have preserved the peace."[68]

Beyond the editorials, what is the historical significance of the Portsmouth draft riot of 1863? It failed to halt for any appreciable time what had already been scheduled; the draft was firmly in place

Joshua Lane Foster, the "Copperhead" editor of Portsmouth's States and Union, *was a controversial figure during the Civil War years. Vehemently anti-Lincoln, antiwar, and racist in his journalistic posture, he repeatedly attacked and ridiculed the Navy Yard in his news coverage and editorials.* Granite Monthly *(April 1900). PA.*

throughout New Hampshire by mid-August 1863.[69]

The Portsmouth riot bore limited resemblance, by comparison, with its more violent counterparts in New York and Boston. In those large cities, twentieth-century historians point to class warfare, ethnic clashes, and prejudicial attacks on black Americans as the primary causes in fomenting the upheavals. By contrast, the Portsmouth riot was more a spontaneous outburst by antiwar protesters and the Democratic Copperhead members against the Union provost marshal's office and the Republican-dominated city leadership. The Navy Yard marines, as an arm of the state, bolstered and upheld the government in power.[70]

The role of Joshua L. Foster and his *States and Union* in instigating the riot remains unclear and nebulous. While Foster clearly regretted the emergence of what he called "mobocracy" in New York City, he felt that the "abolitionist" Lincoln administration had fueled in Portsmouth a combustible situation that inevitably would burst into violence. Defending the arrested men, Foster insisted, "Their only crime is that of being Democrats."[71]

Indeed, the four detainees—all Portsmouth natives, Democrats, and gainfully employed family men—were hardly revolutionary zealots. All four lived and worked either on or near Water (now Marcy) Street in the section of the city known as the South End. Located within the boundaries of Ward 3—often referred to as the "Copperhead Ward" during the war—Water Street was a commercial zone along the riverfront, directly across the Piscataqua from the Navy Yard. Rife with warehouses, saloons, and houses of prostitution, Water Street, in the heart of a poor and transient neighborhood, was plagued with a high crime rate.[72]

Sampson L. Russell, the acknowledged leader of the antidraft protesters, was a thirty-eight-year-old grocer whose store was on Water Street. Described as "one of the most uncompromising Democrats in Ward 3," Russell was "a man who spoke his sentiments freely on all occasions."[73]

Russell's henchman, Richard Walden, also owned and operated a grocery on Water Street. Forty-seven years old at the time of the riot, Walden was serving as moderator of his ward. During the Pierce and Buchanan administrations, he was a foreman caulker at the Navy Yard. (George Fretson, the auxiliary Portsmouth policeman whom Walden struck during the fracas, had also been a caulker at the Yard.)[74]

Augustus Walden, Richard's younger brother, was yet another Water Street grocer. Thirty-three years old in 1863, he was living in the same Pleasant Street boardinghouse as George Fretson.[75]

Richard D. Smart, the fourth person apprehended, was a thirty-five-year-old moulder, grandson of well-known Portsmouth privateer Richard Smart.[76]

It is difficult, in hindsight, to assign to the roles of these four men, given their individual histories, anything more suggestive than the basic charge of "inciting a riot." The fact that the accused men were never brought to trial suggests that the Rockingham County officials were reluctant to prosecute the case. Rather than exacerbate existing tensions, these officials apparently treated the incident as a purely local circumstance to avoid bringing federal charges of treason and sedition.

For the Portsmouth Navy Yard, the impact of the riot was minimal. The Yard lost the services of its marines for several days when the uprising had completely eclipsed the marines' primary responsibility of safeguarding the Yard. Also, the three days of confusion undoubtedly hampered delivery of supplies and travel back and forth across the river for the Yard's work force. This, of course, cost the government time and money.

The Portsmouth riot, albeit regional, was part of a national crisis for the Lincoln administration, and for a brief period, the Northern draft riots sparked an internal civil war within the Union itself.

The wound created by the Portsmouth riot left a legacy of suspicion and distrust, both at the Yard and within Portsmouth, that festered until the end of the war. In time, even Joshua L. Foster himself would experience the poisonous effects of the raw sore that refused to heal.

A Ring of Portsmouth Harbor Forts

During 1863, a mixture of apprehension, fear, and suspicion had renewed efforts toward securing defenses in and around the harbor. Civilian and naval officers were eager to expand and strengthen Forts Constitution and McClary, as well as to build a new one Fort Sullivan, on Seavey's Island. Except for an unfortunate accident during the summer, these forts achieved their purpose. The well-garrisoned forts and Navy Yard batteries "give our harbor a Gibraltar strength," asserted the *Chronicle* on July 4, and gone was the time "when a soldier who staid out beyond his time, was seen to scale the walls at midnight by climbing over cement barrels, into the Fort [Constitution], when no meddlesome sentry was awake to ask his business!"[77]

Determination to ensure an adequate defense had originated from both Washington and Concord. On March 27, 1863, writing to New Hampshire Governor Nathaniel Berry, Secretary of War Edwin M. Stanton asserted, "You are authorized to recruit, for the term of three years, or during the war, a company of heavy Artillery, to be stationed in Fort Constitution."[78]

On Thursday, April 29, Governor-elect Joseph Gilmore and a large entourage visited both the Yard and Fort Constitution. At the time of the visit, the fort was being doubled in size, with the battlements on the south side extending halfway to Fort Point lighthouse. A hundred men were employed full-time. Three weeks later, Fort Constitution was awhirl with activity as iron rails were being laid to transport the stone, cranes, derricks, and new wharving. Despite the cost, the *Chronicle* considered the work imperative, "an important object for the whole seaboard, considering the possibility of foreign war [with Great Britain]."[79]

By July, in addition to heavy armament at Fort Constitution, the federal government provided "some rifle cannon, which will do execution to any invaders which come within five miles circuit." Still

State of New-Hampshire,

EXECUTIVE DEPARTMENT,

Concord. July 18th 1863.

Hon. E. M. Stanton
    Secretary of War,
        Washington DC.

    Sir

    The Fortifications at Portsmouth need for their defence more than one Company of Artillery. Captain Longs Company of Heavy Artillery is now organized and another can be raised within a week by voluntary enlistment. Please grant the necessary authority. They will be of great use for other purposes.

                signed J. A. Gilmore
                        Governor of N.H.

                                                NHDRMA

Gilmore was not satisfied. On July 18, just after the draft riots, he appealed to Secretary of War Stanton for more help, which was quickly authorized.[80]

By late summer of 1863, Fort Constitution had evolved into a small village, even with its own newspaper, the *New Castle Observer*, published by the soldiers. A work force of 160 men—masons, stonecutters, blacksmiths, carpenters, and so forth—was employed on the new fortifications, and a commodious stone shed was completed. The first tier of guns, it was estimated by the *Chronicle* on September 14, "will be mounted. ... next year, and the Fort, when finished, will mount 150 guns." Given this preponderance of ordnance, it probably would have been suicidal for Raphael Semmes and his *Alabama* to pass under the guns of Fort Constitution in any attempt to shell the Navy Yard.[81]

To ensure that the *Alabama* would be intercepted, even if the Confederate raider were to slip by Forts Constitution and McClary, the Navy Department decided that a third fort upriver would maximize protection of the Yard. This meant building Fort Sullivan on Seavey's Island, which would give gunners a commanding position up, down, and across the river. (This strategic site, now occupied by the former naval prison, overlooks the narrows at Pull-and-Be-Damned Point, also known as Henderson's Point.)

"The old earthworks on Jenkins [Seavey's] Island are being renewed," reported the *Chronicle* on April 30, 1863, "and heavy cannon are to be mounted there. During the past week the Engineers at the Portsmouth Navy Yard have been busily at work erecting batteries on the island, and a large gang of men, with teams, have been employed. They expect soon to have in position several large guns that will throw shot far enough, probably, for all practical purposes."[82]

Commandant George Pearson actively oversaw the construction of the new fort. On May 21, Pearson reported to Welles the rapid progress in rushing this important work to completion, mounting "eleven eight-inch guns—one of them on a pivot carriage," building a barracks for the gunners, and digging out an old well to ensure an adequate water supply for the fort. In mid-June, Pearson was notified that Welles was sending "one-hundred contrabands" to man the defenses of Fort Sullivan.[83]

On July 12, the USS *Bermuda* arrived at the Yard with about one hundred prisoners of war and as many contrabands from Fortress Monroe, Virginia. (Two of the prisoners were Portsmouth natives: Captain Joseph Leach, captured aboard his Confederate blockade run-

War Department
Washington City,
July 24th   1863

Governor,

In reply to a resolution of the Legislature of New Hampshire, calling for two heavy rifled cannon with Equipments and ammunition, to be used in the defence of Portsmouth Harbor, I have the honor to state, that the application was referred to the Chief of Ordnance, who reports thereon as follows:

"Two 100 pounder rifled cannon can now be furnished without injury to the service in the field, for the purpose herein stated. The Chief Engineer, General Totten, with whom I have consulted is of the opinion that any large guns, which can be furnished for the defence of Portsmouth Harbor, should be mounted for that purpose at Fort Constitution as part of the regular armament of that fort"

This report has been approved, and instructions given to the Ordnance Bureau to furnish and mount the guns.

Very respectfully
Your Obedient Servant.
Edwin M Stanton
Secretary of War.

His Excellency J. A. Gilmore,
Governor of New Hampshire.
Concord.

NHDRMA

ner *Planter*, along with his clerk, Frank Scott. Leach was the nephew of Representative Daniel Marcy.) "The arrival of these contrabands," commented the *Chronicle* on July 13, "has occasioned no little disqui-

Navy Department,
Washington, Nov 28th 1863

Sir,

Your letter of the 24th inst. has been received, and permission is given you to rate Robert Braiton (colored) as Cook to the Contrabands on Seavy's Island.

Very respectfully,

Gideon Welles,
Secretary of the Navy

Commodore G.F. Pearson
Commandant Navy Yard
Portsmouth
N.H.

NA-NER

etude among the Irish laborers, who think the blacks are to be brought north to take their places. As these blacks are to be trained for soldiers, and in this way to discharge a duty from which the Irish are very willing to be relieved, they should have been received with better feeling."[84]

The Union navy needed manpower, any able-bodied individuals to fill the ranks. The *Chronicle* noted the example of the U.S. revenue cutter *Agassiz*, commanded by Lieutenant Joseph Amazeen of Portsmouth, which arrived at New Bedford, Massachusetts, from New Bern, North Carolina, on July 27 for duty at that station. "She [the *Agassiz*] has a crew of contrabands," reported the *Chronicle*, "white seamen being scarce at Newbern."[85]

Assigned to serve under white officers, the contrabands were trained at Fort Sullivan. Eager to learn to read, they quickly acquired proficiency under the tutelage of some Portsmouth women who went to the fort several times a week. Unfortunately, an incident marred this effort. "A few days since," reported the *Chronicle* on August 18, "while these ladies were engaged in their benevolence work, a boatload of dirty blackguards ... in going down river, stopped to revile and insult the freedman, in the vilest language, regardless of the presence of ladies. At last, a white officer ordered a platoon to load their guns, and told the boat's crew to come on shore or he would fire on them. They thought best to land—and the officer kept them on the island, under guard, all day!"[86]

An Accident and a Runaway Schooner

Given the local draft riot, controversy over the contrabands, and the accelerated work schedule at the Yard during the summer of 1863, Commandant George F. Pearson sought relief from the rigors of his position. In late August, a series of unfortunate events placed onerous demands on Pearson and further tested his mettle. Pearson, in fact, had hoped to leave the Yard. He wrote Secretary Welles on August 27 requesting a transfer to become superintendent at the Naval Academy in Newport, Rhode Island.[87]

Before this letter reached Welles's desk, a serious accident on Friday, August 28, marked perhaps the most severe crisis during Pearson's tenure as Yard commandant. A shot fired from Seavey's Island during target practice hit a boat near Pest Island in Portsmouth Harbor, killing one civilian and wounding four others. Contrabands had fired the gun under the orders from Acting Master William Smith. The incident provoked much comment in the Portsmouth press, both defending and blaming the contrabands, as well as a flurry of reports within the navy itself.[88]

The victim was William J. Trefethen, a twelve-year-old from New Castle. An inquest was held by the selectmen of New Castle, with the verdict that "the boy was killed by a ball fired from the battery on Seavey's Island, by some person to the jury unknown." Printing an explanatory letter about the accident from Acting Master Smith, the *Chronicle* took a middle course in the controversy. Regretting the accident, the *Chronicle* stated "that the boat could not be seen by the gunners; and that the shot took an unexpected and unus[u]al course, passing far beyond where it was expected it would strike. It is also stated that the contrabands did not fire the gun." The *Journal* remained cautious: "We can hardly understand how any body by twenty minutes notice can put himself in a place of safety unless some person is stationed on the ground to tell them which way to flee from random shots."[89]

Joshua L. Foster's *States and Union*, however, seized upon the incident, attacking the contrabands in the most racist terms:

"NIGGER EXPLOITS UPON THE PISCATAQUA," read Foster's headline of September 4. The long article continued in the same vein:

> We had a very striking illustration of the beauties of this present administration through its negro pets, in sight of our city.... There is, as the public are aware, a colony of stolen niggers quartered, with daily rations from Uncle Sam, upon Seavey's Island.
>
> Under special orders from Washington, they have been provided with white officers in uniform, and are being by them instructed in the manly and appropriate business of cannonading up and down and across our river, at random, hitting with their shot anything and everything, or nothing, as the case may be.
>
> We protested against the advent of these creatures here at the time they were imported....
>
> We suppose these niggers and their white officers in whose charge they are and who are in reality responsible for their acts, will be allowed to remain on the island, and indulge in their wonted amusement of shooting over the river, allowing the shots to take an "unexpected and unusual course." This is the nigger millenium, and white folks have no rights which blacks are bound to respect.[90]

The contrabands remained on duty at the battery, but as a result of more stringent safety procedures, there was no further shooting mishap for the rest of the war. Pearson, however, had little time to reflect on the Seavey's Island incident. Two days later, on August 30, another crisis arose. The schooner *Medford*, bound with a load of lumber from Bangor, Maine, to Salem, Massachusetts, put into

Portsmouth's Lower Harbor. In the absence of the captain, who apparently was in town on business, the *Medford* began to spread her sails: The mate had hijacked the vessel. Rushing to the Navy Yard, the master of the *Medford* appealed for help to pursue his runaway vessel, presumably headed south.[91]

Speculation arose that the *Medford* had been bound for the Yard to deliver the lumber when a dispute erupted between the captain and the mate. The latter was said to have learned that he had been drafted. Fortunately for Pearson, he had a fast vessel in the Yard to pursue the *Medford*. The day before the *Medford* hijacking, the USS *Marion*, a school-ship of the United States Naval Academy, and her tender, the USS *America*, the famous racing yacht, had arrived at the Yard. Recounting the circumstances, Pearson on August 31 informed Welles, "Lieutenant Kane went in command of the *America*, with orders to remain out two days if necessary. She left at about 4 p.m. yesterday, and the master of the schooner [*Medford*] went in her."[92]

The effort was futile. On September 2, the *America* returned empty-handed to the Yard, having lost her main topmast. Pearson by this time already had other concerns. That day, Assistant Secretary of the Navy Gustavus V. Fox had alerted him to the impending arrival of an important visitor. "I have the honor to acknowledge ... that the Honorable Secretary of the Navy expects to be at the Rockingham House [Portsmouth's leading hotel] this evening," and will "visit this Navy Yard tomorrow, the 3d instant."[93]

On Thursday, September 3, Secretary of the Navy Gideon Welles toured the Yard in his first and only visit during the Civil War. He and his party of five, including his son, Edgar, arrived in Portsmouth by the noon train from Boston. According to the *Chronicle*, Welles's party "repaired immediately to the Navy Yard, where they were received with ceremony, the officers of the Yard and the U.S. vessels there, being in full uniform: a salute of 17 guns was fired. The vessels, afloat and on the stocks, as well as the other points of interest to the head of the Department, were visited, and their condition afforded him much gratification. He returned to Boston in the evening."[94]

Secretary Welles must have met with Commandant Pearson in private during his inspection tour and convinced Pearson to remain for the time being at the helm of the Yard. Three days after Welles's visit, the USS *Marion* and the USS *America* left the Yard for Newport, Rhode Island, and the Naval Academy. Commandant Pearson was not on board either vessel.[95]

Launchings and Ship Construction

Occasional crises aside, the work of the Portsmouth Navy Yard in building and repairing ships continued unabated. Launchings of the new ships were occasions for considerable festivity.

On March 19, 1863, gentlemen, ladies, and many officials attended the launching of the war steamer *Pawtuxet*, a side-wheeler. Miss Anna M. Vanderbilt of Philadelphia christened the vessel with a bottle of combined wine and sea water. "The launching of war vessels is particularly interesting," commented the *Journal* on March 28, "for such are to vindicate both at home and abroad our national honor.... The company, after the launch, retired to a hall in the Yard where they enjoyed themselves in a social dance, for a few hours. There was a liberal display of female beauty on this occasion, and Portsmouth can boast of as much as any city in the State."[96]

Like almost all the other ships built and commissioned at the Yard during the war—notably the *Ossipee, Kearsarge, Sebago, Mahaska, Conemaugh, Sassacus, Nipsic, Shawmut,* and *Agamenticus*—the new vessel received an Indian name. The American predilection for Indian names was both longstanding and controversial.

The New York *Journal of Commerce* in 1863 noted this continuing practice:

> Some of the Indian names selected by the christening bureau of the Navy Department for the new war vessels, are very harmonious and pretty; some are very rough and unpronounceable; all are unquestionably original, not to say aboriginal. No nation on earth has a larger and richer mine of antique nomenclature to draw upon in the naming of vessels. But there is too much of a good thing—even of Indian—sometimes. Our Naval force has now reached such a number that all the better class of Indian names seems to have been called into play, and only cacophonous ones are left. The *Umpqua, Junxes, Squando,* and *Wambanogue*—specimens taken at random from the latest batch determined upon—are harsh, hard to pronounce, and hard to remember. No human being, but a native Indian, with an extensive knowledge of the dialects of all the extinct tribes, could recollect the names of all the vessels christened within

the past two years.[97]

The custom, nevertheless, continued. On Monday, June 15, two screw gunboats, the *Nipsic* and the *Shawmut*, hit the water, marking the first and only double launching at the Yard during the Civil War. With two christenings, the celebration was elaborate. The Portsmouth Brass Band played, many notables attended, and "Portsmouth contributed lavishly from its wreath of female beauty."[98]

Successfully testing her Hartford-built Woodruff & Beach engines in August, the recently launched *Nipsic* made eleven knots during her sea trials. On Saturday, September 13, the vessel was undergoing final tests preparatory to leaving the Yard for blockade duty. At 11:40 P.M., after performing admirably for more than sixty hours, her machinery abruptly stopped. All the flanges of her propeller had broken, and workmen retrieved bits of iron from the river bottom. On September 15, Pearson wrote to Welles, "I have had the broken blades examined by a competent judge, & he decides without hesitation that the casting was defective.[99]

Such negligence resulted in work delays and much expense. "The steamer *Shawmut*, at the Navy Yard," reported the *Chronicle* on September 25, "is to be taken out of the dock ... to give place to the *Nipsic*, which is to be docked to receive her new propeller. All of her stores, guns, and ordnance have been, or are being taken out, which, together with the delay occasioned by the breakage of her propeller, renders the accident very unfortunate." Finally, on October 15, more than a month after her originally scheduled departure, the ill-fated *Nipsic* left the Yard at 8 A.M. for the Lower Harbor.[100]

Work on the ironclad *Agamenticus* continued throughout 1863, and at times it seemed to be afflicted by the same jinx associated with the *Nipsic*. On August 31, at the Atlantic Iron Works, East Boston, fire destroyed the building in which the turrets for the *Agamenticus* were under construction. The turrets, insured for $2,500 each, apparently suffered little damage. The iron plating for the *Agamenticus* was also slow to arrive, delaying installation, but after the material arrived in mid-October, work on the ship progressed rapidly, "with five layers of wrought iron plating, each plate being a small fraction more than an inch thick," in the *Chronicle*'s description. A new technique for securing the plates made the *Agamenticus* "a formidable ally against the rebels or any other foe." The plating was declared "capable of resisting almost anything in the shape of iron. It was formerly customary, in bolting the iron on the vessels, to drive the bolts through the sides of the ship, and secure them by nuts on the inside. Upon trial, this was found to be an error, the bolts breaking and flying in all directions, rendering the position inside of the vessel nearly as unsafe as exposure to the shot outside.... Now, blunt bolts are used, driven about half or two thirds of the way through."[101]

By December, the huge boilers for the *Agamenticus* had arrived at the Yard, and workmen undertook the task of shifting them to the vessel. "Four of these immense boilers, weighing about forty-five tons each," noted the *Chronicle* on December 21, "are being moved across the Yard on a track laid for the purpose, and in a day or two they will be on the deck of the ship, and lowered into position by means of temporary shears [a hoisting apparatus], erected for this purpose."[102]

The *Agamenticus* looked ahead to the United States Navy of the future, but for its day-to-day operations, the navy still had to rely partly on longtime workhorses from the fleet. In its effort to put every available ship into service, the Union also commissioned a warship from the past, the *Alabama*, which had been rotting on the stocks at the Yard for many years. (This Portsmouth-built warship was not the Confederate raider commanded by Raphael Semmes.) In 1819, when Alabama joined the Union, the keel of this *Alabama* was laid at the Yard. Forty-four years later, she was still there. The impetus to complete the *Alabama* apparently was prompted by Secretary Welles's September 3 tour of the Yard. On his tour, Welles, according to the *Chronicle*, "visited the *Franklin* [on the stocks since 1854] and was of course astonished that such a ship was there, and regretted that she was not launched at the time." Welles must have entertained similar thoughts about the *Alabama*, for on September 21, orders were received from Washington to finish and launch this old ship of the line. "The *Alabama*," commented the *Chronicle* the next day, "compared with the beautifully modeled vessels built now-a-days, is a perfect wash-tub in her proportions, but, nevertheless, will make a good vessel for the purpose for which she was designed, viz., a storeship." Since all her original masts, spars, sails, boats, and other gear had been stripped off for use on other ships, the fitting-out of the *Alabama* would be entirely new.[103]

"The sound of the axe and hammer," reported the *Chronicle* on October 17, "is heard hacking and thumping away on the sides of the old frigate *Alabama*, at the Portsmouth Navy Yard.... Almost one hundred caulkers and reamers are employed on her, besides two hundred

Quarters "A" has been the official residence of the Portsmouth Navy Yard commandants and shipyard commanders since the War of 1812 (when the building was erected for Commodore Isaac Hull). During the Civil War, the home was the site of many post-launch receptions and related functions. Admiral David Farragut died while a guest in Quarters "A" during the summer of 1870. PNSVC

and eighty carpenters, eighty borers and bolters, sixty joiners, forty or fifty laborers, together with smiths, machinists, coopers, mast makers, &c., who make up a large force engaged in finishing this vessel."[104]

Needless to say, the original name of the ship was unacceptable to the Union government, so, on October 30, the Navy Department renamed her the *New Hampshire*. The news created a temporary stir. "An excitement was got up at the Navy Yard a few days since," noted the *Chronicle* on November 13, "when it was reported among the workmen that orders had been received from Washington to stop work on the *Alabama*. The commotion subsided toward night when the joke leaked out, and it was understood that the name of the vessel had been changed to *New Hampshire*." In his annual report, even Welles entertained no illusions about the two sailing sister ships *New*

Hampshire and Boston Navy Yard-built *Vermont*, judging them obsolete as war vessels but satisfactory for service as storeships and for overall defense.[105]

The Yard conducted work as usual even on Christmas, according to the *Chronicle*'s December 25 edition. "Business is not suspended today on the account of a pressure of work caused by the arrival of the *Agawam* [a side-wheel gunboat at the Yard since December 22], *Alabama* [now *New Hampshire*], *Dacotah*, the machinery of the *Agamenticus*, &c., all of which vessels are wanted as soon as it is possible to fit them out."[106]

Safeguarding Government Property

The frenzied activity at the Yard during the wartime construction era created a transient atmosphere conducive to crime. Workmen and naval personnel were always arriving and leaving, and vessels were constantly docking, discharging cargoes, and getting underway. Such a hectic routine fostered conditions favorable for theft of government property and desertion. Commandant Pearson did his best to restrain illegal activities, and vigilance at the Yard caught culprits and prevented loss.

On January 17, 1863, United States Deputy Marshal Adams, alerted by telegraph, came to the Yard to arrest George Donahoe, a three-time deserter from both the army and the navy. After his third desertion, Donahoe had come to Portsmouth and found work at the Yard. "He had been here about a month," reported the *Chronicle* on January 20, "and, in an unlucky moment to him, wrote a letter to a friend in New York State, giving an account of his operations, and stating his present occupation, and even the gang in which he was at work. This letter was the means of his arrest."[107]

A rash of similar incidents followed. On January 20, two seamen, John F. Smith and William Jones, signed up in Boston for duty aboard the USS *Sacramento* at the Portsmouth Navy Yard. After their arrival at the Yard, the pair slipped away and took the train to Portland. "The telegraph, however, was quicker than the locomotive," observed the *Chronicle*, "and when they reached the depot in Portland, they found two gentlemen [the police] in waiting, very anxious to meet them." The deserters, put in irons and accompanied by an officer, were returned to Portsmouth that same afternoon. One day later, Daniel Kelly and Patrick Murphy, two other seamen from the

USS *Sacramento*, were arrested on board ship. They had deserted from a Rhode Island cavalry unit.[108]

Theft of government property at the Navy Yard was an especially serious problem. During May 1863, Pearson had to contend with two major incidents. For some time, copper bolts, iron, and other articles had been reported missing. Finally, Yard authorities became suspicious and organized a watch to catch the offender. They soon caught seaman Timothy F. Allen stealing copper bolts. Pearson had Allen placed in confinement and reported the matter to Secretary of the Navy Welles. After imprisonment at the Yard's Marine Barracks, Allen was sent to Philadelphia Navy Yard for trial at a general court martial, then in session.[109]

On May 16, another case of blatant stealing occurred. "One of the crew of the schooner *Boston*, laying at the Navy Yard," reported the *Chronicle*, "was caught in the act of purloining a coil of rope—about 15 fathoms—having cut it in the middle to secure one end in order to haul it on board. Watchmen were stationed to prevent the crew from coming ashore, and they will not again be allowed the privileges of the Yard."[110]

Becoming "A First-Class Yard"

Throughout 1863, Chief Engineer Benjamin F. Chandler continued his vast construction program, methodically transforming the Yard into a leading naval facility. Without new and improved facilities, it would have been impossible to build and repair as many vessels quickly and efficiently. Although none of the twenty-five vessels built at the Yard during the war years is afloat or preserved today (the *Constellation* is the sole exception among the numerous repaired ships), many of Chandler's construction projects are still intact. By converting the Yard to stone and brick construction, Chandler's legacy endures in numerous shops, reservoirs, a quay, and overall improvements.

By late October, a machine shop and foundry, a smithy, a boathouse and carpenter shop, and a paint shop were completed or nearing completion. Of critical importance was the futtock saw mill, for preparing crooked and beveled timber. Previously, futtocks—curved timbers that form the lower part of a ship's ribs—had been worked out with an axe, so the new futtock saw mill greatly speeded up the process. "The construction of the above buildings," observed the *Chronicle* on October 31, "go far towards making

Wanted,

Ten or twelve first class SHIP SMITHS, for work at the Navy Yard, immediately. Pay from $2.25 to $2.50 per day. Apply to
blw   EPHRAIM OTIS,
w3t ju29   at the Smithery on the Yard.

PC, July 29, 1863

this, what it ought to be, a first-class Yard."[111]

Welles's "Report of the Secretary of the Navy," dated December 7, 1863, described in detail the many Yard construction projects. The cost of materials and labor had come to more than $103,000. Welles gave Chandler and various private and public contractors full credit: "The work on these objects has been prosecuted with vigor, and the progress made is quite satisfactory."[112]

To maintain its recently achieved first-class status, the Yard needed a congressional appropriation for 1864. In mid-December 1863, Secretary Welles submitted his estimates:

Pay of naval officers	$21,170
Pay of seamen	3,024
Pay of civil officers	13,850
Plumbers', coppersmiths' and tin shop	36,858
Quay walls	22,585
Mooring piers	12,330
Iron store	7,668
Extension of ship house	6,549
Machinery and tools	28,465
Repairs on floating dock	4,060
Repairs of all kinds	27,000
Barracks and guard house, Seavey's Island	6,500
Improving Marine Barracks	22,000
Contingent expenses	150,000

Welles's estimates came to $362,059, more than three times the 1862 budget. An additional estimate for defenses included $100,000 for Fort Constitution and the same amount for Fort McClary, bringing the total to a then-staggering sum of well more than half a million dollars.[113]

Confederate Forays at Sea

While the Portsmouth Navy Yard maintained its steady and often frenetic pace of shipbuilding and shop construction, the war at sea continued. Confederate raiders, led by the CSS *Alabama* under Raphael
Semmes, conducted extensive forays, capturing more Portsmouth
prizes. The USS *Kearsarge*, one of the *Alabama*'s chief foes, chased
her around the Atlantic in vain.

The capture and burning of the Portsmouth clipper *Express* by
the *Alabama* in the South Atlantic presented a sticky and unusual
case. Built at a private Piscataqua yard in 1854, the *Express* was
owned by the Marcy brothers and their usual associates. Loaded with
guano from the Chincha Islands, Peru, and commanded by Captain
William Frost of Portsmouth, the *Express* was bound for Antwerp,
Belgium. In waters south of Rio de Janeiro on July 6, 1863, Semmes
seized the *Express*. Immediately, a controversy arose over whether the
Express was protected by Northern registry, Southern registry, or
both. Captain Frost sought to protect his vessel for her owners, claim-
ing that he was carrying a neutral cargo with a certificate from the
French consul on the back of the bill of lading. Captain Semmes was
unconvinced. After seeing the ship's papers, Semmes said to Frost,
"Damn you. I'll burn your ship. You are a traitor, and if it was not for
your wife on board I would shoot you."[114]

After transferring the *Express*'s crew and passengers to the
Alabama, Semmes torched his prize. Despite the burning of the
Express, rumors circulated for months afterward that "Capt. William
Frost exhibited Rebel papers, the *Express* being owned in part by
Peter Marcy of New Orleans." Writing to his father in Portsmouth
from the bark *Herbert* at Boca del Rio, Mexico, on March 8, 1864,
Captain Frost denied the rumor: "Neither Capt. [Daniel] Marcy nor
any one else ever put on board the *Express* anything but papers from
the Customs House in Boston. There was never a confederate register,
flag, or any paper connected with the confederates on board the
Express, and whoever says so, lies."[115]

What seems to be a truthful resolution of these claims and
counterclaims appears in a deposition from John H. Perkins, third
officer of the *Express*, before a notary public in Capetown, South
Africa. The deposition was taken on August 20, 1863, and published
in the *Journal* on April 23, 1864. Under oath with witnesses, Officer

Perkins gave his lengthy account of the *Express*'s encounter with Her Majesty's gunboat *Petrel*, which turned out to be the *Alabama*: "After getting on board the *Alabama*, deponent [John H. Perkins] had a conversation with Mr. Smith, belonging to the *Alabama*, and private Clerk to Captain Semmes;—that said Smith informed him that he had two Registers of the *Express*, the Southern Protection signed by Jefferson Davis, and the Northern Register."[116]

Whatever papers the *Express* possessed, they failed to save her, making it immaterial that Peter Marcy of New Orleans was part-owner of the ship. The only consolation for the Marcys was the $40,000 worth of insurance held on her by several Boston offices.[117]

When Semmes and other Southern raider captains did not burn their prizes, they exercised one of two options. In some instances, Semmes reassigned federal prizes for service in the Confederate navy. After capturing the American bark *Conrad* on June 20, 1863, he armed and reprovisioned and commissioned it as the CSS *Tuscaloosa*, tender to the *Alabama*.[118]

Occasionally they resorted to the practice of bonding captured Northern vessels. Under this arrangement, the captive Union shipmaster provided a bond payable to the Confederate treasury after the end of the war. (Since the North won the conflict, these bonds were never honored.) The reason for this gesture of clemency was very practical. Often the Confederate captains, whose vessels were already overcrowded with prisoners accumulated from destroyed vessels, sought to avoid taking on additional passengers. The option of bonding a vessel allowed the Confederate captains to unload all Northerners.[119]

One advantage of the second Confederate option was to avoid any possible international repercussions involving a captured vessel with a neutral cargo. The Portsmouth-built ship *Santee* was a case in point. Built in 1860, the *Santee* was underway from Akyab (now Sittwe), Burma, with a cargo of rice owned by a London firm. En route to Falmouth, England, the *Santee* reached South Atlantic waters off the coast of Africa, where she encountered the CSS *Tuscaloosa*, which promptly seized her. After discovering that the *Santee* carried a neutral cargo, *Tuscaloosa* Captain John Low bonded the Portsmouth ship for $150,000 and released her.[120]

Numerous burnings, seizures, and bondings of Northern merchant ships prompted New England owners to seek financial restitution, primarily from Great Britain. As early as the summer of 1863, in

Matrimonial.

A young Naval Officer, of good family and some pretensions to good looks, desires to correspond with some YOUNG LADY with a view to MATRIMONY. She must be young, good looking, sociable, and have all the requisites for making home comfortable. Cartes de visite exchanged if desired. Address—O. P. Q., Post Office, Portsmouth, N. H.

PC, Dec. 17, 1863

anticipation of the protracted negotiations between the United States and Great Britain over this issue at the end of the Civil War, the Boston owners of the ship *Nora* sought redress. On August 12, *Chronicle* readers learned:

> Hon. Geo. B. Upton, and George B. Upton, jr., owners of the *Nora*, destroyed by the pirate steamer *Alabama*, have made a protest in reference thereto, and demand of the Government of Great Britain full reparation for the same in the sum of eighty thousand dollars of the coin of the United States, being the value of said ship and freight at the time of her destruction.
>
> They made this demand upon the ground that the *Alabama* was fitted out in an Eng[lish] port, manned mostly by British subjects, has never been in a Confederate port, but has been aided at British Islands, and is, in short, a British pirate and nothing else.[121]

Unfortunately for the Uptons and other Northern shipowners, their complaints about the legal technicalities of the status of the *Alabama* went unheard. With the "pirate" vessel still on the loose, their losses continued to mount without any prospect of diminishing. The USS *Kearsarge*, one of the Union warships assigned to track down and engage the *Alabama*, experienced frustration in her pursuit of the Confederate raiders throughout 1863. Captain John A. Winslow had assumed command of the *Kearsarge* on April 8, 1863, at Fayal, the Azores. Lieutenant Commander James S. Thornton, the new executive officer, recommended improvements to protect the ship's engines and boilers. A native of Merrimack, New Hampshire, and a career naval officer, the thirty-seven-year-old Thornton had served under Admiral David Farragut as executive officer of the USS *Hartford* in running past the Confederate batteries below New Orleans in 1862. Noting that Farragut's ships had been effectively protected by draping chains over the sides, Thornton recommended similar armament for the *Kearsarge* to create a partial ironclad effect. "The engineers' department made the iron work," wrote Second Assistant Engineer William Badlam, "and the ship's carpenter hung the chains. After six days' work, we had the job completed."[122]

After futile attempts to track down the CSS *Florida* off France in September 1863 and the CSS *Georgia* off the coast of Ireland during the late fall, the *Kearsarge* returned to Brest, France, in December. *Kearsarge* sailor John W. Dempsey informed his sister, apparently living in the Boston area, about the ship's activities, especially a diplomatic dispute with Great Britain over stowaways. Writing from Brest on December 14, Dempsey told his sister:

> I suppose you have heard of this ship going to Queenstown, Ireland.... We went there to ship some men as we are pretty short of men we having sent so many home sick and a good many run away from us so we went there and when you got there we were crowded by young men eager to ship here at any rate[.] The English Authorities ordered us to clear out in twenty-four hours after our arrival, but our captain [John A. Winslow] refused to do so. We kept on coaling for three days and then when we got ready we went to sea. So all the English papers are full about the damned saucy "YANKEE" ship. Well that was not all the trouble we got ourselves into. We took 16 men and a boy aboard of us and came back to Brest where we shipped them and everything was going on very well and the men were getting to be good Man of wars men when an order came from England to bring back those men that we took from Ireland[.] We went back there last week and landed them again. I expect that there will be a great deal of trouble on the strength of it, as all of the papers are full about it. Amongst the men was a boy from Watergate, Bandon [in County Cork] by the name of Crowley who knew the Tobins well. They would not ship him so I stowed him away in the coal bunkers till the ship was out to sea[.] I then got him out and got him some clothes and I made him a shirt[,] pants and a cap[.] Well the boy he commenced to cry when he found he had to go ashore again and he was shipped and getting 10 dollars a month, so

when I found out that he was going ashore I got up a subscription for him and we raised him $35 dollars in gold to pay his passage to America and I suppose by the time you get this letter he will be there....

The *Florida* is still laying here afraid of us[.] She would have gone from here long ago only for us[.] Another privateer called the *Georgia* is laying only 69 miles from here at a place called Cherbourg [France][.] Another called the *Rapprahanock* [*Rappahannock*] is in Calias [Calais, France] so you see that we have got our hands full as there is three of them to our one and any of them is a even match for us. I dont see what our government is doing leaving us out here this three months all alone. We cant blockade the Whole Coast of France without assistance and if the whole of them gets at us, there wont be much of us left, but I suppose we will do our best.[123]

USS Dacotah *Pursues the* Chesapeake

In December 1863, the most immediate threat to New England shipping was not from the CSS *Alabama* across the Atlantic, but much closer to home. In the early morning of December 7, a group of seventeen Confederate sympathizers, disguised as passengers, seized the American steamer *Chesapeake* off Cape Cod, Massachusetts. The *Chesapeake* had assisted in tracking down the *Caleb Cushing* off Portland Harbor after a similar Confederate seizure only six months earlier. In the latest Confederate hijacking the *Chesapeake*'s second engineer was killed. The newly expropriated Confederate vessel headed toward Canada and international waters in search of safety.[124]

The Yard sent out the USS *Dacotah*, then at the Yard undergoing minor repairs, to apprehend the *Chesapeake*, the capture of which embarrassed the Lincoln administration. On December 14, in his letter to Welles, Pearson reported:

The *Dacotah* left yesterday morning at 9:30 in pursuit of the *Chesapeake* with orders to search the coasts in the vicinity of Cape Sable [Nova Scotia], & should she find the *Chesapeake* in an English port to demand her of the authorities as an American vessel captured by pirates or other evil-disposed persons. Should she be captured, Commander [Alfred G.] Clary [of the *Dacotah*] was to convey her to the most convenient port, and in the event of her having gone south, he was to return here. I furnished the *Dacotah* with some twenty men from the Rec[eivin]g Ship here, including the firemen & coal heavers intended for the *Agawam*, in order to make up as well as I could for the deficiency of her crew.[125]

Of the numerous Union warships engaged in the search, the USS *Ella and Annie* on December 17 recaptured the *Chesapeake* in Sambro Harbor, near Halifax, Nova Scotia. Commander Clary arrived in the *Dacotah* shortly thereafter. Realizing the gravity of a possible international incident with the British authorities, Clary urged the captain of the *Ella and Annie* "to proceed at once to Halifax, [so] that steps might be taken to legalize the capture." These negotiations were then carried out in Halifax, and the British Vice Admiralty Court ultimately restored the *Chesapeake* to her American owners.[126]

The news of the recapture of the *Chesapeake* elicited an unexpected bonus. "The meeting in Portland, Thursday evening [December 17, 1863]," reported the *Chronicle* on December 19, "for the Freedmen's Relief Association, was earnest and enthusiastic. Just as the services were to begin, the news came of the recapture of the steamer *Chesapeake*, and being announced, was received with great applause. This circumstance gave the meeting a great impulse, and doubtless will swell the receipts. Rev. Mr. Hawkins, collecting agent for this noble charity, has returned to Portsmouth, and will operate here Saturday and Monday."[127]

On December 23, in time for the Christmas holiday, the *Dacotah* returned to the Yard from Halifax, her mission completed. Although neither the North nor the South realized it at the time, Confederate raiding and hijacking operations off the New England coast had ended with the *Chesapeake* incident. Confederate agents and sympathizers bent on seizing Northern ships were no longer capable of raids along the coast of Maine, New Hampshire, Massachusetts, or other Union seaboard states. As dramatic and thrilling as they were in their undertaking and execution, the *Caleb Cushing* and *Chesapeake* seizures were isolated episodes, soon ending in utter failure and quick capture for most of their Confederate instigators. From late December 1863 until the end of the Civil War, New England waters were secure for local shipping and the Union merchant marine.[128]

When Secretary Welles submitted his annual report to

President Lincoln, on December 7, he cited the vast improvement of the United States Navy in all categories during the year. In conclusion, he noted, "I have been constantly cheered and sustained by the assured conviction that the navy of the United States has achieved a great and new historical renown."[129]

Lieutenant George Dewey (in 1863 photo) served at the Yard in 1864 aboard the USS Agawam. *While on government duty, Dewey faced an assault-and-battery charge that was quietly settled before a Kittery judge. In 1876, Dewey married Susan Goodwin, daughter of Portsmouth's Ichabod Goodwin, ex-governor of New Hampshire. Dewey's Civil War combat experience prepared him well for his rendezvous with history at Manila Bay in 1898. NHC*

V 1864: *The USS* Kearsarge *Engages the CSS* Alabama

The Launching of the USS New Hampshire

THE YEAR OF 1864 opened gloomily for the country; the war dragged on," wrote Walter E.H. Fentress in his nineteenth-century history of the Portsmouth Navy Yard. "The Yard continued to teem with work-men," he added, "and the wharves to be crowded with vessels." Fentress's depiction caught the mood of the North. Nevertheless, 1864 marked a pivotal period in the Union's prosecution of the war. Despite war-weariness, the nation's resoluteness to continue did not lessen as the Union navy steeled to end the conflict.[1]

For its part, the Yard in 1864 increased its work force by more than 300 men to a record total of 1,766 employees to meet the acceler-ating demand for new ship construction and repair. In September, Yard Commandant George F. Pearson was relieved of his duties and replaced by Admiral Theodorus Bailey. During 1864, new leadership, more vessels, and significant naval engagements for the Yard and the Union navy accelerated the quest for victory.[2]

In a lead article, a *New York Tribune* correspondent expressed this gritty determination: "On the first day of January, 1864, the United States possessed the fastest Navy in the world. The chief ves-sels composing it have all been constructed during the year 1863.... The first adventures of the *Alabama* so startled the commercial public that there was a general outcry for the fast war vessels." After discussing the numerous new ships with speeds of up to thirteen knots, the correspondent concluded, "The United States [Navy] may stand before the world patiently awaiting the advent of future *Alabamas*."[3]

Contributing to this overall effort the Portsmouth Navy Yard launched the USS *New Hampshire* (formerly the *Alabama*) on Saturday, January 23, 1864. Renaming of the newly completed ship eliminated an embarrassing association with the CSS *Alabama*, and the new name fostered pride among Granite State citizens and inspired a rare wartime poem about a ship from the Yard, "The Launch of the *New Hampshire*."[4]

The *New Hampshire* eventually would serve as a storeship for Union vessels on blockade duty off Port Royal, South Carolina.

Accidents at the Yard

Many accidents during 1864 killed or injured a number of Yard workers. Bad weather during the winter months periodically hampered work on open-air projects. On February 17, trying to cross the Piscataqua in a heavy sea, many workmen "had their boats filled with water, and were obliged to return to Portsmouth," according to the next day's *Chronicle*. The temperature was four degrees below zero, with high winds. A day later, the Piscataqua River above the Portsmouth Bridge froze over. However, the Lower Harbor surrounding the Yard remained clear for navigation.[5]

Spring brought the worst rash of Yard accidents of the wartime period. Until 1864, the Yard's safety record had been excellent, with rarely a mishap. The first accident of 1864 occurred on March 28, when laborer John M. Harvey fell to the ground from the deck of the *Agamenticus*. Although severely injured, Harvey survived.[6]

On April 20, "Patrick Dwyer, a laborer, employed at the Portsmouth Navy Yard while at work scraping the hatchcombings on board the U.S. steamer *Colorado*, was suddenly seized with a fainting fit, and fell from the berth-deck to the fireroom below, a distance of twelve or fifteen feet, striking his head, killing him instantly," the *Chronicle* reported the next day. "We learn that he leaves a widow and two children, residing in this city."[7]

A contractor for the Yard was next. On April 23, three days after Dwyer's accident, "as Mr. George Atchison, of this city, was assisting in unloading a lumber schooner at the Portsmouth Navy

Yard," reported the *Chronicle* on April 27, "a stick of timber which was being drawn out, caught his foot and passing over his body lengthwise, broke his thigh and crushed him so severely that he died of his injuries on Monday [April 25, 1864]. He leaves a wife residing in this city." That same Monday, Captain Hoyt of the schooner *M. Sewall* had his foot severely crushed by a stick of timber at the Yard.[8]

The Indiscretion of Lieutenant George Dewey

An 1864 accident at the Yard involving the gunboat *Agawam* not only caused extensive damage to the vessel but also jeopardized the promising naval career of twenty-six-year-old Lieutenant George Dewey, assigned to the USS *Agawam*.

Dewey's vessel from the start was plagued with problems. Launched in April 1863, the *Agawam* was a Portland-built side-wheel steamer—and a prime example of shoddy workmanship and hasty construction. "If Uncle Sam didn't get pretty well sold on this craft," commented the *Chronicle* on January 9, 1864, "we err in judgment. Her air-port lights have all been taken out to be re-modelled and re-packed, a general store-room is being built, bilge-cocks put in the magazine and ammunition rooms, (the vessel being without any such safe-guard prior to her arrival here,) besides a large amount of general carpentering, caulking and joinering, which must be done before the craft will be seaworthy.... her construction would seem to be rather sham."[9]

Eight days after her commissioning on March 9, the *Agawam* headed down the Piscataqua for sea trials in the Lower Harbor. The ship ran against the rocks on Seavey's Island, at Pull-and-Be-Damned Point just below Fort Sullivan, damaging her port wheel and port quarters. She began leaking immediately and had to limp back to the Yard for repairs. In his two reports of March 18 to Secretary Welles, Commandant Pearson assessed the cause of the accident: "It was a fine afternoon yesterday [March 17], and therefore I have no doubt that the accident occurred by a mistake of the pilot in running too near the Seavey's Island shore without making the necessary calculation of the strength of the tide, or eddy, which striking the vessel upon the starboard bow, forced her against the rocks, although the helm was past aport when he discovered his mistake."[10]

Although Pearson sympathized with the river pilot, Rufus Preble, the Navy Department ordered Preble dismissed from his job of navigating the U.S. naval vessels to and from the Yard.[11]

The conduct of Lieutenant George Dewey likewise underwent close scrutiny in the aftermath of the *Agawam* accident. In his letter of April 8 to Welles, Pearson explained:

> I have respectfully to report that on the 6th inst. while the *Agawam* was being hauled from the Dock to the wharf, some of the Yard laborers performed their work badly, although Lt. Dewey and the officers of the ship endeavored to have them move quicker with the towlines, as the vessel was drifting into shoal waters.
>
> It was then that Lt. Dewey[,] the 1st Lieut.[,] collared one of these men in order to make him do his duty, when another yard laborer [George C. Garland] said "that was too bad," and put himself in an attitude to attack Lt. Dewey, and Lt. Dewey then struck the man who made this remark, with his trumpet, and this was reported to me by the laborer himself, whose name is Geo. C. Garland. I then informed Garland that his conduct was wrong, but that I would investigate the matter....
>
> I ... informed Lt. Dewey that he had no authority whatever to strike or collar any man either of the ship or the Yard unless in self-defense and therefore had rendered himself liable to a court martial; that if the men did not obey his orders promptly, then he should have reported them, & had them discharged, if yard men, at once. I soon found however that the man had complained to the civil authorities of Kittery, and that there, he [Dewey] had been fined some twelve or thirteen dollars for his indiscretion. This being the fact, I have not deemed it necessary to suspend Lt. Dewey from duty or to take any further steps in this matter, unless the [Navy] Department should otherwise direct.
>
> I shall, of course, discharge from the Yard any workmen who neglected their duty while moving the *Agawam*, or who were insolent to her officers.[12]

Under the POLICE COURT heading next day, the *Chronicle* corroborated the legal action taken: "Lieut. George Dewey of the U.S. sloop *Agawam* was brought before Justice Dennett of Kittery Foreside on Thursday [April 7, 1864], to answer to a charge of assault and battery on the person of George C. Garland, of Eliot. Found guilty, and fined $10 and costs."[13]

Dewey is silent on this matter in his *Autobiography*, published a half century later. Had the episode resulted in a court martial, which would have seriously jeopardized or even ended his naval career, he would never have become the Spanish-American War "Hero of the Battle of Manila Bay," and ultimately Admiral of the Fleet.[14]

The accident delayed the *Agawam*'s departure by six weeks. After repairs, the vessel, with Lieutenant George Dewey on board, sailed from the Yard on April 17 for Portland, Maine, where she received her complement and was finally ready for blockade duty. "[The *Agawam* is] a good sea-boat, easily handled, and quite fast," reported the *Portland Advertiser*. "She carries a battery of guns—two 100-pounders, four 9-inch Dahlgrens, and four long range howitzers, besides a plentiful supply of small arms."[15]

As part of the North Atlantic Blockading Squadron at Hampton Roads, Virginia, the *Agawam* conducted operations from June until November. On July 28, 1864, under the temporary command of Lieutenant Dewey, the *Agawam*, together with the USS *Mendota*, shelled Confederate positions across Four Mile Creek on the James River, in concert with U.S. Army operations to re-establish Union control of the river.[16]

The Fast Steamer USS Sassacus

During the first half of 1864, the Portsmouth-built *Sassacus* was assigned to blockade duty off the coast of North Carolina, concentrating on the outer approaches to Wilmington. Closing this strategic Southern port was a major objective of the Union navy throughout the war.

The *Sassacus*'s exploits quickly gained the attention of Union Rear Admiral Samuel Phillips Lee, commander of the North Atlantic Blockading Squadron. At the beginning of the war, eighty-four percent of Southern blockade runners operating out of Wilmington were successful in evading Union offshore vessels. By the end of 1864, thanks to the vigilance and persistence of the *Sassacus* and others in the Squadron, this figure was reduced to fifty percent. The South could not lose half its runners and still expect to continue the war for any length of time.[17]

Writing from Norfolk, Virginia, on March 9, a *Portland Press* correspondent assessed the remarkable speed of the *Sassacus*, "exceeding 16 2/3 miles an hour, with neither tide or current in our favor." The *Sassacus* left Fortress Monroe on January 25, 1864, under Lieutenant Commander Francis A. Roe, headed for her blockading station. On the morning of January 31, Roe pursued a large side-wheel steamer some nine miles distant, closing the gap to about a mile and a half. The chase proved to be a fiasco, as the pursued vessel turned out to be the USS *Keystone State*, which had ignored Roe's warning shots. The episode, Roe told Admiral Lee, caused him to be "taken a long way out of my course and forced to expend an unnecessary amount of coal."[18]

During early February, the *Sassacus*'s chase, capture, and destruction of two fast Confederate blockade runners, *Wild Dayrell* and *Nutfield*, established her reputation. On February 1, at Topsail Inlet, North Carolina, Roe spotted the *Wild Dayrell*, a British-built boat. After chasing the runner ashore, Roe burned the *Wild Dayrell*. Concerning the *Nutfield*, a *Portland Press* reporter recounted:

> When on the morn of February 4th at 7:45, we sighted a steamer burning the suspicious "black smoke," so grateful to the eyes of a Blockader, we started in full expectation of capturing the stranger. She was about 12 miles distant, when we headed for her, running from us at full speed in a Northerly direction. At 1:15 P.M. we were within a mile of her, when she run [ran] on shore, fired and abandoned by her crew in such haste that one of the boats was capsized, and the greater part of her crew were drowned. On boarding the steamer, she proved to be the *Nutfield* of London, new and built expressly for the trade, this being her first attempt at forcing the blockade.... Everything possible was done by the crew of the *Nutfield* to increase the distance between us, by throwing over cargo, and burning oil, and other substances to obtain increased steam.... Her battered hulk now lies on the break [breakers?] of North Carolina, one of the many similar monuments, which bear a silence [silent] but convincing testimony to the vigilance and efficiency of the blockade.[19]

Shortly thereafter, the Navy Department received a report from Admiral S.P. Lee, printed in the *Chronicle* on February 18.

Referring to the recent naval actions, Lee exclaimed:

> The result has equalled my expectations…. Lieut. Com'r Rowe [Roe] estimates the value of the *Wild Dayrell* with her cargo at about $200,000. The *Nutfield*'s cargo consisted of munitions of war, arms, a battery of 8 [English-manufactured] Whitworth guns, and pig lead. The guns and lead were thrown overboard during the chase. Some 700 rifles and a quantity of cavalry sabres, together with other articles, were rescued from her before she was burnt. Lieut Commander Rowe reports that the *Sassacus* attained a speed of 13 1/2 knots, and gained rapidly on one of the fastest steamers yet sent out to run the blockade.[20]

The number of Union naval prizes from 1861 to June 1, 1864, reached a total of 1,227 vessels: Confederate steamers, 232; schooners, 627; sloops, 159; barks, 29; brigs, 32; ships, 15; yachts and small craft, 133. The aggregate value was $12 million, which was distributed among the Union naval captors.[21]

The *Portsmouth Chronicle* summarized the military situation in 1864: "Cotton having abdicated, Iron is king; but it is not yet settled whether in plates or balls."[22]

The Sassacus *and the* Albemarle

In May 1864, the wooden *Sassacus* participated in a celebrated but desperate battle, in engaging the ironclad CSS *Albemarle* in Albemarle Sound, North Carolina. The wooden ship was usually no match for an ironclad enemy, but the *Sassacus*'s captain, Lieutenant Commander Roe, defied conventional naval wisdom. The *Sassacus*'s ramming of the *Albemarle* blunted the Confederate naval offensive in what may have been "the first deliberate attempt to destroy an ironclad by running it down with a wooden ship."[23]

In a detailed letter datelined "U.S. STEAMER *SASSACUS*, ALBEMARLE SOUND, May 8, 1864," a member of the crew (identified only as "E.H.S.") wrote an excellent contemporary account of the fierce action; the *Chronicle* printed it nine days later. The observant participant reported:

The Portsmouth-built wooden steam sloop USS Sassacus *rams the Confederate ironclad* CSS Albemarle *in Albemarle Sound, North Carolina, on May 5, 1864. Hampered by this collision and shelled by other Union vessels, the slightly disabled* Albemarle *withdrew up the Roanoke River the same day, never to engage in battle again. NHC*

... the dreaded ram *Albemarle* hove in sight, accompanied by two Confederate steamers—the *Cotton Planter* and the captured *Bombshell....* The *Cotton Plant* [sic] not having faith in her own abilities, at sight of us turned and skedaddled at a double quick, followed by a parting cheer as we steamed to the attack, 13 knots to the ram's 4 or 5. The flag-ship at a distance of three cables' length poured in her broadside,—our vessel and the *Wyalusing* following suit, and the rebel ram returning with shot and shell. We then went about, and again delivered our fire, the 100 pound shot breaking and rebounding from her sides in every direction—the only acknowledgement being a dense volume of smoke, evidently caused by the concussion.

As our vessel steamed past, the *Bombshell* impudently fired at us, and we gave her a broadside, fairly riddling her. Down came the Confederate rag, and up went the white flag. We told her to fall to the rear and anchor, which she did. We went about, gathered headway, and struck the ram [*Albemarle*] full tilt, (reversing the order of things—the wooden boat doing the ramming). We struck him abeam, settling him down to the water's edge, and smashing our prow. The *Albemarle*, swinging round under our starboard bow, opened her forward port and planted a 100-pound shot into us, which passed through the Yeoman's room, across the berth deck, and out of the port side, forward [of] the beam. This we returned with a shot right in her port, which was shut down with a savage snap. By this time she got under our wheel, opened her after port, and drove another shot into us.... The effect of this shot was terrific: 15 or 17 firemen were fearfully scalded, including Mr. Hobby, 1st Asst. [Engineer], and one man [Thomas Johnson, coalheaver] instantly killed. Two died soon after, and one or two more are sinking fast....

During this time our gallant Commander [Francis A. Roe] and his officers were not idle. Shot and musketry poured into the ram. His flag was shot away, while charges of powder and hand grenades rained on him from the tops as he steamed slowly away, from our crippled but unconquered vessel. The other vessels now closed in upon him, keeping up a running fight till dark, when he escaped in a shattered condition up the Roanoke river. Our losses in killed and wounded are heavy.... By the prompt exertions of our Engineers and gallant firemen, the fires were drawn from under the remaining boiler, thereby preventing an explosion....

We captured 34 prisoners, 5 officers and 23 men in the *Bombshell*.[24]

Although superficially damaged, the *Albemarle* never returned to action. During the fight, she received several hits on her smokestack, which slowed her speed. Taken up the Roanoke River for repairs, the *Albemarle* was awaiting their completion on the night of October 27-28, 1864, when she was torpedoed and sunk in a daring Union night raid.[25]

The *Sassacus*'s ramming of the *Albemarle* quickly caught the attention of the Northern public, and painters, lithographers, and other artists created depictions of the engagement. The Union navy promoted Roe for his distinguished conduct in battle, but his decision to attack the *Albemarle* became a matter of debate, judged either as a courageous and patriotic move or as a foolhardy act of desperation.

In 1899, as a seventy-six-year-old retired admiral, Roe defended his decision: "It is ... my purpose to put on record in my own handwriting the incidents of that fight so much controverted and its glorious results so little understood." Discussing his rationale for his decision to fight, Roe asserted:

> Painfully recognizing the futility of our attack on the slanting iron sides of the enemy, it came to my mind very suddenly that something else must be done than sailing around the Ram and firing useless guns, and that at all hazards this formidable enemy must be crippled, even if I sacrificed my gunboat, myself, my officers, and men to do it. I felt and decided that I could well afford to lose my vessel, if thereby I could work the defeat, or even the disabling of the enemy. There surely was a chance that this craft might be disabled in some way by a collision....

After recounting details of the fight, Roe assessed its result:

> In time of war, victory is conceded to the one remaining in possession of the field, and therefore I claim for the *Sassacus* in this battle, the honors of a Naval victory. The enemy suffered a defeat and fled up the Sound pursued and chased by the vessels of the squadron. When the Ram got near Plymouth [North Carolina] it was leaking so heavily that her Captain ran his vessel on a sand bank to keep it from sinking.... But the ironclad Rebel ram *Albemarle* never emerged again as an enemy after she escaped from the iron grasp of the *Sassacus*.[26]

Roe evaluated the strategic importance of having driven the *Albemarle* from the waters of North Carolina. A Union supply and munitions base at Newbern, North Carolina, to the south on Neuse Sound, would have been subject to capture had the Confederate ram not been stopped. "The action of the *Sassacus* saved this vast storehouse," Roe believed, "and made possible the future efficiency of [Union general William T.] Sherman's Army for a new campaign.... When the *Sassacus* arrived at Newbern on her way north for repairs, I met [Union] General [Innis T.] Palmer, who embraced me and said: 'Captain, you have saved my Army by your heroic action with the *Albemarle*.'"[27]

The USS Colorado, *Prisoners of War, and Deserters*

The USS *Colorado* spent much of 1864 at the Yard out of commission and undergoing repairs. The ship became bedeviled with prisoners of war, accidents, violence, and desertions.

After fourteen months of blockade duty off Mobile Bay, the *Colorado* returned to the Yard on February 4, 1864. Aboard were twenty-eight prisoners, twenty-six of whom were blockade runners.[28]

Following a telegraphic order from Secretary of the Navy Welles on February 6, Commandant Pearson, Commodore Henry Knox Thatcher (captain of the *Colorado*), and Captain George R. Graham of the Yard Marine Corps detachment sought to convey the prisoners to Fort Warren, Massachusetts. On February 6, writing from aboard the *Colorado*, Thatcher informed Pearson:

> With regard to their [the prisoners'] history I have no knowledge except that they were captured by Gun Boats acting under my orders whilst in the act of running the blockade from Mobile, with the exception of two, namely John Hamlin [or Hanlon], a native of Ireland and a ship carpenter by trade who was endeavoring to escape from Confederacy and who immediately after his capture volentirely [*sic*] took the oath of allegiance to the U.S....[;] the other man of whom I have knowledge is William Norvel [or Norval][,] a former Mobile pilot and very useful to the Confederates[,] 34 years of age and a native of Baltimore. If he is permitted to return to the South he will again resume his old calling as he has himself informed me[.]

An attached list of prisoners reads:

Captured on board Schr. *M & Smith* [*Marshall Smith*]   Dec 9th 1863

[Name]	[Ship Duty, Occupation]	[Birthplace]		Age
Thomas L. Nelson	Seaman	Sweden	Age	23
Cha[rle]s Williams	Do [Ditto]	Do	"	38
Cha[rle]s Henson	Cook	Denmark	"	25
H. H. Erickson	Seaman	Do	"	46
John Contoff	Do	Do	"	26

Captured on board Steamer *Grey Jacket*   Dec. 31st. 1863

Jefferson Dugan	Seaman	Ireland	age	23
Peter Hyer	Deck Hand	Germany	"	40

W[illia]m Kelley	Seaman	Ireland	age	27
Richard Welsh	Do	Do	"	48
John Hanlon [Hamlin]	Carpenter	Do Released	"	30
Lewis Johnson	Seaman	Germany	"	27
Joseph Sareto	Do	Italy	"	27
Peter Lawson	Do	Sweden	"	45
Lewis Henrico	Fireman	Spain	"	47
Christian Dobslomick	Coal Heaver	Austria	"	29
Peter Hunt	Fireman	Ireland	"	43
John Deloluinty[?]	Do	Do	"	35
Richard Hyland	Do	Do	"	39
Peter Polonitch	Do	Austria	"	38
Wesley Scott	Steward	Mobile	"	22
Rob[er]t Robinson	Cook	Ireland	"	27
John Pyne	Fireman	"	"	30
Lewis Bartoly	Do	Austria	"	30

Captured from Schr. *John Scott*			Jan. 8th 1864	
Cha[rle]s Johnson	Seaman	Sweden	age	26
John Mahony	Do	England	"	35
Alin Savio	Do	Italy	"	45
W[illia]m Norvel [Norval?} Pilot		Baltimore	"	34
J.D. Hancock	Passenger	Tenessee [*sic*]	"	30

This rare list of blockade-runner captures reveals that the Confederacy was becoming almost totally dependent on foreign-born crews.[29]

At the Yard, Pearson took steps to resolve the status and disposition of the prisoners. Considering the special case of John Hanlon, Pearson judged him a loyal Union man, worthy of reinstatement. After taking the oath of allegiance, Hanlon was released and stayed at the Yard, working as a ship's carpenter aboard the *Colorado*. On February 8, 1864, Pearson ordered the other prisoners to be transported under marine escort by rail to Boston and thence by boat to Fort Warren for their incarceration.[30]

Movement of prisoners of war to, in, around, and from Navy Yards underscored a serious problem. Union Navy Yards had become such transitory places that it became necessary to implement stricter security measures. To regulate the constant traffic of officers, crews, ships' workmen, and prisoners of war, Welles and the Navy

Department sought to eliminate the lax rendering that heretofore had prevailed. Union naval officers were now held accountable for all the personnel and activities aboard their vessels. In May 1864, Pearson issued this important order:

> Officers appointed to command vessels fitting out at this Yard will report to the Lieut. Commander's office every morning at 9 a.m. giving their names and the names of vessels to which ordered. Should a leave be granted them, they will report the fact in the same office, and state who succeeds them as commanding officer, and the commanding officer of a vessel at this Yard will, if he [should] have a sufficient number of officers, detail for daily duty one watch officer and one Engineer to remain on board from bell-ring in the morning untill [sic] bell-ring in the evening, for the purpose of reporting all delinquents among the workers. These officers will have their regular reliefs the same as if the vessel was in commission. The order is reiterated that all officers will remain on board of their vessels during the night, after the vessel is placed in commission.[31]

During the *Colorado*'s long period of repairs, recommissioning, and ultimate departure for sea duty, an accurate daily roll of the personnel was all-important.

On Saturday night, August 27, sixteen seamen deserted from the *Colorado*. "One of them," reported the *Chronicle* a few days later, "was recaptured by the Police on Sunday night, just as he was about to leave by the freight train on the Eastern railroad." On September 2, a day after the recommissioning, "the master at arms [of the USS *Colorado*] was stabbed in the head by a sailor (substitute) inflicting a frightful gash across the face. A number of these bounty jumping rascals are already in irons on board the *Colorado*."[32]

Such incidents continued. On Wednesday night, September 21, fifteen or twenty men attempted to escape from the *Colorado* by jumping overboard and swimming to boats in the river. The *Chronicle* summarized the toll of the night of mayhem: "It is said that one was killed by a musket shot fired by the sentry, two others drowned, and the rest [probably ten to fifteen men] escaped. The larger portion of this crew are a rough set of fellows, being bounty jumpers and cut-throats."[33]

Two of the escapees were caught on September 28. "One steady man on board the *Colorado* had a pass to go on shore," reported the

Chronicle the next day, "and on Tuesday [September 28] night one of these bounty jumpers finding it out, offered the young man $600 for it; the individual, to his credit, be it said, declined the offer."[34]

The *Colorado* sailed to the Lower Harbor on October 1 and put to sea four days later. After clearing Portsmouth, she joined the North Atlantic Blockading Squadron for duty off the coast of North Carolina. A few days after her departure, "The body of an unknown sailor floated ashore in the back cove [Back Channel] near the Navy Yard," according to the *Chronicle*. "A sum of money, roughly estimated at $2000, was found upon him. The body was buried in the cemetery on the Yard on the same day. He is supposed to have been one of the bounty jumpers who escaped from the *Colorado* previous to her sailing." The United States Naval Cemetery of the Portsmouth Navy Yard, established in 1820, was the burial place for navy and marine servicemen and their dependents. The grave of the unknown *Colorado* deserter still remains unmarked.[35]

In another tragic situation, the Yard's vigilance prevented injury or loss of life. On July 18, 1864, a fire broke out at noon along Penhallow Street in downtown Portsmouth. In the largest conflagration since 1845, Portsmouth property losses were estimated at $30,000 to $50,000. Thirty families became homeless and several commercial buildings were destroyed. The office of Joshua L. Foster's *States and Union*, for example, was severely damaged by fire and water. Spurred by a strong wind, the fire would have continued unchecked but for, in the *Chronicle*'s words, "the timely arrival of the little but smart steam fire engine from the Yard." Pearson also sent a steam tub under the supervision of the Yard's Chief Engineer. Yard firemen quickly extinguished the blaze. "Business generally was suspended in the city," concluded the *Chronicle*, "and most of the stores closed—and most of the workmen at the Navy Yard left work for the day—all to assist in staying the conflagration, which threatened the most disastrous consequences."[36]

"Contraband" and White "Galvanized Yankee" Sailors

During 1864, while the South was becoming increasingly dependent upon foreign crews, the Union navy also had to tap every available source of manpower. The manning of two ships at the Yard in the spring of 1864 required not only the transfer of black contraband sailors from the Fort Sullivan Naval Battery, but also a heretofore-unused source of manpower, the nautical equivalent of "galvanized Yankees"—repatriated white Confederate prisoners of war. These white Southerners, in exchange for release from prison, took the oath of allegiance to the United States and enlisted in the Union cause. Since the Union army had already successfully tried this policy, the Union navy undertook the same experiment.[37]

Of the aforementioned categories, black naval personnel were already at the Yard. After ten months of service at Fort Sullivan, the entire contingent of 117 contrabands was split up into two groups in 1864 and transferred to ships being recommissioned at the Yard. Commandant Pearson had long supported the black sailors. On January 22, 1864, he informed Secretary of the Navy Welles, "As the 'Contrabands' here have conducted themselves well, and in my opinion, deserve a little encouragement, I beg leave to recommend that W[illia]m Burril be rated a ship's corporal and W[illia]m Pollard be rated as nurse. As there are now 119 contrabands at the Naval Battery, a nurse there is much needed as well as a ship's corporal." After an attack on three black sailors on leave in Portsmouth, Pearson contacted Portsmouth Mayor Jonathan Dearborn on March 22 to seek redress. Referring "to an assault made upon a boat's crew of 'Contrabands,'" Pearson demanded an investigation of "this diabolical attack upon the black men," and concluded, "It would appear that a few Irishmen were the instigators of this disgraceful affair."[38]

Such incidents of racial violence appear to have been isolated. An article, "TEACHING THE CONTRABANDS TO READ," published in the *Chronicle* on May 24, attests to the positive local reception during their stay:

> Ten months ago about one hundred and seventeen blacks, who had been slaves, were stationed at Fort Sullivan in our harbor. Among them were only three or four who could read a word. [Since the blacks were] showing a desire to learn, several young ladies of this city have visited the island twice a week, formed classes and given them instruction. Among them are two or three advanced in life, and about eight or ten of limited intellect, who could not learn. Of the remainder, about one hundred in number, all can now read and write, and many of them can perform operations in the simple rules of arithmetic. We have seen several letters written by them in which nine words of ten are spelt correctly. All this has been accomplished in ten

months, with two hours instruction only twice a week.... They have now left the Fort and entered upon sea service—able not only to read, but also to correspond with each other.[39]

These newly literate black sailors were needed as part of the complement for the USS *New Hampshire*, which was commissioned on May 13. Also at the Yard to fill out her crew was the USS *Alabama* (not the CSS *Alabama* or the *Alabama* that became the USS *New Hampshire*). A side-wheel steamer purchased by the Union government in 1861, the USS *Alabama* retained her civilian name and was recommissioned at the Yard on May 17. Of the 117 black sailors at the Naval Battery, eighty-seven were assigned to the *New Hampshire* and the remaining thirty to the *Alabama*.[40]

The Navy Department quickly authorized transfers of the black sailors and the "galvanized Yankees." On May 13, Pearson notified Secretary of the Navy Welles, "I have this day received from Baltimore 87 seamen & o[rdinary] seamen for the *New Hampshire*. I have transferred to her 87 contrabands [from Fort Sullivan]." More men were on the way. On May 19, Pearson acknowledged to Commander Albert N. Smith, Bureau Chief of Equipment and Recruiting, the arrival of 195 blacks from Baltimore, 146 of whom he "put on board the *New Hampshire* and the remaining forty-nine on board the *Alabama*." Pearson also confirmed "that 300 rebel prisoners from Rock Island [Illinois, site of a Union prisoner-of-war camp for Confederate captives], are to be enlisted and sent here for the *New Hampshire*." In his third letter of May 19, to Smith, Pearson speculated, "I suppose they [the black sailors from Baltimore] were to go to Port Royal [South Carolina], in order to fill the vacancies in the fleet.... The *New Hampshire* has now 233 contrabands on board."[41]

On May 21, the *Chronicle* noted the arrival of the black sailors from Baltimore at the Yard "via the Eastern Railroad," and added, "One of them, it was feared, had the small pox, and he was taken to the Pest Island, the Hospital at the Navy Yard having just been cleansed from that disease. Every precaution has been taken to prevent the spread of the disease."[42]

On May 31, the *Chronicle* provided a detailed summary of the varied nature of the *New Hampshire*'s crew:

She [the *New Hampshire*] has about 900 men aboard, of whom two hundred are negroes; two hundred and fifty paroled rebel prisoners; and four hundred and fifty enlisted sailors from the receiving ship *North Carolina* at the Brooklyn Navy Yard.... The "rebel" portion of the *New Hampshire*'s crew arrived on Saturday last [May 28, 1864], by rail from Chicago, and were marched from Kittery Depot to the ship under a guard of marines. A prison life of about ten months, exposure, and habits of different kinds, together with varied costumes, have made them a hard looking, pitiable set of men; yet among some of them, rays of intelligence could be discerned through the dirt and rags. One of them remarked that "Uncle Sam was mighty distrustful of them, and he had good reason to be, as one half of them only wanted their bread and butter, and it made no differ- ence to them where they got it." He stated that they had fared very well as prisoners, and instanced the fact that the rations served out to them for their dinner on the day of their arrival on board the *New Hampshire*, were greater than a week's allowance in rebeldom at the time of their capture. He remarked that he had always been a Union man at heart, was impressed in the rebel service, and left a wife and two children in Alabama.... They have all taken the oath of allegiance, and have discarded and thrown overboard their old, dirty garments and donned the navy blue of the United States. We should think this innovation alone might inspire them with a little patriotism, judging from the change it made in their appearance.[43]

On May 31, the USS *Alabama* sailed from the Yard, destined for the North Atlantic Blockading Squadron off Wilmington, North Carolina, followed on June 15 by the USS *New Hampshire* as a depot and supply ship for Port Royal, South Carolina. The contrabands and the nautical galvanized Yankees made excellent crews, as both ships provided outstanding service for the rest of the war.[44]

Tighter Security at Union Yards

The consequences of the draft, the presence of bounty jumpers, and the theft of United States property at the Union Navy Yards com- pelled Secretary of the Navy Gideon Welles to tighten restrictions. With men and matériel disappearing, Welles issued circulars and orders in a concerted effort to halt the thievery.

On February 29, 1864, Pearson responded to Welles, regarding the Navy "Department's circular of the 26th inst., directing the dismissal of any employee, who has at anytime claimed, or shall hereafter claim, exemption from any draft of men that may be ordered by the President of the United States, on the grounds of alienage."[45]

The Navy Department circular was quickly implemented. Three weeks later, on March 19, Pearson reported to Welles, "The following aliens have been discharged from this Navy Yard, because they refuse to serve, should they at anytime be drafted into the military service of the United States." The list named two carpenters, five laborers, and a rigger.[46]

In June, six marines decided to desert. As part of their plan to escape from the Yard, the marines had enlisted two civilian men. The *Chronicle* reported the story on June 29:

> On Tuesday [June 28, 1864], John Dixon of Portsmouth and James Clark of New York were brought up on a charge of tempting six U.S. Marines to desert from the Navy Yard. They were found at midnight on Thursday last [June 23, 1864], the time fixed for the marines to desert,—in separate boats near the Navy Yard landing. The soldiers were kept in their quarters [the Marine Barracks], and four persons went down, representing the would-be deserters. Having taken these on board, they started for Portsmouth, but Capt. Hebb, one of the four, somewhat peremptorily, aided by a revolver, persuaded them to return to the Yard—on arriving at which it was found that they had in their boats portions of six suits of citizens' clothes, intended for the use of the deserters, a part of which clothing was identified as having been worn by one of the would-be deserters when enlisted—a week ago.[47]

Theft of government property from the Yard was much easier than desertion. Ingot copper had been disappearing from the Yard for some time. In August, a schooner arrived, carrying a considerable amount of copper suspected as having come from the Yard. According to the *Chronicle* of September 8, a Boston police officer identified "one Sampson L. Russell, of this city [the 1863 Portsmouth Draft Riot leader] ... as the person who [had] consigned the copper ... to ... T.B. Barnes & Co., of Boston." The officer "then proceeded to Portsmouth, and calling upon Mr. Russell, at his store on Water Street, with a search warrant, found another lot of ingot copper stowed away under the counter." After Russell was served with the writ of arrest, a subsequent search at the Russell store turned up "two musket boxes, partially empty and marked George B. French." A search at the French store yielded four muskets. It was estimated that about $600 worth of copper had been sold to Russell and his brother from the Navy Yard, "stolen by some person or persons yet to be found out." Although a number of Navy Yard workmen were implicated in the theft by Russell, the charges could not be sustained, and the men were released. The case remained unsolved.[48]

The arrival of the U.S. steamer *Shawmut* at the Yard on November 20 presented a totally unexpected security problem. Off the coast of Nova Scotia and in the Bay of Fundy, the *Shawmut* had experienced "a very stormy cruise, with cold weather—ice, cold, sleet and snow." She had come to the Yard for repairs.[49]

The *Shawmut* had been at the Yard only one day when trouble occurred. Acting Master James T. Ross observed:

> At 8 P.M. on the 21st inst. [of November] a boat was discovered near the port bow of this ship. The Officer of the Deck immediately went forward to ascertain why the look-out did not hail her. Finding no look-out (who was there a short time previous) he hailed the boat which answered "passing." Hearing a low whistle he discovered a man clinging to the Cat Fall, under the Starboard bow. The boat was immediately fired into, which rowed rapidly away to Starboard.
>
> The man was brought on Deck and searched. On his person was found a large Bowie Knife and $35.10. By this time it was ascertained that the look out, whose name was Robert Crawford, and three men were missing.
>
> The prisoner, who gave his name as John Williams[,] was then put in double irons. A boat was immediately lowered and four officers, armed, went in pursuit, and continued the search on shore, assisted by the Police, until A.M. of the 22d inst., but the search was unavailing.[50]

In a November 23 letter to Secretary Welles, Rear Admiral Theodorus Bailey (the new commandant of the Yard since September) summarized the incident, adding:

> I request ... that the Dept. will give instructions to the District

Attorney of the U.S.—to prosecute the same, that an example may be made of the offenders and his principals, for a violation of the "Act to Provide a more efficient discipline for the Navy[,] Section 71, Approved March 2d, 1855."[51]

The persistent cases of desertion, the lax procedures for sailors leaving their ships for shore, and the overall vulnerability of the Navy Yards added to the concern at the Navy Department. Welles ordered security tightened even further. In the late fall of 1864, when an officer of a ship at the Brooklyn Navy Yard was severely reprimanded for allowing an enlisted man to remain on shore for a longer time than naval law or custom allowed, the Navy Department took action. Its new shore-leave regulation in early December held each Union ship commander accountable in writing for the whereabouts of his crew, "before absenting himself from his command."[52]

On December 5, Secretary Welles issued an order directing "that no small boats or skiffs can land at the [Portsmouth] Navy Yard on and after 15th inst." On December 13, the *Chronicle* speculated, "This is evidently ... to lessen the number of avenues leading from the Yard, that thieves can more readily be detected." Three days later, the *Chronicle* reported that it was "rumored—only rumored, mind ye,—that the cause of the recent order ... was the detection of several workmen leaving in their boats, before quitting time. Another report has it, that the order originated at Washington, on account of the pilfering discovered at the Philadelphia Yard, and elsewhere."[53]

The *Chronicle* asserted that the order was impractical and inconvenient but hoped "at the same time the interests of the Government be secured." When the deadline of December 15 arrived, the date was extended to give the workmen another week to make the necessary arrangements to comply with the order. After December 26, no boats except those belonging to the Yard were allowed to land. The government provided a landing place at Kittery Foreside, furnishing floating stages and other necessary facilities, as well as evidently paying $150 a year in rent for the docking site. "The new regulation," observed the *Chronicle*, "obliges the workmen to start for the Yard about ten minutes earlier than formerly, and delays their embarkation for this city about the same length of time at night."[54]

These new Navy Department regulations proved successful. Desertion, pilfering, and other security problems at the Yard were virtually eliminated for the rest of the war.

A petty officer and helmsman in the French navy, marine painter Chéri Dubreuil (fl. 1860-1870s), eight years after the famed sea battle off Cherbourg, France, finished his oil painting USS Kearsarge and CSS Alabama in 1872. It has proven to be the most perennially popular Civil War naval scene among American and foreign artists alike— a favorite subject for more than 130 years. Dubreuil's canvas depicts the burning Alabama (foreground) as she begins sinking under the barrage of fire from the guns of the Kearsarge (center), with the English yacht Deerhound and smaller French pilot boats hovering in the background prior to picking up survivors. PEM

William Gurdon Saltonstall (1831-89), a Salem, Massachusetts, merchant at the outbreak of the Civil War, typifies the thousands of Northern civilians who volunteered their services—often at great personal and financial sacrifice—for the Union military effort. In 1862, he commanded the USS Philadelphia, carrying dispatches to other federal ships, before and during the CSS Virginia-USS Monitor battle in Hampton Roads. Resigning his commission in September 1865 with the rank of lieutenant-commander—the highest grade attainable for volunteer naval officers—Saltonstall returned to the world of commerce. Photograph by Phil Scalia, Courtesy Phillips Exeter Academy

(opposite page) Three paintings by Ensign John W. Grattan, assigned to the staff of Rear Admiral David D. Porter, present an eyewitness and sequential rendering of the second Battle of Fort Fisher, January 13-15, 1865. In the first image, the 62-vessel Union fleet bombards the Confederate fortifications. The second portrays the storming of the fort by a 10,000-man Union force, as the fleet stands offshore. The last picture reveals the scene of death and destruction inside the fort after its capture. NHC

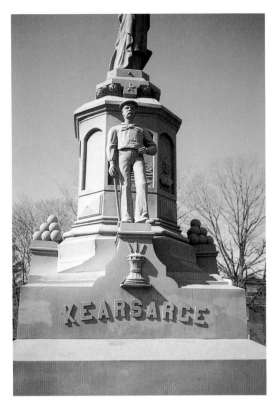

A vigilant USS Kearsarge *crew member surveys the horizon from the side of Portsmouth's Soldiers and Sailors Monument. Located in Goodwin Park on Islington Street, the monument was financed in part by Frank Jones and dedicated in 1888. Author's photo.*

Located in Portsmouth's Harmony Grove cemetery and immediately adjacent to his original gravestone, a Medal of Honor monument commemorates the heroism of carpenter's mate Mark G. Ham, one of the 17 USS Kearsarge *crew members who received this coveted award for their actions in the 1864 sea battle against the CSS* Alabama. *Author's photo.*

Catastrophes to Portsmouth Shipping

During 1864, the number of Portsmouth merchant marine vessels either shipwrecked or destroyed by natural disasters rose sharply. More men were killed as a result of accidents or murders than at the Yard or on Portsmouth-built Union naval vessels in sea battles. Sale or transfer of Portsmouth vessels to foreign registry became rampant.

Bad news arrived from the Indian port of Calcutta. On February 10, 1864, almost two months after the event, Portsmouth learned the fate of one of her most respected ship captains. As the *Chronicle* reported, "Capt. John Hanscom, of the *James Guthrie* of Portsmouth, now at Calcutta, suddenly disappeared on the 18th of December; on the afternoon of the 21st the mate of the ship sent a man down in a little cuddy, under the cabin, for something, when the body of Capt. Hanscom was found with the throat cut from ear to ear." Hanscom's murder was never solved.[55]

Another disaster at Calcutta followed. William Nowell of Portsmouth, the first officer of the ship *Eastern Belle*, was an eyewitness to the October 5 hurricane that devastated Calcutta and the adjacent countryside. Nowell wrote:

> Wrecks strew both banks of the river, as far as the eye can reach..... The *Eastern Belle* is piled up on the banks of the river, with most of her yards and masts gone, and her hull damaged.... I do not doubt that there are upwards of an hundred ships which will prove a total loss.... There were as many vessels destroyed in a few hours by this unexampled hurricane, as the *Alabama* burnt in her whole piratical career, and most of them are English property. I am seriously inclined to deem it a judgement upon them for ungraciously allowing the *Alabama* to slip through their fingers.[56]

Portsmouth shipping men also faced "war-risk" insurance rates. In 1861, before the start of the war, the rate ranged from one-half of one percent of the value of the cargo from the Atlantic Coast, Europe, the West Indies, South America, or the Pacific to 1 1/2 percent for the East Indies. By 1863, due to the successes of the *Alabama* and other Confederate raiders, the American insurance rates had soared to four percent along the Atlantic Coast, three percent for either Europe or the West Indies, and a whopping 7 1/2 percent for the East

Rates of Dockage and Wharfage,

ESTABLISHED BY THE PROPRIETORS, AGENTS AND LESSEES OF WHARVES

FOR THE CITY OF PORTSMOUTH, N. H.

DOCKAGE.

VESSELS of 50 tons and under, 20 cents per day. | VESSELS of 100 to 150 tons, - 40 cents per day.
"   " 50 to 100 tons, - 30 cts. "   "   " 150 to 200 " - 50 cts. "

and 10 cents additional for every additional 50 tons.

WHARFAGE.

	Cents.			Cents.			Cents.	
Anchors and Chains, -	20	per ton.	Chaise, -	20	each.	Shooks, with heading, -	1 1-2	each.
Anvils, - - -	2	each.	Carts, Wagons and Sleighs,	15	"	Timber, -	18	per ton.
Bales of Merchandise, -	6	"	Cart Wheels, -	5	per pair.	Treenails, -	18	per 1000
" " Domestic Goods,	3	"	Chalk, -	15	per ton.	Handspikes, -	15	per 100.
" " Cotton, - -	3	"	Duck, - -	1	per bolt.	Ship Knees, -	1-3	pr inch.
" " Wool, - - -	6	"	Demijohns, -	1-4	pr gal.	Pickets, -	4	per 1000.
" " Hops, - -	5	"	Dye Woods, -	20	per ton.	Mahogany, 20c. per ton of 480 ft.		
" " Feathers, -	4	"	Drums Fish, -	5	each.	Marble, 20c. per ton, measurement.		
" " Rags, 5 each or	15	per ton.	" Figs and Raisins,	1-2	"	Nest Casks, -	6	each.
" " Tobacco, -	1	each.	Dates, -	1	per frail.	" Tubs, -	1 1-2	"
" " Horse & Cow Hides,	12	"	Empty Hogsheads, -	3	each.	" Boxes, -	2	per doz.
" " Leather, -	6	"	Empty Barrels, -	1	"	" Buckets, -	4	" "
" " Moss, - -	3	"	Fish, -	1c	per quintal.	Onions, 3c. per 100 bunches.		
Boxes of Merchandise, -	6	"	Firkins, -	1	each.	Oxen and Cows, -	8	each.
" " Lemons & Oranges,	1	"	Furniture, 12c. per ton, measurement.			Oil, 20c. per ton of 252 galls.		
" " Liquors, -	1	"	Grain, of all kinds, -	1-2	per bush.	Oil Cakes, -	15	per ton.
" " Chocolate, -	1	"	Shorts and Bran, -	1-4	per "	Pipes, -	8	each.
" " Soap and Candles,	1	"	Grindstones, -	20	per ton.	1-2 Pipes, -	4	"
" " Brimstone, -	2	"	Hogsheads, -	7	each.	1-4 " -	2	"
" " Raisins, - -	1	"	Hemp, - 20c per ton, 2240 lbs.			1-8 " -	1	"
" " Figs, - - -	1 1-2	"	Horns, -	6	per 1000.	Pails, -	2	per doz.
" " Herring, -	1-2	"	Hides, -	1-2	each.	Plaster, -	15	per ton.
" " Fish, -	1 1-2	"	Hollow Ware, -	15	per ton.	Plows, -	3	each.
" " Oil, -	1	"	Hay, -	20	" "	Paper, wrapping, -	3-4	per ream.
" " Window Glass,	1	"	Hocs, -	1 1-2	a doz.	" printing, -	3-4	" "
" " Cheese, -	1-2	"	Horses and Mules, -	8	each.	" sheathing, -	20	per ton.
" " Shoes, -	2	"	Iron and Steel, 15c. per ton, 2240 lbs.			Potatoes, -	1-2	per bushel.
" " Hats, -	3	"	Ice, -	6	per ton.	Rakes, -	2	per doz.
" " Cigars, - -	1	per 1000.	Jars of Grapes, Oil and Olives,	1-2	each.	Salt, -	3	" hhd.
" " Tin, -	1	each.	Jugs, -	1-4	pr gal.	" in sacks, -	2	each.
Bags Coffee, Sugar, Nuts, &c.	1 1-2	"	Kegs Butter, -	1	each.	" in bags of 25 lbs.,	1-4	each.
Bones, -	10	per ton.	" Lard, -	1-2	each.	Sugar, in boxes, -	4	per box.
Brooms, -	1	per doz.	" Tobacco, -	2	each.	" in baskets, mats & bags,	20	" ton.
Bundles Twine, -	1	each.	" White Lead, -	20	per ton.	Shot, -	20	" "
Bricks, -	25	per 1000.	Lead, -	15	" "	Slate, -	20	" "
Ballast, -	10	per ton.	Lime, (cask,) -	2	each.	Shovels, -	3	" doz.
Barrels, dry, -	1 1-2	each.	Linseed, -	1-2	bush.	Scythes, -	1 1-2	"
" wet, -	3	each.	Leather, (sides,) -	1-2	each.	Scythe Snaiths, -	1 1-2	"
Cambooses, -	8	"	LUMBER:			Stone for building, -	20	per ton.
Coal, 12c per ton, 2240 lbs.			Boards, -	18	pr 1000 ft	Stoves, -	2 to 4	each.
Cordage, -	15	per ton.	Clapboards, -	18	" " "	Tierces, -	5	"
Chairs, -	1-2	each.	Shingles, -	4	" " "	Tea, in chests, -	4	"
Crates, -	8	"	Oars, -	18	" " ft.	" in 1-2 " -	2	"
Casks Raisins, -	1	"	Hoops, -	25	" "	" in 1-4 " -	1	"
" Currants, -	1	"	Joist, -	18	" " ft.	" in 1-8 " -	1-2	each.
" Cheese, -	2	"	Laths, -	4	" "	Tobacco, in boxes,	1	"
Carboys Vitriol, -	2	"	Staves, -	20	" "	Wood and Bark, -	15	per cord.
Carriages, -	30	"	Shooks, -	1	each.			

PEM, Jan. 1, 1864

Indies. In 1864, the "war-risk" rates continued to rise; on May 4, the *Chronicle* reported that the Portsmouth ship *Sagamore*, sailing from England to New York, was paying an Atlantic war-risk rate of five percent.[57]

    Balking at the increasingly exorbitant war-risk rates, the Portsmouth shipowners decided one by one that it was time to abandon transatlantic trade. Resorting to the familiar tactic of selling their vessels to less-threatened foreign owners who enjoyed much lower insurance rates, New Hampshire shipping investors wisely opted for better times. In March 1864, it was reported that three Portsmouth ships were sold: the *Typhoon*, 1,611 tons, built at Portsmouth in 1851, sold in Singapore for $39,000; the *Albert Gallatin*, 849 tons, built in 1850, sold in London for £4,800; and the *Como*, built in 1858, sold in Singapore for £11,000 cash, "to go under the British flag." The trend continued. In June, the *Coronation*, launched in 1863, was sold in London. Finally, in October, another Portsmouth ship, the *Empire State*, 1,324 tons, completed in 1849 (but not coppered), was sold in London for £5,000.[58]

The Portsmouth "flight from the flag" reflected a national trend. By the end of the war, 1,613 vessels (about 774,000 tons) had been transferred from the American merchant marine fleet.[59]

Daniel Marcy's Many Losses

Daniel Marcy, a Northern merchant vessel owner hoping to win an almost Pyrrhic victory by retaining his holdings, was beset with severe losses. For him, 1864 meant one crushing blow after another.

As a representative in the Thirty-Eighth Congress, Marcy was anticipating his run for re-election on March 14, 1865. His congressional record was basically sound, for, according to the *Granite Monthly*, Marcy was opposed to "schemes...for plundering the public treasury and robbing the people." Marcy's continuing political liability, however, was his inability to shake off the Republican charge that he was a Copperhead.[60]

Moreover, the voting regulations were in the process of changing. From 1864 on, reforms authorized Union army officers and soldiers either to vote in the field or to return on furloughs to their home districts to cast their ballots in the various state, congressional, gubernatorial, and presidential elections. Union military men generally supported the Lincoln administration and the Republican party. Facing a tough re-election, President Lincoln openly solicited the so-called bayonet vote for himself and other Republican candidates. To ensure that soldiers on duty in the South would be able to reach home in time to cast their ballots, the Lincoln administration used United States army transport vessels to expedite their travel to the North.[61]

For Marcy and other Democratic politicians, this development did not bode well. Following the national pattern in the North, the

New Hampshire legislature enacted special laws to encourage this suffrage. While New Hampshire provided for her soldiers to vote, Granite State sailors inexplicably were forgotten and unprovided for in the 1864 election. Election day in New Hampshire was set for Tuesday, March 8, 1864, for the governorship and other state offices. In order to vote, Congressman Marcy decided to absent himself from his Washington duties and return to Portsmouth. Marcy's return was bitterly criticized on March 7 by the *Chronicle*, which declared "the leading newspapers of the copperheads have been full of articles denouncing the administration for permitting our soldier citizens to return and exercise their rights of suffrage."[62]

While many Granite State troops voted in the field, the Thirteenth New Hampshire Volunteers was one of the units that sent representative contingents home to vote. Great fanfare greeted the men. In authorizing the release of men from the front, Virginia Major George Bruce first obtained an order granting a furlough for twelve days, from General Benjamin F. Butler. "There was no attempt to distinguish between Republicans and Democrats," Bruce wrote. "In consequence of many threats, however, that in certain towns the soldiers would not be permitted to vote in case of their return, the order provided that the soldiers should wear side arms, and be considered as on special duty and under military orders, that is, officers were to take their swords and belts, and the men their bayonets and belts, which they were to wear on all occasions during their absence. Free transportation home and return was given to them."[63]

Lieutenant S. Millett Thompson of the Thirteenth New Hampshire, who accompanied his men home, noted in his diary on March 3: "Bullets and ballots are now to shoot at the same target—The Slaveholder's Rebellion. Voters, 390 officers and men of the Thirteenth and Tenth N.H. Vols. take cars [railroad passenger coaches] at 6 P.M.... [as] we start for New Hampshire." On March 4, he noted, "At 7 a.m. embark on the steamer *Guide*."[64]

The United States transport steamers carrying the New Hampshire soldier-voters were bound for Boston. In late February, the *Admiral Dupont* was the first to arrive, disembarking 450 men from various New Hampshire units. After being quartered at Boston's Beach Street barracks until Sunday, February 28, the troops took the railroad to Concord, New Hampshire. Plagued with stormy weather and fog, together with the soldiers' suspicion that the transport steamer captain was a Democrat, the *Guide* finally docked at Boston on March 7, the day before the New Hampshire state election. Describing the tight schedule, Lieutenant Thompson's diary entry for March 8 reads: "All go north on this morning's trains. Those who go via the Boston & Maine Railroad, strike a washout at New Market [Newmarket, New Hampshire], and are further delayed there."[65]

Only about two-thirds of the soldiers aboard the delayed train ever arrived home in time to vote. Citing the example of one Portsmouth-stationed soldier who managed to overcome the rail-transportation breakdown, the *Chronicle* reported: "Josiah B. Kinerson, a private in the First Company of Heavy Artillery, at Fort Constitution, was afraid that he should not reach Manchester in season to vote, trains being irregular on account of the washing away of the road; he accordingly footed it ten miles, run [ran?] a hand car eight, rode six, and after a walk of five miles reached Manchester and added his vote to the fifty six hundred majority for [re-elected Republican Governor] Joseph Gilmore."[66]

Thus the "bayonet vote," going heavily Republican for Gilmore, arose as a significantly crucial factor both in New Hampshire and in national elections throughout the rest of the Civil War. Such circumstances undoubtedly weighed heavily in Democrat Daniel Marcy's mind as he anticipated his congressional re-election bid in the next New Hampshire state election, scheduled for mid-March of 1865.

Other news in 1864 proved even more distressing for Daniel Marcy. As noted earlier, his nephew, William H. Marcy, had joined the Confederate army in 1863. On April 8, 1864, at the Battle of Sabine Cross Roads (or the Battle of Mansfield) in northwestern Louisiana, young Marcy was engaged in combat. Leading up to this clash, Union Major General Nathan P. Banks, in conducting his Red River Campaign, sought to capture Shreveport, headquarters of the Confederate Trans-Mississippi Department. About fifty miles south of this strategically vital city, Confederate Major General Richard Taylor made a stand that blunted Banks's drive and compelled the retreat of the Union army. Among the Confederate dead on the battlefield was Private William H. Marcy, Company A, Crescent Regiment, Louisiana, at the age of nineteen.[67]

In a bitter letter dated August 20, 1864, from New Orleans, Peter Marcy vented his anger to his brother Daniel:

I [k]new that you & Siss and all the family would [have] sworn and weep when you Heard of the death of our Dear and most

Beloved Son. But none Can feel his loss Like his parents. he had few faults and Many vertious [virtues?] and the only consolation which his Sorrowing parents and bereaved Realitions [Relations] have is that he died as a Soldier Should which [is] to die on the field of battle In full view of a great and Glorious victory, without a Stain or a blemish on his Character. Praised by all for his Personal Courage. I take it for granted that to fight and to die in the Service of one['s] Country is the highest attributess [attribute] of Chival[r]y, Courage & Patriotism and Such was the death of our Son William. the regiment To which he was attached was Selected by B[ri]g. G[eneral Richard] Taylor to Capture the Celebrated Sims battery. although Entirely successfull it cost them Dear[ly] In the Loss of So Many brave young men But old Soldiers. the regiment was Small and all young men[,] many from this City[,] fifty Killed and 155 wounded[,] many of them mortal[l]y, whom have died Since. All or overly So where [were?] Born Citizens of This State—all or nearly so of those Soldiers where [were?] Killed by the bullets of hired mercenries—of all Countries Mostly of dutch [should be German] and Irish, who Received from $300 to $1000 Bounty to Come her[e] and Kill the Citizens of this State—not one of which Ever Injured them in the Least—I Call It whole Sale murder and all those who participate with them neither Democrats or fannatich [fanatics] I mean all those who vote [the] means to lay on this Cursed war w[h]ether Democrat or fannatich [fanatic,] Republican or Copperheads[,] all are Equally Guilty of the Same Crime. his remains where [were] decently Intered In the Cemetery at Mansfield two miles from where the Battle Was fought. I have and [an] old acquaintance residing There who has his Effects who promises to take Good Care of them and to Send them to us the First Opportunity[.] these will Be highly prized as mementoes of the lost one.[68]

A month after receiving this tragic family news, Daniel Marcy learned in late September 1864 of the loss of his ship *Frank Pierce*. During the Civil War, the *Frank Pierce*, one of the mainstays in Marcy's fleet, had successfully eluded Confederate raiders for more than three years. She was commanded by Captain John C. Bush, one of Portsmouth's most respected ship captains.[69]

On June 13, 1864, from Port Stanley, Falkland Islands, Captain Bush reported to Supply Clapp, Marcy's business partner: "It is my painful duty to inform you, that the *Frank Pierce* is a total loss & that we arrived here [Port Stanley, Falkland Islands, in the southern Atlantic] today in the Bark *Charles Lambert*, of Sunderland[,] Eng[land], who took us off the wreck on the 7th inst [of June].... It is an unfortunate affair altogether[.][70]

The Rockingham *and the CSS* Alabama

The seizures of Confederate raiders from (in the *Chronicle*'s words) "Jeff. Davis' Bureau of Piracy (or in rebel parlance) 'Navy Department,'" continued to take their toll. The deliberate destruction of the Portsmouth merchant ship *Rockingham* by the CSS *Alabama* brought to New Hampshire citizens anger, indignation, and a desire for vengeance. In the spring of 1864, the CSS *Alabama* was cruising in the Atlantic when Captain Raphael Semmes and his crew chanced upon the *Rockingham*. A seven-year-old vessel of superior construction, the *Rockingham* was flying the Stars and Stripes and carrying a cargo bound for a neutral nation. Semmes showed little concern for the niceties of international maritime law. The *Chronicle* on June 22, 1864, expressed its outrage:

> The ship *Rockingham*, from Callao [Peru] for Queenstown, England [now Cobh, Ireland], was burned by the *Alabama*, April 23, in lat. 15° south, lon. 32° west. The *Alabama* was spoken the following day by a vessel [the *Kent* from Melbourne, Australia] which has arrived at London. The *Rockingham* was commanded by Capt. [Edwin A.] Gerrish, and was on the voyage from Callao for England with a cargo of guano, having sailed from the former port on the 24th of February last. This is the second instance among the various captures by the rebel pirates in which a cargo of Peruvian guano has been destroyed. The pirates heretofore have us[u]ally bonded vessels having cargoes from the Peruvian guano islands, on the ground that the cargo was owned by foreign parties. It is likely that Jeff. Davis has latterly sent more stringent orders to his sea robbers.[71]

Captain Gerrish supplied details of his vessel's demise: "There were twenty-four souls on board, including a lady and a child and a nursemaid; all were transferred on board the steamer [*Alabama*]. As soon as the ship was deserted, [they] made a target of her, both ships being hove to, at 500 yards distance. They fired twenty-four shots, four of which hit the hull and three in the rigging.... After this they went on board and set her on fire." Gerrish also lost the first mate of the *Rockingham*, a Georgian from Savannah who, transferring his allegiance, became a volunteer aboard the *Alabama*.[72]

The *Rockingham* was the next-to-last prize of the *Alabama*. Four days later, on April 24, Semmes spotted the American bark *Tycoon*, bound for San Francisco from New York. He and his men promptly plundered and burned the *Tycoon*. To defend his policy of destruction, Semmes wrote an essay, "The Reasons Why Confederate Cruisers Burn their Prizes, and the Remedy," together with a cover letter, datelined "Confederate States' Steamer *Alabama*, on the High Seas, April, 1864," for submission to the "Editor of the [London] *Times*." Offering a lengthy justification for his policy, Semmes requested publication of his defense "as a reply to the numerous assaults upon me by the English press—not excepting an occasional 'rumble' from yourselves [the London *Times*]—on the subject of my destroying prizes at sea without adjudication by a Prize Court. The London *Evening Star* and kindred negrophilist associates have been particularly virulent and abusive. The term 'pirate' is a favourite epithet with them." On June 16, the *Times* editor printed Semmes's article along with the editor's rebuttal.[73]

After twenty-two months at sea, with only occasional brief stops at friendly ports, the *Alabama* was badly in need of repairs and overhaul. During her spectacular career, she had sunk the U.S. gunboat *Hatteras*, had captured and burned at least fifty-five Union merchant ships (valued at $4.5 million), and had bonded ten others with a value of more than $500,000. On June 11, the Confederate raider landed at Cherbourg, France, and, in the *Chronicle*'s words, was "admitted to free pratique [clearance given to an incoming ship by a health authority of a port], and landed 40 prisoners, the crews of two Federal vessels [*Rockingham* and *Tycoon*].... The *Alabama* was permitted to make extensive repairs at Cherbourg." A few days later, a French steamer transported thirty-seven of the released *Rockingham* and *Tycoon* crew members to Le Havre.[74]

The USS Kearsarge *vs. the CSS* Alabama

Rockingham Captain Edwin A. Gerrish, who had stayed behind at Cherbourg, conveyed crucial intelligence to Edouard Liais, the United States vice-consul there. Gerrish and the *Tycoon*'s captain detailed the *Alabama*'s alterations and overall condition. On the day the *Alabama* reached Cherbourg, Liais quickly telegraphed William L. Dayton, the American minister to France, in Paris. Dayton immediately telegraphed Captain John A. Winslow of the USS *Kearsarge*, then anchored in the Scheldt (or Schelde) River, off Flushing (Vlissingen), Holland, about 300 miles north of Cherbourg.[75]

Until Winslow received this message, the record of the *Kearsarge* during the first half of 1864 had been almost negligible. An embarrassing accident, however, had kept the vessel in the news. On April 17, 1864, while entering the port of Ostend, Belgium, with two local pilots aboard, the *Kearsarge* rammed a fishing boat and careened into a bridge before grounding. The *Kearsarge*, however, sustained no damage in the accident, and the careless pilot was dismissed by Belgian authorities for incompetence. The *Kearsarge*'s crew quickly refloated the beached vessel.[76]

Less than two months later, Minister Dayton's telegram to Flushing, Holland, jolted the *Kearsarge* into action. On Sunday afternoon, June 12, a gun was fired from the *Kearsarge* as a signal for the crew ashore to return to the ship. Captain Winslow then mustered all hands on the quarterdeck to relay the news. "The information was received with three rousing cheers from the crew," wrote First Assistant Engineer William H. Badlam, "and the men[']s eyes glistened with excitement.... They were all eager for the fray." Once the *Kearsarge* was underway, the crew spent every spare minute sharpening swords and cutlasses, keeping the grindstones in constant use. On June 14, the *Kearsarge* steamed through the eastern entrance of Cherbourg Harbor. Captain Winslow and his men could clearly see the *Alabama* at anchor in the distance. Proceeding out through the western passage, the *Kearsarge* moved out beyond the breakwater into international waters, three miles offshore, keeping a sharp lookout for the *Alabama*.[77]

As the *Kearsarge* waited offshore for the battle she had sought for more than two years, the *Alabama* rushed her repairs in a Cherbourg yard.

During their week-long vigil, the men of the *Kearsarge* constantly watched for steamers by day and for signal rockets by night. On June 18, Marine Corporal Austin H.F. Quinby noted in his diary, "The [Cherbourg Harbor] Pilot says he [Semmes] is coming out tomorrow and [will] give us battle[;] we are all ready. [T]here will not be much sleep tonight.... at 11 P.M. all quiet with double lookouts stationed about the ship[.]"[78]

On Sunday, June 19, 1864, the suspense ended. Coalheaver Charles A. Poole wrote in his diary:

> When I was called this morning [I] found the weather fine, with a slight breeze from the Eastward[.] Inspection at quarters as usual[;] we were standing in towards the Land when the Lookout sang out that a Steamer was coming out, and I believe it is the *Alabama*. It was soon made out to be her. we immediate[ly] Beat the drum all hands to quarters and in two minutes every man was at his station ready for action[.] Getting a full head of Steam we steamed off shore, having the appearance of Running away from the *Alabama*. when seven miles from the shore went about and steamed direct for her with a slight sheer to prevent her from Raking us. The order was passed to sand the Decks. This is to prevent the men from slip[p]ing when there is blood on the Decks. I am stationed at the Midships, Shell Room and the armory near the Dispensary of Medicine and the Doctors Station[.] The officers took an affectionate leave of each other and every one was ready to meet the enemy and his Doom if it was to be[.]
>
> The *Alabama* was accompanied by a French Iron Clad [*Couronne*] who came out to see her out of neutral waters. Three Miles from the Land when at that distance she [the *Couronne*] went about and returned to the harbor.[79]

In his letter of June 24, considered by the *Boston Traveller* as "the best account we have seen," an unnamed *Kearsarge* officer noted:

> The *Alabama* came down upon us at full speed until within a distance of about three quarters of a mile, when she opened her guns upon us. We did not reply for several minutes, but ranged up nearer, and then opened our starboard battery, fighting six guns, and leaving only one 32-pounder idle. The *Alabama* fought seven guns, working them with the greatest

The Civil War naval career of Captain John Ancrum Winslow (shown here as a rear admiral) was relatively obscure and uneventful until 1864, when, as the commanding officer of the USS Kearsarge, *he and his men sank the CSS* Alabama. *This episode thrust Winslow into the international lime-light and has secured his place in American naval history. Winslow's tenure as Portsmouth Navy Yard commandant during 1869 and 1870 prompted the naming of a Yard street in his honor. PNSVC*

rapidity, sending shot and shell in a constant stream over our heads. Both vessels used their starboard batteries, the ships being manoeuvered in a circle about each other at a distance of from five hundred to one thousand yards. Witnesses on [the French] shore say that we made seven complete circles during the action, which lasted a little over one hour [from 10:57 a.m. to 12:24 p.m.].

Our shot, particularly the 11-inch shells, made fearful havoc among the enemy. The first one killed three men and wounded nearly the whole gun's crew where it exploded. Finally, we placed a shot in the rudder-port of the *Alabama*, disabling to some extent her steer-apparatus. Almost at the same time another of our shots entered her coal bunker, abreast of her engine, forcing the bunker inboard, and showering the machinery with coal, which prevented her from making progress for a short time, when she set her sails to the breeze and tried to run in toward the French shore.

We were on the watch, and by a rapid movement headed her off, and got into fighting position on her port or weak side, a very successful and decisive manoeuvre. On that side she had but one gun, and we gave our broadside into her with the greatest precision, doing fearful damage to her hull. We shot away her flag, but in a few minutes it was run up again at her mizen truck. A short time longer we kept [up] our cannonade, when she hauled down her flag, and we ceased firing.

In a few minutes she gave us, very unexpectedly, a couple of shots more, and again we opened our batteries upon her. This however continued but a very short time, for she soon showed a white flag, in token of surrender, and sent a boat on board of us to ask for assistance in saving the wounded, as she was in a sinking condition. We immediately launched two boats, the other two having been riddled by shot, and sent for the wounded, but before the boats got alongside the once formidable *Alabama* settled by the stern, thrust her bow far out of the water, and then disappeared beneath the waves, carrying down no one will ever know how many of the poor victims.

Previously to this, after the firing had ceased, and it was evident that the *Alabama* was sinking, an English steam-yacht [the *Deerhound*], which had been observing the fight at a distance, came up alongside of us, and asked permission to assist in picking up the wounded. Of course it was granted, as an act of humanity, but by so doing we were robbed of half the fruits of our hard earned contest; for the yacht moved up ahead of us, lowered her boat, picked up Semmes and several of his officers and crew, and then stood away with all haste for the English coast. Then we saw through the ruse that Semmes had no doubt planned beforehand for his escape in case of his defeat, but we could not follow and leave the poor unfortunates still in the water, so we remained by them until all were picked up. Thereafter we steamed into this port [Cherbourg] and came to anchor.

We had picked up in our boats sixty-five of her crew and firemen, and five officers living and one dead. Of the men fifteen were seriously wounded, two dying on board of us. We had only three men severely wounded. As soon as we came into Cherbourg the wounded were all sent to the hospital, as our accom[m]odations on board were not so convenient for their proper treatment. We paroled all the other prisoners except the officers, for we were unable to keep so many on board, or send them to the States.

According to the account of the master of the British steam-yacht (*Deerhound*) she landed forty at Southampton. Probably this is exaggerated. But taking it as true, and adding those we picked up, and nine which a French pilot boat rescued, there are about 120 accounted for, leaving over 30 who inevitably went down with her when she sunk. The officers of the *Alabama* say they numbered on board about 150 all told, but they give no account of those who joined her after she arrived here at Cherbourg. The number of these will never be known, but several of the most experienced gunners of the English naval reserve went on board the night before the action on purpose to point the guns. They were old, practiced seamen, who had seen service in the English navy, and were supposed to be able to sink the *Kearsarge* or disable her guns in half an hour. Semmes promised them that before noon they should be on board of us....

Our commander, Capt. Winslow, after the action was over, and during the afternoon, had all hands mustered on the quarter-deck, and there was offered solemn prayers and thanksgiving to God, who had given us so signal a victory.[80]

Devoting six pages to the events on June 19, Austin Quinby's diary concludes with his own interpretation:

When the *Alabama* raised her head out of the water for her final plunge to the depths below the Captain [Winslow]

ordered no cheers to be given as it would do no good to cheer
over a fal[l]en foe[,] so none was given[,] but I presume that if
the victory had been on the other side you could have he[a]rd
the cheers all over England and the south. The Sinking of the
Alabama was as much or more a victory over the English than
the south, for she was an English built Regular Man of War
Armed with the most improved English guns Manned by Men
from the Naval Reserve[;] only about 20 Men on bo[a]rd
belonged to the U. States[;] then the yacht *Deerhound*
bro[ugh]t seven of their best gunners, called the Crack gunners
of the English Navy, but they found their match as they always
have for the past one hundred years or so since 1776[.]

The English were very bitter against the North and
were praying that the *Alabama* might win but they found the
Yankees were enough for them even to this day[.] The destruction of the *Alabama* will ever be handed down in history as the
greatest battle of Modern times and I may say of Ancient
times[;] it was the first deep sea fight between steam vessels
that is on record....

The land around and back of Cherbourg is very high
and the H[e]ights were literally covered.... [A]bout the whole
city [was] there to see a genuine Naval Battle[.] There were
two large excursion trains [which] came down from Parris [*sic*]
this morning to witness the fight when we came to anchor in
the harbor. You could see [them] returning to the city like a big
army[.] All the Prisoners were paroled and the wounded sent
on shore to the Hospittle where they were made as comfortable
as French skill could do[;] our three men and the *Alabama* men
were all in the same ward. A large fleet of boats are around us
to gaze at the Black Cruiser of the Isle [the *Kearsarge*:] the
American Consul [Edouard Liais] and the Minister Dayton['s]
son [William Lewis Dayton, Jr.] came on bo[a]rd to congratu-
late Captain Winslow and Crew for the great Victory over the
Pirate *Alabama*[;] Minister Dayton[']s son won 10[,]000 Franks
[francs] on the fight[;] his Father Telegraphed him to take all
the bets he could get. Every one is happy tonight and the sole
topic is about the fight, decks swept down and one would not
know but what we had just come in from a short cruise. [S]o
ends the memoriable [*sic*] 19th day of June A.D. 1864
Cherbourg France[.][81]

Undoubtedly the most elated eyewitness to the epic sea battle was Captain Edwin A. Gerrish of the *Rockingham*, the last vessel burned by the *Alabama*. As the *Journal* recalled years later (November 6, 1897), "Capt. Gerrish offered to fight on the *Kearsarge*, but as this was against the rules of the navy he had to content himself in standing on a [Cherbourg] hill to watch the action... which ended the career of the *Alabama*.[82]

In his four-page letter of June 19, sent to his uncle back in his home village of Newington, New Hampshire, *Kearsarge* landsman Martin V. Hoyt exulted: "As I watched the end of her [*Alabama*'s] flying jib-boom sink beneath the waters, I think it was the proudest moment of my life.... When we go to England now, we can tell them if they choose to build any more ships for the Confederates that we will serve them in the same way by sinking them to rise no more."[83]

The Kearsarge *Legend*

The *Alabama-Kearsarge* sea battle instantly captured the attention of the civilized world. For days and weeks after the event, Northern, Southern, English, and French journalists devoted many columns to the fight. Politicians discussed its ramifications in the British House of Lords. Writers and artists rushed to depict the action. Diplomats and businessmen exploited its international repercussions. Naval experts assessed the relative merits of both ships. For the North, the *Kearsarge*'s victory came at exactly the right time to offset the sagging Union army fortunes in northern Virginia.

On July 5, the steamship *City of Baltimore*, having left Liverpool on June 22, arrived in New York, bringing the news of the sea battle fought two weeks earlier. Northern exuberance was instantaneous. On July 6, the *Chronicle* exclaimed: "THE PIRATE *ALABAMA* was sunk... after a fair open-sea fight.... The pirates took to their boats, and Semmes with 40 of his men was picked up by an English vessel which ran away with them—another example of John Bull's ardent love of fair play."[84]

In the 130 years since the event, evaluations and opinions about the sea battle have been numerous. An early assessment, in the form of a telegram received in Liverpool just after the battle, was voiced by an unidentified *Alabama* officer saved by the *Deerhound*. The survivor observed, "The *Alabama* was in first-rate trim. We have been deceived in the *Kearsarge*. Work hot and heavy, but weight of the damned metal of *Kearsarge* too much. Her shots went slap through below water line. Hell could not stand it. Yankee far too fast for Semmes, who held his men too cheap." In "THE LAST OF THE *ALABAMA*," the London *Saturday Review* on June 25 stressed the far-reaching value of the Union Navy Yards, declaring, "If the *Kearsarge* had been lost, the Federal dockyards could have supplied as many ships as powerful; while the Confederacy... had but one *Alabama*."[85]

Two of the most direct American comments, representing both Union and Confederate viewpoints, were penned shortly after the event. Writing in his diary on July 6, Secretary of the Treasury Salmon P. Chase grasped its effect on the North's standing abroad: "[News has arrived of] the glorious victory of the *Kearsarge* in combat with the *Alabama*, which came ought [out] to fight and went to the bottom. All looked well. The last event particularly [is] worth millions in the improvement of our prestige and credit in Europe."[86]

In a July 25 diary entry, Mary Boykin Chesnut recorded the Southern reaction: "Semmes, of whom we have been so proud—he is a fool after all—risked the *Alabama* in a sort of duel of ships! He has lowered the flag of the famous *Alabama* to the *Kearsarge*. Forgive who may! I cannot."[87]

The naval career of Captain Semmes was effectively over. Although English press reaction to Semmes was generally sympathetic, that still could not restore his former luster. On June 23, the *Illustrated London News* published Semmes's report to John Mason, the Confederate agent in England, blaming Captain Winslow for firing "upon me five times after my colours were struck. It is charitable to suppose that a ship of war of a Christian nation could not have done this intentionally." Notwithstanding his self-serving and fallacious explanation, Captain Semmes never again commanded a Confederate warship. Had Semmes been captured, the North certainly would have pressed for his trial, perhaps even his execution, on charges of piracy.

With the sinking of the CSS *Alabama*, the Union breathed more easily, despite the Confederate warships *Tallahassee*, *Shenandoah*, and *Stonewall* still patrolling the high seas during the final months of the war. With the *Alabama*'s demise, the symbol of Confederate naval power lay at the bottom of the English Channel.[88]

Captain Winslow and the officers and crew of the *Kearsarge* overnight became heroes in the North, basking in a fame that increased with time. Winslow and the *Kearsarge* never sank or captured another Confederate ship, but to the adoring Northern public, their exploits on June 19 were sufficient and enduring proof of Union naval power and superiority.

The exhilaration of the officers and men aboard the *Kearsarge* in their place in naval history was captured in *Kearsarge* Marine Corporal Austin Quinby's diary entry of June 20:

> Morning pleasant[.] The old Ro[u]tine of Duty[.] Washed decks and everything in its place[.] If a stranger had come in bored [on board] he would not have suspected that we had been in one of the greatest battles on record[.] The French Admiral said that he had been through the Crimean war and all the French wars for 50 years and had seen a good many battl[e]s but he had never seen one to equal it[.]... the Harbor is black with boats filled with people to have a look at the *Kearsarge*[.] [P]lenty of visitors on bored.[89]

French visitors thronged to inspect the *Kearsarge*. The *Journal* in 1867 revealed that these were not merely curiosity seekers:

> Some days after the sinking of the *Alabama*, when the *Kearsarge* was in port at Cherbourg, Commandant Winslow being absent in Paris, the charge of the vessel was with Lieut[.] Commander [James S.] Thornton. While below at dinner, he was informed that some visiters [*sic*] on deck wished to see him. He sent an invitation for them to meet him in the cabin. They declined, wishing to see him on deck. He ascended and found several officers who from their dress he soon discovered were of the highest rank in the French navy. They apologized for their intrusion, saying they had some curiosity to see the vessel which came so well out of the fight, and asked the privilege of examining her. This was readily granted, and they made a scrutinizing examination, particularly of her armament. They asked many questions, the answers to which were translated to one who appeared to be an engeneer [engineer] or their secretary, who was in citizens' dress, and took notes of what was seen. After staying sometime on deck, Capt. Thornton invited them below. The hat of the citizen coming in contact with a beam was suddenly knocked off, and the unmistakable countenance of the Emperor of France [Napoleon III]

was recognized at once by Capt. Thornton! Napoleon finding himself discovered, now freely talked in English, satisfying his curiosity by his personal inquiries, and obtaining with his Navy Board, such knowledge of the prowess of our ship, that in a few weeks several of the ships in the French Navy had their old armaments removed, to be supplied by such guns as were found on board the *Kearsarge*.[90]

Despite rumors that Semmes would soon obtain another ship, French enthusiasm for supplying war vessels or port facilities, or even recognizing the Confederacy, waned rapidly in the aftermath of the sea battle they had viewed for themselves from the Cherbourg heights. Portsmouth newspapers followed these shifts in French policy closely. "A letter in the *Paris Patrie*," reported the *Chronicle* on July 8, "states that Semmes has announced that on the 15th of August he will again embark on a new *Alabama*, which will then be completed. The seamen of the old *Alabama* will continue to receive the pay and form part of the new cruiser. Rumor points to the steamer *Rappahannock*, the ex-British war-vessel which stole away from Sheerness [England] to Calais, as likely to be Semmes' next vessel." That story proved fictitious. "The *Rappahannock*," noted the *Chronicle* on July 21, "is under strict surveillance at Calais, and not permitted to leave." Fading Confederate hopes turned in vain toward acquisition of a French-built ship. "The steamer *Yeddo*, built at Bordeaux, supposed for the rebels," noted the *Chronicle* in the same issue, "has been purchased by Prussia, and is now fitting out for service at Bremerhaven." On August 6, the *Journal* concluded the matter. "All speculations about the iron clad *Yeddo*, that it was feared was designed for the rebels, have been put to rest, the vessel having been quietly sold to the Prussians. It is a question whether Semmes or his accomplice [John] Kell [executive officer of the *Alabama*], get another ship. Semmes it is said is sick and will spend the summer at some of the German watering places. He has had enough of Cherbourg as a *watering* place."[91]

In Washington, President Lincoln and Secretary Welles publicized and rewarded the *Kearsarge*'s victory. On July 6, Welles wrote to Winslow: "The President has signified his intentions... to recommend that ... you may be advanced to the grade of commodore. Lieutenant Commander James S. Thornton... will be recommended to the Senate for advancement ten numbers in grade, and you will report... the

Published by Ch* Magnus 12 Frankfort St.N.Y.

THE SINKING OF THE

PIRATE ALABAMA

By the U. S. Gunboat "Kearsarge," Captain WINSLOW, June 19th, 1864.

Written by SILAS S STEELE, Esq. *Tune: "Teddy the Tiler," or "Cannibal Islands."*

I sing the doom and dark career
Of the Rebel Pirate, made to steer
And plunder our ships, both far and near
    The terrible "*Alabama*!
She was built by "*neutral* Johnny Bull,"
Who threatened Yankee ears to pull,
Because they dealt in nigger wool ;
Tho' *cotton* filled his pockets full.
But when *Rebellion* showed its face
Brave Mr. Bull soon "*changed his base*,"
And on the *sly.* to his disgrace,
    Built the Rebels *Alabamas*!

CHORUS : Launch and arm upon the sly,
    Hit Uncle Sam, but do it shy,
    But you couldn't shut up his eye,
    For he sunk *your Alabama*!

She roved the Ocean fierce and free,
And changed her flag in every sea,
Upon our un-armed ships to prey,
    This valiant *Alabama*!
Our cruisers sought her round and round,
She dodged them like a dastard hound
Until her name was quite renowned,
As a witch-craft never to be found
But the bold *Kearsarge* got in her wake,
And kept her track without mistake,
Till in *Cherbourg* port, coiled like a snake
    She found the *Alabama*l

CHORUS : Rob and plunder night and day
    Scuttle or burn then skulk away
    But you've a *reckoning* yet to pay,
    My valiant *Alabama*!

Famed Captain *Semmes* was in a plight,
He found there was no chance for flight,
So he must either yield or fight,
    With his terrible *Alabama*!
So he piped up his piratic crew
Of French and English, fierce and true,
Says he "*we'll put the Kearsarge through*"

And sink her with all France to view.
But *Win slow*, famed for *win*-ning *fast*,
Soon nailed our Stars unto the mast
While his brave crew shouted, like a blast,
    Death or the *Alabama*!

CHORUS : Load away, fire away shot and shell,
    That's the tune brave tars to tell,
    Stand by—and let her rip, pell mell,
    Death or the *Alabama*!

Now larboard and starboard seven rounds
With our 32's and 100 pounds,
We shook the French who lined the ground
    To cheer the *Alabama*!
We struck her 'neath the water line,
And through her hull let in the brine,
Till through the smoke we saw a sign
That we had crippled her in the spine,
A shout resounded from our crew,
A *cock* upon our smoke stack flew,
And in his "cock-a-doodle-do—
Cried how are you Alabama."

CHORUS : Load away, fire away shot and shell, &c.

Another broadside made her "cave,"
She stood for France her wreck to save
When down she sunk into the wave,
    The used up Alabama.
We lowered boats to save the crew,
And could have nabbed the captain too,
But her tender "*Deer-hound*" hove in view
And *stole* our prisoners not a few.
But there's a reckoning yet to come,
We'll make these sympathizers hum,
Give them what Paddy gave the drum,
    As we did the "*Alabama*?"

CHORUS : Here's glory to our Navy true
    To *Winslow* and brave *Thornton* too
    And three cheers for the *Kearsarge* crew
    That sunk the *Alabama*!

PEM

names of any others of the officers and crew whose good conduct on the occasion entitles them to especial mention."[92]

Along with Winslow, Thornton became a popular hero, and Admiral David G. Farragut took a personal interest in Thornton. Writing from off Mobile Bay, Alabama, to his son on July 20, 1864, Farragut exclaimed, "The victory of the *Kearsarge* over the *Alabama* raised me up.... Winslow had my old First Lieutenant of the *Hartford*, Thornton, in the *Kearsarge*. He is as brave as a lion, and as cool as a parson." The *Chronicle* and the *Journal* quickly printed stories about Thornton, "a native of this State, and a descendant [grandson] of Hon. Matthew Thornton, one of the signers of the Declaration of Independence." Both papers published a doubtlessly erroneous story about Thornton that nevertheless nourished the growing *Kearsarge* legend and Thornton's new-found fame: "A month or so before the *Alabama* came out of the harbor of Cherbourg, James S. Thornton, the lieutenant commander of the *Kearsarge*, leaving that vessel on the watch at a near point, disguised himself in a French blouse and the general apparel of a French artisan, and succe[e]ded in getting admission on board the rebel vessel, and examining fully every part of her, taking notes of machinery, armament, &c." Thornton never denied the tale. On more solid ground was the recognition accorded to another New Hampshire son, the grandson of another Declaration of Independence signer, Josiah Bartlett. In one of his reports to the Navy Department, Winslow wrote, "I am happy to commend [*Kearsarge*] Acting Master's Mate Ezra Bartlett, in charge of the shell supply, for his coolness and efficiency." Sailor Bartlett was a native and resident of the village of Stratham, near Portsmouth.[93]

Captain Winslow's letter of June 25 to Welles, listing "the names of the men who... exhibited marked coolness and good conduct," contributed the most lasting legacy to Civil War naval history. Winslow listed seventeen men, all subsequently awarded the Congressional Medal of Honor. Considering that 1,520 such medals were awarded for Civil War service, the vast bulk going to the United States Army, with only 307 bestowed on the U.S. Navy, the *Kearsarge* earned a lion's share, perhaps a record, for a single engagement.

The seventeen men included Quartermaster William Smith, born in Ireland and a resident of Concord, New Hampshire. His citation reads, "Acting as captain of the 11-inch pivot gun of the second division, Smith carried out his duties courageously.... It is stated by rebel officers that this was more destructive and did more damage than any other gun of *Kearsarge*." Winslow also noted that "A reward was offered by Captain Semmes to silence his [William Smith's] gun." Another recipient of the medal was Joachim Pease, a seaman from Long Island, New York. A loader on the no. 2 gun, Pease was one of five of the 29,000 black men serving in the Union Navy during the Civil War who achieved this distinction. Mark G. Ham, a carpenter's mate from Portsmouth, also won this coveted honor.[94]

Along with official recognition, the *Kearsarge-Alabama* battle quickly became transformed into the cultural expression of nineteenth-century America, a phenomenon continuing to the present day. Frederick Milnes Edge, an English journalist, was the first to seize the opportunity. After interviewing the *Kearsarge*'s officers and the *Alabama*'s wounded survivors and paroled prisoners within days of the event, Edge produced a forty-eight-page pamphlet, *The Alabama and the Kearsarge*, published in London about a month after the battle. To ensure accuracy, Edge had sent his proof sheets to Captain Winslow for checking. Responding on July 13, Winslow informed Edge, "I can fully endorse the pamphlet as giving a fair, unvarnished statement of all the facts both prior and subsequent to the engagement." Shortly after publication of the London first edition, Edge's pamphlet was reprinted in New York for American readers.[95]

On August 18, 1864, the influential, widely circulated *Washington Intelligencer* reprinted Edge's pamphlet in full and appended an editorial, "Achievements of Our Navy." The article praised the performance of the *Kearsarge*, chiding in turn critics of Gideon Welles's "Rip Van Winkle's tubs," as they had dubbed the newly constructed vessels of the Navy Department. Welles himself included Edge's pamphlet reprinted in full in his "Report of the Secretary of the Navy" for 1864. Fifteen years later, the *Journal* reprinted the pamphlet in two consecutive issues, November 1 and 8, 1879. Over the years, other reprintings of Edge's piece, along with similar articles, reminiscences, and anecdotes, have appeared in American newspapers, magazines, and Civil War histories.[96]

Artists quickly sensed a dramatic subject with wide appeal. Led by French artist Edouard Manet, who had traveled from Paris to Cherbourg for the event depicted in *The Battle of the Kearsarge and the Alabama* (1864), generations of painters still execute this perennially popular theme. The typical image features a burning *Alabama* with red flames and billowing black smoke enveloping her shattered masts and tilted deck, the *Kearsarge* hovering intact in the background, with the *Deerhound* picking up survivors clinging to broken timbers in the choppy green sea.[97]

Poets, printmakers, and sheet-music publishers also joined the popular craze. Well known for his patriotic war verses, George Henry Boker wrote the satirical "Captain Semmes, C.S.A.N., June 19, 1864," published in the *Philadelphia North American* shortly after the news of the battle reached the United States. Boker's poem was widely reprinted in newspapers throughout the North. Appearing in the *Boston Transcript* and also receiving wide distribution, the religious and patriotic ballad *"Kearsarge"* exclaimed, "Hurrah for Winslow, Thornton and tars!" Currier & Ives, the noted American printmaking firm, quickly rendered its artistic depiction of the action off Cherbourg. J. Marsh of Philadelphia published the sheet-music score, "Last of the *Alabama*, or COMMODORE WINSLOW'S GRAND VICTORY MARCH," with a lithograph of the famous scene on the front sheet. In ten stanzas, the songwriter described the battle, ending his doggerel with these verses:

> Then mes[s]mates let your voices swell
> And let us now in music tell,
> Of Winslow whom we love so well
> Who sunk the *Alabama*.[98]

The *Kearsarge* docked at the Boston Navy Yard on November 7, the night before the 1864 presidential election. The timing was politically opportune, creating a crescendo of excitement for the National Union Party, the name used by the Republicans specifically for this election. The magic name of the *Kearsarge* would soon be translated into votes to retain the Lincoln administration in power.

Bolstered in part by the *Kearsarge*'s return to the United States, stimulating a flurry of public dinners and speeches, the resultant surge of Union patriotism could not help but be reflected in election results. Running against Major General George B. McClellan, the Democratic candidate, President Lincoln was buoyed by recent military successes in his bid for a second term. As a wartime president, he needed victories to remain in office. Along with the civilian turnout, Lincoln cultivated the Union military vote. No longer were token contingents of New Hampshire regiments required to return to their home districts via U.S. Army transports or by rail to cast their ballots. Union soldiers, taking advantage of state laws respecting their rights of franchise, were now entitled to vote in the field, as well as at the posts and camps where they were stationed.[99]

The Union naval officers and sailors were also carefully solicited by the Lincoln administration for their votes. As election day drew near, Secretary Welles took measures to expedite voting procedures at yards and naval facilities throughout the North. On October 31, he wrote the commandant of the Portsmouth Navy Yard concerning arrangements for agents visiting the Yard "for the purpose of receiving the sailors' votes." Three days later, Welles reiterated, "It is not doubted that every [Yard] mechanic and laboring man who is entitled to the privilege of voting to attend the polls and discharge his duty; no impediment will therefore be placed in the way of his doing so." A brief order issued by the Yard's executive officer on November 5 removed all remaining obstacles: "On Tuesday the 8th instant (being the day of the Presidential election), no work will be done in the yard, and there will be no muster."[100]

On November 8, 1864, for the first time in an American presidential election, Union army and naval officers, soldiers, sailors, and Navy Yard workers were legally authorized to cast their votes—in the field, on receiving ships, and at the Navy Yards. Early returns indicated the trend. On November 4, the *Chronicle* reported, "A letter from Sherman's army says that nine-tenths of the soldiers in it have voted for Lincoln. McClellan stood no sight whatsoever." Perhaps influenced by the soldiers' and sailors' response, Portsmouth and New Hampshire went for Lincoln. On November 10, the Republican *Chronicle* recorded its satisfaction with the election results: "Gen. McClellan sent in his resignation to the Secretary of War [Edwin M. Stanton] on Tuesday evening. Good by[e], Mac." In its December 3 issue, the *Journal* tallied the bayonet vote: "NEW HAMPSHIRE—SOLDIERS' VOTE.—In 18 Regiments returned, Lincoln has 1998, McClellan 679. L's majority 1819. In the 5th Reg. McClellan got 8 majority, and in the 10th (Irish) 37. Lincoln majorities in all the others."[101]

Above and beyond her purely military and naval role in freeing the seas, for the most part, for Union shipping, the *Kearsarge*'s victory precipitated far-reaching political, diplomatic, commercial, economic, and financial consequences. Perhaps the *Kearsarge*'s most important contribution was in restoring much-needed confidence for winning the battle of Union home morale.

Yellow Fever Strikes the Yard

Competing with the elation over the *Kearsarge-Alabama* duel was the fear in Portsmouth over the outbreak and spread of yellow fever, brought to the Yard by the USS *De Soto* in mid-June 1864. The well-meaning measures taken to fight the deadly disease were medically worthless, and yellow fever cost more lives and resulted in more lost work hours at the Yard than any other single cause during the Civil War.[102]

After seventeen blockade-runner captures while serving with the West Gulf Blockading Squadron, the *De Soto* had departed Key West, Florida, on June 10, on orders from Rear Admiral Theodorus Bailey, squadron commandant, for repairs at the Portsmouth Navy Yard. On June 18, the *Chronicle* reported:

> Quite a panic has been created among some of the workmen at the Portsmouth Navy Yard, by the death of three or four seamen, by fever, on board the U.S. steamer *DeSota* [*sic*].... There is considerable complaint because the vessel was not detained at quarantine the length of time prescribed by law, these complaints being occasioned by the belief that the disease among the officers and crew is contagious, and often fatal. We are informed that the Asst. Surgeon [of the *De Soto*], Geo. Parker, of Concord, died on Friday morning,—and that two of the crew also died on that day.[103]

Much of the ensuing controversy in 1864 centered on whether the United States Navy should have allowed the *De Soto* to proceed upriver to the Yard. On June 16, Pearson sought the medical opinion of Yard Surgeon Michael Delaney, who in turn had consulted with the *De Soto*'s ship's surgeon. It was the judgment of the latter physician that the only prevailing disease aboard the *De Soto* was "Bilious Remittent Fever." With this medical assurance, Pearson on that same day reported to Secretary Welles, "I have ordered her to the yard after consulting with the surgeon [Michael Delaney] and shall proceed to cleanse her at once and then prepare her for sea unless otherwise ordered. The Sick I propose to remove to the Barracks at Seavey's Island and transfer the remainder of her crew to the Receiving ship [USS *Vandalia*], discharging any whose term of service has expired." Four days later, Pearson suggested to Welles, "I beg to leave to recommend their discharge, although a portion of them are in debt to the Government."[104]

Although completely caught off guard by the *De Soto* crisis, Pearson acted decisively a few days later on June 27 when the side-wheel steamer USS *Tioga* of the East Gulf Blockading Squadron arrived at the Portsmouth Lower Harbor. Anxious to avoid a repetition of the situation created by the *De Soto*, Pearson immediately ordered the incoming *Tioga* quarantined downriver, off Clark's Island. The *Tioga* flew "the yellow fever flag at her mizzen mast," reported the *Journal* on June 28, "indicating that there is no mistake about the character of the sickness on board this craft. Three or more officers, including the Paymaster, besides several seamen, have died of this disease on the way home. She will be detained at quarantine until cleansed." Explaining why the *Tioga* was sent to the Yard in the first place, her captain [Edward Y. McCauley] in his letter of June 28 to Welles asserted, "The Yellow fever having broken out on board during the middle of the month, [was] accompanied by malignant symptoms. Rear Admiral [Theodorus] Bailey [commandant of the East Gulf Squadron and later yard commandant] ordered her, on the 19th Instant., to proceed to this Port in hopes that a speedy removal to a cold climate might arrest the disease." The same day, Pearson advised Welles, "As there is no place provided by the [Portsmouth] Board of Health for landing the crew of any ship of war when afflicted with yellow fever, I have arranged with said board to land the whole crew of the *Tioga* at the Barracks of Seavey's Island Battery."[105]

In his letter to Welles on June 29, citing the military exigency, Pearson defended his original decision to allow the *De Soto* to land at the Yard. Noting that no Portsmouth health officer had come to visit the naval vessel in the Lower Harbor, Pearson elaborated:

> It is apparent that the Board of health [*sic*] here is not sufficient for the necessities of the Government in times like the present, when nearly if not all the U.S. Ships arriving here are from Southern ports; and the delays in visiting them and the long delays of the quarantine in their retention, will prevent their returning to service for months.... Besides, (as shown in the case of the *Tioga*) the Board of Health has no suitable "Lazaretto" [a hospital ship used for quarantine of contagious diseases] or place to contain the crew of a U.S. Vessel....

Pearson also reported that Portsmouth civilian authorities were resolved to prohibit "any workman from this Yard who goes on board the *De Soto* from entering the city."[106]

The next week to ten days, from late June into early July, marked the height of the yellow fever panic. The Navy Department, the Portsmouth Navy Yard, the Portsmouth Board of Health, the Portsmouth Board of Aldermen, and private citizens, along with the *Chronicle* and the *Journal*, became embroiled in a flurry of correspondence, health notices, resolutions, editorials, charges, and countercharges. The Yard was unofficially closed for about a week. Eventually, between fourteen and sixteen people died of the fever, including several associated with the Yard: Captain Jacob P. Morrill, clerk of the master carpenter; Greenleaf J. Prescott, master machinist; a Mr. Poor, a lodgeman or boatman aboard the *De Soto*; Andrew Grace, a watchman aboard the *De Soto*; Seldon E. Garland, Yard boatman; and Capt. Black of the schooner *J.E. Gamage*, docked at the Yard. At the request of the Board of Aldermen, Pearson ordered the *De Soto* to quarantine grounds in the Lower Harbor. Starting on July 6, the *Chronicle* published a running notice from the newly appointed Sanitary Committee, public health regulations in an attempt to curb the epidemic. Orders dealt with treating decayed fruit or vegetables, swill tubs, sink and cellar drains, pigsties, fish entrails, manure, and privies. One resolution read, "No lobsters will be boiled or sold within the limits of the city, the dealers having consented thereto."[107]

By mid-July, the ravages of yellow fever mercifully and abruptly ended. "The fever-ish excitement is over," punned the *Chronicle* on July 16, "and about two-thirds of the workmen have returned to duty; the rolls now embracing 1200 of the 1800 recently employed, and numbers returning daily." In a report printed in a parallel column in the same issue of the *Chronicle*, the Board of Aldermen blamed the Yard for the outbreak of disease. Fingers were pointed at Yard Surgeon Delaney, Commandant Pearson, and especially at the *De Soto*'s ship's surgeon, who seemed unaware that at least forty cases had been on board when the ship left Key West for Portsmouth.[108]

The summer of 1864 passed without a recurrence of yellow fever in Portsmouth. After both vessels had been in quarantine for almost three months, the *Tioga* (on October 22) and the *De Soto* (on October 24) left Clark's Island to return to the Yard, with the approval of the Board of Health. Voicing the then-current medical belief, the *Chronicle* on October 25 commented, "The late severe frosts have probably destroyed the direful disease which caused such an excitement in our midst last summer, yet even now, in breaking out the holds of these vessels, too much care cannot be exercised, as it is possible that some of the articles of clothing or furniture may still be infected."[109]

Both the *De Soto* and the *Tioga* continued to attract controversy. Captain Theodorus Bailey, Pearson's successor at the Yard in the late fall of 1864 (and, ironically, the officer who had ordered the *De Soto* north), objected to Welles on November 26 that the quarantine of the two ships was too costly, complaining about the "very exorbitant expenses that I cannot approve ... without the instructions of the Department." Citing the added compensation and the subsistence charges for the sailors assigned aboard both ships during the long quarantine period, as well as theft of government funds and property from the *De Soto*'s paymaster's office and other departments of the ships, Bailey was particularly incensed about the excessive fees charged by the Portsmouth Board of Health officers: "I can only say, that I am informed that Health Officers are, by the laws of New Hampshire, entitled to 'reasonable compensation' for their services. The chairman of the Board of Health, B[enjamin] S. Goodwin, who certifies these bills, is an Indian or Root [herbal] Doctor in Portsmouth."[110]

In December 1864, as it turned out, Dr. Goodwin also charged the City of Portsmouth for additional services during the yellow fever epidemic. When the city refused to pay what it considered an exorbitant fee, Goodwin sued for his money. The result favored the city, and Goodwin eventually received a reduced amount for his services.[111]

The Union Fleet at Mobile Bay

On August 5, 1864, Commander Tunis Augustus Macdonough Craven, a native of Portsmouth and a second-generation career naval officer, was among the Union ship commanders engaged in a massive effort to seal off Mobile, Alabama, the last major Confederate port on the Gulf Coast. Commander Craven's vessel, the ironclad USS *Tecumseh*, lay at anchor in Pensacola, Florida. After receiving orders from Admiral David Glasgow Farragut to reinforce the assembled fleet, the *Tecumseh* arrived outside the entrance to Mobile Bay the evening before the scheduled attack.[112]

Crossing the bar at flood tide at 6:00 a.m., the Union attack force, with the *Tecumseh* heading the column, moved into Mobile Bay.

At 6:47 a.m., Craven opened fire on Fort Morgan, which guarded the eastern approach. The action quickly became widespread. After passing beyond Fort Morgan, Craven decided to engage the CSS *Tennessee*, a heavy ironclad and the most formidable warship in the Confederate squadron defending the bay. The *Tecumseh* continued advancing, but suddenly, without warning, a tremendous explosion rocked her. She had hit a Confederate torpedo (submerged mine) and was doomed. All hands hastened to abandon ship.[113]

Craven's biographer describes the last dramatic moments aboard the *Tecumseh*: "The captain [Tunis A.M. Craven] and the pilot were in the conning tower directly over the turret, whence there was no escape save through a narrow opening. Upon reaching this[,] Commander Craven turned to the pilot and said, 'You first, sir.' The pilot John Collins escaped and[,] as he related, the vessel sank under him, carrying her crew of one hundred and sixteen in all, save himself and the few that were able to escape through the port holes." The *Tecumseh* sank a mere twenty-five seconds after the initial impact. Variously recorded as "You first, sir," "After you, sir," and "After you, pilot," Craven's last words were among the noted quotations that emerged from the Civil War. Craven's biography notes, "A buoy in Mobile Bay marks the spot where the *Tecumseh* lies, the iron-bound tomb of the gallant Craven and his devoted crew."[114]

After the *Tecumseh*'s sinking, the remaining Union vessels drifted in confusion toward the guns of Fort Morgan. From his flagship *Hartford*, Farragut rallied the fleet with his famous command, "Damn the torpedoes! Full speed ahead!" As the Union vessels proceeded, duds bounced harmlessly against their hulls. With many Union vessels ramming against or firing accurate shots at the *Tennessee*, the battered Confederate warship surrendered at 10:00 a.m. One by one, Confederate forts in the bay, believed by the Southerners to be impregnable, surrendered. Fort Morgan, the last to hold out, surrendered on August 23.

The Union naval victory at Mobile Bay—the largest naval battle of the war—effectively closed the Confederate port to shipping. Trapped Mobile blockade runners had no hope for escape. Although the city itself remained in Confederate hands until the following spring, Mobile was strategically isolated and militarily neutralized, a port in name only. Following the *Kearsarge*'s success six weeks earlier, the Battle of Mobile Bay was another triumph that raised Lincoln's stock in the November 1864 presidential election.[115]

Gustavus V. Fox, proved indispensable as Navy Secretary Gideon Welles's right-hand man, serving as assistant secretary of the navy from 1861 to 1866. Married to a Portsmouth woman, Fox frequently toured the Navy Yard during the war years. NHC

The sacrifice of Commander Tunis A.M. Craven, his men, and the USS *Tecumseh* was not forgotten. On September 3, President Lincoln ordered the Union Navy Yards to fire salutes during the week, with the following Sunday designated as a day of national thanksgiving. On September 9, the *Chronicle* reported that "a salute of 100 guns, in honor of the victory at Mobile, was fired at the Navy Yard on Thursday noon; and the bells of the city for an hour rang out their joyful peals. The flags were displayed on the U.S. vessels at the Navy

Yard."[116]

Changes at the Yard

"Engineer [Benjamin F.] Chandler," reported the *Chronicle* on July 18, 1864, "is projecting great improvements on the Yard." In order to respond to increasing wartime demands, the Navy Department, the bureau chiefs, the commandants, and Chandler himself undertook needed, often long-overdue changes at the Portsmouth Navy Yard. The Yard constructed new facilities, experimented with new equipment, and implemented new services. As the work force expanded to 2,900 men by December 1864, Yard employees had to adjust to new transportation and housing arrangements.[117]

For some years, the Marine Barracks had been hampered by limited space. On August 4, 1864, the Quartermaster's Office of the Marine Corps in Washington, by public notice, solicited "SEALED PROPOSALS ... for REBUILDING and REMODELING the MARINE BARRACKS at the NAVY YARD, Portsmouth, NH. Bidders are referred to Constructing Engineer CHANDLER, of the Portsmouth Yard, for examination of Plans and Specifications." On Monday, August 15, noon, the deadline for acceptance of the competitive bids, the Marine Office opened the sealed envelopes. Three and one half hours later, it was announced that the contract was awarded to a Lawrence, Massachusetts, firm. "The work is to be commenced at once," reported the *Chronicle* on August 20, "and is under the superintendence of Civil Engineer B.F. Chandler."[118]

Construction at the barracks was underway for the next several months, resulting in a vast improvement. According to the *Chronicle* on December 23, the "former quarters were 'narrow-contracted,' poorly-ventilated, seven-by-nine [foot] compartments, inconvenient and uncomfortable." In line with Chandler's plans, the new facilities included raised wings for officers' quarters: a center section with a cook room, mess room, and cells (compartments for military prisoners serving short terms for minor infractions) on the first floor; and a second floor consisting of "large sleeping apartments, good enough for anybody." Two porches in front overlooked the river and the parade lawn and provided views of the sea. Upon completion in early 1865, the new barracks, according to the *Chronicle* on January 31, presented "a comfortable and cleanly appearance."[119]

Flanked by the Iron Plating Shop (left) and the Engine House (right), the Head House held machinery for the Yard's marine railway, which extended from the front of the building to Dock Basin (off photograph at left center), an artificial indentation of the Piscataqua River. The marine railway was used to haul ships onto dry land for thorough hull inspections before repair crews on staging platforms began their work. PNSVC

While appropriating money for necessary improvements, the Navy Department also strove to eliminate excess expenditure. In a circular issued on October 10, Commodore Joseph Smith, Bureau Chief of Yards and Docks, instructed the various Navy Yard commandants: "Where there are hot houses or conservatories at Navy Yards attached to Officers Quarters, they must be cared for and supported at the expense of officers on whose premises they are located, and who enjoy the fruits of them."[120]

In addition to the Marine Barracks, other improvements, alterations, additions, or completely new structures underway included a naval stores building, timber shed, ordnance park, porter's house, ordnance building, and futtock saw mill. At the naval stores building, the *Journal* reported on September 3, "We noticed several boxes labelled 'roast beef.' These boxes are filled with tin canisters hermetically sealed, each containing four pounds of beef, roasted in Portland, which may be kept in this way for years.—Other provisions, perishable on exposure to the air, are packed in like manner."[121]

Captain John Lenthall, Bureau Chief of Construction and Repair, ordered another economical measure: "The screenings and sweepings of the brass foundry, finishing shop, and the plumber's shop, must be carefully collected, and all the metal extracted, that it may be used again. The proper master workmen must make a monthly return to the Commandant to be entered on the Storekeeper's books."[122]

Engineer Chandler also undertook a salvage project. During the summer of 1864, he sought to recover an anchor lost from the steamer USS *Colorado* on her earlier passage up the river. Describing the newly acquired diving gear used for the operation, the *Chronicle* reported on August 16:

> The apparatus consists of a suit of canvas, covering the whole body, except the head, which is protected by a large globe-shaped copper armor, with a tube leading to the inside for the purpose of conveying fresh air to the wearer who presents a hideous appearance when in full dress. Accompanying this rig is a large air pump, with a number of feet of hose attached....
>
> The diver is compelled to append a weight of ninety-two pounds to his shoulders to counteract the density of the water.[123]

Reuben Wiley, the diver, was employed in the Carpenter's Department at the Yard. No novice in the business, Wiley, during the aftermath of the Crimean War, had made many successful dives to the bottom of Sebastopol Harbor on the Black Sea to raise sunken vessels in that Russian port. On Saturday, August 13, Wiley began salvage operations in the Piscataqua, but the strong tide and heavy undercurrent thwarted his initial attempt.[124]

A few days later, Wiley tried again. After two attempts, he fastened a chain around a fluke of the anchor. Workmen on the surface used scows and rigging to raise the anchor. "For this perilous job," commented the *Chronicle* on August 22, "the diver gets $50. If he had not succeeded in finding it [the anchor] he was to receive nothing."[125]

The next month, another situation arose that required the services of a diver. On September 17, the steamer USS *Franklin* was

The Ordnance Building at the Portsmouth Navy Yard, built in 1857, was a gun-carriage factory during the Civil War. Cannon lined up in Gun Park (foreground), and their carriages were shipped by rail to the front for the Union army. Now Building 22, this structure currently serves as the Officers' Club. PNSVC

launched at the Yard with great fanfare. Thousands of spectators lined the banks of the Piscataqua: there was a large press contingent: and a poem, "Launch of the Frigate *Franklin*," was written for the occasion. A problem arose, however, when the packing (the timber on which a vessel rests before launching) did not float out from beneath the *Franklin*. Somehow the packing remained secured to the vessel by ropes. Five days after the launch, Mr. Wilmot of New York, a professional but inexperienced diver, went down with a knife to cut the lines. He became entangled in his air hose, and his surface crew, misunderstanding his signals, compounded the problem. In desperation, Wilmot cut the hose and ultimately surfaced. According to the *Chronicle*, "he was in an exhausted condition when pulled up, and could not have survived much longer."[126]

The launch of the *Franklin* marked Commandant George F. Pearson's last major ceremonial function at the Yard. On September 14, Pearson had responded to Secretary Welles's transfer orders, "directing me, on being relieved of this command by Commodore [Rear Admiral Theodorus] Bailey on the 30th instant, to proceed as soon as practicable thereafter to Panama, N[ew] G[ranada] [then Colombia], via Aspinwall, and relieve Acting R[ear] Admiral Charles H. Bell of the command of the Pacific Squadron, when I am to hoist my flag as Acting Rear Admiral in command of that squadron." On Friday afternoon, September 30, in a brief ceremony at the Yard, Pearson, according to the *Chronicle*, "assembled the officers and men, read to them his orders to report for duty on the Pacific coast, thanked all for their courtesy and attention to duty during his four years pleasant stay at the Yard as Commandant, and bade them farewell."[127]

Pearson then introduced Bailey, who read his orders to report to the Yard, thereby officially taking command. A worthy successor to Pearson, Bailey had served as Farragut's second-in-command at the capture of New Orleans in 1862. Later, as commandant of the East Gulf Blockading Squadron, Bailey coordinated a Union naval force that captured 150 blockade runners.[128]

Commandant Bailey immediately addressed a long-standing problem: the lack of an efficient and dependable commuting service for Portsmouth Navy Yard employees. For years, Yard workers had relied upon their own often inadequate and frequently unsafe rowboats, wherries, and other craft for their river crossings. To remedy this deficiency, the United States Navy in October 1864 purchased a small steam yacht for both ferry and mail service. After a rough passage from Philadelphia, the steamer arrived at the Yard on October 30. Officially named the *Emerald* and serving in a noncommissioned status, the yacht could accommodate about fifty passengers. After repairs to the *Emerald* and preparation of landing sites on both sides of the Piscataqua, the *Emerald* began regular trips to and from the Yard. On January 14, 1865, the *Chronicle* published the ferry schedule: "She leaves the Navy Yard slip, at the foot of Daniel Street [on the Portsmouth side] for the present [time], at 9 and 11 A.M., and 1 1/2 [1:30 p.m.], 4, and 5 1/2, or on arrival of the mails." The Yard ferry ser-

LAUNCH OF THE FRIGATE FRANKLIN,

AT PORTSMOUTH, SEPT. 17, 1864.

Staunch old frigate! sleeping monster!
  Many years thou'st been as dead;
But this day with new-found valor
  Thou wilt lift thy war like head!
From thy prison-house escaping
  Forth thou'lt bound to greet the day;
Classic Neptune! crown the service;
  Wed her, proud Piscataqua!

Fitting time, while fair Astræa
  Reigns in gracious equity;
Another golden age divining
  For the universal free!
At this hopeful time auspicious,
  Namesake of a noble man!
Hail we thy presageful advent:
  Thou may'st speed God's perfect plan!

Matchless glories of the zenith,
  Bathe in splendor all the scene;
Whilst the thousands of spectators
  Breathless gaze o'er flood-tide sheen:
Lo! she moves! the waters riving,
  On, the ship majestic strides,
Till her home she safely reaches,
  Where glad waves caress her sides!

Soon our gallant tars will man thee,
  And thou'lt cleave the billows blue,
Striking terror to the lawless, —
  How they'll fear thee and thy crew!
Hurl among them crashing broadsides,
  Monarch of the strife-swept sea!
And in honor help establish
  Justice, Law and Liberty!   E. P. N

PJ, Oct. 1, 1864

vice was an immediate success, and the *Emerald* carried commuters regularly until her retirement in 1883.[129]

Increasing wartime demand for housing and rail transportation for Yard workers prompted additional changes. Since the beginning of the war, all the low-priced tenements for Navy Yard workers in the Portsmouth area had been rented. The lack of housing became especially acute in 1863 and 1864. In late September 1864, in an attempt to accommodate the surplus of workers who lacked

Rear Admiral Theodorus Bailey (shown here as a captain in a carte-de-visite photo, circa 1861-62) served as Portsmouth Navy Yard commandant from 1864 to 1867, toward the end of a distinguished 46-year naval career. Bailey accepted the surrender of New Orleans from Confederate authorities in 1862 and later that year became the commander of the East Gulf Blockading Squadron, which captured 150 blockade runners. Much of his tenure at the Yard coincided with the postwar reduction of the U.S. Navy and a downsizing of the Yard's activities. NHC

Portsmouth housing, a drive was initiated to run a special daily train to and from Great Falls (now Somersworth), where more housing was available and rents were lower. About 200 men endorsed the plan. On Monday, December 5, 1864, a special Navy Yard commuter train between Great Falls and Portsmouth began operation. On December 3, the *Chronicle* had observed, "While boarding for men in this city [Portsmouth], we believe, is from $5 to $7 per week, at the lowest; and for women $2.50 to $4—the rate for the host of workmen from our Navy Yard, who live at Great Falls now, we are told is to be $3.50, including washing. They bring dinner down with them, of course."[130]

As Christmas 1864 approached, the war-weary gloom prevalent at the beginning of the year had largely dissipated. An expectation of imminent victory now filled the air at the Yard, within the United States Navy, and throughout the Union. During 1864, orator Edward Everett in a major address ("The Navy in the War"), shipbuilder Donald McKay in a public letter, and Gideon Welles in his annual "Report of the Secretary of the Navy" cited the gains and massive strength of the Union fleet. Also during that year, the Port of Portsmouth tallied an impressive 750 ship arrivals. On Christmas Eve, the *Journal* provided holiday cheer with a story of a captured blockade runner with barrels marked "Epsom Salt," destined for the Confederacy. The cargo was discovered instead to be pulverized saltpeter, used in the manufacture of gunpowder. This timely interception had "undoubtedly saved much suffering and many lives."[131]

During 1864, the ongoing wartime expansion of the Navy Yard continued to stimulate a boom in Portsmouth. Shortly before Christmas, the Yard labor force of more than 2,900 workmen received a total of $147,000. Most of this money, as the *Chronicle* noted on December 20, "is distributed among the traders and businessmen of this city and its immediate vicinity, thus keeping up the tumult of business."[132]

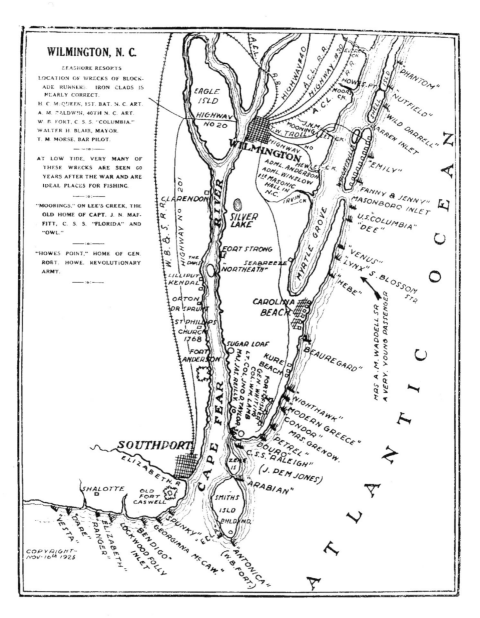

This map pinpoints the location of 77 wrecks of Confederate blockade runners near Wilmington, North Carolina. Note at Shell Island (upper right) the sites of the Nutfield and Wild Darrell (should be Dayrell), driven aground by the Portsmouth-built USS Sassacus in early February 1864. PEM

VI 1865: The Yard's Transition

The Capture of Fort Fisher

THE YEAR OF 1865 boded well for the Union. "At the New Year's Reception at the White House," reported the *Journal* on January 14, 1865, "Mr. Lincoln was dressed in a full suit of black, and appeared in the best humor." By contrast, the same issue reprinted an article from the *Richmond Whig* that reflected an increasingly gloomy outlook in the Confederacy. The *Whig* reporter commented, "She [England] has no ships that could encounter the Yankee monitors with any prospect of success, and although she might build such, yet the probability is that they could cross the ocean and not even break up the blockade, far less send an army and fleet here to assist us."[1]

In early 1865, the Union navy was ready to take Fort Fisher, which guarded the Confederacy's last remaining Atlantic blockade-running port—Wilmington, North Carolina. Bristling with defensive bastions, Fort Fisher stood on Federal Point (renamed Confederate Point by its defenders), eighteen miles south of Wilmington. Despite the fort's strength, its strategic value to the Confederacy had begun waning as early as autumn 1864. On October 24, the *Chronicle* observed, "The *Richmond* [Virginia] *Dispatch* learns from a gentleman just from Wilmington, N.C., 'that the blockade of that port is as effective as Yankee ingenuity and an unlimited force of gunboats can make it. They have now established two lines of picket boats in the offing to give the alarm of the attempted egress of blockade runners, and as soon as the latter make their appearance, the boats throw up [signal]

273

rockets and burn blue lights.'" In late December 1864, a combined Union army and navy expedition, consisting of fifty-six warships, together with troop transports and landing barges, assembled in an attempt to take Fort Fisher. Included in this armada were the Portsmouth-built or -repaired ships *Sassacus, Minnesota, Colorado,* and *R.R. Cuyler.* Led jointly by Rear Admiral David D. Porter and Major General Benjamin F. Butler, the ill-coordinated attack failed.[2]

On January 7, 1865, the *Journal* reprinted an account from the *Philadelphia Ledger,* written by journalist Benson J. Lossing, who accompanied the expedition. Believing that the fort could not be taken, Lossing wrote:

> Fort Fisher is a large work, covering about six acres at Federal Point, at New Inlet, mounting 60 guns. It is built of earth and logs. The bombardment, unequalled in the number of vessels engaged, the weight of metal and length of duration, by anything, it is believed, recorded in history, has demonstrated the fact that forts of earth and logs may be so constructed as to defy naval attack. All the barracks and other buildings in the fort were fired by our shells and consumed, while the men were so safely hidden in the traverses that very few casualties, it is believed, occurred.[3]

For his part, General Butler also held that Fort Fisher was impregnable. Evaluating the chances of success of an assault upon Fort Fisher, Butler later contended, "I had been definitely told by the most skillful engineers, that if I had ordered it, it would be murder." Brushing aside criticism, Butler publicly stated that his epitaph should read, "Here lies the General who saved the lives of his soldiers at Fort Fisher and Big Bethel."[4]

Butler, however, was dismissed—and replaced by Major General Alfred H. Terry. Admiral Porter and the Union stiffened their resolve to take Fort Fisher. Assembling a squadron of sixty-two Union vessels—almost the identical naval force that had participated in the December debacle—Porter and Terry mounted an expedition of 8,000 soldiers and 2,000 sailors and marines. An innovator who embraced the latest training tactics, Porter had organized a special landing party of naval and marine forces, well rehearsed in mock amphibious exercises for the second operation.[5]

For three days, January 13 through 15, 1865, the Union naval

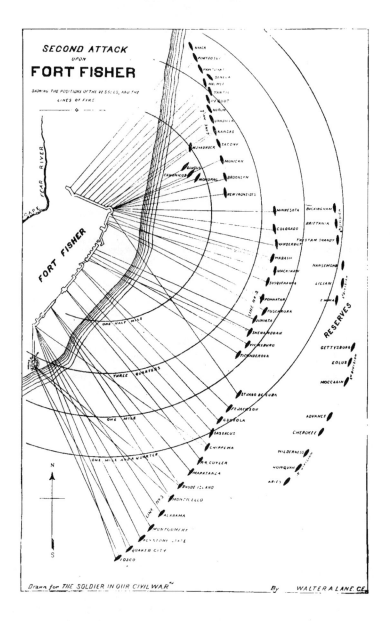

Coordinated fields of fire from the 62-vessel Union fleet during a three-day bombardment (January 13-15, 1865) reduced the defenses of Fort Fisher, North Carolina, thus enabling an amphibious force of 10,000 federal soldiers, sailors, and marines to capture this strategic Confederate stronghold. This action closed the port of Wilmington and its blockade-running operations. NHC

bombardment of Fort Fisher was merciless, sometimes at the rate of a hundred shells a minute. In his handwritten report to Admiral Porter, Portsmouth Commander Enoch G. Parrott, captain of the USS *Monadnock*, observed:

> While the ironclads were alone opposed to the fort, the rebels attempt to contend with them, and opened a fire rather severe and obstinate, but less accurate than ours; but their guns, as they successively showed activity, were invariably reduced to silence. We aimed almost wholly at their guns, watching the effect of each shot, and waiting for the smoke to clear away before firing another. As their disabled guns generally remained in place, it was an inconvenience during the latter part of the fight, as the rebels did not fire often enough to show us which were the remaining efficient ones. We saw one of them tumbled over by our fire, and I have no doubt that most of them or their carriages received disabling shots over and over again from the ironclads. Never was a work better prepared for an assault.... At the moment of the assault we had the satisfaction to see that the guns on this face could not be used against our advancing men.[6]

Parrott's devastating shelling contributed to the success of the Union assault conducted against the Fort Fisher works during the afternoon of January 15. By 10 p.m., the Confederate defenders, 1,500 strong, were overwhelmed by the 10,000-man Union force. "Fort Fisher is ours," read Porter's telegram sent that evening to Navy Secretary Gideon Welles.[7]

Demonstrating the ability of concentrated and superior naval gunpower to reduce stationary land defenses, the second Fort Fisher expedition was the largest amphibious operation, prior to World War II, in American history—its basic execution anticipated American military strategy and tactics in the South Pacific more than seventy-five years later. In January 1865, the *Boston Herald* stressed the importance of the capture of Fort Fisher, which signified that the Union blockade was now virtually complete. Its reporter wrote, "By the sealing of the harbor of Wilmington the rebels are completely isolated from commercial communication with the outer world. They are now hemmed in on every side, as it were, by a wall of fire, and must rely on their own resources to carry on the war, unaided by any foreign power." With Wilmington sealed, outlying British island ports, once humming with blockade-running activities, were rendered useless. "The closing of the port of Wilmington," noted the *Chronicle* on February 20, "has been a sad blow to Nassau. All is starvation there now." On March 10, the *Chronicle* added, "It is said [that] there are 35 blockade-runners lying in the port of Nassau, whose occupation is gone. They represent capital to the amount of $15,000,000."[8]

On January 16, the morning after the capture of Fort Fisher, an explosion rocked the magazine within the fort. About a hundred casualties resulted from the blast. Although a rumor held that the Confederates had rigged a detonation wire leading to the shells, a New York correspondent maintained that the explosion "was caused by the carelessness of our men, who were indiscreet enough to go in with lighted cigars and lighted candles. They were cautioned but paid no heed to it."[9]

Among the casualties was Portsmouth's Alfred Laighton, a USS *Gettysburg* officer who had come ashore. Ordered to gather the dead and wounded, Laighton was complying when the explosion killed him. Before the battle, Laighton and a fellow officer had agreed that, in the event that either might fall, the survivor would visit the friends of the deceased. Laighton's unidentified comrade arrived in Portsmouth about two weeks later with his sad news. "It is our painful duty," announced the *Journal* on January 28, "to record the death of another of the sons of Portsmouth, who has just fallen in his country's service at the post of duty and danger—viz. Acting Ensign ALFRED STOWE LAIGHTON, U.S.N., who was killed at the capture of Fort Fisher. He was the only son of Wm. F. Laighton, Esq. of this city; and his death makes a sore breach in the large circle of friends here; where his sacrifice on the altar of our country will be remembered and honored. His age was 28, and he was married but 18 months ago."[10]

On January 18, the Portsmouth Navy Yard fired a salute of thirty-one guns in honor of the capture of Fort Fisher. A few days later, various military and Masonic delegations gathered for graveside services to pay respects to the memory of Ensign Laighton, the highest-ranking local naval officer to fall in the war.[11]

Symbolizing the costly Union sacrifice—more than 1,000 casualties—for Fort Fisher, the epitaph on Laighton's white tombstone in Portsmouth's Harmony Grove Cemetery reads:

278 "Constructing Munitions of War"

In man's regret he lives and woman's tears,
More sacred than in life, and nobler far
For having perished in the front of war.[12]

The USS Minnesota *Undergoes Repairs*

After the capture of Fort Fisher, the USS *Minnesota*, hit by
Confederate shelling during the battle, limped north for repairs at the
Portsmouth Navy Yard. As this latest Union naval victory raised
expectations that the war was drawing to a close, activity at the various Navy Yards and within the Navy Department was soon increasingly cut back to handle only the most essential work. "It is a gratifying fact in regard to the rebellion," declared the *Boston Traveller* in
February 1865, "that the Navy has now done the heaviest part of the
work that will be required of it, and that the expenses of that department will now be lessened. No more vessels will be bought and few
contracted for. There are now, for the first time, all the seamen that
are wanted. Charleston [South Carolina] is the only port this side of
Texas, in rebel hands, and will soon be sealed up. The blockading vessels can now be put to other uses—some will be repaired, and others
sent to Europe."[13]

In the Navy Department's judgment, the USS *Minnesota* was
one of the ones deemed worth repairing. Both the *Chronicle* and the
Journal ran the same article, noting the ship's value: "She is a first
class frigate of 3,307 tons, and carries 49 guns. This steamer comes
direct from Fort Fisher and being considerably damaged in the fight
at that place, will need a thorough overhauling."[14]

A day or two after the *Minnesota*'s arrival, an agent visited the
ship to inquire about the seamen's prize money. "In talking with an
old tar, who was in both attacks on Fort Fisher, and has been in seventeen engagements," reported the *Chronicle* on February 14, the prize
agent "asked him 'whether he had any body to whom to leave his
money if he got his head blown off?' Jack replied that 'Jeff Davis had
not made the shot yet that is to do that little business.'"[15]

Yard Commandant Theodorus Bailey's efforts to repair the
Minnesota, decommissioned on February 16, proved formidable. In
frequent correspondence with John Lenthall, Chief of the U.S. Navy's
Bureau of Construction and Repair, Bailey fretted about the "dimensions or projections of spars," distilling tanks, and so forth. "The
steamer *Minnesota* is being rapidly dismantled," noted the *Chronicle*

This 1865 photograph shows the USS Minnesota *undergoing repairs and overhaul at the Portsmouth Navy Yard floating dry dock. Severely damaged during the second Fort Fisher expedition in mid-January 1865, the badly leaking* Minnesota *limped northward. She arrived at the Yard on February 10, only to be decommissioned six days later. Hampered by postwar U.S. Navy budget cuts, the* Minnesota *was not recommissioned until June 3, 1867. PNSVC*

on February 24, "and will be soon docked [placed in dry dock] for examination. It is reported that she leaks considerably." Bad luck continued. On the evening of February 18, a marine on guard duty fractured his skull in a fall, and on March 28, according to the *Chronicle* three days later, "a fire was discovered on board the *Minnesota* in a Dry Dock at the Navy Yard, by a watchman while going his usual rounds.... The fire was occasioned by a lot of cotton waste having been thrown on a lamp—either accidentally or designedly—and after smouldering for an hour or more, it burst out and had it not been for the arrival of the watchman, the steamer must have been destroyed." In his letter of April 3 to Lenthall, Bailey confided, "The repairs of the

Engines & Boilers of this ship will probably require five months from this date."[16]

The *Minnesota* was not recommissioned until June 3, 1867, more than two years later.[17]

Accidents, Deserters, and Senator Hale

Expectation of imminent Union victory was not enough. Although the Confederacy, increasingly diminished fort by fort, city by city, and ship by ship, tottered on the verge of collapse in early 1865, the conflict nevertheless went on. The Portsmouth Navy Yard maintained its day-by-day press of activity, but casualties, expenditures, and political accusations continued to plague the Yard.

"On Monday [January 2, 1865]," reported the *Chronicle* two days later, "a boat's crew belonging to the *Merrimac* or *Albatross*, with Mr. Hingerty, Boatswain of the Navy Yard, and one or two other officers as passengers, started from the Navy Yard slip at the foot of Daniel Street, about five o'clock P.M., and when nearly across, encountered such a strong tide near the ship *Franklin*, as to sweep the boat on her bow mooring chains, with such force as to capsize her, with her crew. All were fortunately saved, except one—a colored seaman, who was drowned."[18]

The difficulties of the USS *Merrimac* (not the more famous *Merrimack*/CSS *Virginia*) had barely begun. On February 1, she left the Yard for the Lower Harbor, where she lay for a few days before heading down the Atlantic Coast, for blockade duty off Florida. As the *Chronicle* reported on February 3, "Six substitute sailors seized the opportunity to escape. A number of shots were fired at them, but none seemed effectual to induce them to return. Two of them were caught, however, by some of the soldiers at Fort McClary. The remainder are at large."[19]

The next news of the *Merrimac*, three weeks later, was even more alarming. "We regret to learn that the noble U.S. Str. *Merrimac*, recently refitted at this Navy Yard," announced the *Chronicle* on February 21, "is reported lost at sea. A steamer arrived at Port Royal [South Carolina], brings the officers and crew, who were taken off after laying by her all night, and abandoning her in a sinking condition, with engines disabled and fires out. No other particulars." Additional details soon became known. Overwhelmed by a gale, the *Merrimac* took on water off the coast of Florida. The mail steamer

Morning Star successfully rescued the entire crew.[20]

Incidents at the Yard jeopardized and ultimately cost human lives. Several attempts at desertion involved the Yard's receiving ship USS *Vandalia*. The reason for these numerous attempted escapes was not recorded; perhaps a number of green and disillusioned naval substitutes, sensing that the war was almost over and feeling no patriotic incentive to remain aboard for training, chafed under military discipline. On January 3, 1865, two (possibly three) sailor substitutes aboard the *Vandalia* attempted to escape by swimming ashore. Guards instantly fired at them, killing one; the other was captured in the water. The hat belonging to the deceased deserter drifted ashore on the Kittery side of the river, whereupon it was picked up by a little boy and found to contain $900 in greenbacks.[21]

At the end of the week, on January 7, a crew of one hundred substitute sailors was taken from the *Vandalia* for transfer to the USS *De Soto*, the ship associated with the outbreak of yellow fever the previous summer. "Upon being examined," noted the *Chronicle* on January 9, "it was found that a large number of the men had on citizens' clothes beneath their outer dress. Whiskey and various kinds of weapons were also found concealed upon them; all this undoubtedly for the purpose of effecting their escape at some time.... All those deemed suspicious were sent below, and the hatches fastened down." The *De Soto* then sailed for Baltimore.[22]

On January 17, in a similar situation, a draft of fifty seamen from the *Vandalia* was sent aboard the USS *Shawmut*. One or two tried to escape, but they failed. "One completely covered himself with coal," reported the *Chronicle*, "but was discovered by a marine, upon which he showed a little fight, but a pair of handcuffs induced him to yield."[23]

A grim reminder of these escape attempts occurred on January 21, when the body of an unknown man, apparently having been in the water for a long time, washed up on the Kittery shore. The remains were buried in the Kittery Almshouse. "It is supposed to be," noted the *Chronicle*, "that one of the bounty-jumping sailors from the *Vandalia*, who was drowned or shot while attempting to desert. Was about 5 feet 9 inches in height, and dressed in checked shirt, dark pants, and boots, with a plaid scarf around his waist. The [Kittery] Aldermen deemed it unnecessary to hold an inquest."[24]

In the midst of these disruptive events, a political salvo fired from Washington sought to discredit the work of the Yard and the Navy Department. Defeated in his bid for a fourth term in the United States Senate, Dover's John Parker Hale, chairman of the Senate Committee on Naval Affairs, had baited the Navy Department repeatedly during the war years. He detested Welles and Gustavus Fox. During his January and February speeches on the Senate floor before leaving office on March 3, Hale lashed out against alleged graft, corruption, and mismanagement in the Navy Department. On February 17, Hale charged:

> I found out, and found out by accident, that the most enormous frauds were being perpetrated right under my nose in the [Portsmouth] navy-yard within ten miles of where I live. I found there that monkey-wrenches, the fair price of which was from twelve to fifteen dollars a dozen, were bought by the Navy Department at Portsmouth for $150 a dozen.... Take the item of anvils, weighing about two hundred pounds, the fair market value of which was thirty dollars; the Government paid fifty dollars. Axes, handled, worth $1.25 each, were obtained at three dollars. Small axes, the fair price of which was seventy-five cents, were furnished to the Government for $1.50. Grindstones worth $4.50 each, were sold to the Government for thirty dollars each. Scale-beams worth $6.50, were sold for fifty dollars; and so on the prices ranged throughout.[25]

Hale also repeated his charges, first articulated the previous year, that the Navy Department had attempted to circumvent a congressional law for an appropriation of $14,000 for the purchase of Seavey's Island for the Yard, coupled with similar allegations that the Navy Department had tried to evade a congressional appropriation of $25,000 for the construction of a hospital.[26]

Gleefully reprinting Hale's comments pertaining to the Yard, Joshua L. Foster's *States and Union* editorialized, "And all this money wrung from the pockets of the hard-working people to go into the coffers of the cormorants who are fattening upon the blood and sinews of the laboring classes. But who are these fellows? We have hardware and copper contractors right here in Portsmouth to say nothing of our very pious Navy Agent [Thomas Tullock]."[27]

Hale's contention that war profiteers defrauded the Navy Department during the war was basically true, but Hale relished this final parting shot to besmirch Welles's and Fox's reputations. Hale's departure brought tremendous relief to Welles.

Prisoner of War Thomas Gay

Although Confederate prisoner-of-war camps were located hundreds of miles from the Portsmouth Navy Yard, their existence and reputation were well known at the Yard. The care and treatment accorded to Northern prisoners of war, constantly trumpeted by the Portsmouth press, produced bitter accusations. It is estimated that 195,000 Union soldiers and 215,000 Confederates were incarcerated at various times during the war. In Union and Confederate camps alike, prisoner death rates were high. Few federal naval and marine officers and men were captured; no separate statistics, however, appear to have been compiled to establish their number or the percentage of the total Union prisoner list.[28]

Thomas S. Gay was an unlucky exception. Of English birth but raised in Portsmouth, Gay went to sea early in life. After entering the U.S. Navy at age twenty-seven in March 1864, Gay was appointed acting master's mate the following month; ultimately he was assigned to the USS *Otsego*. A few months later, while still attached to this ship, Gay participated in an expedition that attempted to destroy the Confederate ironclad *Albemarle*, then lying in the Roanoke River at Plymouth, North Carolina. Lieutenant William B. Cushing led a party of six officers and eight seamen. Early in the morning of October 27, Cushing and his men blew up the *Albemarle*. Of the fourteen Union commandos, only Cushing and one other escaped—one drowned, another was shot, and Gay and the rest were captured. For months, nothing was known in Portsmouth about Gay's fate. Most of his friends feared he had been killed.[29]

Released in a prisoner exchange on February 25, 1865, Gay was promoted by the navy four days later to acting ensign for "gallant service." When he returned to Portsmouth in mid-March for duty aboard the USS *Vandalia*, the Yard's receiving ship, Gay responded to requests by the editors of the *Journal* for an article about his experiences. Published on the *Journal's* front page on March 25, Gay's narrative offers a graphic, emotional account of his ordeal, replete with universal contemporary observations articulated by Northern and Southern prisoners alike: poor or meager rations, inadequate or nonexistent shelter, lack of medical care, sadistic guards, confiscation of personal property—all culminating in either ruined health or death.[30]

After describing the destruction of the *Albemarle* and his capture the same day, Gay records: "We were ... sent to Salisbury prison [North Carolina], where we arrived on the 5th of November [1864]. The gate of the stockade was thrown open to us, and we were received by upwards of 10,000 of our fellow prisoners, all in a wretched condition. I could call this no other than a living grave yard."[31]

During his eight days of incarceration there, Gay observed, "Deaths would average thirty per day. Most of these died from mere starvation. A very painful occurrence transpired one day during my stay. One of our poor fellows stepped over the dead line [a fence or barrier marking the boundary of a prison camp] to gain a few acorns to satisfy the cravings of hunger and was deliberately shot by the sentry without a moment's warning."[32]

On November 13, 1864, Gay and a party of Northern prisoners were sent by train to another camp at Danville, Virginia, where they endured similarly wretched conditions. After a month at Danville, the group was transferred to Richmond and taken to "Hotel de Libby"—as the best-known Confederate prisoner-of-war facility was dubbed throughout the North. Outraged by the systematic stripping of all valuables from the incoming lot of prisoners by Libby guards, Gay observed that the Northerners were "divested of their overcoats, boots and money, and more particularly, which is the first demand, 'Come, pass over that watch, Yank.'"[33]

In late December 1864, Gay witnessed the arrival at Libby of about 200 Union prisoners, recently captured at the Petersburg, Virginia, front. More than two-thirds had no overcoats or boots, and many suffered frozen feet and later death. Finally, on February 20, news of an exchange arrived at Libby. Gay concluded:

> On the following morning some fifteen hundred privates, all in a most wretched condition, many unable to move without the assistance of some of their comrades who were scarcely able to help themselves, marched down to the rebel flag-of-truce boat, many with only a blanket round them to cover their person. After getting on board the boat, two poor fellows died on the way down the [James] river. At 11 A.M. we arrived in sight of our lines, where so many anxious eyes were gazing, each eager to catch the first glimpse of the old flag, that has been tram-

pled by so many traitors. The moment it was seen, our voices ascended up ten times louder than in Libby, notwithstanding we were still under rebels, but now we had no dread or fear of them. So great was our exultation that we almost forgot that we had but just been released from rebel dungeons. We were soon under the protection of our flag, where we were received with abundance of every thing to make us comfortable, and all en route for Annapolis on our flag-of-truce steamer *New York*, where we received the best of care, and eatables of all kinds, furnished by the Sanitary Commission.[34]

A "First-Class Yard"

Before the Civil War, Portsmouth citizens, New Hampshire politicians, and naval officers stationed locally often clamored for the creation of a "first-class Navy Yard." Support from Washington for a modern comprehensive facility, local interests contended, not only was long overdue but also was essential to enable the Portsmouth Navy Yard to compete on an equal footing for contracts with the Boston Navy Yard, the Brooklyn Navy Yard, and other government installations. The exigencies brought on by the Civil War triggered a building boom that transformed the Yard permanently. From its prewar, sleepy, and second-class status, the Yard had evolved by 1865 into a first-class establishment.

No person was more responsible for this transition than Civil Engineer Benjamin F. Chandler. "Our friend Chandler," observed the *Chronicle* on January 24, 1865, "has been rewarded for his fidelity and shrewd management of the business of his department, by a liberal increase of salary." On February 11, the *Journal* added, "The many well-built public buildings and works of a permanent character at this yard projected by Mr. Chandler and constructed under his supervision, testify to great improvements made in the capacity of the yard for efficiency since he has been located here."[35]

Although the war was rapidly coming to an end, Chandler and Bailey kept pushing in early 1865 for authorization from Washington to undertake new projects. One serious deficiency warranting attention concerned an inadequate water supply. On January 30, Commandant Bailey alerted Rear Admiral Joseph Smith, chief of the Bureau of Yards and Docks: "In consequence of the increased amount of engines & work in this Yard, the reservoirs supplying the water to

The establishment of the Iron Plating Shop at the Portsmouth Navy Yard in 1862 signaled a new era in naval construction. After the clash of the two ironclads, CSS Virginia *and USS* Monitor—*which demonstrated the obsolescence of wooden warships—the world's navies turned to iron (and, later, steel) construction. To build the Yard's first ironclad, the USS* Agamenticus, *beginning in the fall of 1862, the Yard erected the plating shop and stocked it with immense lathes and other metal-fabricating machinery. PNSVC*

help the various establishments in motion, have run dry, and we have been obliged the last week to melt snow to supply the engines.... I would respectfully suggest that a condensing apparatus be provided for such contingencies, which are liable to occur during a drought in summer, or in the absence of rain in the winter. Enclosed I send you communications made to me on the subject, by [Naval] Chief Engineer [Richard M.] Bartleton & Civil Engineer Chandler." Negotiations proceeded. On February 21, Bailey reported to Smith, "The Bureau... directed me to construct new and larger cisterns. I accordingly directed [the] Civil Engineer to commence the construction of a reservoir to contain not less than 200,000 gallons."[36]

On February 24, Smith responded, "You will be authorized to expend the amount asked for a cistern, and the condensing machine may go on although it will be unnecessary I hope, after the cistern shall have been completed."[37]

The Yard succeeded in obtaining funds for both projects. In the Bureau of Yards and Docks annual report, issued in October 1865, the list of expenditures included a condenser. The Navy Department budget for fiscal year 1865-66 appropriated "For reservoir, gutters ... $17,000."[38]

Alterations to "Timber Shed No. 27" created the Iron Platers' Department. The new classes of ships being built were longer, necessitating longer building ways. The extension of the shiphouse over the ironclad *Passaconaway*, then under construction, was plagued during January and February with cold weather. The exterior work on the addition was frequently delayed, but it was completed with the coming of spring. Chandler, Bailey, and the local press also promoted the building of an iron foundry. "The establishment of a good iron-foundry on this Yard," commented the *Chronicle* on March 18, "will be a 'big thing' for the yard itself, and a step of economy on the part of the government. We need also a good ropewalk, and when that is completed, and put in good running order, the Portsmouth Navy Yard will be first-class in point of merit, if it is not 'rated' as such." All of these projects eventually were funded in the naval appropriations.[39]

Conducting this extensive undertaking required many skills. On March 20, the *Chronicle* itemized the various occupations and trades at the Yard, an indication of how all-encompassing the Yard's role had become by 1865:

> The work on the Portsmouth Navy Yard is divided into 37 different classes, in the following order: 22 writing clerks, 2 draughtsmen, 1 receiver of provisions and clothing, 2 receivers of naval stores, 1 examiner of bills, 170 borers, 30 boat-builders, 626 ship carpenters, 23 yard carpenters, 5 coopers, 34 gun carriage makers, 191 joiners, 40 sawyers, 16 spar-makers, 55 boiler-makers, 48 iron-platers; 225 machinists, armorers, brass founders, plumbers, coppersmiths, and pattern-makers, (all of which are included under the head of Machinist's Dept.); 139 smiths and helpers; 72 ca[u]lkers and reamers, 103 gunner's riggers, 343 laborers, 108 masons and helpers, 1 messenger, 25 painters, 42 boatswain's riggers, 50 master's riggers, 47 sailmakers, 32 teamsters, 54 watchmen; 41 helpers for yard purposes, in civil engineer's department; 4 timber markers; 2

on ordnance tug boat; 6 helpers at the naval store. Besides the above, there are 11 civil officers, which include all salaried civilians, from the naval constructor to the porter for the Yard.[40]

Chandler met his objectives. On May 27, in a major article, "NAVY YARD AFFAIRS," the *Journal* effectively summarized the Yard's accomplishments. In addition to elaborating on the Yard's shipbuilding program and physical transformation, the reporter also praised its beautification: "The tastefully laid out esplanade, and fine parade ground are well worthy [of] mention, and reflect credit on their projectors." More important, in its coming of age during the Civil War, the Yard had achieved its long-sought status relative to the other government Navy Yards. "A large sum of money was appropriated, by the last Congress, for 'Repairs,'" concluded the *Journal*, "and the coming summer new buildings will be erected, and improvements made which will tend to effect the consummation so long desired, i.e. a first class yard."[41]

The Demise of Portsmouth's Merchant Marine

In contrast to the improved situation of the Yard, the American merchant marine dropped to third- or fourth-class status. Portsmouth citizens freely understood the significance of this development. "It has been ascertained that more than six hundred sea-going vessels belonging to citizens of the United States," noted the *Journal* on August 19, 1865, "have been sold to subjects of Great Britain during the war. Men of other countries have also bought American ships in large numbers, and it is estimated that a thousand vessels in all that were four years ago carrying the stars and stripes, are now sailing under foreign colors. The capacity of the vessels transferred is estimated at five hundred thousand tons."[42]

Among those affected by the various developments that brought Port of Portsmouth commerce close to ruin, Portsmouth shipping magnate Daniel Marcy suffered both financially and politically. Despite his wealth, Marcy's "Copperhead" sympathies hurt his bid for re-election to Congress. In early January—the state elections would be held on March 14, 1865—the arrival of a controversial visitor further hurt Marcy politically. "Capt. Joseph Leach," reported the *Journal* on January 14, "formerly of the ship *Frank Pierce* [a Marcy vessel], and subsequently captured as a blockade runner, or for some other impropriety against the laws of Father Abraham, and held as a prisoner by Uncle Sam, has been in town of late, the guest of Hon. Daniel Marcy, member of Congress from this District. Whether our Representative has succeeded in obtaining a pardon and allowing Joseph to sojourn with his brethen we are not informed."[43]

Marcy's unpopularity resulted in his expected defeat at the polls on March 14. General Gilman Marston, the Republican candidate and a popular war hero, thrashed Marcy by a 1,500-vote plurality in a three-man congressional race; Marcy failed to take a single ward in Portsmouth. The soldiers' vote went heavily against Marcy.[44]

Shipping trends proved equally disastrous for Marcy's interests. As his namesake ship was sailing across the Pacific, Marcy received news from his Boston office "the unfortunate news of the failure of the charterers of the *Daniel Marcy*. As the largest shipments of rice are usually made in February[,] it may be that the *D.M.* would get her cargo before this news reaches Akyab [Burma, now Sittwe, Thailand] & I only hope by the next mail from India we may get such good news."[45]

On April 22, the *Chronicle* reported: "A letter from the first officer of ship *Daniel Marcy* of New York, dated Akyab, Feb. 12, announces the death of George B. Worth, Jr. of New Bedford, second officer of the ship, he having been stabbed through the heart in December by one of the seamen, and died in half an hour. The ship was in the Strait of Malacca at the time of the murder. The murderer had been sent to Calcutta to be hung. Mr. Worth was ... 26 years of age."[46]

The tragic incident aboard the *Daniel Marcy* resulted from the increasingly common practice of allowing sailors to carry sheath knives or pistols. "Although shipowners are slow to arm their ships to protect themselves against the depredations of British pirates," commented the Boston *Commercial Bulletin*, "the sailors are not slow to arm themselves to resist their own officers. We are credibly informed that hardly a ship of a thousand tons leaves any of our large seaports without a majority of her crew being armed with revolvers."[47]

The general availability and acceptance of individual weapons aboard ship—ostensibly for emergency use against the Confederate enemy—cost the life of at least one Piscataqua-area captain. On April 27, the *Chronicle* reported, "the murder of W.W. French, the master of ... [the ship *William Tell*], off Pernambuco [Recife, Brazil], on the 19th of March." In his reprinted letter, first mate Charles A.C. Harris reported the fatal stabbing of French in his hammock in the after cabin, and the less serious assault on the second mate. With the help of loyal crew members, Harris seized six conspirators and placed them in irons. Upon arriving in Pernambuco, Harris placed the second mate in the hospital, and, with the aid of the American consul, the murderers in prison to await trial. "Capt. French belonged [resided] in Newmarket, N.H.," concluded the *Chronicle*, "and leaves a wife and three children."[48]

Still another New Hampshire ship captain presumably perished at sea. Joshua Hickey, the well-respected Portsmouth mariner who before the war had commanded the *Alice Ball* and the *Henrietta Marcy* for the Marcy empire, sailed again near the end of the war, this time for new owners. "The ship *Eagle Wing*, a noted Boston clipper," announced the *Chronicle* on October 27, "sailed from that city for Bombay in April last, under the command of Capt. Joshua Hickey of this city; and from that time to this, upwards of eight months, no tidings whatever have been received from or of her or the crew." The *Eagle Wing*, together with Captain Hickey and his men, apparently was lost at sea without a trace.[49]

One by one, Portsmouth ships suffered similar fates or changes of status. According to the *Chronicle* on June 28, the clipper *Wild Pigeon*, built in Portsmouth in 1851, was sold for $35,000 in Valparaiso, Chile, to Spanish interests. Regarding the fate of the Portsmouth-built ship *Isaac H. Boardman* and others constructed for the same owners, the *Chronicle* on October 26 reported:

> The British ship *Commander-in-Chief*, formerly the *Isaac H. Boardman*, which was burnt while loading in the dock at Cardiff [Wales] for Callao [Peru], was built in Portsmouth in 1855, for Isaac H. Boardman, Henry Cook, J.B. Morse and others, and registered 1432 tons. At the outbreak of the rebellion she was sold in England, and hailed from Bristol at the time of her loss.... The parties who owned her had quite a fleet of ships in 1860, only one of which, the *Merrimac*, survives. Three of them have gone by fire: first, the *Crown Point*, burnt by the Confederates; second, the *North Atlantic*, burnt at Calcutta, probably by her crew; and now the *Isaac H. Boardman*.[50]

Sources vary as to the price the American merchant marine

paid for the war, but all agree it was enormous. In their 1942 book, American maritime scholars Robert Greenhalgh Albion and Jennie Barnes Pope increased the early estimates. They cited the flight to foreign registry, with 990 ships and barks "sold foreign"; 213 vessels "lost at sea" (probably half of them destroyed by Confederate raiders); fifty-five condemned as unseaworthy; the decline of whaling and whalers (with animal oil preempted by the advent of the petroleum industry); the surge of rail transportation; and lower shipbuilding costs in Canada and elsewhere. Albion and Pope estimated the total loss in all ship categories to the Northern merchant marine fleet at 1,613 vessels, or about 744,000 tons.[51]

The Cruise of the CSS Shenandoah

Although the war had decimated the American merchant marine fleet, and Portsmouth was affected proportionately, the Appomattox Courthouse surrender on April 9, 1865, did not halt Northern maritime losses. Until late June of that year, the war at sea continued. In the era before instantaneous communication, the saga of the CSS *Shenandoah* followed a familiar pattern in pre-twentieth-century naval warfare. Cruises and captures by warships and privateers were often conducted under their captains' mistaken belief (or deliberate pretense) that the conflict was still going on. The CSS *Shenandoah*, under Lieutenant James I. Waddell, who claimed to be unaware of any peace, carried on for the Southern cause. The *Shenandoah* had succeeded the *Alabama* as the scourge of Yankee shipping. By early 1865, the *Alabama*'s once-feared Raphael Semmes had become an object of Northern ridicule. "Semmes, whose pirate ship was sunk by the *Kearsarge*," reported the *Journal* on March 4, 1865, "has been made a Vice Admiral of the rebel navy, and will command the James River [Virginia] fleet!—which fleet has free passage way at present as far towards the sea as Fort Darling, say six miles. A formidable field of operation for an Admiral." By that time, in the eyes of Portsmouth citizens, Waddell had replaced Semmes as a plundering villain on the high seas.[52]

In a career resembling that of Semmes, Waddell, an ex-United States naval officer, took command of the British Indiaman *Sea King* in October 1864, off the island of Porto Santo, near the Portuguese island of Madeira. Renaming his 790-ton vessel the CSS *Shenandoah*, Waddell hoisted the Confederate flag and set out, armed with six guns and manned by an English crew. His orders were to concentrate upon New England whaling fleets in the Pacific. Whaling, in fact, was on the decline. "The whale fishery has nearly given out," reported the *Journal* on January 21, 1865. "Last year the fleet decreased 27 vessels of 8375 tons.... Petroleum has superseded whale oil, and shortly the whales will be left to a more peaceful life." The *Shenandoah's* objective was to attack the almost defenseless whaling vessels in remote waters, where a Confederate raider would be least expected. This concerted policy of destruction was designed to sap Northern commerce and morale.[53]

To reach the Arctic whaling grounds, Waddell initially sailed across the Atlantic toward South America. While still in the mid-Atlantic on November 12, the *Shenandoah's* log records, "At 12:15 a.m., fired a gun and hove ... to and boarded her. She proved to be the *Kate Prince* of Portsmouth, N.H., but having a neutral cargo was bonded for $40,000; sent all prisoners on board for passage to Bahia, Brazil." Ship captain Henry Libbey of Portsmouth, master of the *Kate Prince*, was relieved to save his ship. He had left Cardiff, Wales, carrying a cargo of coal for Bahia, with a certified bill of lading. "Captain Waddell and officers," wrote Libbey in his report, "treated myself and mate with such civilities as were consistent with the circumstances." It was not until early January 1865, a month and a half later, that, through newspaper accounts, Portsmouth learned about the ransoming of the *Kate Prince*. (The vessel had arrived at Bahia on November 28.)[54]

Although she was safely docked in a neutral port, the ordeal of the *Kate Prince* had not ended. By law, she required proper identification papers, so on January 24, 1865, representing the firm of William Jones & Son, part owners and agents for the *Kate Prince*, an unnamed secretary wrote Port of Portsmouth Collector Timothy Upham in an effort to replace the stolen documents. After reviewing the details of the ship's seizure, the secretary asserted, "The Register ... of the *Kate Prince* was kept back by Capt. Wardell [*sic*] & the *K.P.* was forced to take the prisoners [previously captured American merchant sailors] from the *Shenandoah* & convey them to Bahia. We now write to ask that you grant us a new Register for the *Kate Prince* and we desire to obtain such as soon as possible as the ship will be sailing without any proper papers & might not be able to make her position clear, or to show that she is an American vessel." Three days later, the Treasury Department contacted Upham, acknowledged that the *Kate*

CSS Shenandoah, *the last Confederate raider on the high seas, continued to destroy Union shipping after the war officially ended. PEM*

Prince was "robbed of ships-papers," and authorized him "to grant the new Register as requested." After unloading her coal in Bahia and receiving the new documents, the *Kate Prince* sailed for Calcutta.[55]

Waddell sailed the *Shenandoah* in the opposite direction. After rounding Cape Horn and crossing the Pacific, the *Shenandoah* arrived at Melbourne, Australia, on January 25, 1865. After undergoing repairs and reacting to American diplomatic pressure, she set sail before dawn on February 18. Less than two weeks later, on March 1, the Portsmouth-built ship *James Montgomery* arrived unexpectedly at the same port. An article appearing in a Melbourne newspaper, reprinted by the *Chronicle* three months later, observed:

> Considerable excitement was manifested yesterday morning [February 28, 1865] in Collins street, and till about noon it was supposed by many that the *Shenandoah* had made her first capture in Australian waters. The ship *James Montgomery*, with tobacco, kerosene, and lumber, from Boston—one of the American ships expected for sometime past—was reported at five o'clock on the previous evening as being off Cape Otway,

with a fair wind for the Heads. It was expected she would reach the entrance of the [Port Phillip] Bay [Melbourne] at daylight, but as nothing was heard of her from Queenscliff at a late hour in the forenoon, the suspicion became strong that she had been pounced upon by the Confederate cruiser. This conjecture was supported by the fact that the owner of the *James Montgomery* is believed to be so thoroughly Federal in his principles that his ship would sail under the stars and stripes, and no other flag. Shortly before noon, however, anxiety was set at rest by the arrival of the ship, unseen and unmolested by the enemy. It was stated in town yesterday that the *Shenandoah* is at anchor in a bay on the Tasmanian coast, where she is having a double deck laid down, and being made stronger and more formidable as a fighting ship.[56]

While the *James Montgomery* had managed to evade capture, the *Shenandoah*, repaired and reprovisioned, was now free to pursue American whalers. Waddell headed north, capturing barks off Ascension Island, and in the Sea of Okhotsk. By mid-June, the *Shenandoah* had reached the Bering Sea, where the American whaling fleet out of New Bedford had congregated. In actions on June 22, 25, and 28, Waddell captured twenty-four whalers and burned all but four, virtually and effectively closing down Yankee whaling operations in Arctic waters. Six weeks later, sketchy reports of the *Shenandoah*'s Bering Sea exploits reached Portsmouth. "The Rebel Privateer," headlined the *Journal*'s story on August 5, with the conclusion, "Her Commander [Waddell] was informed of Lee's surrender and the collapse of the rebellion, but did not believe it. He believed in Mr. Lincoln's assassination, for he expected it."[57]

Not until August 26 did Portsmouth captain Orlando G. Robinson, master of the whaling bark *Gypsey* (or *Gipsey* in Waddell's reports), arrive home. Two months earlier, on June 26, the *Shenandoah* had captured the *Gypsey*, confiscated her nautical instruments, burned the whaler, and removed Robinson's crew for boarding the ransomed *General Pike*. On August 28, the *Chronicle* published an interview with the *Gypsey* captain: "He [Robinson] mentions the fact that after getting on board of the ship *Gen. Pike* (the only vessel that was bonded, and into which 252 men were crowded to be sent home) he (Capt. Robinson) remarked to the captain of another whaler in the hearing of the pirate captain Waddell, that they wouldn't have provi-

"Destruction of Whaleships off Cape Thaddeus, Arctic Ocean, June 23, 1865, by the Confederate Steamer Shenandoah," *an 1874 watercolor by Benjamin Russell, depicts an action that occurred two months after the war ended, a series of engagements that was vilified by the Union and has remained controversial ever since. New Bedford Whaling Museum.*

sions enough to last them to San Francisco, whereupon the pirate chief said, 'Kill your Kanakas [Hawaiian sailors] and eat them; you have plenty of 'em!'"[58]

"A beautiful specimen of Southern chivalry," editorialized the *Chronicle*. "Two hundred and fifty two men robbed of everything, crowded on board a small whaling barque, with the advice to resort to cannibalism in case their provisions gave out! ... We, with the numerous friends of Capt. Robinson, rejoice with his family in the fact of his safe arrival home once more, and express the hope that he may live to see Waddell hung higher than Haman [in the Old Testament, a man executed as an enemy of the Jewish people]."[59]

In Portsmouth, passions against Waddell continued to run high. On September 8, the *Chronicle* reprinted a story from the *Sag Harbor* (New York) *Express*, which stated that "when the pirate [Waddell] boarded the *Favorite* [a whaler captured on June 28], Capt. Young of that vessel attempted to shoot Waddell ... with a bomb-gun, but unfortunately the mate had removed the cap from the gun, unknown to the Captain. He was told that it was sure death for him to shoot. He replied, 'I die willingly, could I kill that wretch.' The pirates immediately handcuffed him, and put him in the coal-hole of the pirate." For his part, Waddell claimed that Captain Young was drunk during the incident.[60]

Unwilling to take his chances were he to surrender at an American port, Waddell completed a global circumnavigation. In November 1865, he sailed to Liverpool, England, to deliver his ship to British authorities. Paraphrasing an article in the *Liverpool Post*, the *Chronicle* on November 23 noted, "The crew of the pirate *Shenandoah* brought on shore a quantity of luggage, and appeared to have no lack of money—facts which appear to attest that their long cruise did not go unrewarded. Many of the crew were Liverpool men, and these, immediately on being landed, drove to their homes."[61]

From Waddell's and the Confederacy's perspective, it was, indeed, a highly successful cruise. Waddell had captured thirty-eight ships, destroying all but four. The *Shenandoah* took 1,053 prisoners. Damage to Union commerce was judged at $1.3 million, and as a result of the *Shenandoah*'s actions, the world market price of whale oil jumped from $140 to $240 a ton.[62]

The Portsmouth press immediately denounced the destruction of the Yankee whaling fleet as legally and morally unjustifiable. Receiving the "latest news from Liverpool, [on] November 9," the *Chronicle* reported on November 21, "Capt. Waddell says the first information he received of the close of the war was on August 30th, from the British vessel *Banacouta*, and that he immediately consigned his guns to the hold and steered for Liverpool." The *Chronicle*'s reaction to Waddell's story was blunt: "Capt. Waddell lies; he knew it long before, but it was appropriate for him to wait for British information." The *Journal* was equally skeptical. Criticizing an article that appeared in the *London Times*, the *Journal* on December 2 scoffed at Waddell's posture of innocence: "Her Captain (Waddell) continued his depredations long after being informed of the surrender of the Confederate armies, but *would not* be convinced until a *British* vessel had confirmed. He then steers for Liverpool, and gives up his vessel to the English Government. These facts make that Government justly answerable, and she cannot fail to be so officially notified. The crew, 180 in number, have all been liberated, with the special plunder of each, and no questions asked; some boasting that the *Shenandoah* was the last to pull down the Confederate flag."[63]

Victory Amid Violence

Despite the distant forays of the CSS *Shenandoah*, the capture of Fort Fisher in mid-January 1865 had been the last major U.S. Navy campaign in the Civil War. By April, less than three months later, the conflict, for all intents and purposes, had ended. Until peace took hold, however, minor naval expeditions, routine seizures of the dwindling numbers of blockade runners, and the completion of nearly finished construction projects—interspersed with the usual rumors and overblown alarms—occupied the day-to-day, almost anticlimactic attention of the Union navy and the Portsmouth Navy Yard.

During the final months of war, Portsmouth sailors sent encouraging news from their ships. In a private letter, dated "Key West [Florida], Feb. 22," an unnamed officer or sailor related:

We [on board the USS *Alliance*] arrived at this port this morning, from a trip up the coast, and to-morrow morning we leave for St. Marks [a port of entry south of Tallahassee], with Gen. [John] Newton and staff on board. We are to attack that place, as it is the only port open to blockade runners, except Galveston [Texas]. We are to take 300 troops, and 1200 have gone to-day, in two vessels. Eight armed vessels are to take a part in this expedition, and the land force to co-operate with the navy. The rebels there have one ram and a floating battery.

We brought down 17 rebel prisoners from U.S. bark *Midnight*, who were taken by a boat expedition from that vessel. The sailors took their launch 24 miles overland, got *above* the Johnnys [rebels], and surprised them. These rebel soldiers were stationed as a guard to keep the negroes from escaping down river, but our sailors took 150 negroes, with the guard, and we brought them all to Key West together....

On our way here we spoke the army transport *Reliance*, a few hours from Fort Myers, with intelligence that the Fort was invested by 4000 rebels. We put our prisoners and negroes on board the R. [*Reliance*], and steered for the place, where we arrived on the morning of the 20th, but could not get up within five miles of the fort. We therefore sent up two boats—*Launch* and *Second Cutter*—with a 24-lb boat howitzer, which soon cleaned out the rebels. Our loss was eight negro soldiers killed and as many wounded. The rebels caught one negro, killed and quartered him. Our darkeys say they will not be taken, and threaten to retaliate at St. Marks, if they get a chance.

We remained till Fort Myers was reinforced, and then left for Key West.[64]

This speculation proved accurate. On March 3 and 4, a joint Union army-navy expedition succeeded in crossing the bar to blockade the mouth of the St. Marks River. The port of St. Marks thus was effectively closed to Confederate shipping.[65]

A similar letter also reflected the impending-end-of-the-war mood. After the USS *Albatross* had been recommissioned at the Portsmouth Navy Yard in late December 1864, she sailed on January 6, 1865, for reassignment with the West Gulf Blockading Squadron. From aboard the *Albatross* in New Orleans, on February 23, an officer, signing only as "IOTA," related, almost cavalierly, the latest news. After describing the rescue of 300 troops aboard the grounded U.S. transport *Empire City* at Elbow Key, Florida, he wrote:

We shaped our course for Key West, Florida, where we arrived about 8 o'clock Saturday morning [February 21]. Here Captain Du Bois received instructions to proceed to New Orleans with the soldiers, via [the Dry] Tortugas, where he would leave the prisoners [at Fort Jefferson]. While lying at the wharf at Key West a plot was discovered among the prisoners to escape. They had procured a key to unlock their irons, but the plot was discovered in season to prevent its consummation.

We left Key West that night about 11 o'clock and steered for the Dry Tortugas, which we reached about 10 the next day. Here we landed the prisoners, and glad enough [we] were to get rid of them. Having finished this part of our work we steered for New Orleans, where we arrived at 11:30 Monday night [February 23]. The next day we landed our ship-wrecked soldiers. During our passage up the river, the officers that we took from the wreck held a meeting and invited the officers of the *Albatross* to a supper at the St. Charles Hotel, New Orleans.

After enjoying ourselves until about 1 o'clock we broke up our meeting by singing Auld Lang Syne.... You see that we have some good times. The health of the officers and crew is good, very few cases of sickness, and these light. Where we are bound is not decided yet....[66]

At the Portsmouth Navy Yard, daily activities also assumed a more relaxed mood. In contrast to the frenzy of accelerated ship construction and repair associated with the earlier wartime years, attention now centered on payrolls, legal questions, and religious services. "The disbursements at the Portsmouth Navy Yard, (including $159,000 distributed last week,) on the payroll for wages and salaries alone, for the past year, we are informed have amounted to upwards of two and a half millions of dollars," the *Chronicle* reported on February 21. The next month, the story was about the same. "There are 2645 names on the February Roll," noted the *Chronicle* on March 18, "and $144,840 are required to pay this body of workmen."[67]

The draft status of Yard workers was interpreted differently in Maine and New Hampshire. A circular issued by Maine's provost general granted draft exemption to skilled government workers; New Hampshire, by contrast, was less lenient on this issue. Quoting the Maine directive, the *Chronicle* on March 25 addressed the controversy: "The original intent of the law was not to exempt every first class mechanic employed on Navy Yards or elsewhere for the Government; but *only* [those] so very skillful that their services could not be replaced, thereby depriving the government of the services of the right man in the right place. It would be absurd to suppose that the services of one or two hundred first class carpenters, joiners, or machinists could not be replaced by twice the number of equally well skilled men glad enough to fill those places."[68]

Another yard-related situation provoked a response. A spirit of social reform sought to counteract the influence of Portsmouth's notorious Water Street, which continued to attract off-duty Navy Yard workers. To divert attention from Water Street, a daily prayer meeting was instituted near Number 27 Timber Shed and attended by many Yard workmen. "There has been a growing necessity for such an 'institution' for the past few months," commented the *Chronicle* on March 27, "owing to such a large number of strangers employed on the Yard from neighboring towns, who, having left their families and become free from the restraining influences of home, are careless in their habits, and allow themselves to become demoralized to a greater or less extent." Some individuals were "recklessly sacrificing their religion, reputation and honor, by plunging into these vices and scenes of dissipation common to communities created with a mushroom rapidity."[69]

The end of the war apparently eliminated or reduced these concerns. In the early spring of 1865, news of union victories in Virginia produced immediate elation at the Yard. The Yard Log for April 4 reads, "21 guns were fired at noon in honor of the capture of Richmond." Lee's surrender at Appomattox Courthouse on April 9 triggered an even greater celebration. At noon on Monday, April 10, Yard workmen, assembled under a flagstaff, gave three hearty cheers for the flag, as well as additional ones for the Yard Commandant. "In consequence of the welcome intelligence from General [Ulysses S.] Grant," Admiral Bailey proclaimed to the crowd, "work on the Yard will be suspended for the remainder of the day."[70]

That afternoon, a fracas occurred in Portsmouth that remains embroiled in controversy. The role of the Yard workers in this event also appears blurred. In an article entitled, "Riot and Mobocracy in Portsmouth—The *States and Union* Printing Office Destroyed," editor Joshua L. Foster declared:

> Work on the Navy Yard was suspended at noon and the plan was deliberately concocted of destroying our office. Large numbers of the men there employed came to the streets and visited the [Water Street] rumholes of our city, got well liquored up and soon commenced the scene of the riot which raged from about 2 P.M. to 4 or 5 P.M. without restraint or any effective effort at restraint by the authorities whose sworn duty it is to guard and protect the public peace and save the property of citizens from destruction.[71]

When a half dozen men appeared on the street below Foster's second-story office, they urged him to display his loyalty to the Union by unfurling the American flag. Since Foster did not have a flag at hand, he could not immediately comply. A crowd gathered, shouting such threats as "Clean out the office," "Hang him," and "String him up." Before long, the mob swelled to more than 2,000 people, becoming increasingly impatient. At this point, Provost Marshal Daniel Hall intervened, pleading with the mob not to molest Foster.[72]

When Foster disappeared monetarily from the window, the crowd turned ugly, smashing through the doors of the newspaper office. Once inside, the rioters hurled type, presses, ink, paper, and other supplies and equipment to the street below. Foster barely escaped with his life.[73]

The editors of both the *Chronicle* and the *Journal* promptly condemned the anarchy and praised Portsmouth Mayor John H. Bailey for reading the text of the Riot Act, ordering the mob to disperse, and closing all the saloons in the city. In his next issue, delayed until April 19 and printed by the *Manchester* (NH) *Union* presses, Foster rendered his account of the riot: "What a craven set are those fellows on the Navy Yard and their aiders and abettors in Portsmouth." Notwithstanding Foster's accusations, the following month he submitted a claim for $15,000 in damages—suing not the Navy Yard but rather the City of Portsmouth, represented by the mayor and the board of aldermen. (Portsmouth Navy Yard records during this period are utterly silent on the incident.) Urged by the board of aldermen to withdraw his petition for redress, Foster evidently complied. In any case, Foster never collected.[74]

In retrospect, the 1865 riot, lacking any evidence of a concerted plot, appears to have been an almost spontaneous action. Unlike the 1863 Portsmouth Draft Riot, which represented a more organized clash against city and United States government authorities, the 1865 violence was targeted against a single individual. Through his Copperhead-oriented *States and Union*, Foster had greatly alienated the pro-Union, Republican majority in the city, and the end of the war impulsively unleashed these long-pent-up frustrations, focusing on Foster as the enemy personified.

Only hours after the attack on Foster on April 10, Yard workers and citizens of Portsmouth gathered in Market Square to celebrate the Union victory. Culminating a day of bell ringing, band playing, bonfires, and fireworks, Yard personnel fired a salute of one hundred guns in Market Square. John McGraw (also described as McGrath or Magraw), a leather worker in the Yard's Ordnance Department, was assisting in firing the salutes. McGraw was holding a ramrod in the gun, the cannon discharged prematurely and blew off his hands.[75]

Mangled as he was, McGraw survived, but with a wife and several small children to support, the wounded man required immediate financial assistance. During the lunch hour on April 12, a large number of Yard workmen assembled and unanimously pledged half a day's wages per man to benefit McGraw and his family. This campaign raised $3,000. At the same time, the officers and men of the Yard's

No. 444.   U. S. Navy Yard, Portsmouth, N. H.

Commandant's Office, April 11, 1865.

Sir:

    I have the honor to acknowledge the receipt of your order of the 10th inst. (by telegraph,) directing me to fire a national salute in honor of the capture of the rebel General Lee and the army of northern Virginia. — Which order was carried into execution last evening.

      I am most respectfully,
        Your obt. servt.,

           T. Bailey
           Comdr.

Hon. Gideon Welles,
   Secretary of the Navy
     Washington,
       D.C.

NA-DC

receiving ship, USS *Vandalia*, collected a purse of about \$330.[76]

On Saturday, April 15, news of President Abraham Lincoln's assassination reached the Yard. Work was suspended immediately until further notice. "I received the Department's telegram," Commandant Bailey wrote Secretary Welles on April 18, acknowledging Welles's order, "directing that, on Wednesday, the 19th inst., the day of the funeral solemnities of the late President, work be suspended, the flags kept at half-mast, and twenty-one minute guns fired at meridian." The next day, a company of marines, along with naval and marine officers in uniform, marched in a memorial procession in Portsmouth. Gunners on the USS *Vandalia* fired a one-gun salute every half hour between sunrise and sunset. On Friday, April 21, work at the Yard finally resumed. Peace had begun, but the country remained in mourning.[77]

Peacetime Priorities

Peace ushered in a more sobering time of unemployment and economic transition. For four heady years, the frenzy of wartime activity at the Yard had provided a boom for Portsmouth and its environs. With peace, that situation changed overnight. The United States Navy also retrenched. The war boom, in short, became the peace bust.

Secretary of the Navy Gideon Welles was determined to slash costs. On May 2, he informed Commandant Bailey, "It is important that the expenses of the Navy should be reduced to the lowest possible limit, and to do this there must be rigid economy in all matters connected with Navy Yards and Naval Stations. All superfluous writers [clerks] and employees of every description attached to the Yard must be discharged and you will put no repairs on vessels of the Navy, except those of the Navy proper, without especial authority from the Department."[78]

From April on, the message from Washington, bureau by bureau, and within the Yard itself, was clear. "Suspend until further orders," wrote Bureau Chief of Equipment and Recruiting Andrew Smith to Bailey on April 17, "all naval enlistments, except those of persons having Honorable Discharges." A week later, on April 24, Smith slashed even further: "You will order the Rendezvous at Kittery closed permanently, and employees discharged. Men are to be enlisted on board the Rec[eivin]g Ship [USS *Vandalia*], where the Books,

Blanks, Stationery &c. are to be transferred. Store the furniture in the yard." Captain Percival Drayton, Farragut's fleet captain during the Battle of Mobile Bay and now assigned to a desk job as Bureau Chief of the Navigation Department, sent Bailey two circular orders, dated May 6 and 8. In the latter, Drayton ordered that "no further purchases of articles in any Department Supplies ... will be made." Furthermore, "All orders for the purchases of Navigation Supplies, not predicated upon instructions from this Bureau, issued since the last 1st instant [May 1, 1865], will be and are revoked." Directives from Captain John Lenthall, Bureau Chief of Construction and Repair, canceled all new construction.[79]

This policy had an immediate impact on the Portsmouth Navy Yard's workforce. By May 5, 1865, employment at the Yard had reached its zenith, with 2,563 men on the rolls, the largest number heretofore in the Yard's history. Five days later, on May 10, Engineer Benjamin Chandler reported to Bailey, "As works (on which I am now occupied) are completed[,] I shall recommend the discharge of mechanics and laborers and reduce my employees to the lowest possible number."[80]

Reductions began forthwith. "About seven hundred and fifty Navy Yard workmen were discharged from the Yard on Monday [May 22] and Tuesday [May 23] of this week," reported the *Chronicle* a day later. "This number includes carpenters, borers, joiners, spar makers, calkers, gunner's riggers, boatswain's riggers, machinists, watchmen, boat-builders, smiths, yard carpenters and sail makers. Discharges from other departments are soon to follow, which will reduce the force to about 33 per cent. The suspension of so large a number of working-men will necessarily affect the interests of this city, and a reduction in prices of rents must immediately ensue." In June, 2,300 workmen were employed; by July, the Yard payroll of mechanics and laborers dipped to $97,000, about one-half of the amount for March. As the end of 1865 approached, the workforce continued to drop. "The number of men employed there [the Yard] at the present time," noted the *Chronicle* on November 25, "is about nineteen hundred, one thousand of whom will probably receive a 'ticket-of-leave.' Every department under the cognizance of the Bureau of Construction and Repair have had their 'quotas' assigned them in relation to the number to retain or discharge." In 1866, as the result of successive layoffs, the Yard's workforce totaled 876 men.[81]

Among those affected by the workforce reduction was

Benjamin F. Martin, master spar maker at the Yard. On November 21, 1865, citing Welles's instructions, Commandant Bailey informed Martin: "Your services as Master Spar Maker will be dispensed with after the 30th inst. The work will then be superintended by a Quarterman.—If agreeable to you, you can remain in charge of the work with the rate and pay of Quarterman." Protesting his demotion in a two-page response to Bailey on November 27, Martin argued, "Four years ago last May I had the honor to receive the appointment which I now hold as Master Spar Maker in this Yard, at which time I left my business in Portsmouth, N.H. to attend to its duties, and invite inspection to the manner in which I endeavored to discharge its duties.… My being disrated is against all precedent while so large a number of workmen are employed, and [so] that he [Gideon Welles] will revoke the order in relation thereto I respectfully ask that you will refer this communication for his consideration and decision." Martin's appeal, if it ever reached Washington, went unheeded. In the end, he remained at the Yard as a block maker.[82]

Within the United States Navy itself, large numbers of officers and men were leaving the service or adjusting to new conditions. Paraphrasing an article from the *Army and Navy Journal*, the *Chronicle* on August 11 noted, "Volunteer naval officers of every grade are being dismissed [from] the service as rapidly as possible. Nearly all are granted four months' leave, preparatory to their dismissal." For those inclined to join the U.S. Navy as enlisted personnel, compensation was limited. Two notices in the *Chronicle*, dated April 25 and August 2, solicited enlistees. The first read: "To ship for ONE YEAR, on Receiving Ship *Vandalia*, one YEOMAN writing a good hand, at $30 per month; one QUARTER GUNNER, at $25 per month; two BOATSWAINS, at $25 per month; one MASTER-AT-ARMS, at $35 per month. No Bounty given." Featuring a drawing of a ship and the caption, "All Hands Ahoy!" the August notice offered even less money for naval service: "WANTED—Three Years' Men for the U.S. Naval Service. SEAMEN—$20 per month. Ordinary Seamen—$16 per month. Landsmen—$14 per month. Three Months' Advance Paid. Apply on board the U.S. Receiving Ship *Vandalia*, Portsmouth, N.H."[83]

During these months of transition, the navy, the Yard, and the governor of New Hampshire reviewed numerous appeals relative to discharges and employment. The United States Navy was reverting to peacetime status so rapidly that it was difficult to provide immediate satisfaction for individual cases.

Government hiring policy favored returning veterans. "Returning soldiers have the preference when vacancies are to be filled in Navy Yards and government work," reported the *Chronicle* on May 3. "Their names are registered, their former employment stated, and when requisitions are made for men in the respective departments, master workmen are obliged to first consult this register, and employ those there recorded, if such be found. About four hundred have registered their names on the Portsmouth Navy Yard."[84]

Letters directed to public officials reflect postwar anxieties. Typical was an appeal sent to incoming New Hampshire Governor Frederick Smythe. Writing Smythe from the USS *Ohio* on June 12, sailor Oliver P. Cross, a native of Charlestown, New Hampshire, reviewed his case: "I expected to get my discharge as soon as the war was over[.] I entered on Board of the *Vandalia* receiving Ship at Portsmouth but have since been transfered to the *Ohio* where I now am[.] I left my property with my father who is over seventy years old[,] his health is very poor this spring and he is unable to at[t]end to it, so sir if you would use your great influence to get my discharge you will releive [*sic*] the state from paying my family state aid and confer on me a favour that can never be forgot[.]"[85]

John S. Frost and William J. Frost wished to return to work at the Yard. Writing from New Castle, New Hampshire, on November 20, 1865, they initially addressed their request to Secretary of War Edwin M. Stanton, but wrote Secretary Welles's name over Stanton's: "My brother and myself served in the Navy on board the *Vandalia* one year. We each received an honorable discharge Sept. 1st 1865. Since that time we have been out of employment, and we are induced to write you hoping you will aid us in getting employment at the Forts in this harbor or the Navy Yard."[86]

Even if Welles responded to their request, he had little to offer. The Navy Department had tightened hiring procedures. "The secretary of the Navy has issued an order," reported the *Chronicle* on October 11, "directing that hereafter all applications for the position of master workmen in navy yards must be addressed to the Chief of the Bureau of Yards and Docks in Washington, accompanied by recommendations and a statement of qualifications, and whenever a vacancy occurs in any yard, selection for the place will be made from the applicants accepted as competent, without regard to State or locality."[87]

During early October 1865, another Washington directive

ordered the reduction of wages at the Yard for each category of workman for the months of October and November. Pay for carpenters, blacksmiths, coppersmiths, machinists, and masons, for example, was reduced from $3 per day to $2.75. On Wednesday, October 18, four hundred machinists met at a Portsmouth hall to protest, listen to speakers, and to draft a petition (then called a "memorial") addressed to Secretary Welles. A delegation of workers presented the "memorial" to Bailey, who forwarded the document to Washington. Rumors persisted that a committee would travel to Washington in an effort to restore the wage rate to its old standard. However, the lobbying trip never materialized and wages remained reduced.[88]

As a direct result of the cost-cutting measures within the United States Navy and at the various Yards, the wage structure of the American merchant marine also plummeted. During June, when more than a thousand navy men were discharged, former sailors scrambled for any available job with private shipping companies. According to one perceptive article, "The Supply of Seamen," reprinted from the *New York Journal of Commerce* by the *Chronicle* on July 29, the outlook was grim: "Owing to the discharge from employment in the navy of large numbers of seamen, the mercantile marine has been better supplied than ever before, and generally with men possessing good qualifications. For the same reason seamen's wages have fallen about 50 per cent. Six months ago the advance [in wages] to Liverpool was $130, now it is only $25. Then seamen received $50 per month, now they get only half that sum. The decline is greater than has taken place in any other of the industrial vocations."[89]

Praise for the Yard's War Effort

In the days following Portsmouth's Market Square victory celebration of April 10, the scent of war—not peace—still lingered. The last unaccounted-for Confederate ram was still loose on the high seas. Writing from Washington on April 28, Secretary of the Navy Welles ordered Commandant Bailey, "Hurry forward the work on the *Agamenticus....* The departure of the [Confederate] ram *Stonewall* from Teneriffe [Canary Islands], as is supposed, for our own coast renders it important that all the available formidable force at our command should be in readiness...." On May 3, the *Chronicle* expressed confidence: "Orders have been received at the Portsmouth Navy Yard to prepare the iron-clad *Agamenticus* for sea. A rumor prevails that a rebel ram has been seen outside on the coast, which probably occasioned the haste in fitting her out. Her machinery [during a 96-hour trial conducted at the Yard] works admirably, and if she is stationed at the mouth of our harbor, we need ask no other means of defence from rebel incursions."[90]

The logbook of the USS *Agamenticus* on May 5 records her initial sea trials: "Started fires under all the Boilers, & made preparations for proceeding to the Lower Anchorage.... At 3:45 Left the Navy Yard & steamed down to center Buoy off Fort Constitution & made fast with [illegible word] at 4:05. Banked fires. Stationed crew." The sea trials were successful, and the ironclad was commissioned the same day. "We will risk her [the *Agamenticus*]," reported the *Chronicle* on May 6, "against anything foreign or domestic, in the shape of a naval battery."[91]

Commander Charles H. Cushman, captain of the *Agamenticus*, was still recovering from wounds sustained at Fort Fisher, so Secretary Welles on May 6 selected Commander Enoch G. Parrott, then in New York, to take permanent command, ordering him to "proceed to Portsmouth, N.H., without delay." On May 12, Parrott reported to the Yard and the *Agamenticus* for duty. The alarm over the *Stonewall* lasted only another week, however. On May 19, the Confederate ram arrived in Havana and was handed over to Spanish authorities. In return for this transfer, the *Stonewall* commander received $16,000, the amount needed to pay off his officers and crew. With the neutralization of the *Stonewall*, the *Agamenticus* returned to the Yard on May 29. There, operating under a less demanding schedule, workmen completed the final outfitting of the Portsmouth ironclad. Finally, on August 13, 1865, the *Agamenticus*, requiring three years of construction and costing slightly more than $1 million, steamed out of the Yard for sea duty.[92]

In mid-1865, the Yard's daily routine assumed a more relaxed pace. During June, for example, a number of Union warships were declared surplus: the *Winona*, the *Dawn*, the *Ethan Allen*, the *Galena*, the *Wamsutta*, the *Arkansas*, and the *Henry Janes* arrived at the Yard for decommissioning. Unlike the previous summer, when the *De Soto* had docked without proper quarantine, the Portsmouth Board of Health enforced the regulations, detaining the vessels briefly in the Lower Harbor before allowing them to proceed to the Yard itself. Perhaps because of these precautions, no cases of yellow fever were reported at the Yard or in Portsmouth in 1865.[93]

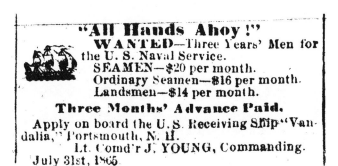

"All Hands Ahoy!"
WANTED—Three Years' Men for
the U. S. Naval Service.
SEAMEN—$20 per month.
Ordinary Seamen—$16 per month.
Landsmen—$14 per month.
Three Months' Advance Paid.
Apply on board the U. S. Receiving Ship "Vandalia," Portsmouth, N. H.
Lt. Comd'r J. YOUNG, Commanding.
July 31st, 1865.

PC, Aug. 2, 1865

On July 8, Commandant Bailey placed an advertisement in the *Journal*, announcing an auction on Thursday, July 20, at the Yard to dispose of the vessels. Reporting the results on July 22, the *Journal* noted, "Five of the six vessels ... were sold by Auction.... The sale was attended by a large number of the heavy business men from New York, Boston, Portland, and smaller cities.... Bidding was quite brisk on the sailing vessels, opening moderate on the steamers, and closing dull." At various times during the summer, the Yard also sold other ships, as well as "50 CORDS MANURE," "TURPENTINE BARRELS," tools, life preservers, linseed oil, and other expendable items that would fetch a price.[94]

The USS *Agamenticus*, on which the Yard had invested so much time, money, and effort over the years, was also affected by the navy cutback. After operating off the northern New England Coast for less than two months, the *Agamenticus* was decommissioned on September 30, 1865, at the Boston Navy Yard. There she lay "in ordinary" (in modern parlance, "in mothballs") for five years. Renamed the *Terror*, the warship finally rejoined the North Atlantic fleet in 1870.[95]

Other evidence of the slower pace at the Yard was the fact that for two days, July 18 and 19, extreme heat spurred the suspension of all work—a circumstance that never would have occurred during the war. Other activities were of a similar nature. "The firing of cannon on Monday [July 31, 1865] morning about 9 o'clock," reported the *Chronicle* the next day, "was at the Fort on Sullivan's [should be Seavey's] Island, preparatory to removing them, no further use being anticipated for these weapons of war." At the end of August, by proclamation of President Andrew Johnson, all restrictions were removed on trade with the South. To aid navigation for naval and commercial ships, lighthouses along the southern coast, sabotaged or destroyed

---

No Charge for Services.

U. S. SANITARY COMMISSION

ARMY & NAVY CLAIM AGENCY.

By appointment of the National Commission at Washington, the subscriber has opened an office in Portsmouth, N. H., and will attend to the

COLLECTION OF

Soldiers' and Sailors' Claims

on the Government for PENSIONS, BACK-PAY, PRIZE MONEY, &c., without charge for services.

Having a central office in Washington, the Commission have unusual facilities to give prompt attention to these matters. Apply to

S. HOLMAN, Local Agent,   )
No 5 Congress St. (Up Stairs.
Portsmouth, N. H., June 28, 1865.

PC, June 28, 1865

during the war, were restored. On December 7, the *Chronicle* announced, "The Lighthouse Board gives notice of the re-establishment, since the 8th of October, of a fixed red light on Southwest Reef, Atchafalaya Bay, La.; of a fixed white light on Shell Keys, south point of Marsh Island, La.; of a fixed white light on Timballier [*sic*] Island, La.; and of a fixed white light at Matagorda, Texas." In December 1865, an additional eighty-six lighthouses on the South Atlantic and Gulf Coasts, however, still needed to be re-established.[96]

Undoubtedly the most exciting event of the summer at the Yard was the visit of Vice Admiral David G. Farragut. During June and July of 1865, the architect of the Union naval victory had undertaken a triumphal tour throughout the Northeast, attending a round of banquets, receptions, and public appearances in New York, Boston, and the White Mountains. Upon arriving in Portsmouth on July 20, Farragut and his family proceeded to Quarters "A," the commandant's residence, as the guests of Rear Admiral Bailey.[97]

On July 24, Farragut, Bailey, and their aides prepared to leave the Yard aboard the steam tug *Portfire* for a short voyage down the coast to Rye Beach, where the "old hero" was to spend a few restful days. The next day, the *Chronicle* captured the dramatic occasion:

In the Yard all the workmen congregated on the wharf to witness the departure of the greatest naval hero of the war.

Admiral Bailey introduced him to the crowd present—numbering upwards of fifteen hundred workmen—in the following manner: "Gentlemen, I take pleasure in introducing to you Vice Admiral Farragut, the hero of many hard-fought battles, and one who has done as much to crush the rebellion as any other man in the country. Gentlemen, I propose three times three cheers for Admiral Farragut." This was done with a will, the effect being almost deafening.

The "hero of the Mississippi" then responded in a neat and appropriate manner as follows: "Gentlemen, I thank you for the honor you have done me on this occasion in thus assembling and by your enthusiastic cheers, testifying your esteem and well wishes toward one of your fellows. And allow me to say that while you have been constructing munitions of war at home during the last four years, you have contributed as much as those of us who have used them and tried to render them effective in crushing the late wicked rebellion. And I hope, gentlemen, that as long as the labor is performed as faithfully and as honestly as it has been done in the past, if the Government needs your services that you may continue in its employ. (Cheers) But whatever our lot may be cast[,] let us strive to do what in us lies to further the interests of the best and strongest government on the face of the earth. (Cheers) Gentlemen, I bid you a kind adieu." Three more cheers were given and the party embarked for Rye Beach, the workmen returning to their labor.[98]

During the rest of 1865, despite the budget cuts and the reduced labor force, the remaining Yard workmen, for their part, fulfilled Farragut's exhortation in finishing half-completed or otherwise essential projects. Secretary Welles's "Report of the Secretary of the Navy" for 1865, together with bureau reports, devoted many paragraphs to the many major improvements at the Portsmouth Navy Yard: new buildings, new shops, new shiphouses, an immense derrick capable of raising one hundred tons, and a large "cupola blast," for melting iron in a new furnace. Commandant Bailey also undertook sanitation measures to make the Yard a cleaner and healthier place. On December 16, 1865, in a major article, the *Journal* noted: "It is the

Reported May 12th 1865.
J. Bailey
Comdt

NAVY DEPARTMENT,

6 May 1865

Sir:

You are hereby detached from the Command of the *Miantonomah* and you will proceed to *Portsmouth, N.H., without delay,* and report to *Commodore Bailey* for the Command of the *U. S. Steamer Agamenticus, (3d Rate)*

I am, very respectfully,

Your obedient servant,

Secretary of the Navy.

Commander
E. G. Parrott,
U. S. Navy,
New York.

view of Admiral Bailey to have the Yard put in as complete order as possible … removing chips [manure], stowing timber, &c." so that the cleaned-up facility began "to look something more like the Navy Yard before the war."[99]

Welles's annual report elicited interest beyond the Yard and the navy. Analyzing at length the Union navy's wartime experience, the *London Times* early in 1866 recognized the value of what England might learn:

Seven thousand five hundred of these [Northern merchant marine volunteers during 1861] in all submitted to examination and received appointments, being first instructed in gunnery and nautical routine by means of schools established for the purpose. Most have since returned to the merchant service, and the experiment of temporary commissions thus tried by the United States in the hour of need is not without interest for ourselves as a maritime power. Nor is this the only subject on which our Admiralty might derive valuable information from the American Navy Department. The war has been fruitful in experience of all kinds, except in engagements at sea on a large scale. It is regretted that we only know the operations of Admirals [David D.] Porter, [John A.] Dahlgren, and [David G.] Farragut from published reports, and that no scientific officer of the British Navy was specially deputed to watch any of them on the spot. There must, however, be means of ascertaining such facts as may save us many costly failures in naval construction.[100]

The Civil War galvanized the United States Navy into a first-class force, led by first-class officers and supported by first-class yards, in approaching Great Britain's traditional ranking as the world's leading naval power. In this regard, one Western orator flaunted American patriotism: "Where is Europe, compared to America? Nowhar! Where is England? Nowhar! They call England the mistress of the sea; but what makes the sea? This Mississippi river makes it. And all we've got to do is turn the Mississippi into the Mammoth Cave, and the English navy will be floundering in the mud."[101]

Postwar American disdain toward England's maritime standing was likewise evident in connection with the controversial *Trent*, the British mail packet associated with the celebrated 1861 diplomatic crisis. "The *Trent*, the historic vessel associated with the seizure of [Confederate diplomats James M.] Mason and [John] Slidell," reported the *Chronicle* on December 21, 1865, "has not long survived the American war. At last accounts she was at the Isle of Dogs [a peninsula formed by the Thames near London, where English kings once kept their hounds], where she was to be broken up. Her career is ended."[102]

The Record of the Union Navy and the Yard

By almost all historical appraisals, and by this author's assessment, the Union navy, its officers and men, the Navy Department, and the various federal Navy Yards, on the whole, performed admirably during the Civil War years. The Portsmouth Navy Yard, as part of this overall historical process, contributed proportionately to the effort.

BUREAU OF ORDNANCE.
NAVY DEPARTMENT, Washington City, Dec. 4 1865.

Sale of

A lot of condemned and unserviceable

Navy Cannon, Small Arms, and

AMMUNITION & ORDNANCE STORES,

At THE NAVY YARD, BOSTON.

NOTICE is hereby given that there will be sold by Public Auction, at the Navy Yard, Boston,

On the 21st Day of December, 1865, at noon.

A lot of condemned and unserviceable Navy Cannon, Small Arms, Small Arm Ammunition, and miscellaneous Ordnance Stores.

The Cannon will be sold by the pound, and the remainder of the articles in lots to suit purchasers.

Terms cash in Government funds, one-half of the purchase money to be paid at the end of the sale, and the remainder within ten (10) days afterwards, at which time the articles must be removed, otherwise they will revert to the Government.

For more particular information parties are referred to the Inspector of Ordnance at the Boston Navy Yard.

H. A. WISE,
Chief of Bureau of Ordnance, Navy Dpt.

BUREAU OF ORDNANCE.
NAVY DEPART'T, Washington City, Dec. 4, 1865.

SALE OF A LOT OF

Condemned Navy Cannon,

At the NAVY YARD, PORTSMOUTH, N. H.

NOTICE is hereby given that there will be sold at the Navy Yard, Portsmouth, N. H. at Public Auction

On the 28th Day of December, 1865, at noon.

A large lot of old Navy Cannon.

These Cannon will be sold by the pound to the highest bidder. Terms cash, in Government funds, one-half of the purchase money to be at the end of the sale, and the remainder within ten days afterwards, at which time the Cannon must be removed from the Navy Yard, otherwise they will revert to the Government.

Further information regarding the sale will be given on application to the Ordnance Officer at the Portsmouth Navy Yard. H. A. WISE,
Chief of the Bureau of Ordnance, Navy Dpt.

PJ, Dec. 16, 1865

According to a modern estimate, the Civil War resulted in about 360,000 Union dead, the vast majority of whom were in the army. The navy's loss, by contrast, was much less. A Washington source in November 1865 stated, "During the entire war the Navy lost only 1406 men killed and 1638 wounded, out of 75,000 sailors and marines on the rolls. The whole expense of the Navy since the beginning of the war was less than $230,000,000."[103]

Casualties among New Hampshire men serving in the U.S.

Navy or the Marine Corps also were relatively light. From a modern, adjusted estimate of 1,200 citizens who served in these two military branches, nine were killed in action and fifty died of disease.[104]

At the cost of these sacrifices, the Union navy practically annihilated Confederate shipping. According to Secretary of the Navy Welles's 1865 annual report, partly reprinted in the *Chronicle* on December 7, "The number of [Confederate] vessels captured or sent to courts for adjudication from May 1, 1861, to the close of the rebellion, is 1151; whole number captured and destroyed, 1504." In financial terms, the "gross proceeds of the property captured since the blockade ... $21,829,542.96."[105]

The staggering Confederate losses were closely monitored by Union naval personnel eager to claim their individual shares of prize money. In early January 1866, flag officers of squadrons, commanders of warships, and enlisted men began to collect their payments. By that month, $9.5 million in prize money already had been paid, with 600 Confederate vessels still pending adjudication. Prize money eventually amounted to about $15 million. On March 24, 1866, the *Journal* carried a partial list of awards with some familiar names: Vice Admiral Farragut received $56,448 in prize money; Rear Admiral Theodorus Bailey, $39,098; and Rear Admiral Charles Wilkes, associated with the *Trent* controversy, $7,943. The destruction of the CSS *Albemarle*, in which Thomas Gay had been a participant, netted $1,934 for each member of Lieutenant Cushing's picket-boat crew. Sums awarded to officers varied from $500 to $54,000; payments to enlisted men ranged from thirteen cents to $1,900.[106]

Admiral Theodorus Bailey, in particular, kept a careful accounting of such matters. In his personal sixty-page notebook, "Memorandum of Prizes taken & sent into Key West," he listed in chronological order the names of the captured ships and their cargoes during the time he served as commander of the East Gulf Blockading Squadron. On one page, Bailey noted, "Wrote to Mr[.] H. J. Planter[?] Dist. Atty. Feby 28th, 1865, for information about the prizes condemned & what prizes have been adjudicated & declared ready for distribution by the Court[,] giving him a list of those of which no information has been received." Bailey apparently believed that he had never received the full amount of the prize money legally due him.[107]

Other money matters were scrupulously and unimpeachably documented. Relative to the Portsmouth Navy Yard and outlying harbor defenses, United States expenditures from July 1, 1860, to July 1,

1865, were funds well spent:

Custom House, Portsmouth	$5,779.02
Light-house, Whales' Back	1,000.00
Navy Yard, Portsmouth,	651,804.66
Marine Barracks,	22,000.00
Fort Constitution,	131,000.00
Fort McClary,	100,500.00
Temporary works in harbor,	295,600.00
Total,	$1,207,683.68[108]

In return for this investment, the federal government and the United States Navy received twenty-six new ships, repair facilities, and a recruiting vessel from a strategically located naval base. The Yard remained a stable workhorse installation, which was never threatened, let alone captured or subjected to ransom throughout the war. Moreover, the base operated almost without interruption during this period—except for a few days during the 1864 yellow-fever scare—and remained free from such natural disasters as fire, flood, or earthquakes. The Yard's contribution to the blockade—the most effective and most extensive up to that time in naval history—was keenly felt and highly regarded.

In the months immediately after the war, the common concern focused on peacetime adjustment, and war memories tended to recede. A perceptive *Kennebec* [Augusta, Maine] *Journal* article, appearing in early November 1865, gauged the nation's priorities for the years ahead. Envisioning the future of the Union soldier—which by inference might include sailors, Yard workers, and others whose lives were uprooted by the war—the anonymous journalist wrote:

The Englishmen were asking before the close of the war, "What will the American soldiers do when let loose?" As they have been let loose, they can now see. They are at work in all the departments of business, on the farms, in workshops, on the railroads, and whatever labor or attention is required, as before the war. The time spent in the army was simply like a journey, an excursion, which, for the most of the soldiers, had no influence to break up the habits of their lives, or their expectations as to their mode of support. The new regions of the country [including the American West], visited by the army has shown attractions to some of our Northern young men, and they will plant their homes at the South, under the new system of free labor. This is the answer as to the American soldiers—they are industrious citizens again, turning as naturally to civil life as the needle to the pole.[109]

The federal triumph reversed the direction of the temporarily diverted national needle to swing again toward peace. After a four-year interruption, the Union navy and the Portsmouth Navy Yard were free, once again, to resume more tranquil pursuits. Their numerous contributions and accomplishments during the Civil War represented, in naval parlance, "a job well done."

★★★★

DIED IN THIS HOUSE
AUGUST 14, 1870

DAVID GLASGOW FARRAGUT

ADMIRAL
IN THE UNITED STATES NAVY

FAITHFUL AND FEARLESS

★★★★

Dedicated in 1908, an iron tablet on the fence in front of Quarters "A" honors the memory of Admiral David G. Farragut; the inscription was written by Admiral George Dewey. The entry pertaining to Farragut's death was duly entered in the Portsmouth Navy Yard Log. Three days later, the Log reads: "Work suspended on account of the funeral of Admiral Farragut, which took place at 2 P.M. from St. John's Church, Portsmouth. The escort and body left the Yard at 11:45 A.M. on the Speedwell, Emerald, *and* Cohasset." *PNSVC*

Epilogue
1866-1995: The Civil War Legacy

Decline of Piscataqua Shipbuilding

FOR DECADES, PORTSMOUTH and the Yard continued to feel the effects of the Civil War. The Portsmouth merchant marine struggled for survival, and new ship construction along the Piscataqua waterfront was almost nonexistent. "We trust that our shipbuilders," stated the *Chronicle* on November 22, 1865, "in anticipation of the coming discharge [of much of the labor force] at the Navy Yard, will make preparations for the resumption of work in our private yards, so that the ring of the axe and the clang of the hammer shall once more awaken the long silent echoes of the Piscataqua."[1]

The expected "clang of the hammer" amounted to little more than a muffled tapping, a reminder of a bygone age. In a major article, "Our Home Shipping—Why Is Ship Building At a Stand?" the *Journal* on June 9, 1866, addressed the grim realities: high duties on imported materials, high labor costs, and foreign competition that undercut American prices. With obsolete designs, the American merchant marine was at a disadvantage when the Suez Canal, a waterway requiring shallower-draft vessels, opened for shipping on November 17, 1869.[2]

The era of shipbuilding in private Piscataqua yards was, in fact, nearing the end. Such yards turned out only six ships during the late 1860s and only eight during the 1870s. In 1875, Daniel and Peter

319

Marcy honored the memory of their relative killed in the war with the completion of the ship *William H. Marcy*. The ship *Paul Jones*, launched in 1877, was the last of the hundreds of wooden, three-masted, square-rigged sailing vessels built on the Piscataqua or its tributaries.[3]

Portsmouth and the "Alabama Claims"

After the war, the legacy of the depredations of the CSS *Alabama* and other Confederate cruisers soured diplomatic relations between the United States and Great Britain. Emerging from the Civil War in a position of strength, the United States claimed that Great Britain, in offering covert aid to the South, had failed to enforce her neutrality obligations. For her part, Great Britain realized it was in her best national interest as the world's leading maritime trading power to continue trade with America and to follow a policy of freedom of the seas regarding neutral cargoes. The British, in short, sought rapprochement with the United States. The American demands on Great Britain, collectively called the "Alabama Claims" in reference to the Confederate cruiser, required protracted negotiations.

Pressing these claims against Great Britain, Portsmouth citizens encountered continual delays and frustrations, and they harbored few illusions. Since 1801, Portsmouth claimants who had suffered losses in the Quasi-War with France (1798-1801) had futilely sought reimbursement for their French spoliation claims. The prospects for a just settlement of the Alabama Claims must have seemed equally insurmountable.

Finally, in 1871, six years after the end of the Civil War, an Anglo-American commission signed the Treaty of Washington, an agreement to submit the claims for international arbitration. On September 14, 1872, in Geneva, Switzerland, four arbiters, representing the United States, Great Britain, Italy, and Brazil (the latter two as neutral parties), rendered their decision: Great Britain was to pay $15,500,000 in gold to the United States as compensation. During the Geneva negotiations, New Hampshire interests were represented, in part, by Frank Warren Hackett, a Portsmouth native and lawyer who had served in the Union navy during the war.[4]

The next step involved the release of money to the American claimants. Again a Portsmouth man was on the scene. During his two terms in the U.S. House of Representatives (1875 to 1879),

Portsmouth's Frank Jones led the fight for the passage of the Geneva Award Bill to free funds for companies and individuals with legitimate claims. A driven business tycoon in private life, Jones was a power in Congress, serving on the prestigious Committee on Naval Affairs. For years before and after his Congressional service, Jones frequently traveled to Washington to lobby for Portsmouth's interests and his own. Even when he was merely a private citizen, Jones's presence was influential. His persistence was rewarded. According to Speaker of the House Samuel J. Randall, the passage of the Geneva Award Bill was due as much "to Mr. Jones as to any other man, and that but the efforts and influence of Mr. Jones and one other son of New England, the bill would have totally failed in the House."[5]

The overall Treaty of Washington settlement, however, was a diplomatic compromise between the United States and Great Britain, with the Portsmouth claimants maintaining that they had been shortchanged. The treaty had whittled collectible damages down to a few Confederate ships. Those held liable included the *Alabama*; the *Florida* and her tenders; and the *Shenandoah*, the latter not for her entire cruise but only after she left Australia in February 1865. This incomplete accounting, for example, left no recourse for the Portsmouth owners of the *Kate Prince*, captured and ransomed by the *Shenandoah* in November 1864. In their definitive study, *Sea Lanes in Wartime* (1942), Robert Greenhalgh Albion and Jennie Barnes Pope rightly concluded that the Treaty of Washington settlement "was a good bargain for England at that—to have reduced so effectively the competition of the American merchant marine, not only during the war but for a half century thereafter."[6]

The Court of Commissioners of the Alabama Claims finally began to disburse the Geneva Award Act money during the mid-1870s, thanks to an act of Congress in 1874. By January 1, 1877, judgments of the court paid out more than $9 million, mostly to shipowners. However, the sheer number of claims, some undoubtedly fraudulent, and the volume of testimony, overwhelmed the commissioners as they attempted to process the many petitions quickly and fairly. In an attempt to handle the enormous backlog of claims, another act of Congress in 1882 extended the deadline for filing claims and established additional categories for compensation. On November 17, 1883, the *Chronicle* declared, "The report of the Commissioners of Alabama Claims shows that 5,751 claims amounting to $28,061,997 [about double the Geneva Award Act amount] have been filed.... Commissions to take testimony have been issued in 4,950 cases, and testimony under stipulations of counsel is being taken in about 200 cases.... The report says it will be impossible to dispose of all the pending cases within the term prescribed by the act."[7]

On March 5, 1884, thirty-nine leading citizens of Portsmouth—a number of them acting as administrators and executors of estates for deceased claimants—submitted a joint letter to their New Hampshire congressmen. Hoping to ward off attempts by others seeking reimbursement, the Portsmouth men opposed any further slicing of the already meager Geneva Award compensation pie, declaring:

> The undersigned residents of Portsmouth beg to suggest that any proposed enlargement of the participants in the sum now held to be awarded among ship owners, masters, shippers, and others, who have established their claims under the [Geneva Award] act of June 5th, 1882, by increasing the jurisdiction of the Court of Commissioners of Alabama Claims and reorganizing claims for losses within four miles of the shore and on the Mississippi river [sic] and inland waters ... is not only highly prejudicial to our rights under the existing law, but will in effect so materially reduce the amounts to which we are legally entitled, and for which we have at no little expenditure of time and money adduced proper legal proofs, that our claims will become nearly valueless.[8]

Between 1885 and 1888, successful claims under the 1882 Geneva Award Act released money long awaited by Portsmouth ship investors or their heirs. On March 12, 1885, for example, sums ranging from $62 to $1,330 went to the owners of the ships *Piscataqua*, *Portsmouth*, and *Granite State* and of the bark *Mary Annah*. Regardless of the total sums, or whatever behind-the-scenes influence such powerful men as Frank Jones might have exerted, no pressure or infusion of money was adequate to revive the moribund Portsmouth merchant marine.[9]

Adjustment of War Heroes to Peace

After the conflict, Union naval officers and sailors and Portsmouth Navy Yard personnel quickly and quietly settled into a peacetime routine that almost always seemed anticlimactic after their wartime experiences and exploits. With very few exceptions, the principal actors in the Civil War drama resumed their pre-1861 military, business, political, or journalistic roles. Leaders in peace as well as in war, such diverse figures as Naval Secretaries Welles and Fox; Yard Commandants Pope, Pearson, and Bailey; career naval officers Farragut, Dewey, Parrott, and Pickering; politicians and business men Daniel Marcy, Peter Marcy, and Goodwin; and newspaper editor Foster adjusted to the new era and became respected and prosperous. When they died, their obituaries were duly printed in the national and local press. When Admiral Farragut died at the Portsmouth Navy Yard's Quarters "A" in 1870, he was mourned as a national hero.[10]

When Secretary of the Navy Gideon Welles retired in 1869, he organized his departure in much the same way as he had run his department during the war—ever practical, occasionally bumbling, but inevitably successful. The saga originally was published in the *New York Tribune*, then reprinted in the *Journal* on May 15, 1869:

When that excellent gentleman, the Hon. Gideon Welles, retired from the government of the Navy, he was a good deal bothered about the expense of moving his furniture and baggage back to Hartford. The franking [free mailing] privilege not being quite elastic enough to cover his case, he was permitted to take one of the Government vessels [USS *Tallapoosa*]. Who permitted him—whether he did it himself, or his successor [Adolph E. Borie]—we are not informed [it actually was Vice Admiral David D. Porter]; but the vessel was loaded, and off the gallant old salt sailed for the Connecticut River. When he got there he found that vessels drawing more than six feet of water could not get into the Connecticut River whereas his drew eleven! Mr. Welles has [had] never been so much astonished in his life. His chagrin was only equaled by the Vicar of Wakefield's when that delightful person found that he had ordered a portrait so big that he could not get it into the house. The result of it all was that Mr. Welles had to go beating along the coast [of Long Island Sound] until he found water enough at New London to float his goods, and thence he sent them home by rail, at just double the cost of shipping them from Washington in the regular way. It may seem rather singular that a gentleman who had been eight years Secretary of the

Navy should have not know[n] something about the depth of water on Saybrook bar [at the mouth of the Connecticut River], and still more singular that he could send a vessel on a voyage without inquiring whether she could possibly get into [her] port of destination. But then Mr. Welles always was a very remarkable man.[11]

The newspapers also provided sketches of the postwar careers of a few of the lesser-known naval officers. Commodore John S. Missroon, a South Carolinian, exemplified many Southern officers who remained loyal to the Union, at considerable sacrifice. He died on October 23, 1865, at Charlestown, Massachusetts, and on October 28, the *Journal* noted:

During the year 1860, in the latter part of July, while he was stationed at this [Portsmouth] Navy Yard as Executive Officer, he had a private conversation with a friend, in relation to how the people of the South would probably conduct themselves, in the event of the election of Abraham Lincoln as President. He was strongly solicited by his friends in South Carolina, to resign his position in the U.S. Navy and return home, otherwise the consequence to his property would be disastrous—as the citizens were privately making active preparations for the resistance to the government of Mr. Lincoln, should he be elected. The loyal and steadfast course which he pursued there, after abandoning friends and property, the loss of which was very great, will cause his name to be registered and recollected among the heroes of our country.[12]

To honor Rear Admiral John A. Winslow, who served as the Portsmouth Navy Yard commandant during 1869 and 1870, a street in the Yard bears his name. After his death in 1873, the arrangement for Winslow's final resting place in Forest Hills Cemetery in Boston further enhanced the *Kearsarge* legend. On June 11, 1875, Winslow's widow climbed Mount Kearsarge and selected a large boulder near the summit. The citizens of nearby Warner, New Hampshire, hauled the boulder down the mountainside to the local rail depot, and the railroad transported the rock to Boston free of charge. The epitaph on the metal plaque bolted to Winslow's gravestone explains the boulder's link to the ship's name.[13]

Captain James S. Thornton, also connected to the *Kearsarge*, was stationed at the Yard from 1865 to 1873, as executive officer. According to the Thornton family history, in August 1873:

> ... he ... was sent in command of the U.S.S. *Monongahela* to Kerguelen [an island in the southern Indian Ocean] with the transit of Venus expedition [which observed the astronomical phenomenon of the transit, or crossing, of this planet in front of the sun on December 9, 1874]. The only available charts for this dangerous voyage were the original charts made by Captain [James] Cook, which were placed at Thornton's disposal by the British government. He accomplished his difficult mission successfully, but upon the return voyage, while studying his copy of the Cook chart in his cabin, he was thrown down by a sudden lurch of the ship and received serious injuries to the spine. He was at once invalidated [invalided] home, but died on May 14, 1875, at Germantown, Pennsylvania, within a few weeks after his arrival.[14]

Commander Samuel Dana Greene, the *Monitor* hero, also saw postwar duty at the Portsmouth Navy Yard, serving as equipment officer in 1884. On the afternoon of December 11, when Greene unaccountably was missing, an extensive search was conducted, and his body was found in the upper loft of the Franklin Shiphouse. He had died of self-inflicted head wounds from a Colt naval revolver. The next day, Portsmouth's *Penny Post* noted, "At the time of his death he had been engaged in writing a history of the *Monitor*'s achievements [for *Century Magazine*] in refutation of unjust and unwarranted reports. It has been thought that he was physically affected by the concussion sustained by the *Monitor*, and dwelling too much upon the injustice of unkind criticism had contributed to a temporary mental derangement."[15]

Other naval personnel fared much better. Taking advantage of new opportunities for black Union sailors, Stephen Goodman had embarked upon a life of freedom. As one of the contrabands stationed at Seavey's Island during 1863, Goodman had first learned reading and writing in classes conducted by Portsmouth women. On March 22, 1866, from the USS *Sagamore*, in Key West, Florida, Goodman used excellent penmanship to write to one of his former teachers about his status:

I have often thought that I would write to you to let you know how I was get[t]ing along in the world. I have no just reason to complain for my health is good and has been since I left Portsmouth.

I have been shifted from one Ship to another until last May [1865] since I have been at[ta]ched to this Vessel and I sup[p]ose shall be until my time of servis [sic] expires which will be next June and should I be spared until then and as soon as I can I am going to Portsmouth....

God is a good God for He has brought me through dangers seen and unseen for which I have a thankfull heart and fully appreciate His blessing.[16]

The subsequent lives of most of the "*Kearsarge* boys," or the "*Kearsarge* heroes," as the press had dubbed them, also appeared blessed. To the end, the *Kearsarge* sailors relished their exalted position in naval history. After his discharge, Martin Hoyt, the ship's barber, returned to Portsmouth to open his shop in Market Square, where he never tired of remarking to his customers that "while in the service it was his good fortune to be one of the crew of the U.S.S. *Kearsarge* when that vessel struck the *Alabama*." In 1875, one of his patrons had a startled reaction to this, for he had been an officer aboard the *Alabama* during the 1864 sea battle.

On June 19, 1884, Hoyt and sixteen other *Kearsarge* veterans living in the Portsmouth area held their first formal reunion at the Kearsarge House, a leading Portsmouth hotel. Meeting annually on or about that date in Portsmouth or at private homes elsewhere in New England, they signed a charter in January 1893 for the *Kearsarge* Naval Veterans Association, dedicated to commemorating the June 19, 1864, event with annual dinners, parades, excursions, group photographs, and exhibitions of relics. Henry S. Hobson, a member of the *Kearsarge* Survivors' Association of Boston, an allied organization, preserved his memories with his privately printed book, *The Famous Cruise of the Kearsarge* (1894).[17]

As years passed, the "*Kearsarge* boys" still exhibited their rambunctious nature. During World War I, on March 6, 1918, on the occasion of his eightieth birthday, Austin H. F. Quinby told reporters at his Ossipee, New Hampshire, home that he "would be very happy if he could re-enter the navy, so that he might take a shot at a [German] submarine."[18]

One by one, the old heroes passed on. Martin Hoyt, the last Portsmouth-area *Kearsarge* survivor, died in December 1918. In 1935, at Orogrande, New Mexico, far from the sea, ninety-one-year-old *Kearsarge* veteran William Alsdorf died—the last participant from either side of the celebrated sea battle fought seventy-one years earlier.[19]

The Kearsarge's *Last Mission*

Of the many Civil War vessels associated with the Portsmouth Navy Yard, the *Kearsarge* continued after the war to command the most respect and attention from American citizens. For almost thirty years, the *Kearsarge* cruised worldwide as an instrument of American foreign policy. It was assumed that she would eventually be retired by the navy as a historic vessel. When the USS *Brooklyn*, remembered for her performance in the Battle of Mobile Bay, was decommissioned, sold, and burned in Boston Harbor in July 1891 to salvage the copper used in her construction, the *Journal* editorialized: "There are three naval vessels which the American people will never willingly allow to be sold or broken up, and for the preservation of which they will be ever willing to grant whatever funds may be necessary; and those are the *Hartford* [which sank at her berth at the Norfolk Navy Yard in 1956], the *Kearsarge* and the *Constitution* [still in commission at the Boston Navy Yard, Charlestown, Massachusetts]."[20]

But retirement was not to be her fate; in 1894, the *Kearsarge* ended her illustrious career in active service, still protecting American interests. An article, "Wreck of the *Kearsarge*," in the *Colon* (then Colombia, now Panama) *Telegram*, on Friday, February 9, relates perhaps the earliest account of this sad event:

> The U.S. Ship of War *Kearsarge*, under command of Captain [Oscar F.] Hey[er]man is wrecked on Roncador Reef [now Roncador Cay, a Colombian island in the Caribbean] 80 miles from Old Providence [another Colombian island] and about 300 miles north of this Port.
>
> The *Kearsarge* was from Port au Prince, Haiti bound to Greytown [now San Juan del Norte], Nicaragua [,] to protect the Nicaragua Canal [then under construction but later abandoned] from harm in the disturbance between Honduras and that Republic, having on board Acting Rear Admiral [Oscar F.]

Dramatic overhead view of the USS Kearsarge *during overhaul at the Portsmouth Navy Yard (1877 and 1878). Renowned for her 1864 sea battle, the* Kearsarge *served the United States during the postwar era by sailing to distant ports on diplomatic missions to advance American foreign policy. Honoring the ship's place in American naval history, successive U.S. Navy vessels have borne the* Kearsarge *name, a practice continuing to this day. PNSVC*

Stanton ordered by the Washington Government to proceed on that mission.

On Friday the 2nd instant [February 2, 1894] at 7 P.M., a heavy running sea prevailing, she struck on the reefs and from that moment strenuous efforts were made to retrieve her from her dangerous position. The guns were thrown overboard and other materials in order to lighthen [*sic*] the vessel, but it soon became evident that all efforts to get her off would be useless as the keel was broken amidships.

On Saturday [February 3] Admiral Stanton and the entire crew landed on the barren reef with two weeks provisions and 10 days water, but without their personal effects and accoutrements. The vessel's steam launch and three boats were lost during the transfer of the crew. There has fortunately been no loss of life....

By the loss of the *Kearsarge* the United States loses a historical relic of the highest value. She it was who dealt the death blow to the terrible confederate cruiser *Alabama* during the war of secession; and although as a warship she was of no value, she was yet maintained in commission and was constantly cruising in the Caribbean sea.[21]

This account is basically accurate, making the *Kearsarge* yet another of the many vessels that had been wrecked on Roncador, a Caribbean ship graveyard. As it turned out, however, there was one casualty: Fireman Andrew Ribbins drowned after he stepped into a deep hole while walking in shallow water. "The loss of this ship is a most deplorable disaster," lamented the *Chronicle* on February 9, "as it removes one of the two historical ships [the other was either the *Hartford* or the *Constitution*] that the people and Congress both

An unsigned wash drawing portrays the last battle of the USS Kearsarge as she founders on Roncador Reef in the Caribbean on February 2, 1894. The wreck of this famed Civil War ship, slated for preservation by the United States, deprived the nation of a historic vessel. This painting was owned by Franklin D. Roosevelt, an avid collector of American naval and maritime art. Courtesy Franklin D. Roosevelt Library, Hyde Park, NY

WRECK OF KEARSARGE.

Severe Loss to Government—Plans to Supply the Place She Filled.

WASHINGTON, Feb. 23.—In the wreck of
the Kearsarge the navy and state departments have sustained a severe loss. It
was one of the valuable points of the old
wooded cruisers that they could be put
into condition for service in a very short
time, as the materials for repairs could
be found in any navy yard, or any port,
even in a foreign country. This is not
true of the complicated steel ships with
their extensive machinery, requiring a
high grade of expert skill to repair.

So, even in late years, whenever a vessel was wanted in great haste, the wooden
ships were called into service. Already
there is talk in the navy department
about supplying the Kearsarge's place,
and several projects have been broached
that may find their way to congress. One
contemplates the construction of a mag-
nificent battleship worthy to perpetuate
the name of the Kearsarge on the naval
lists. Another project is to build two or
three light draught steel gunboats about
the size of the Petrel, now doing valuable
service in Chinese waters.

Two of these vessels could be built for
about half a million dollars, and if they
were stationed in the Gulf of Mexico, at
Mobile, or Galveston, they would be of in-
estimable value to the United States commercial interests, as they could be sent to
any central American port in a day or two,
and from their small size would be very
economical to maintain. From their light
draught they would be able to reach many
points that are inaccessible to our large
cruisers.

THE KEARSARGE

PC, Feb. 24, 1894

intended to preserve forever."[22]

To one *Kearsarge* battle survivor, sailor Henry S. Hobson, the ship's fate, although highly regrettable, was a fitting end to her service to her country. "We are glad," wrote Hobson in 1894, that "she died in the harness [in active service]—much better than be laid up in 'Rotten Row' [where worn-out vessels are moored in a navy yard]."[23]

The dramatic end of the *Kearsarge*'s career attracted the attention of American artists, poets, and journalists. New Hampshire poet George Bancroft Griffith, in "The *Kearsarge*," declared that the ship's name and reputation could never be slurred by "calling her pensioner." Franklin D. Roosevelt—collector of American naval art and a frequent visitor to the Yard in his roles as assistant secretary of the navy and as president—took pride in owning the painting *U.S.S. Kearsarge on Roncador Reef, February, 1894*. In the unknown artist's rendering of the *Kearsarge*'s last battle, the ship is shown defiantly fighting to the end.[24]

The Yard Overcomes Adversity

Although the men and ships associated with the Civil War era have passed into history and legend, the Portsmouth Naval Shipyard (as the facility is known today) continues as an active and vital component of the Department of the Navy. Its longevity and survival, however, have been neither automatic nor easy. The Yard's fortunes have been inevitably tied to the cyclical fluctuations of American foreign policy—hectic expansion and feverish productivity during war, budget cutbacks and few contracts during peace.

The post-Civil War era was no exception. Attempting to compete with the nation's preoccupation with the Westward Movement, Reconstruction, industrialization, and the money-making frenzy that Mark Twain and Charles Dudley Warner labeled "the Gilded Age," the neglected United States Navy fell upon hard times. Satirizing the congressional lack of concern for the Yard, the *Journal* in a mock announcement on July 15, 1876, suggested that this notice be inserted in the London *Times* or in another influential European journal:

> A Navy Yard with all appliances for build-
> ing and repairing Naval vessels and machinery.
>   Apply to FRANK JONES
>   or JNO BURLEIGH
> of the [Congressional] Committee upon Naval Expenditures.[25]

Despite its doldrums and the fact that its workforce dipped to just seventy-one employees in 1877, the Navy Yard was hardly ready to be leased out to a foreign power. Not content to limp along, the Yard fought for appropriations and modernized its physical plant. During the Spanish-American War in 1898, Camp Long was established at the Yard to house nearly a thousand Spanish prisoners. The early 1900s brought the construction of a stone dry dock; a detonation at Henderson's Point was needed to remove the navigational obstacle there.

In 1905, President Theodore Roosevelt called upon the Yard to host a crucial diplomatic conference. Acting in the role of peacemaker in an attempt to end the Russo-Japanese War, Roosevelt arranged for the plenipotentiaries of the belligerents to meet at the Yard, free from Washington's summer heat and from outside distractions. The President's peace initiative had the desired results. On September 5, 1905, in Building 86, after a month of negotiations, the Russian and

Portsmouth business tycoon Frank Jones (1832-1902), in his roles as a Gilded Age congressman and a private lobbyist, sought to restore the post-war navy and the port to their former eminence. PPL

Japanese delegates signed the Treaty of Portsmouth, thereby establishing peace and defusing international tensions. Roosevelt had thus engineered a great diplomatic victory, had put the Portsmouth Navy Yard on the map, and had incidentally secured for himself the Nobel Peace Prize.[26]

Three years later, the naval prison was commissioned; it remained in service until 1974. World War I ushered in the age of submarine construction; between 1914 and 1971, 134 "Portsmouth-built" submarines were launched. Since 1962, the Yard has specialized in nuclear submarine repair and overhaul.[27]

With the approach of the year 2000, marking 200 years of service to the Navy Department, the Yard can look back on success in overcoming cutbacks, closure orders, and reduction-in-force (RIF) policies. During one especially difficult time, the Yard in 1964 received an order to phase out closure over a ten-year period. In 1971, however, three years before the planned closing, the Nixon administration rescinded the order. More than twenty years later, the Yard faced another crisis during yet another round of projected military base closings. Again the Yard gained another reprieve when on June 25, 1993, the Base Closure and Realignment Commission (BRAC) unanimously voted to remove the Yard from the closure list. Maine's senior senator, William Cohen, remarked to reporters at the time, "We had the law on our side, we also had the facts and, in addition, we had the future of the Navy."[28]

Despite the news, the battle to save the Yard was temporarily, but not permanently, won. The third and final review dragged on over the next two years and created uncertainty. As the eight-member BRAC panel continued its deliberations, rumors abounded in the Portsmouth area that the Yard, facing intense competition from other military bases, was being targeted for closure. Placing his office and reputation on the line in order to bolster the Yard's chances for survival, Admiral Jeremy Boorda, Chief of Naval Operations, flew up from Washington on May 12, 1995, to attend a Yard change-of-command ceremony (with Capt. Carl Strawbridge replacing Capt. Lance Horne). Speaking before a cheering crowd in the standing-room-only Yard auditorium, Boorda vowed, "Maybe they [the BRAC panel members] got confused. We will unconfuse them."[29]

On Friday, June 23, 1995, at 12:30 P.M., the BRAC chairman at a Washington meeting, "asked for a motion to close Portsmouth, mentioning that in the absense of a motion, the shipyard would stay open. The commissioners remained silent." The chairman "asked again, and received no motion. Seconds later, he gaveled the meeting closed for a lunch recess." The panel's silence saved 4,000 jobs at the Yard. "Shipyard stays Open. Closure Panel Ends 5-Year Ordeal," headlined the *Portsmouth Herald*'s Extra Edition. Many ranking Maine and New Hampshire politicians judged Boorda's brave stand as the turning point in shifting the tide in favor of the Yard. Senator Cohen reflected, "Because we had the support of the Navy, we prevailed. Hopefully this is the last time we have to go through this. I've had more admirals in my office this year than in my entire [twenty-three congressional and senatorial] career."[30]

Senator Cohen understood the Yard's ongoing purpose and raison d'être. Throughout its long history, the Portsmouth Naval

Shipyard adjusted technologically to unforeseen contingencies in the defense of the United States. During the Civil War years in particular, the Yard rapidly reorganized its resources, as Admiral Farragut had put it, for "constructing munitions of war." That dedication on behalf of the officers, sailors, and workers materially aided the Union in winning the naval war.

Notes

CHAPTER 1

1. *PJ*, April 30, 1859.

2. *Ibid.*, February 6, 1864.

3. *PC*, October 26, 1860.

4. Saltonstall, *Port of Piscataqua*; Brighton, *Port of Portsmouth Ships and the Cotton Trade, 1783-1829*; Brighton, *Clippers of the Port of Portsmouth and the Men Who Built Them*; Brighton, *Tall Ships of the Piscataqua, 1830-1877*; Winslow, *"Wealth and Honour": Portsmouth During the Golden Age of Privateering, 1775-1815*.

5. *PJ*, September 28, October 19, 1861; Pickett, pp. 56, 114-16; Brighton, *Tall Ships of the Piscataqua*, pp. 159, 267-68.

6. Nelson, 2:82, 90 with quotation, 94-101 with annual statistics; *Portsmouth Directory, 1860-61*, pp. 127-41.

7. *PJ*, July 14, 1860.

8. *PC*, December 28, 1860.

9. *Ibid.*, August 14, 1860.

10. *Ibid.*, November 17, 1860.

11. Fentress, pp. 1-68; Preble, pp. 1-91; *Cradle of American Shipbuilding*, pp. 3-23; Tawresey, pp. 28-30; *PJ*, June 13, 1846, November 22, 1879.

12. *Cradle of American Shipbuilding*, p. 20.

13. Fentress, p. 68.

14. *PJ*, September 1, 1860.

15.   *ACAB*, 5:68; John Pope, U.S. Steamer *Richmond* off Pass a Loutre, Louisiana, October 22, 1861, to Captain William W. McKean, Commanding Gulf Blockading Squadron, U.S. Flag Ship *Niagara* (original letter and typescript copy), with enclosure, Statement of A.A. Henderson, Surgeon, October 22, 1861, ZB File, John Pope Folder, Archives, NHC.

16.   *PC*, October 2, 1860; *ACAB*, 4:692; *PC*, July 2, 4, 1867; *PJ*, July 6, 27, 1867 (the last four citations are obituaries and funeral orations on George F. Pearson).

17.   *PJ*, November 6, 1886, and *PC*, November 2, 1886 (obituaries of Benjamin F. Chandler); Preble, pp. 90-91.

18.   *PJ*, July 14, November 24, 1860.

19.   "LOG BOOK, U.S. NAVY YARD, KITTERY, MAINE," entry for September 29, 1860, PNSVC; Boyd, *Extracts*, entry for September 29, 1860.

20.   *PC*, October 16, 1860.

21.   *Executive Documents*, No. 1, 36th Congress, 2nd Session, "Report of the Secretary of the Navy," 3:1.

22.   Long, pp. 1-14, 308-9, 319-20, with an excellent bibliography of the African Squadron and the international slave trade, pp. 473-74; Spears, pp. 117-21.

23.   *PC*, October 4, 6, 1860.

24.   *PC*, October 8, 1860.

25.   *PJ,* April 24, 1847.

26.   Eason, "U.S.S. *Marion*, Journal, Jan. 1858 - Sept. 1860," ink drawings of "Fernando Po Island" and "St. Pauls de Loando," White Library, MSM, Mystic, CT.

27.   *DANFS*, 5:360-61; Rogers, p. 117; *PJ*, December 15, 1860.

28.   *PC*, November 7, 1860.

29.   Goodwin, "Hon. Ichabod Goodwin," pp. 292-97; *DAB*, 8:408-9; Nelson, 3:114-15; *PH*, April 15, 22, 1990; Brighton, *Rambles about Portsmouth*, pp. 21-28.

30.   *PC*, November 20, 1860, with excerpts from the *Nashua Gazette, Concord Standard,* and *Salem Gazette*.

31.   *ACAB*, 6:142; *DAB*, 18:600-601; Niven, pp. 303-20.

32.   *DANFS*, 4:179-80; Fentress, p. 68; Preble, p. 90; George Magruder, Washington, DC, November 16, 1860, to George Pearson, Portsmouth, NH, RG 181, Entry 24, Letters Received from the Bureau of Ordnance, NA-NER.

33. *Ibid.*, Circular letter from Magruder, December 6, 1860, with printed enclosure, "TABLE OF ALLOWANCE OF BOOKS for Libraries of Vessels of War and Navy Yards ... Navy Department, October 27, 1860."

34. Horatio Bridge, Washington, DC, November 16, 1860, to George Pearson, Portsmouth, NH, Letters Received from the Bureau of Provisions and Clothing, RG 181, Entry 26, NA-NER.

35. George Magruder, Washington, DC, December 1, 1860, to George Pearson, Portsmouth, NH, RG 181, Entry 24, Letters Received from the Bureau of Ordnance, NA-NER; Pearson, November 28, December 10, 17, 1860, to Magruder, RG 181, Entry 23, Letters Sent to the Bureau of Ordnance, NA-NER.

36. *Ibid.*, Pearson, December 19, 1860, to Magruder, RG 181, Entry 23, Letters Sent, NA-NER; Magruder, December 21, 1860, to Pearson, RG 181, Entry 24, Letters Received, NA-NER.

37. George Pearson, Portsmouth, NH, December 26, 1860, to William L. Hudson, Boston, MA, RG 181, Entry 2, Miscellaneous Letters Sent, NA-NER.

38. *PC*, December 27, 1860.

39. Niven, p. 324.

40. *Ibid.*, p. 612; Hayes, ed., 1:1.

41. *PC*, January 14, 1861.

42. *DANFS*, 4:179; *CWNC*, I:2; Roberts, pp. 195-98.

43. Brighton, *Tall Ships of the Piscataqua*, p. 130; *PJ*, August 26, 1876; "Hon. Daniel Marcy," p. 354.

44. *Ibid.*, pp. 353-55; "Captain Daniel Marcy" (obituary), *Granite Monthly* 15 (December 1893): 391; *PJ*, November 13, 1893 (obituary of Marcy); Nelson, 3:185-86; Brighton, four articles, "Daniel Marcy was One of Portsmouth's Pillars"; "'Copperhead' Marcy was Elected to Congress"; "Criticism of the Statesman Marcy Flourished"; "Marcy Enjoyed Ship Building to Politics," *PH*, March 4, 11, 18, 25, 1990, reprinted in slightly different form in Brighton, *Rambles about Portsmouth*, pp. 1-6.

45. *PC*, November 17, December 31, 1860; *PJ*, September 29, 1860.

46. Brighton, *Tall Ships of the Piscataqua*, pp. 260-61; James H. Salter, Queenstown, Ireland, December 16, 1860, to Supply Clapp Thwing, Boston, MA, Box 3, Folder 5, Marcy Papers, NHHS. For Supply Clapp Thwing, business partner of the Marcys, see Thwing, pp. 86-89.

47. *PC*, December 28, 1860; *PJ*, December 29, 1860.

48. *PC*, December 28, 1860.

49. *PJ*, March 26, 1859, reprinted from the *Boston Courier.*

50. Boyd, *Extracts*, entry for January 4, 1861.

CHAPTER 2

1. "LOG BOOK, U.S. NAVY YARD, KITTERY, MAINE," entry for January 12, 1861. PNSVC, Portsmouth, NH.

2. *PC*, January 2, 12 with quotation, 14, 1861.

3. *Ibid.*, March 14, September 9, 1861.

4. *PJ*, February 9, 1861.

5. *PC*, January 28, 1861, reprinted in *PJ*, February 9, 1861.

6. *Ibid.*, Benjamin F. Chandler, Civil Engineers [*sic*] Office, U.S. Navy Yard, Portsmouth, NH, January 25, 1861, to George F. Pearson, Commandant's Office, Portsmouth Navy Yard, Portsmouth, NH, RG 45, Entry 32, Letters Received, Yards and Docks, NA-NER.

7. John Missroon, Portsmouth Navy Yard, Portsmouth, NH, February 4, 1861, to George Pearson, Portsmouth Navy Yard, Portsmouth, NH, Civil War Folder, 1861-1865, PNSVC.

8. George F. Pearson, Commandant's Office, Navy Yard, Portsmouth, NH, February 8 and 14, 1861 (two letters), to Isaac Toucey, Secretary of the Navy, Washington, DC, RG 181, Entry 8, Letters Sent to the Secretary of the Navy, NA-NER.

9. *PC*, February 8, 9, 16, 1861; Log, entry for February 7, 1861, PNSVC.

10. George Pearson, Commandant's Office, Navy Yard, Portsmouth, NH, February 14, 1861, to John Lenthall, Chief of the Bureau of Construction and Repair, Washington, DC, RG 181, Entry 15, Letters Sent to the Bureau of Construction and Repair, NA-NER.

11. DANFS, 2:233; Boyd, *Extracts*, entries for April 20, July 17, 1861; *PC*, July 18, 21, 1861.

12. *PC*, April 5, 1861, which reprints Goodwin's Proclamation, dated March 28, 1861.

13. Preble, p. 92; Niven, pp. 321-23; *DAB*, 19:629-30.

14. *PC*, April 11, 1861.

15. Log, entries for April 11, 12, 1861, PNSVC; *PC*, April 13, 1861.

16. George Pearson, Commandant's Office, Portsmouth Navy Yard, Portsmouth, NH, April 18, 1861, to Joseph Smith, Chief of the Bureau of Yards and Docks, Washington, DC, RG 34, Entry 34, Commandants' Letters, 1861, NA-DC.

17. *PC*, April 25, 29, 1861.

18.   *Ibid.*, April 27, May 24, 1861.

19.   *Ibid.*, June 4, 1861.

20.   *Biographical Directory of the American Congress, 1774-1927*, p. 1387; *PJ*, March 16 (which reprints Parris's letter), April 27, 1861; *PC*, February 19, April 23, 24, 29, May 6, 1861; George Pearson, Commandant's Office, Portsmouth Navy Yard, Portsmouth, NH, April 23, 1861, to Gideon Welles, Washington, DC, RG 45, Entry 8, Letters Sent to the Secretary of the Navy, NA-NER.

21.   Boyd, *Extracts*, entries for May 20, 22, 1861; Log, entry for May 22, 1861, PNSVC; *PC*, May 2, 24, 1861.

22.   *Ibid.*

23.   *CWNC*, I:5-6; Nevin, pp. 327-28, 350-54.

24.   *Ibid.*; *DAB*, 1:339-40, 6:568-69; *PC*, June 5, August 3 (excerpted from *Boston Transcript*), 1861; Niven, p. 327.

25.   Goodwin, "Hon. Ichabod Goodwin," pp. 296-97, reprinted in *Sketches of Successful New Hampshire Men*, pp. 133-36.

26.   George Pearson, Commandant's Office, Portsmouth Navy Yard, Portsmouth, NH, April 23, 1861, to Gideon Welles, Washington, DC, RG 45, Entry 8, Letters Sent to the Secretary of the Navy, NA-NER.

27.   George Pearson, Commandant's Office, Portsmouth Navy Yard, Portsmouth, NH, April 27, 1861, to Lt. Col. William Dulany, Commanding Marines, Portsmouth Navy Yard, Portsmouth, NH, with Dulany's return letter of the same date, RG 45, Entry 34, Commandants' Letters, NA-DC.

28.   George Pearson, Commandant's Office, Portsmouth Navy Yard, Portsmouth, NH, April 29, 1861, to Gideon Welles, Washington, DC, RG 45, Entry 8, Letters Sent to the Secretary of the Navy, NA-NER.

29.   George Pearson, Commandant's Office, Portsmouth Navy Yard, Portsmouth, NH, April 29, 1861, to Captain William L. Hudson, Commandant, Boston Navy Yard, Boston, MA, RG 45, Entry 2, Miscellaneous Letters Sent NA-NER (two letters sent on the same day).

30.   Wade, pp. 25-51; *PJ*, May 4, 1861; *PC*, April 27, May 4, 13, 1861; Gideon Welles, Navy Department, Washington, DC, May 1, 1861, to George Pearson, Portsmouth Navy Yard, Portsmouth, NH, RG 181, Entry 10, Letters Received from the Secretary of the Navy, NA-NER.

31.   "Order of the Day, Camp Constitution, Portsmouth, May 6, 1861, General Order, No. 3." Early Documents, Executive Records, Correspondence and Messages, RG 1, Box 26, Folder: Executive Correspondence, May 1861, NHDRMA.

32.   *PC*, November 26, 1860, which reports the ration contracts for the year of 1861 for the Yard marines; May 21, July 18, August 6, 1861.

33.   *Ibid.,* June 15, 1861.

34.   *Ibid.,* May 4, August 13, 1861; *PJ*, May 4, 1861; George Pearson, Commandant's Office, Portsmouth Navy Yard, Portsmouth, NH, April 29, 1861, to Gideon Welles, Washington, DC, RG 181, Entry 8, Letters Sent to the Secretary of the Navy, NA-NER.

35.   *PJ*, May 4, 1861; *PC*, July 3, 6, September 4, 1861.

36.   George Pearson, Commandant's Office, Portsmouth Navy Yard, Portsmouth, NH, to Gideon Welles, Washington, DC, RG 181, Entry 8, Letters Sent to the Secretary of the Navy, NA-NER; Gideon Welles, Washington, DC, May 2, 1861, to George Pearson, Commandant's Office, Portsmouth Navy Yard, Portsmouth, NH, RG 181, Entry 10, Letters Received from the Secretary of the Navy, NA-NER.

37.   *PJ*, December 14, 1861; "Enlistment of Seamen for the United States Navy," *Executive Documents First Session of the Thirty-Seventh Congress*, Executive Document No. 7, pp. 1-2.

38.   *PC*, December 24, 1861.

39.   Quarles, pp. 229-30; McPherson, pp. 563-64; Aptheker, pp. 169-76, 200; Browning, pp. 203-4.

40.   *PC*, May 2, 8, 1861; G.B. Russell, Phillips Exeter Academy, Exeter, NH, April 27, 1861, to Ichabod Goodwin [Concord, NH], Executive Records: Correspondence & Messages, RG 1, Box 26, Folder: Executive Correspondence, Governor Goodwin, April 1861, NHDR-MA.

41.   *PC*, May 2, 8, 9, 1861.

42.   George Pearson, Commandant's Office, Portsmouth Navy Yard, Portsmouth, NH, August 3, 1861, to William R. Hathaway, Acting Master, U.S. Navy, Nantucket, MA, RG 181, Entry 2, Miscellaneous Letters Sent, NA-NER.

43.   Gideon Welles, Navy Department, Washington, DC, July 24, 1861, to George Pearson, Navy Yard, Portsmouth, NH, RG 181, Entry 10, Letters Received from the Secretary of the Navy, NA-NER.

44.   *PC*, October 8, 1861, excerpted from the *Boston Advertiser*.

45.   George Pearson, Navy Yard, Portsmouth, NH, November 1, 1861, to Gideon Welles, Navy Department, Washington, DC, RG 45, Entry 34, Commandants' Letters, 1861, NA-DC.

46.   *Ancestry and Descendants of Sir Richard Saltonstall*, pp. 31, 198-204; Saltonstall, "Autobiography and Reminiscences" (1886), Typescript original, MHS, Boston, MA, pp. 1-2, with paragraphing supplied.

47. *PC*, October 1, 1861.

48. *Ibid.*, December 28, 1861, *PJ*, January 11, 1862.

49. G[ustavus] V[asa] Fox, Navy Department [Washington, DC], December 6, 1861, to "Editor[,] *Boston Journal.*" Manuscript 861656, Baker Memorial Library, Dartmouth College, Hanover, NH.

50. *PJ*, December 14, 1861.

51. Long, p. 320; *DANFS*, 2:171.

52. *PC*, February 19, 1861.

53. *Ibid.*, June 18, 1861; Brighton, *Clippers of the Port of Portsmouth*, pp. 127-33; Spears, p. 227; *DANFS*, 6:336-39.

54. *PC*, August 13, 1861.

55. *Ibid.*, September 25, 1861; *PJ*, September 28, 1861; Boyd, *Extracts*, entry for September 24, 1861.

56. *PJ*, October 12, 1861; *ACAB*, 1:689. The treaty of April 21, 1861, at Ambrizette, Angola, is not listed in Clive Parry's *Consolidated Treaty Series*, Vols. 1-10, or in other similar multivolume compilations of American treaties.

57. *PC*, October 16, 17 (two articles), November 18, 1861: *PJ*, October 26, 1861.

58. *Ibid.*, *PC*, October 21, 1861.

59. Boyd, *Extracts*, entry for December 11, 1861: *DANFS*, 5:360; *ACAB*, 6:5.

60. *PC*, September 30, October 4, 18, 1861; *DANFS*, 2:171; *CWNC*, I:14.

61. *Ibid.*, *PC*, December 23, 1861, February 10, 27 (two articles), 1862; *PJ*, March 15, 1862.

62. *PC*, June 27, October 25, 1861; *DANFS*, 4:408.

63. Long, pp. 319-20.

64. For the most definite, comprehensive study of the blockade, see Robert M. Browning, Jr., *From Cape Charles to Cape Fear: The North Atlantic Blockading Squadron During the Civil War* (1993). Other sources include: Time-Life Books, *The Blockade: Runners and Raiders*; Wise, *Lifeline of the Confederacy: Blockade Running During the Civil War*; Wait, pp. 914-16; Heffernan, pp. 23-26; Albion and Pope, pp. 148-50; Laas, pp. 24-38.

65. *PJ*, June 22, 1861.

66. *PC*, May 3, 1861; Hall pp. 52-62; George Pearson, Commandant's Office, Portsmouth Navy Yard, Portsmouth, NH, September 19, 1861, to John Lenthall, Chief of the Bureau of Construction and Repair,

Washington, DC, Letters Sent to the Bureau of Construction and Repair, RG 181, Entry 15, NA-NER.

67.   *PC*, June 24, August 9 (two articles), 1861; Boyd, *Extracts*, entry for August 8, 1861.

68.   George Pearson, Commandant's Office, Portsmouth Navy Yard, Portsmouth, NH, September 19, 1861, to G[ustavus] V. Fox, Navy Department, Washington, DC; Similar letter to Gideon Welles, same day. RG 45, Entry 34, Commandants' Letters, 1861, NA-DC.

69.   *DANFS*, 1:74; *DAB*, 14:260. Commander Enoch Greenleafe Parrott's orders to take "command of the U.S. Steamer *Augusta*," Navy Department form, Washington, DC, August 10, 1861, signed by Gideon Welles, Parrott Papers, Beinecke Library, Yale University, New Haven, CT.

70.   E[noch] G. Parrott, "North River off the Battery" [New York, NY], October 1, 1861, to Susan——, n.p., Parrott Papers, Beinecke Library, Yale University, New Haven, CT.

71.   *DAB*, 14:260-61; *Report of the Secretary of the Navy in Relation to Armored Vessels*, p. 574.

72.   *PC*, August 12, 1861, excerpted from the *Boston Transcript*.

73.   *DAB*, 6:508-9; *PC*, June 7, 1861.

74.   Merrill, pp. 49-50; *CWNC*, I:9-12; *PC*, May 4, 1861, with paragraphing supplied.

75.   *DANFS*, 5:325; *PJ*, May 11, June 15, 1861; *PC*, April 27, May 6, June 10, 1861.

76.   *PC*, June 19, 1861; Boyd, *Extracts*, entry for June 18, 1861; George Pearson, Commandant's Office, Portsmouth Navy Yard, Portsmouth, NH, June 19, 1961, to Gideon Welles, Navy Department, Washington, DC, with enclosure of Henry Eagle, USS *Santee*, Portsmouth Navy Yard, Portsmouth, NH, June 19, 1861, to George Pearson, RG 45, Entry 34, Commandants' Letters, 1861, NA-DC.

77.   *PC*, June 20, 24, 1861.

78.   *Ibid.*, December 19, 20, 1861; *DANFS*, 6:325; *CWNC*, VI:295-96.

79.   Woodman, pp. 233-59; *PC*, December 7, 1861; *CWNC*, I:19, 22, 39, II:10, 15; Melville, pp. 31-32, 245, with quotation on p. 32.

80.   *PC*, December 24, 1861.

81.   *Ibid.*, April 11, 1861; *PJ*, September 1, 1861, reprinted in Brighton, *Tall Ships of the Piscataqua*, p. 269.

82.   Tarleton, p. 166; *PC*, March 29, 1878 (obituary of James Neal Tarlton); James N. Tarlton, Portsmouth, NH, May 13, 1861, to

Richard Hawley Tucker, Wiscasset, ME, typescript copy, Tucker Papers, Hawthorne-Longfellow Library, Bowdoin College, Brunswick, ME.

83. *PC*, August 19, 1861.

84. *Ibid.*, George Harrington, Treasury Department [Washington, DC], November 14, 1861, to "the Collector of Customs," Portsmouth, NH, United States Customs Service, RG 36, Entry 315, Letters Received, 1850-1863, Box 3, Folder: 1861, NA-DC.

85. *PJ*, July 27, 1861; *PC*, October 9, 18, 1861.

86. Long, pp. 322-28; *PC*, December 3, 19 (excerpted from the *Boston Post*), 1861.

87. *PJ*, December 7, 1861; *DAB*, 9:626-27.

88. Peter Marcy, New Orleans, LA, February 14 and 25, 1861 (two letters), to Daniel Marcy, Portsmouth, NH, Marcy Papers, Box 3, Folder 17, NHHS, Concord, NH.

89. Robinson, p. 243.

90. Albion and Pope, pp. 151-52; *CWNC*, VI:252, 328-29 (Annex A, "Privateers Commissioned by the Confederate States Government"); *PC*, April 24, 1861, excerpted from the *New York Commercial*; *PJ*, May 25, 1861.

91. *PJ*, June 8, July 27, 1861.

92. Brighton, *Tall Ships of the Piscataqua*, pp. 251-54; *PC*, June 12, 1861, excerpted from *New Orleans Delta*; *PJ*, July 27, 1861.

93. H.L. Townsend, Pass l'Outre, LA, May 4, 1861, to Peter Marcy, New Orleans, LA, Marcy Papers, Box 3, Folder 21, NHHS, Concord, NH; W.L. Frost, Eastport, ME, August 31, 1861, to Daniel Marcy, Portsmouth, NH. Telegram, Item VFM #799, White Library, MSM, Mystic, CT; *PC*, July 17, September 2, 3, 6, 18, 1861; *PJ*, September 7, 1861.

94. *PJ*, October 5, 1861; Brighton, *Tall Ships of the Piscataqua*, pp. 241-44, 257-58; James N. Tarlton, Portsmouth, NH, September 23, 1861, to Richard H. Tucker, Wiscasset, ME, Tucker Papers, Hawthorne-Longfellow Library, Bowdoin College, Brunswick, ME.

95. James N. Tarlton, New York, NY, November 16, 1861, to Richard H. Tucker, Wiscasset, ME, Tucker Papers, Hawthorne-Longfellow Library, Bowdoin College, Brunswick, ME.

96. Charles H. Brooks, Havre de Grace [now Le Havre], France, December 11, 1861, to Daniel Marcy, Liverpool, England, Marcy Papers, Box 3, Folder 26, NHHS, Concord, NH.

97. Robinson, pp. 243-44; *PJ*, May 11, 1861.

98.   *Ibid.,* August 10 (excerpted from *Boston Courier*), 24, 1861.

99.   *PC*, March 21, 1861.

100.   *Ibid.,* December 28, 1861.

101.   Brighton, *Tall Ships of the Piscataqua*, pp. 234-36; *PC*, August 28, September 16, 1861; *PJ*, August 31, September 21, 1861.

102.   *PC*, May 2, June 10, July 30, August 6, September 17, 23, October 22, December 6, 1861.

103.   George Pearson, Commandant's Office, Portsmouth Navy Yard, Portsmouth, NH, May 8, 1861, to Benjamin F. Martin, Portsmouth, NH, Martin Papers. One folder, NHHS, Concord, NH.

104.   *Ibid.*, "Abstracts of Monthly reports of Labor performed in the spar makers department since the breaking out of the Rebellion commencing April 25th 1861," Martin Papers. One folder, NHHS, Concord, NH.

105.   Samuel Colt, Hartford, CT, April 24, 1861, to Ichabod Goodwin [Concord, NH], Early Documents, Executive Records, Correspondence and Messages, RG 1, Box 26, Folder: Executive Correspondence, April 19-May 31, 1861, NHHS, Concord, NH; *PC*, June 10, 1861.

106.   *Ibid.*, October 24, 1861; H[enry] A. Wise [Ordnance Department], Washington, DC, September 5, 1861, 11 P.M., to [George Pearson,] Commandant, Portsmouth Navy Yard, Portsmouth, NH. Copy of Telegram. RG 181, Entry 24, Letters Received, Ordnance Department, NA-NER.

107.   *Ibid.,* Andrew A. Harwood [Ordnance Department], Washington, DC, September 6, 1861, to [George Pearson,] Commandant, Portsmouth Navy Yard, Portsmouth, NH. Telegram. RG 181, Entry 24, Letters Received, Ordnance Department, NA-NER.

108.   *Ibid.,* Andrew A. Harwood, Ordnance Department, Washington, DC, September 7, 1861, to [George Pearson,] Commandant, Portsmouth Navy Yard, Portsmouth, NH. Telegram. RG 181, Entry 24, Letters Received, Ordnance Department, NA-NER.

109.   *Ibid.,* Andrew A. Harwood, Ordnance Department, Washington, DC, September 9, 1861, to George Pearson, Commandant, Portsmouth Navy Yard, Portsmouth, NH, RG 181, Entry 24, Letters Received, Ordnance Department, NA-NER; G[ustavus] V. Fox, Navy Department, Washington, DC, September 9, 1861, to George Pearson, Commandant, Portsmouth Navy Yard, Portsmouth, NH, RG 181, Entry 10, Letters Received from the Secretary of the Navy, NA-NER.

110.   George Pearson, Commandant's Office, Portsmouth Navy Yard, Portsmouth, NH, May 25 and July 18 (two letters), 1861, to Joseph

Smith, Chief of the Bureau of Yards and Docks, Washington, DC, RG 181, Entry 31, Letters Sent, Yards and Docks, NA-NER.

111. Log, entry for July 27, 1861, PNSVC.

112. *PJ*, September 28, 1861, with Moses's quotations reconstructed from the article.

113. Gideon Welles, Navy Department, September 20, 1861, to George Pearson, Commandant, Portsmouth Navy Yard, Portsmouth, NH, RG 181, Entry 10, Letters Received from the Secretary of the Navy, NA-NER.

114. *PJ*, August 24, 1861.

115. *PC*, May 14, July 30, September 11, December 6, 1861.

116. Canney, pp. 74-78, with ship and sail plans of the *Kearsarge*; Silverstone, pp. 38-39, with photographs of the *Kearsarge*; Marvel, "The Pride of Portsmouth: The Cruise of the U.S.S. *Kearsarge*," pp. 1-6.

117. Log, entry for May 25, 1861, PNSVC; *DAB*, 6:173; John Lenthall, Navy Department, Bureau of Construction and Repair, Washington, DC, June 4 and 13 (two letters), 1861, to George Pearson, Commandant, Portsmouth Navy Yard, Portsmouth, NH, RG 181, Entry 16, Letters Received from the Bureau of Construction and Repair, NA-NER.

118. Marvel, "The Pride of Portsmouth: The Cruise of the U.S.S. *Kearsarge*," pp. 2-6; *New Hampshire Statesman*, May 11, June 18, 1861.

119. *PC*, June 10, 1861; *DANFS*, 3:609-10; *Union Leader*, February 10, 1993; *Boston Sunday Globe*, October 24, 1993.

120. *PJ*, June 15, 1861.

121. *Ibid.*, August 24, 1861; *PC*, September 12, 14, 1861; Boyd, *Extracts*, entry for September 11, 1861.

122. *PJ*, November 23, 1861; *PC*, October 7, 10, 26, 1861; Log, entries for October 5, December 1, 1861; Boyd, *Extracts*, entries for October 5, December 1, 1861, PNSVC; George Pearson, Commandant's Office, Portsmouth Navy Yard, Portsmouth, NH, October 5, 1861, to Gideon Welles, Navy Department, Washington, DC, RG 45, Entry 34, Commandants' Letters, 1861, NA-DC; Preble, p. 92.

123. *PJ*, November 23, 1861; *ACAB*, 5:1.

124. "Report of the Secretary of the Navy," with tabular columns for 1861 and 1862, *Executive Document No. 1, Message of the President of the United States* (1862), 3:22-46.

125. *PC*, December 6, 1861; *DANFS*, 2:227-28.

126. *Ibid.*, July 3, 10, 1861; Boyd, *Extracts*, entry for July 4, 1861.

127. *PC*, July 13, 17, 1861; *PJ*, July 6, 1861.

128. *PC*, August 31, September 13, 17, 1861; Boyd, *Extracts*, entries for August 30, September 15, 1861; *DANFS*, 6:215-16.

129. *PC*, November 19, 1861; *DAB*, 2:227-28.

130. *PC*, January 1, 1862; *DAB*, 6:173; *CWNC*, I:5, 21, 26.

CHAPTER 3

1. *PC*, October 17, 29, 31, 1862.

2. Boyd, *Extracts*, entry for January 6, 1862; George F. Pearson, Portsmouth Navy Yard, Portsmouth, NH, January 6, 1862, to Gideon Welles, Navy Department, Washington, DC, United States Military Telegraph, RG 45, Entry 34, Commandants' Letters, 1862, NA-DC.

3. *PC*, January 7, 1862; *PJ*, January 11, 1862.

4. Preble, p. 94; *PC*, January 16, 1862, which reprints the entire text of the eighth section of the law.

5. *PC*, January 1, 14, 16, 18, 1862; Boyd, *Extracts*, entry for January 14, 1862; Marvel, "The Pride of Portsmouth: The Cruise of the U.S.S. *Kearsarge*," p. 7.

6. *PC*, January 10, 14, 15, 16, 17, 22, 1862; *PJ*, January 18, 1862.

7. George F. Pearson, Commandant's Office, Portsmouth Navy Yard, Portsmouth, NH, January 14 (two letters on this date), 15, 16, 1862, to Joseph F. Smith, Bureau of Yards and Docks, Washington, DC, RG 181, Entry 31, Letters Sent to the Bureau of Yards and Docks, NA-NER.

8. John R. Holbrook, Portsmouth, NH, January 8, 1862; M.J. and W.A. Vaughan, Portsmouth, NH, January 8, 1862; Amos Paul, South Newmarket, NH, January 9, 1862; Nathaniel L. Thompson, Kennebunk, Maine, January 8, 1862; Hamson Loring, City Point Works, Boston, MA, January 9, 1862; and John Currier, Newburyport, MA, January 10, 1862. All letters to George F. Pearson, Navy Yard, Portsmouth, NH. Folder: "Years of 1860-69," PNSVC, Portsmouth, NH.

9. *PC*, February 4, 1862.

10. Preble, p. 94.

11. *PC*, October 22, 25, 1862.

12. Marvel, "The Pride of Portsmouth: The Cruise of the U.S.S. *Kearsarge*," pp. 7-8; Preble, p. 92; Canney, pp. 74-75; *PJ*, February 1, 1862.

13. George F. Pearson, Navy Yard, Portsmouth, NH, February 4, 1862, to John Lenthall, Chief of Bureau of Construction and Repair, Washington, DC, RG 181, Entry 15, Letters Sent to the Bureau of Construction and Repair, NA-NER; George F. Pearson, Navy Yard, Portsmouth, NH, February 5, 1862, to Gideon Welles, Washington, DC, RG 45, Entry 34, Commandants' Letters, 1862, NA-DC.

14. Gideon Welles, Navy Department, Washington, DC, January 18, 1862, to Charles W. Pickering, USS *Kearsarge*, Portsmouth, NH, Pickering Letterbook, NHHS; *PC*, February 4, 5, 1862.

15. *Ibid.*, February 8, 1862.

16. Marvel, "The Pride of Portsmouth: The Cruise of the U.S.S. *Kearsarge*," p. 9; "Extract of a Letter, dated Madeira, Fe[bruar]y 22, 1862, from Commander C[harles] W. Pickering, Commanding Steam Sloop *Kearsarge*, Copy given to the Constructors, March 31, 1862," RG 181, Entry 16, Letters Received from the Bureau of Construction and Repair, NA-NER.

17. *Ibid.*; *PC*, April 1, 1862.

18. *Ibid.*, April 12, 1862; Hill, p. 360; Badlam, p. 11.

19. *PC*, February 11, 1862, excerpted from the *New York Tribune*.

20. *Ibid.*, August 15, 1862; Marvel, p. 10; Charles W. Pickering, USS *Kearsarge*, off Algeciras, Spain, July 14, 1862, to Gideon Welles, Navy Department, Washington, DC, Pickering Letterbook, NHHS.

21. *Ibid.*, October 6, 1862, excerpted from the *Boston Traveller*.

22. Badlam, p. 12; Marvel, "The Pride of Portsmouth: The Cruise of the U.S.S. *Kearsarge*," p. 10; *PC*, October 25, 1862.

23. *Ibid.*, December 9, 1862; Badlam, p. 12; *A Naval Encyclopaedia*, p. 103, under Cadiz entry.

24. *PC*, December 9, 1862.

25. *CWNC*, I:23; *DANFS*, 2:214-15; *PC*, March 18, 1862.

26. Saltonstall, "Autobiography and Reminiscences," pp. 6-7, MsHS, Boston, MA.

27. *Official Records of the Union and Confederate Navies of the War of the Rebellion* (hereinafter referred to as *ORN*), Series I, 7:3-73. Report of Lieut. George U. Morris.

28. *Ibid.*, pp. 23-24. Report of Lieut. Austin Pendergrast.

29. *Ibid.*, p. 21. Report of Lieut. George U. Morris.

30. J.P. Morse, "Fort Munrow" [Fortress Monroe, Virginia], March 13, 1862, to "Will," no place, manuscript with typescript copy. Papers of

the Civil War—Miscellany, one folder, Phillips Library, PEM, Salem, MA.

31.   *PC*, March 11, 1862; *DAB*, 4:573-74; *ACAB*, 2:749; S[amuel] D[ana] Greene, Hampton Roads, Virginia, March 14, 1862, to his "Mother." Seven pages. Papers of the Civil War, Box 2, Phillips Library, PEM, Salem, MA.

32.   *Ibid.*, J.P. Morse, *op. cit.*, letter of March 13, 1862; *CWNC*, II:31 (Dahlgren quotation), 34-35, with facsimile of a letter, Samuel Dana Greene, "U.S. Iron-Clad Steamer *Monitor*, Hampton Roads [Virginia], March 12, 1862, to Gideon Welles, Secretary of the Navy, Washington, DC.

33.   *Ibid.*

34.   Saltonstall, *op. cit.*, pp. 16-17.

35.   *ORN*, Series I, 7:22, 24. Casualty statistics of the USS *Cumberland* and the USS *Congress*; *PC*, March 18, 1862; reprinted in *PJ*, March 22, 1862.

36.   *PC*, April 3, 1862.

37.   *PJ*, March 11, 22, 1862.

38.   *PC*, March 18, 1862.

39.   *CWNC*, II:30, reproducing a painting depicting the sinking of the *Cumberland*; *PC*, August 20, 1862; Longfellow, p. 202; Melville, pp. 53-54.

40.   Allard, pp. 114-16; Silverstone, p. 3.

41.   *PC*, March 17, 1862; *PJ*, March 22, August 23, 1862.

42.   Silverstone, p. 3; *DANFS*, 1:15, 7:105-6.

43.   *PC*, September 17, 29, 1862.

44.   *Ibid.*, October 6, 17, 1862.

45.   *Ibid.*, October 29, 1862; George F. Pearson, Navy Yard, Portsmouth, NH, October 30, 1862, to Francis H. Gregory, New York, NY, PNSVC, Portsmouth, NH; *ACAB*, 2:760.

46.   *PC*, December 19, 1862; Boyd, *Extracts*, entry for December 23, 1862.

47.   Joseph Smith, Bureau of Yards and Docks, Washington, DC, January 30, 1862, to George F. Pearson, Navy Yard, Portsmouth, NH, RG 181, Entry 32, Letters Received from the Bureau of Yards and Docks, NA-NER.

48.   *PC*, March 15, 1862.

49.   Wait, p. 920, reprinted in Commager, 2:853-54.

50. John Lenthall, Bureau of Construction and Repair, Washington, DC, July 31, 1862, to George Pearson, Navy Yard, Portsmouth, NH, RG 181, Entry 16, Letters Received from the Bureau of Construction and Repair, NA-NER.

51. *PC*, September 10, 27, October 8, 1862; *PJ*, October 4, 1862; Boyd, *Extracts*, entries for September 6, October 9, 1862.

52. [Andrew H. Foote,] Bureau of Equipment and Recruiting, Washington, DC, November 20, 1862, to George Pearson, Navy Yard, Portsmouth, NH, RG 181, Entry 18, Letters Received from the Bureau of Equipment and Recruiting, NA-NER; *DAB*, 6:499-500; *ACAB*, 2:496-97.

53. George F. Pearson, Navy Yard, Portsmouth, NH, December 16, 1862, to Andrew H. Foote, Bureau of Equipment and Recruiting, Washington, DC, RG 181, Entry 17, Letters Sent to the Bureau of Equipment and Recruiting, NA-NER.

54. Andrew H. Foote, Bureau of Equipment and Recruiting, Washington, DC, December 18, 1862, to George Pearson, Navy Yard, Portsmouth, NH, RG 181, Entry 18, Letters Received from the Bureau of Equipment and Recruiting, NA-NER.

55. *Ibid.*, A[lbert] N. Smith, February 2, 1864, to George Pearson.

56. *Cradle of American Shipbuilding*, pp. 4-8, with maps on pp. 4-5; Fentress, p. 69.

57. *Ibid.*; Preble, pp. 90-91.

58. *PC*, January 11, 1862.

59. *Ibid.*, February 19, 21, 1862.

60. *Ibid.*, May 23, 1862; *PJ*, May 24, 1862.

61. *Ibid.*

62. George F. Pearson, Navy Yard, Portsmouth, NH, August 25, 1862, to Joseph Smith, Bureau of Yards and Docks, RG 181, Entry 31, Letters Sent to the Bureau of Yards and Docks, NA-NER; *ACAB*, 1:372-73; Preble, p. 90.

63. *Ibid.*, George F. Pearson, September 1, 1862, to Joseph Smith.

64. *Cradle of American Shipbuilding*, p. 27; Preble, pp. 99-101; *PJ*, June 16, 1866.

65. *PC,* September 26, December 17, 1862.

66. *DAB*, 16:579-82; *PJ*, October 25, 1862. For the three pirates, see Nash, 2:1307 (Gibbs); 3:1811-15 (Kidd); and 3:1872-73 (Lafitte). For local assessment of Gibbs, see Snow, pp. 273-87; *PJ*, April 30, 1831, with a description of Gibbs's execution.

67. Long, p. 321.

68. *PJ*, October 25, 1862.

69. Brighton, *Clippers of the Port of Portsmouth*, pp. 59-61; *PJ*, October 18, 1862; Hackett, "A Reminiscence of the *Alabama*," pp. 382-830.

70. *Ibid.*, October 25, 1862; *PC*, October 20, 1862; Albion and Pope, pp. 152-53.

71. *Ibid.*; *PJ*, October 25, 1862, excerpted from the *New York Herald*.

72. Thomas P. Salter, New York, NY, October 17, 1862, to Daniel Marcy, Portsmouth, NH, Marcy Papers, Box 4, Folder 9, NHHS.

73. *PJ*, November 15, 1862; Submitted Bill, Receipt, and Deposition of Captain Nathan Parker Simes and owners of the Ship *Emily Farnum*, October 25, 31, 1862, before Thomas H. Dudley, U.S. Consul at Liverpool, England. One-page copy. RG 36, Bureau of Customs, Entry 315, Portsmouth, NH, Letters Received, 1850-1863, Box 3, Folder: 1862, NA-DC.

74. *PC*, November 4, 1862; Brighton, *Tall Ships of the Piscataqua*, p. 272.

75. *PJ*, October 25, 1862, three articles, with one excerpted from the *New York Express*.

76. *PC*, December 31, 1862, excerpted from the *Boston Traveller*.

77. *PC*, April 21, 1862.

78. Roland, pp. 159-65; Pelzer, pp. 46-52; *PJ*, October 4, 1862.

79. Wait, p. 917.

80. *PJ*, January 25, 1862, with paragraphing supplied.

81. Pelzer, pp. 50-51, with bibliography on p. 52.

82. *PC*, March 15, May 20, 1862; Brighton, *Tall Ships of the Piscataqua*, pp. 220-21, 275-77; *A Naval Encyclopaedia*, pp. 13, 132-35.

83. *Ibid.*, September 15, 1862.

84. *Ibid.*, May 1, 1862, excerpted from the *Boston Post*; Printed Sheet, "GENERAL ORDER," Navy Department, April 22, 1862, RG 181, Entry 10, Letters Received from the Secretary of the Navy, handnumbered on p. 235, NA-NER.

85. *PJ*, January 25, 1862; *DANFS*, 5:64; *CWNC*, I:40. The capture of the *Gipsey* does not appear in *ORN*.

86. *PJ*, January 25, 1862.

87. *CWNC*, II:50-56; *PJ*, July 12, 1862.

88. Thomas P. Salter, New York, NY, July 9, 1862, to Daniel Marcy [Portsmouth, NH], Marcy Papers, Box 4, Folder 6, NHHS.

89. New Orleans *Daily Picayune*, May 2, 1872 (obituary of Samuel Marcy).

90. James N. Tarlton, Portsmouth, NH, April 29, 1862, to Richard Hawley Tucker, Wiscasset, ME, Tucker Papers, Hawthorne-Longfellow Library, Bowdoin College, Brunswick, ME. For the *Alice Ball*, see Brighton, *Tall Ships of the Piscataqua*, pp. 242-43, and *PJ*, April 19, 1862.

91. James N. Tarlton, *op. cit.*, August 28, 1862, to Richard Hawley Tucker.

92. *Ibid.*, Tobey & Littlefield, Portsmouth, NH, September 8, 1862, to Richard Hawley Tucker.

93. James N. Tarlton, *op. cit.*, September 13, 1862, to Richard Hawley Tucker.

94. *PC*, October 24, 1862, excerpted from the *Dover Enquirer*.

95. Roland, pp. 230-31; Low and Clift, pp. 834-35.

96. George F. Pearson, Navy Yard, Portsmouth, NH, October 30, 1862, to Gideon Welles, Navy Department, Washington, DC, Letters Sent to the Secretary of the Navy, RG 181, Entry 8, NA-NER; *PC*, October 29, 31, 1862.

97. *Ibid.,* November 7, 1862.

98. *Ibid.*, March 15, 17, November 11, 24, 1862.

99. *Ibid.,* March 15, 17, October 11, 17, November 24, 1862.

100. *Ibid.*, November 29, 1862.

101. *Ibid.*, May 27, June 21, 1862.

102. *Ibid.*, May 3, 1862, excerpted from the *New York Evening Post*; Laas, pp. 33-37; Plowman, pp. 197-205.

103. *PJ*, July 1, 1893 (obituary of Thomas Aston Harris).

104. *Revised Register of the Soldiers and Sailors of New Hampshire in the War of the Rebellion 1861-1865*, p. 1128; *DANFS*, 3:303, 5:249.

105. Thomas A. Harris, USS *Penguin* off St. Augustine, FL, March 16, 1862, to Albert Ruyter Hatch [Portsmouth, NH], Hatch Papers, Box 1, Folder 8, NHHS.

106. *Ibid.*, Thomas A. Harris, USS *Henry Andrews*, New Smyrna, FL, March 20 [30?], 1862, to Alfred R. Hatch, Portsmouth, NH; *ORN*, Series I, 12:648-51.

107. *Ibid.*, Series I, 12:649.

108. *DANFS*, 4:197-98; *PC*, March 8, May 9, 12, 16, 1862.

109. *Ibid.*, May 16, 31, October 18, 1862; *DAB*, 14:220-21; *CWNC*, II:102.

110. *Ibid.*, II:110; *ORN*, Series I, 8:227-30.

111. *PC*, December 15, 1862.

112. *PJ*, July 12, 1862.

113. *PC*, February 10, 1862; *Navy Register*, 1862, p. 110.

114. George F. Pearson, Navy Yard, Portsmouth, NH, February 27, 1862, to Gideon Welles, Navy Department, Washington, DC, RG 45, Entry 34, Commandants' Letters, 1862, NA-DC.

115. *Ibid.,* Ward Marston, Marines Barracks, Navy Yard, Portsmouth, NH, February 27, 1862, to George F. Pearson, Navy Yard, Portsmouth, NH. Enclosure to accompany Pearson's letter of February 27, 1862, to Welles.

116. *PC*, February 22, 1862; *PJ*, February 22, 1862.

117. *PC*, November 18, 1862; Basler, 5:497-98.

118. *PC*, August 4, 23, 1862.

119. James Brooks, Manchester, NH, July 29, 1862, "To the British Consul in Portsmouth [NH]," RG 36, Entry 317, Bureau of Customs, Portsmouth, NH, Folder: Letters Received from British Consuls, 1849-1869, NA-DC.

120. *Ibid.*, George B. Starr[?]. Vice Consul at Portland, ME, Portsmouth, NH, August 1, 1862, to [Joseph M.] Edmonds, n.p.

121. *DAB*, 6:499-500; *ACAB*, 2:496-97; *PJ*, August 23, 1863; Printed circular letter, from Gideon Welles, Washington, DC, September 16, 1862, RG 181, Entry 10, Letters Received from the Secretary of the Navy, NA-NER.

122. *PJ*, October 11, 1862, excerpted from the *New York Tribune*.

123. *Ibid.,* December 6, 1862, with quotation taken from the *New York Observer*; *ACAB*, 5:683-84.

124. *PC*, February 21, July 2, 1862; *PJ*, July 4, 1862.

125. *PC*, May 7, 1862.

126. *Ibid.*, December 27, 1862.

127. *PJ*, October 11, 1862.

128. Arthur Winslow, pp. 330-39; *DANFS*, 6:9; Boyd, *Extracts*, entry for September 9, 1862.

129. S[imeon] N. Freeman, "U.S. Steamer *R.R. Cuyler*, Portsmouth Navy Yard," NH, September 16, 1862, to George F. Pearson, Navy Yard, Portsmouth, NH, RG 45, Entry 34, Commandants' Letters, 1862, NA-DC.

130. Thomas Williamson, Chief Engineer [Navy Yard, Portsmouth, NH],
      September 20, 1862, to [George F. Pearson?,] Navy Yard, Portsmouth,
      NH, Civil War Folder, 1860-1865, PNSVC, Portsmouth, NH.

131. *Ibid.,* M.G. Delany, Surgeon, Navy Yard, Portsmouth, NH, September
      24, 1862, to George F. Pearson, Navy Yard, Portsmouth, NH.

132. *PC*, October 8, 18, 1862.

133. *Ibid.,* April 23, June 7, 1862.

134. *Ibid.,* August 7, 1862.

135. *Ibid.,* September 6, 19, October 18, 1862; *PJ*, September 13, 1862.

136. Boyd, *Extracts*, entry for February 26, 1862; *DANFS*, 2:171; *PC*,
      February 10, 1862; *DAB*, 9:393-94; *ACAB*, 6:71.

137. *PC*, May 8, 1862.

138. Field, pp. 293-96; Tibawi, pp. 150-52; *PC*, September 27, 1862.

139. Field, pp. 296-97, 306; *PC*, November 12, December 2, 1862, January
      19, 1863.

140. *CWNC*, II:107.

141. Ayling, p. 110; *PC*, December 23, 27, 1862.

142. *Ibid.,* January 19, 1863.

143. *CWNC*, II:116.

144. *PC*, December 13, 1862, with lengthy excerpts from the "Report of the
      Secretary of the Navy."

145. Preble, p. 94: *Cradle of American Shipbuilding*, p. 80; *PC*, July 26,
      August 19, December 19, 1862.

146. Preble, p. 94; *PC*, July 29, 1862.

147. *Ibid.,* November 14, 1862; *PJ*, August 9, 16, 1862.

148. *PJ*, January 17, 1863.

149. *DANFS*, 1:40; Boswell, pp. 1-77, with quotation on p. 74; Stone, *et al.*,
      pp. 1-19.

150. *Ibid.*; Wilmerding, p. 11; *CWNC*, II:42.

151. *PC*, November 18, December 29, 1862.

CHAPTER 4

1.   *DAB*, 8:105-7; Niven, pp. 348-49, 374-77.

2.   *PJ*, January 10, 1863, two articles, one of which reprints John P.
      Hale's letter, "Senate Chamber [Washington, DC], December 29th,
      1862," to Gideon Welles.

3. *Ibid.*

4. *PC*, January 3, 10, 1863.

5. *Ibid.*, February 5 (two articles), 6, 1863; Boyd, *Extracts*, entry for February 4, 1863; Preble, p. 95.

6. *PC*, March 16, 1863.

7. *Ibid.*, March 13, 1863.

8. *Ibid.*, May 8, 1863; *PJ*, May 23, 30, 1863; *DANFS*, 5:368.

9. *PJ*, May 30, 1863, excerpted from the *Boston Transcript*.

10. *PC*, April 21, 1863.

11. *Ibid.*, April 21, 1863, excerpted from the *Newburyport Herald*.

12. *PC*, January 10, 21, February 10, 1863; *DANFS*, 6:222-23; *DAB*, 2:408-9.

13. *PC*, April 22, 1863.

14. *CWNC*, II:75; *DAB*, 2:409.

15. *CWNC*, II:32, 34.

16. *PC*, February 28, 1863.

17. Roland, pp. 91-92; Peter Marcy, New Orleans, LA, January 15, 1863, and February 21, 1863 (two letters), to Daniel Marcy, Portsmouth, NH, Daniel Marcy Papers, Box 4, Folders 12 and 14, NHHS.

18. Booth, *Louisiana Confederate Soldiers and Louisiana Confederate Commands*, entry for "Marcy, W.H."; *New Orleans Daily Crescent*, August 2, 1866, funeral notice for William Henry Marcy.

19. *PH*, March 11, 1990, "'Copperhead' Marcy was elected to Congress," by Ray Brighton; *PJ*, February 23, 1863; "Hon. Daniel Marcy," p. 355; Bell, pp. 329-31.

20. *Biographical Directory of the United States Congress, 1774-1989*, p. 1422; *PH*, March 11, 1990; *States and Union*, March 13, 1863.

21. Booth, entry for Samuel Marcy; *New Orleans Daily Picayune*, May 2, 1872, obituary and funeral notice for Samuel Marcy; Daniel Marcy, Portsmouth, NH, July 7, 1863, to Edwin M. Stanton, Secretary of War, Washington, DC, Daniel Marcy Papers, Box 5, Folder 1, NHHS.

22. Samuel Marcy, Fort Warren, Boston Harbor, MA, July 30, 1863, to Daniel Marcy, Portsmouth, NH, Daniel Marcy Papers, Box 5, Folder 2, NHHS.

23. Samuel Marcy, August 12, 1863, to Daniel Marcy, *op. cit.*

24. *ORN*, Series I, 2:156-57, 161-62; *CWNC*, III:66.

25.   Brighton, *Tall Ships of the Piscataqua*, pp. 257-58; Joshua W. Hickey, "Hamburgh" [Germany], September 21, 1863, to Daniel Marcy, Portsmouth, NH, Daniel Marcy Papers, Box 5, Folder 5, NHHS.

26.   Numerous documents, letters, memos, copies, and extracts, between and among Daniel Marcy, Supply C. Thwing, Joshua W. Hickey, Robert W. Sloman, and other parties, relating to the negotiations relative to the sale of the *Orozimbo*, September, October, and November 1863, Daniel Marcy Papers, Box 5, Folders 5-8, NHHS. The quotation is from Joshua W. Hickey, Ship *Morena*, Hamburg [Germany], November 11, 1863, to Supply C. Thwing, Boston, MA, Daniel Marcy papers, Box 5, Folder 8, NHHS.

27.   *PC*, March 26, 1863; Brighton, *Tall Ships of the Piscataqua*, pp. 232-33.

28.   *List of United States Vessels Sold and Transferred to British Subjects in the Year 1863*, p. 4.

29.   *PC*, February 7, March 6, 1863.

30.   *Ibid.*, February 16, 17, 18, 19, 1863; *PJ*, February 21, 1863.

31.   *PC*, June 16, 1863.

32.   *Ibid.*, August 1, 1863.

33.   *Ibid.*, July 15, 20, 1863.

34.   *Ibid.*, July 18, 1863.

35.   *Ibid.*, July 23, 1863; *PJ*, August 1, 1863.

36.   *PC*, August 26, 1863.

37.   *DAB*, 2:257-58; Bulloch, 1:408-12; Roland, pp. 166-71.

38.   *ORN*, Series II, 2:455-57; *CWNC*, III:112, 116 (photograph of the CSS *Stonewall*), 117; VI:209, 304.

39.   *CWNC*, III:93-94, 97-99; Mason Philip Smith, pp. 70-82.

40.   Adams, pp. 26-36; Mason Philip Smith, pp. 83-110; *CWNC*, III:101, 104; *PC*, June 29, 30, July 2, 1863; *PJ*, July 4, 1863.

41.   *PC*, June 29, 30, 1863, the latter excerpted from the *Portland Argus*.

42.   *PJ*, July 8, 1863, excerpted from the *Portland Press*.

43.   *PC*, July 8, 1863.

44.   Mason Philip Smith, pp. 111-29; Alexander, pp. 208-13.

45.   *Ibid.*, p. 211.

46.   *PJ*, August 22, 1863.

47.   George F. Pearson, Navy Yard, Portsmouth, NH, August 24, 1863, to Gideon Welles, Secretary of the Navy, Washington, DC,

Commandants' Letters, RG 45, Entry 34, NA-DC; Boyd, *Extracts*, entry for August 20, 1863.

48.   *PC*, August 22, 1863; *PJ*, August 22, 1863.

49.   *Ibid.*; Mason Philip Smith, pp. 126-29.

50.   Boatner, pp. 245-46; Bernstein, *The New York Draft Riots*; Hanna, pp. 262-73.

51.   Hurd, p. 98; "Joshua L. Foster," obituary, *Granite Monthly*, 28 (February 1900), pp. 118-19; *States and Union*, May 8, 1863; *PJ*, February 3, 1900, obituary of Joshua L. Foster.

52.   Roland, p. 93; Marvel, "New Hampshire and the Draft, 1863," pp. 58-60.

53.   *PJ*, October 11, 1865, "Provost Marshal's Office Closed. Its History" (article summarizing its activities).

54.   *DAB*, 4:311; Marvel, "New Hampshire and the Draft, 1863," p. 61.

55.   *PC*, May 15, 18, 1863.

56.   *Ibid.*, June 23, 1863.

57.   Marvel, "New Hampshire and the Draft, 1863," pp. 63-64; Brighton, *They Came to Fish*, 1:160; *States and Union*, July 17, 1863.

58.   Joshua L. Foster, "Sec[re]t[a]ry," Portsmouth, NH, July 14, 1863, to Joseph A. Gilmore [Concord, NH], Early Documents, Executive Records: Correspondence and Messages, RG 1, Executive, Box 30, Folder: Exec. Corr. 1863, July 11-15, 1863. NHDRMA, Concord, NH.

59.   Handbill attached to Joshua L. Foster's letter, Portsmouth, NH, July 14, 1863, to Joseph A. Gilmore, Concord, NH, with notation in Foster's hand, "Adopted at a citizens meeting in Portsmouth[,] N.H.[,] July 13, 1863," *op. cit.* Also printed in *The States and Union*, July 17, 1863.

60.   Charles Robinson, Portsmouth [NH], July 14, 1863, to Governor [Joseph A.] Gilmore, Concord, NH, Early Documents, Executive Records, Correspondence and Messages, RG 1, Executive, Box 30, Folder: Exec. Corr. 1863, July 11-15, 1863. NHDRMA, Concord, NH.

61.   Robinson, July 17, 1863, to Gilmore, *op. cit.*

62.   *PC*, July 15, 1863; *PJ*, July 18, 1863; Marvel, "New Hampshire and the Draft, 1863," p. 65.

63.   Brighton, *They Came to Fish*, 1:160-61; *PC*, July 18, 22, 27, 1863; *PJ*, July 25, 1863; *States and Union*, July 24, 1863.

64.   *PC*, July 17, 1863; *PJ*, July 18, 1863.

65.   *PC*, July 17, 1863, in "THE PORTSMOUTH MOB," excerpted in *PJ*, July 18, 1863.

66. Charles Robinson, Portsmouth, NH, July 17, 1863, to Joseph Gilmore [Concord, NH], Early Documents, Executive Records, Correspondence and Messages, RG 1, Executive, Box 30, Folder: Exec. Corr. 1863, July 15-20, 1863, NHDRMA, Concord, NH.

67. *PC*, July 21, 1863; Brighton, *They Came to Fish*, 1:162; *States and Union*, April 26, 1865.

68. *PC*, July 17, 18, 22, 23, 25, 1863; *PJ*, July 18, 1863; *States and Union*, July 24, 1863.

69. Marvel, "New Hampshire and the Draft, 1863," pp. 68-69.

70. Bernstein, *The New York Draft Riots*; Hanna, pp. 272-73.

71. *States and Union*, July 24, 1863.

72. Brighton, *The Prescott Story*, pp. 53-57.

73. *Portsmouth Directory,* 1861 and 1864, for residential and occupational information on Sampson L. Russell, Richard Walden, George Fretson, Augustus Walden, and Richard D. Smart; *PT*, August 5, 1871 (obituary of Sampson L. Russell).

74. *PC*, November 20, 1878; *PJ*, November 23, 1878 (obituaries of Richard Walden).

75. *PH*, September 19, 1910 (obituary of Augustus Walden).

76. *PH*, April 3, 1905 (obituary of Richard D. Smart).

77. *PC*, July 4, 1863.

78. Edwin M. Stanton, War Department, Washington, DC, March 27, 1863, to N[athaniel] Berry [Concord, NH], Early Documents, Executive Records, Correspondence and Messages, RG 1, Box 30, Folder: Executive Correspondence, March-April, 1863, NHDRMA, Concord, NH.

79. *PC*, May 2, 25, 1863.

80. *Ibid.*, July 4, 1863; J[oseph] A. Gilmore, Concord, NH; July 18, 1863, to E[dwin] M. Stanton, Washington, DC, Early Documents, Executive Records, Correspondence and Messages, RG 1, Box 30, Folder: Executive Correspondence, July 16-20, 1863, NHDRMA, Concord, NH; Edwin M. Stanton, Washington, DC, July 24, 1863, to J[oseph] A. Gilmore, Concord [,NH], *op. cit.*, Folder: Executive Correspondence, July 21-24, 1863. NHDRMA, Concord, NH.

81. *PC*, September 16, 1863.

82. *Ibid.*, April 30, 1863.

83. George F. Pearson, Navy Yard, Portsmouth, NH, May 21, June 12, 1863 (two letters) to Gideon Welles, Washington, DC, RG 45, Entry 34, Commandants' Letters, 1863, NA-DC.

84.   Boyd, *Extracts*, entry for July 12, 1863; *PC*, July 13, 1863; *PJ*, July 18, 1863.

85.   *PC*, July 29, 1863.

86.   *Ibid.*, August 18, 1863.

87.   George Pearson, Navy Yard, Portsmouth, NH, August 27, 1863, to Gideon Welles, Washington, DC, RG 45, Entry 34, Commandants' Letters, 1863, NA-DC.

88.   George F. Pearson, Navy Yard, Portsmouth, NH, August 28, 1863, to Gideon Welles, Washington, DC, with enclosure; W[illiam] H. Smith, Acting Master Commanding, Seavey's Island Battery, Portsmouth, NH, August 28, 1863, to Commandant George F. Pearson, Navy Yard, Portsmouth, NH, *op. cit.*; *PH*, August 20, 1989.

89.   *PC*, August 29, 31, 1863; *PJ*, September 5, 1863.

90.   *States and Union*, September 4, 1863.

91.   *PC*, September 1, 1863.

92.   *Ibid.*, August 28, 1863; George F. Pearson, Navy Yard, Portsmouth, NH, August 31, 1863, to Gideon Welles, Washington, DC, RG 181, Entry 7, Letters Sent to the Secretary of the Navy, 1863, NA-NER. Reprinted in *ORN*, Series I, 1:434; Boyd, *Extracts*, entry for August 30, 1863.

93.   Boyd, *Extracts*, entry for September 2, 1863; *ORN*, Series I, Vol. 2:436; George F. Pearson, Navy Yard, Portsmouth, NH, September 2, 1863, to Gustavus V. Fox, Washington, DC, RG 181, Entry 8, Copies of Letters and Endorsements Sent to the Secretary of the Navy, NA-NER.

94.   *PC*, September 3, 4, 11, 1863.

95.   *ORN*, Series I, 2:436; *ACAB*, 1:284.

96.   *PJ*, March 28, 1863.

97.   *Ibid.*, October 31, 1863, excerpted from the *New York Journal of Commerce*.

98.   *PJ*, June 20, 1863.

99.   George F. Pearson, Navy Yard, Portsmouth, NH, September 14, 15, 1863 (two letters), to Gideon Welles, Washington, DC, RG 45, Entry 34, Commandants' Letters, 1863, NA-DC; *PC*, May 15, August 13, September 15, 1863.

100.   *Ibid.*, September 25, October 16, 1863; Silverstone, p. 54.

101.   *PC*, September 1, October 17, 29, 31, 1863.

102.   *Ibid.*, December 21, 1863; *PJ*, December 19, 1963.

103. Wood, pp. 19-20; *DANFS*, 5:56; *PC*, September 11, 22, 1863.

104. *Ibid.*, October 17, 31, 1863, the latter reprinted in *PJ*, October 31, 1863.

105. *PC*, October 31, November 13, 1863; *PJ*, December 19, 1863; Preble, p. 96; *DANFS*, 7:486.

106. *PC*, December 25, 1863.

107. *Ibid.*, January 20, 1863.

108. *Ibid.*, January 23, 1863.

109. *Ibid.*, May 20, 1863; George F. Pearson, Navy Yard, Portsmouth, NH, May 30, June 8 (two letters), 1863, to Gideon Welles, Washington, DC, RG 181, Entry 8, Letters Sent to the Secretary of the Navy, NA-NER.

110. *PC*, May 20, 1863.

111. *Ibid.*, October 29, 31, 1863, the latter reprinted in *PJ*, same date.

112. *Message of the President of the United States and Accompanying Documents*, "Report of the Secretary of the Navy" (1863), pp. xxviii, 615-16, 849, 1058, 1077-78, reprinted in *Executive Documents Printed by Order of the House of Representatives ... 1863-'64* (1864), same pagination, with quotation on p. 615.

113. *PC*, December 12, 1863.

114. Brighton, *Clippers of the Port of Portsmouth*, pp. 96-99; *PC*, October 6, 10, 1863; *CWNC*, III:111.

115. *PJ*, April 9, 1864.

116. *Ibid.*, April 23, 1864.

117. *PC*, October 8, 1863.

118. *CWNC*, III:97; VI:317.

119. Albion and Pope, pp. 152-53.

120. CWNC, III:122; Brighton, *Tall Ships of the Piscataqua*, pp. 273-74; *PC*, October 8, 1863.

121. *PC*, August 12, 1863, excerpted from the *Salem Register*.

122. Badlam, pp. 12-13; Marvel, "The Pride of Portsmouth: The Cruise of the U.S.S. *Kearsarge*," p. 11; *ACAB*, 6:104.

123. Badlam, pp. 12-13; John W. Dempsey, U.S. Steamer *Kearsarge*, Brest, France, December 14, 1863, to "Dear Sister," n.p., one letter, Miscellaneous Manuscripts, MsHS, Boston, MA.

124. Smith, pp. 141-57; *CWNC*, III:162-63; VI:209-11; *PJ*, December 12, 1863.

125.   *PC*, December 12, 1863; *ORN*, Series I, 2:515-16, 518, 520, 522-23, the latter a reprint of George F. Pearson, Navy Yard, Portsmouth, NH, December 14, 1863, to Gideon Welles, Washington, DC, RG 45, Entry 34, Commandants' Letters, 1863, NA-DC.

126.   Smith, pp. 158-73; *ORN*, Series I, 2:521, 524, 528-29.

127.   *PC*, December 19, 1863.

128.   *Message of the President of the United States, and Accompanying Documents at the Commencement of the First Session of the Thirty-Eighth Congress.* "Report of the Secretary of the Navy," pp. i-xxvi, with quotation from p. xxxvi, and pp. 615-16, 849, 1058, 1070, 1077-78, relating to the Portsmouth Navy Yard. Reprinted with same pagination in *Executive Documents ... during the First Session of the Thirty-Eighth Congress, 1863-'64.* "Volume 4, No. 1 Navy."

CHAPTER 5

1.   Fentress, pp. 72-73.

2.   *Cradle of American Shipbuilding*, p. 76.

3.   *PJ*, January 16, 1864, excerpted from the *New York Tribune*.

4.   *DANFS*, 5:56; Wood, pp. 19-21; *PC*, January 23, 1864; *PJ*, January 30, 1864.

5.   *PC*, February 18, 20, 1864.

6.   *Ibid.*, March 29, 1864.

7.   *Ibid.*, April 21, 1864, reprinted in *PJ*, April 23, 1864.

8.   *PC*, April 27, 1864.

9.   *DANFS*, 1:15; *PC*, January 9, 1864.

10.   Boyd, *Extracts*, entries for March 9, March 17, April 18, 1864; George F. Pearson, Navy Yard, Portsmouth, NH, March 18, 1864 (two letters), to Gideon Welles, Secretary of the Navy, Washington, DC, RG 45, Entry 34, Commandants' Letters, 1864, NA-DC; *PC*, March 21, 1864.

11.   Pearson to Welles, May 30, 1864, *op. cit.*; *PC*, March 21, 1864.

12.   Pearson to Welles, April 8, 1864, *op. cit.*

13.   *PC*, April 9, 1864.

14.   Dewey, *Autobiography*.

15.   *PC*, April 19, 20, 1864, the latter excerpted from the *Portland Advertiser*.

16.   *CWNC*, IV:92; Silverstone, pp. 62-63, with photograph and caption, "The gunboat *Agawam* in the James River, 1864-1865," on p. 62.

17. *DANFS*, 6:350-51; Laas, pp. 24-38; Roland, p. 243.

18. *DAB*, 16:85-86; *PC*, March 23, 1864, excerpted from the *Portland Press*; *ORN*, Series I, 9:422-23; Wise, pp. 278, 280, 314, 326; *CWNC*, IV:12, 15.

19. *PC*, March 23, 1864, excerpted from the *Portland Press*.

20. *PC*, February 18, 1864, reprinted in *PJ*, February 20, 1864; *ORN*, Series I, 9:437-39, 459-60, 481-83.

21. *PC*, June 10, 1864.

22. *Ibid.*, October 12, 1864.

23. *ORN*, Series I, 9:*passim*, especially Francis A. Roe's reports, pp. 737-40, 743-44, 746, 757, 759-60, 767, including a map depicting the site of the *Albemarle-Sassacus* collision on p. 766; Holden, pp. 96-107, with quotation on p. 96. Holden's article is reprinted as "The *Sassacus* Fight," undated clipping, Box 3, Folder: "Newspaper Clippings, 1858-1888," Francis Asbury Roe Papers, Manuscript Division, LC. See also *Battles and Leaders*, 4:625-42, including another version of Holden's article, pp. 628-33, with maps on pp. 629-30.

24. Holden, pp. 100-103; *PC*, May 17, 21, 1864; Bennett, pp. 460, 463, for drawings of the battle.

25. *CWNC*, IV:54, 124-26, VI:193-95, with an illustration of the battle, IV:56.

26. Roe, "*Sassacus* and *Albemarle*, May 5, 1864, Sounds of North Carolina," Box 3, Folder: "Accounts, USS *Sassacus* & CSS *Albemarle*, 1864," Francis Asbury Roe Papers, Manuscript Division, LC, pp. 1, 4-9.

27. *Ibid.*, p. 9.

28. *DANFS*, 2:144-45; *PC*, January 26, 1864; Boyd, *Extracts*, entry for February 4, 1864.

29. Henry Knox Thatcher, "U.S. Steam Frigate *Colorado*, Navy Yard, Portsmouth, NH, February 6, 1864," to George F. Pearson, Navy Yard, Portsmouth, NH, with attached list of prisoners, RG 45, Entry 34, Commandants' Letters, 1864, NA-DC.

30. George F. Pearson, Navy Yard, Portsmouth, NH, February 8, 1864, to Gideon Welles, Washington, DC, RG 181, Entry 8, Letters Sent to the Secretary of the Navy, 1864, NA-NER; George F. Pearson, Navy Yard, Portsmouth, NH, February 8, 1864, to Captain George R. Graham, U.S. Marine Corps, Navy Yard, Portsmouth, NH, RG 181, Entry 36, Orders, NA-NER.

31. *PC*, May 30, 1864.

32. *Ibid.*, August 30, 1864.

33. Frederic F. Baury, Acting Volunteer Lieutenant, U.S. Frigate *Colorado*, September 22, 1864, to Commodore Henry Knox Thatcher, USS *Colorado*, Navy Yard, Portsmouth, NH, RG 45, Entry 34, Commandants' Letters, 1864, NA-DC; *PC*, September 24, 1864.

34. *PC*, September 29, 1864.

35. *Ibid.*, October 13, 1864; *DANFS*, 2:144; Doyle, "U.S. Naval Cemetery, 1820-1986," p. 1.

36. *PC*, July 19, 1864.

37. Brown, *The Galvanized Yankees*, pp. 7-9.

38. George F. Pearson, Navy Yard, Portsmouth, NH, January 22, 1864, to Gideon Welles, Navy Department, Washington, DC, RG 181, Entry 8, Letters Sent to the Secretary of the Navy, NA-NER; G.F. Pearson, Commandant, Navy Yard, Portsmouth, NH, March 22, 1864, to Jonathan Dearborn, Mayor of Portsmouth, Portsmouth, NH, PNSVC.

39. *PJ*, May 21, 1864, reprinted in *PC*, May 24, 1864.

40. *DANFS*, 1:18, 5:56; Boyd, *Extracts*, entries for May 13, 17, 1864; *PC*, May 14, 1864.

41. George F. Pearson, Commandant, Navy Yard, Portsmouth, NH, May 13, 1864, to Gideon Welles, Secretary of the Navy, Washington, DC, RG 181, Entry 8, Letters Sent to the Secretary of the Navy, NA-NER; George F. Pearson, Commandant, Navy Yard, Portsmouth, NH, May 16, 19 (three letters), 21, 1864, to Albert N. Smith, Commander, Chief of Bureau of Equipment and Recruiting, *ad. inst.*, Washington, DC, RG 181, Entry 17, Letters Sent to the Bureau of Equipment and Recruiting, NA-NER.

42. *PC*, May 21, 1864.

43. *Ibid.*, May 31, 1864, reprinted in *PJ*, June 4, 1864.

44. Boyd, *Extracts*, entries for May 13, 17, 18, 31, June 6, 15, 1864.

45. George F. Pearson, Navy Yard, Portsmouth, NH, February 29, 1864, to Gideon Welles, Secretary of the Navy, Washington, DC, RG 45, Commandants' Letters, 1864, NA-DC.

46. Pearson, March 19, 1864, to Welles, *op. cit.*

47. *PC*, June 29, 1864.

48. *Ibid.*, September 8, 1864.

49. *Ibid.*, November 26, 1864.

50. Theodorus Bailey, Commandant, Navy Yard, Portsmouth, NH, November 23, 1864, to Gideon Welles, Secretary of the Navy, Washington, DC, with enclosure, James T. Ross, Executive Officer, USS *Shawmut*, Portsmouth Navy Yard, Portsmouth, NH, November

23, 1864, to Theodorus Bailey, Commandant, Portsmouth Navy Yard, Portsmouth, NH, RG 45, Entry 34, Commandants' Letters, 1864, NA-DC.

51.   *Ibid.*

52.   *PC*, December 3, 1864.

53.   *Ibid.*, December 13, 16, 1864.

54.   *Ibid.*, December 15, 19, 24, 26, 1864.

55.   *Ibid.*, February 10, March 12, 1864.

56.   *PJ*, December 3, 1864, reprinted in *PC*, same date.

57.   *PC*, May 4, 1864; Brighton, *Tall Ships of the Piscataqua*, pp. 238-41; Albion and Pope, pp. 168-71.

58.   *PC*, March 7, 21, 26, June 6, October 1, 1864; *PJ*, April 2, 1864.

59.   Albion and Pope, p. 171.

60.   "Hon. Daniel Marcy," pp. 355-56; "Criticism of the Statesman Marcy Flourished," by Ray Brighton, *PH*, March 18, 1990; *Biographical Directory of the United States Congress, 1774-1989*, p. 1422.

61.   Benton, pp. 204-21; Roland, p. 196.

62.   Benton, pp. 221-22; *PC*, March 7, 1864.

63.   Benton, p. 221.

64.   Thompson, pp. 237-42, with quotation on p. 238.

65.   *Ibid.*, pp. 239-40.

66.   *PC*, March 1, 9, 17, 1864; Pillsbury, 2:548; Stackpole, 4:85-86.

67.   Booth, *Louisiana Confederate Soldiers and Louisiana Confederate Commands*, entry for W.H. Marcy; *New Orleans Daily Picayune*, August 2, 1866; *New Orleans Crescent*, same date, both concerning the reburial of William H. Marcy; Taylor, pp. 192-98; Kennedy, ed., "The Red River Campaign," pp. 163-66, and "Mansfield and Pleasant Hill," pp. 167-70, with two maps on p. 168.

68.   Peter Marcy, New Orleans, LA, August 20, 1864, to Daniel Marcy [Portsmouth, NH, or Washington, DC], Daniel Marcy Papers, Box 5, Folder 15, July-August 1864, NHHS, Concord, NH.

69.   *PC*, September 5, 6, 1864; *PJ*, September 24, 1864; Brighton, *Tall Ships of the Piscataqua*, pp. 188-96.

70.   John C. Bush, [Port] Stanley, Falkland Islands, June 13, 1864, to Supply Clapp Thwing, Boston, MA, with a copy to Daniel Marcy, as well as other related letters, protests, and legal papers concerning the sinking of the *Frank Pierce*, Daniel Marcy Papers, Box 5, Folder 14, NHHS, Concord, NH.

71.   Hackett, "A Reminiscence of the *Alabama*," p. 382; Brighton, *Tall Ships of the Piscataqua*, pp. 244-47; *PC*, June 22, December 16, 1864; *ORN*, Series I, 3:55.

72.   *ORN*, Series I, 3:53.

73.   London *Times*, June 16, 1864, three items including Semmes's April letter, his essay, and a *Times* editorial; *PC*, June 29, 1864.

74.   *CWNC*, IV:78, VI:193; *PC*, June 29, July 1, 8, 1864.

75.   *ORN*, Series I, 3:50-53.

76.   *PC*, February 17, March 28, May 18, 1864; Marvel, "The Pride of Portsmouth: The Cruise of the U.S.S. *Kearsarge*," pp. 14-15.

77.   Badlam, p. 18.

78.   Quinby, "Cruise of the *Kearsarge*," Phillips Library, PEM, Salem, MA, entry for June 18, 1864.

79.   Poole, "Cruise of the United States Steam Sloop *Kearsarge* In se[a]rch of rebel Privateers in 1862, 63 & 64," Log 432, Vol. 2, G.W. Blunt White Library, MSM, Mystic CT, entry for June 19, 1864.

80.   *PJ*, July 16, 1864, excerpted from the *Boston Traveller*, from a "letter dated Cherbourg [France], June 24, [1864]...written by an Officer of the *Kearsarge*." There are many printed and manuscript sources relating to the *Kearsarge-Alabama* sea battle. Books and articles emphasizing the role of the *Kearsarge* include: *Executive Documents Printed by Order of the House of Representatives...1864-'65*, Vol. 6, No. 1, Navy, "Report of the Secretary of the Navy," which includes "Sinking of the *Alabama*," pp. 617-79; *ORN*, Series I, 3:50-85; *Papers Relating to Foreign Affairs, Accompanying the Annual Message of the President to the Second Session Thirty-Eighth Congress*, Parts II-III; Edge, *The* Alabama *and the* Kearsarge; Hobson, *The Famous Cruise of the* Kearsarge; *Battles and Leaders of the Civil War*, 4:600-625; Ellicott, *The Life of John Ancrum Winslow*; Hill, "The *Kearsarge*," in Hill, *Twenty-Six Historic Ships*, pp. 359-74; and Taylor, "The U.S.S. *Kearsarge* Versus the *Alabama*: Showdown off Cherbourg," in *Yankee*, 48:72-77, 133-38.

      The four most recent studies are: Marvel, "The Pride of Portsmouth: The Cruise of the U.S.S. *Kearsarge*," in *Historical New Hampshire* 41 (Spring/Summer 1986):1-20; Delaney, *Ghost Ship: The Confederate Raider* Alabama (1989); Brighton, three articles in *PH*: "The Sea Battle That was Decided by Friends" (June 11, 1989), "*Kearsarge* [should be *Alabama*] Out-Maneuvered in Final Sea Battle" (June 18, 1989), and "Namesakes of the Civil War Vessels Unite a Nation" (June 25, 1989); and Robinson, *Shark of the Confederacy: The Story of the CSS* Alabama (1994).

In addition to *PC* and *PJ*, for contemporary newspaper and periodical accounts, with articles and letters frequently reprinted from other American, British, and French sources, see: *Andover* (MA) *Advertiser*, July 30, 1864; *Charleston* (SC) *Mercury*, July 11, 16, 23, 27, 28, 30, August 10, 17, 20, October 1, 1864; *Chicago Tribune*, July 27, 31, 1864; *Exeter* (NH) *News-Letter*, July 11, 25, August 15, 1864, January 5, 1865; *The Guardian* (London), June 22, 29, 1864; *Harper's Weekly*, July 23, 1864; *Journal des Débats* (Paris), June 20-23, 1864; *Le Moniteur Universel* (Paris), June 21-22, 24-25, 1864; *New York Daily Tribune*, July 12, 18, 21, 1864; *Saturday Review* (London), June 25, 1864; *Scientific American*, July 16, 1864; and *The Watchman and Wesleyan Advertiser* (London), June 22, 29, 1864.

For manuscripts in the form of logs, letters, and diaries, see "Abstract Log: U.S. Steam S[hip] *Kearsarge* of Capt. Jno. A. Winslow, Commanding," and the Bartlett, DeWitt, Poole, and Quinby collections.

81. Quinby, *op. cit.*, entry of June 19, 1864; Southwick, p. 225, for identification of William Lewis Dayton and his son, William Lewis Dayton, Jr.

82. *PJ*, November 6, 1897, excerpted from the *Boston Sunday Globe*.

83. Martin V. Hoyt, USS *Kearsarge*, Cherbourg, France, June 19, 1864, to "Dear Uncle" [Samuel Hoyt, Newington, NH], John Paul Jones House, PHS, Portsmouth, NH. Another version of Hoyt's account is Hoyt, Martin, "Naval Engagement between the U.S.S. *Kearsarge* and the Confederate Steamer *Alabama*," two-page typescript, Civil War file, Langdon Library, Newington, NH, reprinted in Rowe, pp. 167-69.

84. *PC*, July 6 (with quotation), 7, 8, 11, 13, 1864; *PJ*, July 9 (two articles), 16, 1864.

85. *Exeter News-Letter*, July 11, 1864; *Saturday Review*, 17 (June 25, 1864):769.

86. Donald, ed., Salmon P. Chase's diary entry for July 6, 1864, pp. 234-35.

87. Woodward, ed., Mary Boykin Chesnut's diary entry for July 25, 1864, pp. 622-23.

88. *PJ*, July 9, 1864, excerpted from the *London Daily News* and the London *Times*; *Illustrated London News*, June 25, 1864, with quotation; London *Times*, June 16, 20-21, 1864; *London Observer*, June 26, July 3, 1864; Ellicott, pp. 33-35, 45-46.

89. Quinby, *op. cit.*, entry of June 20, 1864.

90. *PJ*, June 15, 1867.

91.   *Ibid.*, August 6, 1864; *PC*, July 8, 21, 1864; Leary, pp. 167-73; Spencer, pp. 190-92; Case and Spencer, pp. 509-15.

92.   *ORN*, Series I, 3:72-73, partially reprinted in *PC*, July 12, 1864.

93.   Farragut, pp. 403-4; *PC*, July 12, 26, 1864; *PJ*, July 23, 1864, June 15, 1867.

94.   *ORN*, Series I, 3:68, contains the list of the seventeen *Kearsarge* crewmen awarded the Congressional Medal of Honor; *Medal of Honor, 1861-1949: The Navy*, pp. 11-13, 15-16, 27 (citation of Mark G. Ham), 29, 35, 40, 43 (citation of Joachim Pease), 45-46, 49 (citation of William Smith), 50; *Above and Beyond*, pp. 50-51, 322-24; Foster, *The Soldiers' Memorial*, pp. 42, 49; Lowe and Clift, pp. 835-36.

95.   Edge, *The* Alabama *and the* Kearsarge, reprinted as *An Englishman's View of the Battle*; reprinted also in *Executive Documents...The House of Representatives...1864-'65*, pp. 666-79; and in *PJ*, November 1, 8, 1879 (two installments), November 15, 1879, which reprints a letter, "Capt. John A. Winslow, U.S.S. *Kearsarge*, off Dover [England], July 13th, 1864, to Fred[eric]k M. Edge, London."

96.   *PC*, August 20, 1864, excerpted from the Washington *National Intelligencer*, August 18, 1864, which includes Edge's pamphlet reprinted in full.

97.   Holzer and Neely, p. 98, with a reproduction of Edouard Manet's painting, *The Battle of the* Kearsarge *and the* Alabama, original in the John G. Johnson Collection, Philadelphia Museum of Art, Philadelphia, PA; also reproduced in Schneider, p. 73; Miller, p. 182; Gay, plate 78, p. 97; Hanson, following p. 222, plate 85 (Manet's picture); and Delany, cover of book, and Gronberg, plate 21, p. 86, with another Manet picture, an 1864 watercolor, *The* Kearsa[r]ge *at Boulogne*, p. 128. Other depictions of the battle include Xanthus Russell Smith's *Engagement Between the Pirate* Alabama *and the U.S.S.* Kearsarge *off Cherbourg, June 19, 1864*, original at the Union League of Philadelphia, Philadelphia, PA, reproduced in Holzer and Neely, p. 102; *The American Heritage History of the Civil War*; Cheri Dubreuil's *U.S.S.* Kearsarge and *C.S.S.* Alabama, in Brewington, p. 110; James Edward Buttersworth's Kearsarge *and* Alabama (two images), in Schaefer, pp. 152-53; and John Frink Rowe's *The* Kearsarge *and the* Alabama, original at the Langdon Library, Newington, NH, and reproduced in Rowe, p. 168. Other paintings, woodcuts, and lithographs are reproduced in Holzer and Neely, pp. 103, 104, 107 (two images); Hanson, following p. 222, plate 86; Gronberg, p. 127; *Battles and Leaders*, 4:612-14, 620, 622-23; and *CWNC*, IV:77 (two images).

98. For Boker, see *DAB*, 2:415-18, with his poem *"Captain Semmes, C.S.A.N., June 19, 1864,"* in *Chicago Tribune*, July 27, 1864, and in *Exeter News-Letter*, August 15, 1864; "The Sinking of the Rebel Corsair," by an unnamed poet, in *Harper's Weekly* 8 (July 23, 1864):466; the poem *"Kearsarge,"* originally published in the *Boston Transcript*, reprinted in *PC*, December 19, 1864, and in *Exeter News-Letter*, January 9, 1865. For the Currier & Ives print, see Peters, 2:385, and its reproduction in Holzer and Neely, p. 103. Broadsides include: "Welcome Song...." signed, "Jno. A. Winslow, Captain, *Kearsarge*, Nov. 14th/64" and "The Sinking of the Pirate *Alabama*;" both at Phillips Library, PEM, Salem, MA. For a rare poem on the *Kearsarge*'s opponent, see *"Alabama," Charleston Mercury*, July 27, 1864. The sheet-music composition and lyrics, "Last of the *Alabama*," in *CWNC*, VI:166-69.

99. Benton, pp. 217-22.

100. Gideon Welles, Navy Department, Washington, October 31, November 2 (two letters), 1864, to Theodorus Bailey, Commandant, Navy Yard, Portsmouth, NH, Letters Received from the Secretary of the Navy, RG 181, Entry 10, NA-NER; "Order" issued by A[lexander] Murray, Commandant, "P.T. [pro tempore]," November, 5, 1864, Navy Yard, Portsmouth, NH, Copies of "Orders"...Sent to Yard Officials and Heads of Departments, RG 181, Entry 36, NA-NER.

101. *PC*, November 4, 10, 1864; *PJ*, November 12, December 3, 1864; Pillsbury, 2:548; Stackpole, 4:86-87.

102. Estes and Goodman, pp. 142-44; *PH*, July 2, 1989, "Yellow Fever Sails into the City on the *DeSoto* [*De Soto*] in 1864," article by Ray Brighton; Brighton, *They Came to Fish*, 1:164-65, 2:248.

103. *PC*, June 18, 1864; *DANFS*, 2:267.

104. George Pearson, Commandant, Navy Yard, Portsmouth, NH, June 16, 20 (two letters), 1864, to Gideon Welles, Secretary of the Navy, Washington, DC, Letters Sent to the Secretary of the Navy, RG 181, Entry 8, NA-BB; *PC*, July 11, 1864.

105. *PJ*, June 28, 1864; Lieutenant Commander Edward Y. McCauley, Commanding, USS *Tioga*, Portsmouth, NH, June 27, 1864, to Gideon Welles, Secretary of the Navy, Washington, DC, RG 45, Entry 34, Commandants' Letters, 1864, NA-DC; Pearson, June 28, 1864, to Welles, Letters Sent, *op. cit.*

106. Pearson, June 29, 1864, to Welles, Letters Sent, *op. cit.*

107. *PC*, June 29, 30, July 1, 4, 6, 8, 9, 1864; *PJ*, July 9, 1864; Pearson, July 2, 4, 5, 6, 7 (five letters), 1864, to Welles, Letters Sent, *op. cit.*; "City of Portsmouth, In Board of Aldermen, June 28, 1864, THE FOLLOWING PREAMBLE AND RESOLUTIONS WERE PASSED

AND ORDERED TO BE PRINTED," Broadside, copy in RG 45, Entry 34, Commandants' Letters, 1864, NA-DC.

108. *PC*, July 7, 16, 1864, including Board of Aldermen's Report, dated July 14, 1864.

109. *Ibid.*, August 23, October 17, 25, 1864; Boyd, *Extracts*, entries for October 22, 24, 1864.

110. T[heodorus A.] Bailey, Commandant, Navy Yard, Portsmouth, NH, November 26, 1864, to Gideon Welles, Secretary of the Navy, Letters Sent to the Secretary of the Navy, RG 181, Entry 8, NA-NER; *DAB*, 1:501-2.

111. Estes and Goodman, p. 143.

112. *DAB*, 4:518-19; *ACAB*, 2:3-4; Introduction to "Notes from the Journal of Lieutenant T.A.M. Craven, U.S.N.," in *Proceedings of the United States Naval Institute* (1888), 14:119-20; *PJ*, August 20, 27, 1864, the latter excerpted from *The New York Times*.

113. *CWNC*, IV:92-97, VI:86-97, the latter, "An August Morning with Farragut at Mobile Bay," by Harrie Webster; Farragut, pp. 412-25; *DANFS*, 7:78; *ORN*, Series I, 21:405-519; *PC*, August 16, 1864.

114. "Notes" in *Proceedings, op. cit.*, p. 120; *CWNC*, 4:95-96, with contemporary drawing of Craven and Collins aboard the *Tecumseh* on p. 96.

115. *ORN*, Series I, 21:405-519; *CWNC*, 4:95-100, 5:83; Wise, pp. 179-81; Love, pp. 309-11.

116. *ORN*, Series I, 21:543; Boyd, *Extracts*, entry for September 8, 1864; *PC*, September 9, 1864.

117. *PC*, July 18, 1864.

118. *Ibid.*, August 13, 20, September 3, 1864; Preble, pp. 96-97.

119. *PC*, December 23, 1864, January 31, 1865.

120. Joseph Smith, Chief of the Bureau of Yards and Docks, Navy Department, Washington, DC, October 10, 1864, to T[heodorus] Bailey, Commandant, Navy Yard, Portsmouth, NH, RG 181, Entry 32, Letters Received, Yards and Docks, NA-NER.

121. *PJ*, September 3, 1864.

122. *Ibid.*, John Lenthall, Chief of Bureau of Construction and Repair, Washington, DC, December 30, 1864, to Theodorus Bailey, Commandant, Navy Yard, Portsmouth, NH, RG 181, Entry 16, Letters Received, Bureau of Construction and Repair, NA-NER.

123. *PC*, August 16, 1864.

124. *Ibid.*

125. *Ibid.*, August 22, 1864.

126. *Ibid.*, July 16, September 19, 24, 26, 1864; *PJ*, September 3 (excerpted from the *Boston Traveller*), September 17, 24, October 1, 1864, the latter containing the poem, "Launch of the Frigate *Franklin*, at Portsmouth, Sept. 17, 1864"; *DANFS*, 2:443.

127. George F. Pearson, Commandant, Navy Yard, Portsmouth, NH, September 14, 30 (two letters), 1864, to Gideon Welles, Secretary of the Navy, Washington, DC, RG 45, Entry 34, Commandants' Letters, 1864, NA-DC; *PC*, October 3, 1864; *PJ*, October 8, 1864.

128. *PC*, September 28, 1864, excerpted from the *New York Herald*, and reprinted in *PJ*, October 1, 1864, biographical sketch of Theodorus Bailey; *DAB*, 1:501-2; *ACAB*, 1:138-39.

129. Boyd, *Extracts*, entry for October 30, 1864; *DANFS*, 2:347; *PC*, October 15, December 5, 1864, January 14, 1865; *PJ*, November 5, 1864.

130. *PC*, September 21, December 2, 3, 19, 20, 1864.

131. Everett, 4:666-67, excerpted in *PJ*, April 2, 1864; *DAB*, 6:223-26; *CAB*, 2:387-89; *Executive Documents...1864-'65*, Vol. 6, "Report of the Secretary of the Navy," pp. 715-18; Letter of Donald McKay, East Boston, MA, October 29, 1864, "To the Editor of the *Boston Daily Advertiser*," partially reprinted in *PJ*, November 22, 1864. "Report of the Secretary of the Navy" is excerpted in *PC*, December 8, 1864, and *PJ*, December 24, 1864. For Port of Portsmouth arrivals, see *PC*, January 14, 1865. For the "Epsom salt" story, see *PJ*, December 24, 1864, excerpted from the *Portland Press*.

132. *PC*, December 20, 1864.

CHAPTER 6

1. *PC*, January 14, 1865 (two articles).

2. Material on Fort Fisher is extensive. See Gragg, *Confederate Goliath: The Battle of Fort Fisher*; Porter, pp. 683-754; Love, pp. 316-21; Parker, pp. 104-17; Wise, pp. 205-10; Roberts, pp. 614-15; *CWNC*, IV:149-51, V:6-20; *ORN*, Series I, 11:245-378, 425-596; *PC*, October 24, 1864.

3. *PJ*, January 7, 1865, including an excerpt from the *Philadelphia Ledger*.

4. *PJ*, January 11, 1865, the first quotation reconstructed from the text.

5. Love, pp. 318-19.

6. E[noch] G. Parrott, "U.S. Iron Clad *Monadnock*, off Morris Island, S.C., Jan. 30, 1865," to David D. Porter, Commanding North Atlantic Squadron (South Carolina), "Report of the Capture of Fort Fisher,"

rough draft, Parrott Papers, Beinecke Library, Yale University, New Haven, CT; printed in *ORN*, Series I, 2:462-63; and in *Report of the Secretary of the Navy*, December 1865, pp. 132-33.

7.   *CWNC*, V:19, facsimile of Porter's telegram to Welles.

8.   *Ibid.*, p. V:13; *DANFS*, 4:4111, pertaining to the USS *Monadnock* and accompanying analysis; *PC*, January 20, February 20, March 10, 1865, the first excerpted from the *Boston Herald*.

9.   Gragg, pp. 230-35; *PJ*, January 28, 1865.

10.   *Ibid.*, another article in the same *PJ* issue; *PC*, January 27, 1865.

11.   *PJ*, January 21, 1865; Boyd, *Extracts*, entry for January 18, 1865.

12.   Foster, *The Soldiers' Memorial*, pp. 18, 40, the latter reproducing the lettering on Laighton's stone in Harmony Grove Cemetery, Portsmouth, NH.

13.   *PJ*, February 18, 1865, excerpted from the *Boston Traveller*.

14.   T[heodorus] Bailey, "U.S. Navy Yard, Portsmouth, N.H., Commandant's Office, Feb. 9, 1865," to Gideon Welles, Navy Department, Washington, DC, RG 45, Entry 34, Commandants' Letters, 1865, NA-DC; *PC*, February 10, 1865, partially reprinted in *PJ*, February 11, 1865.

15.   *PC*, February 11 (two articles), 14, 1865.

16.   T[heodorus] Bailey, Portsmouth Navy Yard, Portsmouth, NH, February 9, 20, April 3, 1865 (three letters), to John Lenthall, Chief of the Bureau of Construction and Repair, Washington, DC, RG 181, Entry 5, Letters Sent to the Bureau of Construction and Repair, NA-NER; *PC*, February 21, 24, March 31, 1865, the latter reprinted in *PJ*, April 1, 1865.

17.   *DANFS*, 4:372-74; Boyd, *Extracts*, entries for June 3, 27, 1867.

18.   *PC*, January 4, 1865, reprinted in *PJ*, January 7, 1865.

19.   *PC*, February 3, 1865, reprinted in *PJ*, February 4, 1865.

20.   *PC*, February 21, 1865, reprinted in *PJ*, February 25, 1865; *DANFS*, 4:336; *CWNC*, V:39.

21.   *PJ*, January 7, 1865.

22.   *PC*, January 9, 1865; Boyd, *Extracts*, entries for January 7 and 8, 1865.

23.   *PC*, January 21, 1865.

24.   *Ibid.*, January 23, 1865.

25.   *The Congressional Globe*, entries for January 28, 30, February 17, 1865, which reprint Hale's speeches, the latter excerpted in *States*

and Union, March 10, 1865. For Hale, see *Biographical Directory of the United States Congress, 1774-1989*, p. 1111; and *DAB*, 4:105-7. For an analysis of the speeches, see Niven, pp. 478-80; Sewell, pp. 220-21.

26. *States and Union*, March 10, 1865.

27. *Ibid.*

28. Roland, pp. 108-9.

29. *Revised Register of the Soldiers and Sailors of New Hampshire in the War of the Rebellion 1861-1866*, p.1123; Foster, *The Soldiers' Memorial*, p. 26; *PJ*, March 11, 25, April 1, 1865, April 3, 1886; *PT*, March 30, 1886, the latter two being obituaries of Thomas S. Gay.

30. *PJ*, March 25, 1865, "NARRATIVE OF ENSIGN THOMAS S. GAY, OF THIS CITY, Who accompanied Lieut. Cushing in the *Albemarle* Expedition, fell into the hands of the Rebels and was an inmate at the Salisbury, Danville, and Libby Prisons." Dated "Portsmouth, N.H., March 18, 1865."

31. *Ibid.*

32. *Ibid.*

33. *Ibid.*

34. *Ibid.*

35. *PC*, January 24, 1865; *PJ*, February 11, 1865.

36. T[heodorus] Bailey, Commandant's Office, U.S. Navy Yard, Portsmouth, NH, January 24, 30, February 14, 21, 1865 (four letters), to Joseph Smith, Chief, Bureau of Yards and Docks, Washington, DC, RG 181, Entry 31, Letters Sent to the Bureau of Yards and Docks, NA-NER.

37. Joseph Smith, Chief, Bureau of Yards and Docks, Washington, DC, February 24, 1865, to T[heodorus] Bailey, Commandant, Navy Yard, Portsmouth, NH, RG 181, Entry 32, Letters Received from the Bureau of Yards and Docks, NA-NER.

38. *Message of the President of the United States* (1865), "Report of the Secretary of the Navy," pp. 5-6; Preble, p. 98.

39. *PC*, February 24, March 18, 1865; *PJ*, March 25, May 27, 1865; Preble, p. 98.

40. *PC*, March 20, 1865.

41. *PJ*, May 27, 1865, article, "NAVY YARD AFFAIRS."

42. *PJ*, August 19, 1865; Brighton, *Tall Ships of the Piscataqua*, pp. 269-71, 299-301.

43. *PC*, January 13, 1865; *PJ*, January 14, 1865.

44.   *PJ*, January 28, March 3 (three articles), 18 (three articles), 1865.

45.   James Brown & Co., Liverpool, England, March 25, 1865, to S[upply] C. Thwing, Boston, MA, with copy of telegram, March 25, 1865, both as enclosures from "S.C. Thwing, by John Thomas," Boston, MA, April 8, 1865, to Daniel Marcy, Portsmouth, NH, Daniel Marcy Papers, Box 5, Folder 20, NHHS, Concord, NH.

46.   Brighton, *Tall Ships of the Piscataqua*, pp. 281-83; *PC*, April 22, 1865, excerpted from the *New Bedford Standard*, reprinted in *PJ*, April 29, 1865.

47.   *PC*, January 29, 1865, excerpted from the Boston *Commercial Bulletin*.

48.   *PC*, April 27, 1865, excerpted from the *Boston Journal*, and reprinted in *PJ*, May 6, 1865.

49.   *PC*, October 27, 1865.

50.   *Ibid.*, June 28, September 28, October 26, 1865; Brighton, *Clippers of the Port of Portsmouth*, p. 36.

51.   *PJ*, August 19, 1865; Albion and Pope, pp. 171-73.

52.   *PJ*, March 4, 1865.

53.   Materials on the CSS *Shenandoah* are extensive. See Horan, ed., *C.S.S. Shenandoah*; Hunt, *The Shenandoah*; *ORN*, Series I, 3:passim; *DAB*, 10:302-3; *PC*, January 23, August 7, 1865, "THE PIRATE SHENANDOAH"; *PJ*, January 21 (with quotation), November 25, 1865, "THE HISTORY OF THE SHENANDOAH."

54.   Gilbert, p. 300; Brighton, *Tall Ships of the Piscataqua*, pp. 320-32; *ORN*, Series I, 3:402, Report of Henry Libbey, Master of the *Kate Prince*; *PC*, January 3, 1865; *PJ*, January 7, 1865; *CWNC*, IV:133.

55.   "Wm Jones & Son, part owners & agents of Ship, *Kate Prince*," Portsmouth, NH, January 24, 1865, "to the Collector of Customs for the Port of Portsmouth, NH," RG 36, Entry 315, Bureau of Customs, Portsmouth, NH, Letters Received, 1865-1908, Box 5, Folder 1865, NA-DC. Geo[rge] Harwinton[?], Assistant Secretary of the Treasury, Washington, DC, January 27, 1865, to T[imothy] A. Upham, Collector, Port of Portsmouth, Portsmouth, NH, *op. cit.*; Brighton, *Tall Ships of the Piscataqua*, p. 231.

56.   Brighton, *op. cit.*, pp. 182-84; *PC*, June 1, 1865, excerpted from an unnamed Melbourne, Australia, newspaper; Kennett, Fuqua, and Fuqua, pp. 50-54.

57.   *ORN*, Series I, 3:790-92, the last page an itemized list, "Vessels captured, bonded, and destroyed by the C.S.S. *Shenandoah*, from October 30, 1864, to June 28, 1865." Hunt, pp. 272-73, "List of Prizes

Captured by the Confederate S.S. *Shenandoah*." A revised table is in Horan, ed., pp. 195-98. Kennett, Fuqua, and Fuqua, p. 53; *PC*, July 31, 1865; *PJ*, August 5, 1865, with quotation.

58. *PC*, August 28, 1865.

59. *Ibid*.

60. *Ibid*., September 8, 1865, with excerpts from the *Sag Harbor* (New York) *Express; ORN*, Series I, 3:829-30, for Waddell's version of the incident.

61. *PC*, November 23, 1865, with excerpts from the *Liverpool Post*.

62. Kennett, Fuqua, and Fuqua, p. 54; *PC*, September 19, November 23, 1865; *ORN*, Series I, 3:792.

63. *PC*, November 21, 1865; *PJ*, December 2, 1865, excerpted in part from the *London Times*.

64. *PC*, March 4, 1865; *DANFS*, 4:354.

65. *ORN*, Series I, 17:812-19, with map on p. 813; *CWNC*, V:56.

66. Boyd, *Extracts*, entries for December 26, 1864, and January 6, 1865; *DANFS*, 1:22; *PC*, March 10, 1865.

67. *PC*, February 21, March 18, 1865.

68. *Ibid*., March 25, 1865.

69. *Ibid*., March 27, 1865.

70. *Ibid*., April 11, 1865, with quotation reconstructed from text of article; Boyd, *Extracts*, entry for April 4, 1865.

71. *PH*, April 8, 1990, Brighton, "Confederate *States and Union* was Destroyed"; *States and Union*, April 19, 1865.

72. *PC*, April 11, 1865; *PJ*, April 15, 1865.

73. *Ibid*.; *PC*, April 23, 1865.

74. *States and Union*, April 19, 1865; *PC*, May 19, 1865; *PH*, April 8, 1990.

75. Fentress, p. 73; Preble, p. 98; Theodorus Bailey, Commandant, Navy Yard, Portsmouth, NH, April 11, 1865, to Gideon Welles, Secretary of the Navy, Washington, DC, RG 45, Entry 34, Commandants' Letters, 1865, NA-DC; *PC*, April 11, 1865.

76. *PC*, April 11, 13, 23, 1865; *PJ*, April 15, 1865.

77. Theodorus Bailey, Commandant, Navy Yard, Portsmouth, NH, April 18, 1865, to Gideon Welles, Secretary of the Navy, Washington, DC, RG 45, Entry 34, Commandants' Letters, 1865, NA-DC; *PC*, April 17, 19, 1865; Boyd, *Extracts*, entry for April 17, 1865; Preble, p. 98.

78. Niven, p. 507; Gideon Welles, Navy Department, Washington, DC, May 2, 1865, to Theodorus Bailey, Commandant, Navy Yard, Portsmouth, NH, RG 181, Entry 10, Letters Received from the Secretary of the Navy, NA-NER.

79. A[ndrew] Smith, Chief, Bureau of Equipment and Recruiting, Washington, DC, April 17, 24, 1865 (two letters), to Theodorus Bailey, Commandant, Navy Yard, Portsmouth, NH, RG 181, Entry 18, Letters Received from the Bureau of Equipment and Recruiting, NA-NER; Joseph Smith, Chief, Bureau of Yards and Docks, Washington, DC, May 9, 1865, "Circular," to Theodorus Bailey, Commandant, Navy Yard, Portsmouth, NH, RG 181, Entry 32, Letters Received, Yards and Docks, NA-NER; P[ercival] Drayton, Chief, Bureau of Navigation, Washington, DC, May 6, 8, 1865 (two letters, both as "Circular Order"), to Theodorus Bailey, Commandant, Navy Yard, Portsmouth, NH, RG 181, Entry 22, Letters Received, Bureau of Navigation, NA-NER; Theodorus Bailey, Commandant, Navy Yard, Portsmouth, NH, April 21, 1865, to John Lenthall, Chief, Bureau of Construction and Repair, Washington, DC, RG 181, Entry 15, Letters Sent to the Bureau of Construction and Repair, NA-NER.

80. Preble, p. 98; B[enjamin] F. Chandler, Civil Engineers [sic] Office, Navy Yard, Portsmouth, NH, May 10, 1865, to Theodorus Bailey, Commandant, Navy Yard, Portsmouth, NH, Civil War Folder, 1860-1865, PNSVC, Portsmouth Naval Shipyard, Portsmouth, NH.

81. *PC*, May 24, June 6, August 10, November 25, 1865, the first article reprinted in *PJ*, May 27, 1865; *Cradle of American Shipbuilding*, p. 76.

82. Theodorus Bailey, Commandant, Navy Yard, Portsmouth, NH, November 27, 1865, to Benjamin F. Martin, "Master Spar Maker" [Portsmouth Navy Yard, Portsmouth, NH]; Martin, November 27, 1865, to Bailey, *loc. cit.*, Benjamin F. Martin Papers, one folder, NHHS, Concord, NH.

83. *PC*, April 25, August 2, 11, 1865, the latter excerpted from the *Army and Navy Journal*.

84. *PC*, May 3, 1865.

85. Oliver P. Cross, U.S. Ship *Ohio*, June 12, 1865 [to Governor Frederick Smythe, Concord, NH], RG 1, Executive, Box 33, Folder, Executive Correspondence, June 1865, Gov. Smythe, NHDRMA, Concord, NH.

86. John S. Frost and William J. Frost, New Castle, NH, November 20, 1865, to "Hon. G. Welles, Secretary of the Navy" (originally written as "Hon. E. M. Stanton, Secretary of War"), PNSVC, Portsmouth Naval Shipyard, Portsmouth, NH.

87. *PC*, October 11, 1865.

88. *Ibid.*, October 11 (another article), 17, 20, 1865; *PJ*, October 21, 28, 1865.

89. *PC*, June 15, 1865; *PJ*, June 24, July 29, 1865, the latter excerpted from the New York *Journal of Commerce*.

90. "USS AGAMENTICUS," *Periscope*, March 9, 1990; *DANFS*, 6:105-6; *ORN*, Series I, 3:502; *PC*, April 23, May 3, 1865, the former reprinted in *PJ*, April 29, 1865; Boyd, *Extracts*, entry for April 21, 1865.

91. "THE LOG OF UNITED STATES Ironclad *Agamenticus*," May 5, 1865—June 5, 1865, entry of May 5, 1865, original manuscript in PNSVC, Portsmouth Naval Shipyard, Portsmouth, NH, with copy in possession of the author; Boyd, *Extracts*, entry for May 5, 1865; *PC*, May 6, 1865.

92. *Periscope*, May 9, 1990; Gideon Welles, May 6, 1865, Navy Department, Washington, DC, filled-in form of orders to Enoch G. Parrott, New York, NY, Parrott Papers, Beinecke Library, Yale University, New Haven, CT; *PC*, May 15, 1865; Boyd, *Extracts*, entries for May 29, June 27, July 3, August 3, 9, 13, 1865; *CWNC*, V:98, VI:304.

93. Boyd, *Extracts*, entries for June 1, 6, 7, 8, 10, 17-18, 20-21, 26-27, 30, July 12, 1865; *PC*, June 13, 1865, reprinted in *PJ*, June 17, 1865.

94. Preble, p. 98; *PJ*, July 8, 22, 1865; *PC*, July 21, 1865.

95. *DANFS*, 7:105; *Periscope*, March 9, 1990.

96. *PJ*, July 22, 1865; *PC*, August 1, 31, December 7 (two articles), 1865.

97. Mahan, p. 297; Lewis, p. 330; *PC*, July 21, 25, 1865.

98. *PC*, July 25, 1865.

99. *Ibid.*, August 29, September 22, December 7, 1865; *PJ*, December 16, 1865.

100. *PJ*, February 3, 1866, excerpted from the London *Times*.

101. *PC*, September 30, 1865.

102. *PC*, December 21, 1865; Heilprin, *A Complete Pronouncing Gazetteer or Geographical Dictionary of the World*, 1:888.

103. Roland, p. 262; *PC*, November 7, 1865.

104. Cleveland, pp. 13, 181.

105. *PC*, December 7, 1865.

106. *Ibid.*, January 4, 1866; *PJ*, March 24, 1866.

107. Theodorus Bailey, "Memorandum of Prizes taken & sent into Key West by the Vessels composing the East Gulf Blockading Squadron under the Command of Theodorus Bailey, Act[in]g Rear Admiral," 60-

page handwritten booklet, original in possession of Dudley W. Stoddard, New York, NY, and copy in possession of the author.

108. *PC*, July 21, 1866.

109. *Ibid.*, November 6, 1865, excerpted from the *Kennebec* (Augusta, ME) *Journal*.

EPILOGUE

1. *PC*, November 22, 1865.

2. *PJ*, June 9, 1866; Dalzell, pp. 237-62.

3. Brighton, *Tall Ships of the Piscataqua*, pp. 267-355; Brighton, *Rambles about Portsmouth*, p. 15.

4. Material on the Alabama Claims issue is extensive. See (in order of publication): Frank Warren Hackett, *The Geneva Award Acts* (1882), and Hackett's second book, *Reminiscences of the Geneva Tribunal* (1911), both with excellent bibliographies and copies of the various treaties and acts. The treaties also appear in Israel, ed., *Major Peace Treaties of Modern History, 1648-1967* (1967), 2:803-42. See also Albion and Pope, *Sea Lanes in Wartime* (1942), pp. 172-73; Cook, *The Alabama Claims* (1973); and Long, *Gold Braid and Foreign Relations* (1988), pp. 336-37. Pertinent articles include: Prime, "An Incident Connected with the Alabama Claims Arbitration," pp. 66-78, in *Personal Recollections of the War of the Rebellion* (1912); and Williams, "Yankee Fleets Raided by Confederate Cruisers," in *American Neptune* 27 (October 1967):263-78, especially pp. 276-78; *DAB*, 4:71-72.

5. *PC*, March 14, 1879; Brighton, *Frank Jones*, pp. 89-102; Winslow, "Frank Jones of New Hampshire," pp. 45-52; *DAB*, 10:168-69.

6. Albion and Pope, p. 173.

7. For the texts of the two Geneva Award Acts, see Hackett, *The Geneva Award Acts*, pp. 130-37 (Act of June 23, 1874), and pp. 127-29 (Act of June 5, 1882), the latter in *PJ*, June 24, 1882. For the disbursement under the 1874 act, see Hackett, *op. cit.*, "Preface," pp. iii-iv. See also Coale, pp. 76-96; Manning, pp. 283-97; Sedgwick, pp. 136-37; *PJ*, September 28, 1872; November 28, 1874; January 17, February 7, 14, 1880; May 30, 1882; *PC*, October 27, 1874; June 6, 1882; October 18, November 17, 1883.

8. *PC,* March 10, 1884, reprinted in *PJ,* March 15, 1884.

9. *PC,* March 14, 1885. Other *Chronicle* articles relating to the Geneva Award legislation and subsequent released funds appeared on February 21, 1883; March 6, 11, 21, 30, April 16, July 11, August 14,

1885; January 20, 1887; and October 27, 1888. For the settlement regarding the ship *Express*, see *PT*, June 4, 1875.

10. Farragut, pp. 540-42; *PC*, August 15, 1870; Brighton, "Grand Funeral Marked Old Hero's Death," *PH*, April 21, 1991.

11. *PJ*, May 15, 1869, excerpted from the *New York Tribune*; Niven, pp. 567-68.

12. *PJ*, October 28, 1865.

13. Ellicott, pp. 274-75; Chandler, p. 200; *PJ*, October 11, 1873; July 3, 1875; *PT*, June 14, 1875.

14. *The Family of James Thornton, Father of Hon. Matthew Thornton*, pp. 8-11, with quotation on p. 11; *PC*, October 14, 1865; May 17, 25, 1875; *PJ*, March 8 (excerpted from the *Southern African Mail*), May 22, 1875; *Nashua Gazette*, May 13, 20, 27, 1875; *Manchester Daily Union*, May 17, 1875.

15. *DAB*, 4:573-74; *ACAB*, 2:749; *PJ*, December 13, 1884; *Penny Post* (Portsmouth, NH), December 12, 1884; Still, *Ironclad Captains*, pp. 22-23.

16. *PJ*, April 14, 1866.

17. Chandler, pp. 208-9; *PC*, May 17, 1875; *PJ*, June 28, 1884, June 27, 1885; June 26, 1886; January 7, 21, June 17, 24, 1893; September 19, 1896; Gurney, pp. 214-15; Brighton, "Namesakes of Civil War Vessels Unite a Nation," *PH*, June 25, 1989; Hobson, *The Famous Cruise of the* Kearsarge. For perhaps the final reunion, see *PH*, June 21, 1922.

18. *PH*, March 6, 1918; Quinby, *The Quinby-Quimby Family*, pp. 291-93.

19. For a list of the fourteen Portsmouth-area *Kearsarge* veterans, their ranks, dates of death, and burial sites, see Foster, *The Soldiers' Memorial*, p. 49, with additional information on pp. 50-101. Selected obituaries of the *Kearsarge* crew include: Carsten B. De Witt, *PC*, May 17, 1865, and *PJ*, May 20, 1865; Mark Ham, *PJ*, March 13, 1869, and *PC*, March 17, 1869; William Barnes, *PJ*, February 16, 1884; True W. Priest, *PH*, February 23, 1909; Martin Hoyt, *PH*, December 27, 30, 1918; William Wainwright, *PH*, April 14, 1920; Henry S. Hobson, *PH*, March 24, 1923. For William Alsdorf, see Taylor, "The U.S.S. *Kearsarge* versus the *Alabama*: Showdown off Cherbourg," p. 138.

20. *PJ*, August 1, 1891; *DANFS*, 1:162, 3:261-63.

21. *PJ*, February 17, 1894; *PC*, February 9 (two articles), 22, 24, 1894; *Colon Telegram*, February 9, 1894; Walling, pp. 671-90; Hobson, p. 167; Hill, p. 371.

22. *PC*, February 9 (with quotation), 22, 1894.

23. Hobson, p. 167.

24. Black-and-white reproduction of the painting, *U.S.S.* Kearsarge *on Roncador Reef, February, 1894*, with caption, "From the collection of Franklin D. Roosevelt. Reproduced by permission of the President," in Dalzell, *The Flight from the Flag*, frontispiece. Poems: "The *Kearsarge*," by George Bancroft Griffith, in *PJ*, March 10, 1894; and "*Kearsarge*," by Noah Davis, in *Granite Monthly* 17 (October 1894):220-22.

25. Long, pp. 338-39; *PJ*, July 15, 1876.

26. *Cradle of American Shipbuilding*, pp. 27-87. Randall, *There Are No Victors Here: A Local Perspective on the Treaty of Portsmouth*.

27. Winslow, *Portsmouth-Built: Submarines of the Portsmouth Naval Shipyard*.

28. *PH*, June 26, 1993.

29. *Ibid.*, May 12-13, 17-18, 20, 1995.

30. *Ibid.*, June 22-23, 1995; *Boston Globe*, June 24, 1995.

Bibliography

IN HIS EXCELLENT ESSAY on "Sources" for *The American Iliad: The Story of the Civil War* (1991), Charles P. Roland estimated the number of Civil War books and articles at roughly 90,000 items. With the ongoing interest in the Civil War, that figure continues to accelerate at an astonishing rate. Scholarly monographs, articles in newspapers, popular magazines and professional journals, battlefield maps, and museum guides appear daily. New manuscript sources likewise constantly surface. The same booming phenomenon is true with newly discovered Civil War photographs, paintings, and sketches, and related materials. Modern artists add their work to this category. During the six years of researching and writing this book, I have been constantly updating my bibliography right up to press time.

I have concentrated on the Union sources germane to my topic. The extensive Record Groups at the National Archives, Washington, and Waltham, Massachusetts; the Portsmouth Navy Yard logbooks; and the *Official Records of the Union and Confederate Navies in the War of the Rebellion* provide the most reliable, day-by-day administrative accounts relative to running a navy yard, operating a ship, or directing a blockade. Personal and business letters, frequently revealing their writers' private prejudices and sympathies, offer unguarded insights into the navy and the war. I have also relied heavily on Civil War-era newspapers and magazines, not only for the reprinting of many essential contemporary documents, but also for their editors' lively, often critical, assessment of the day's happenings and governmental policies. Such slanted and provocative journalism oftentimes offsets the conventional Union party-line documentation and affords the modern historian contrasting viewpoints in arriving at a more balanced interpretation. Less satisfactory in some instances but still valuable are memoirs written or lectures delivered years after the event; such sources, subject to faulty memory or deliberate embellishment, may lack immediacy. All these materials, taken as a whole, fashion a reasonable synthesis of the times. The following bibliography, stressing United States Navy, Union, New Hampshire, and Portsmouth sources, is as comprehensive as I can make it. This list is intended as well to facilitate further investigation and work in this fascinating field.

BIBLIOGRAPHIES

Albion, Robert Greenhalgh. *Naval and Maritime History: An Annotated Bibliography*. 4th ed., rev. and enl. Mystic, CT: Marine Historical Assn., 1972.

Allard, Dean C., Martha L. Crawley, and Mary W. Edmison, comps. and eds. *U.S. Naval History Sources in the United States*. Washington: Naval History Division, Department of the Navy, U.S. Government Printing Office, 1979.

Carman, Harry J., and Arthur W. Thompson. *A Guide to the Principal Sources for American Civilization, 1800-1900, in the City of New York: Manuscripts*. New York: Columbia University Press, 1960.

Cherpak, Evelyn M., comp. *A Guide to Archives, Manuscripts, and Oral Histories in the Naval Historical Collection*. Newport, RI: Naval War College, 1987. 70-page finding-aid pamphlet.

———. *Register of Papers of Stephen B. Luce*. Manuscript Register Series No. 14. Newport, RI: Naval Historical Collection, Naval War College, 1986. 26-page finding-aid pamphlet.

Cole, Garold L. *Civil War Eyewitnesses: An Annotated Bibliography of Books and Articles, 1955-1986*. Columbia, SC: University of South Carolina Press, 1988.

Coletta, Paolo E., comp. *A Bibliography of American Naval History*. Annapolis, MD: Naval Institute Press, 1981.

DeWitt, Donald L., comp. *Guides to Archives and Manuscript Collections in the United States: An Annotated Bibliography*. Westport, CT, and London: Greenwood Press, 1994. See especially "Marine Corps and Navy," pp. 146-52; and "Civil War," pp. 158-63.

Dolph, James. "The Portsmouth Naval Shipyard: A Bibliography." [Portsmouth, NH, Portsmouth Naval Shipyard], March 1989. 17-page typescript. Copies at Portsmouth Naval Shipyard Visitor Center, Portsmouth Naval Shipyard, Portsmouth, NH, and at Naval Historical Center, Washington Navy Yard, Washington.

Emery, George, comp. "Subject Cards to the Library's Collection of Manuscripts." Manuscripts housed in file cabinets at library's Rare Book Room. Naval Historical Center, Washington Navy Yard, Washington, ca. 1990. 21-page typescript.

Harbeck, Charles T., comp. *A Contribution to the Bibliography of the History of the United States Navy*. Cambridge, MA: Privately printed, Riverside Press, 1906.

Haskell, John D., Jr., and T.D. Seymour Bassett, eds. *New Hampshire: A Bibliography of Its History*. Hanover, NH, and London: University Press of New England, 1979, 1983.

Higham, Robin, ed. *A Guide to the Sources of United States Military History*. Hamden, CT: Archon Books, 1975. 559-page bibliography.

Higham, Robin, and Donald J. Mrozek, eds. *A Guide to the Sources of United States Military History: Supplement I*. Hamden, CT: Archon Books, 1981. 300-page bibliography.

———, eds. *A Guide to the Sources of United States Military History: Supplement II*. Hamden, CT: Archon Books, 1986.

Jordan, William B., Jr. *Maine in the Civil War: A Bibliographical Guide*. [Portland, ME?] Maine Historical Society. In preparation.

Kinnell, Susan K., and Suzanne R. Ontiveros, eds. *American Maritime History: A Bibliography*. Santa Barbara, CA, and Oxford: ABC-Clio, 1986.

Labaree, Benjamin W. *A Supplement (1971-1986) to Robert G. Albion's* Naval and Maritime History: An Annotated Bibliography. Mystic, CT: Mystic Seaport Museum, 1988.

Library of Congress. *Naval Historical Foundation, Manuscript Collection: A Catalog*. Washington: Library of Congress, U.S. Government Printing Office, 1974.

Lynch, Barbara A., and John E. Vajda, revs. *United States Naval History: A Bibliography*. 7th ed. Washington: Naval Historical Center, Department of the Navy, 1993.

Munden, Kenneth W., and Henry Putney Beers. *Guide to Federal Archives Relating to the Civil War*. Washington: National Archives, National Archives and Record Service, General Services Administration, 1962.

Murdock, Eugene C. *The Civil War in the North: A Selective Annotated Bibliography*. New York and London: Garland Publishing, 1987.

Naval Historical Foundation: Manuscript Collection, 1975-1994. n.p.: [1994]. Update of the 1974 catalog, *Naval Historical Foundation Manuscript Collection*. 60-page pamphlet with index.

Neeser, Robert Wilden. *Statistical and Chronological History of the United States Navy, 1775-1907*. 2 vols. New York: Macmillan, 1909. A bibliographical compilation.

Nevins, Allan, James I. Robertson, Jr., and Bell I. Wiley, eds. *Civil War Books: A Critical Bibliography*. Baton Rouge, LA: Louisiana State

University Press, 1967. Vol. 2, especially chap. 6, "The Navies," by Thomas Wells, pp. 217-39.

Sellers, John R., comp. *Civil War Manuscripts: A Guide to Collections in the Manuscript Division of the Library of Congress*. Washington: Library of Congress, 1986.

Smith, Myron J., Jr. *American Civil War Navies: A Bibliography*. American Naval Bibliography, vol. III. Metuchen, NJ: Scarecrow Press, 1972.

BOOKS

Adams, Charles Thornton. *The Family of James Thornton, Father of Matthew Thornton*. New York: n.p., 1905. Copy at New Hampshire Historical Society, Concord, NH.

The Alabama *and the* Kearsarge: *An Account of the Naval Engagement in the British Channel, on Sunday, June 19th, 1864*. Boston: Alfred Mudge & Son, 1870. 24-page pamphlet, copy at New Hampshire Historical Society, Concord, NH.

Albion, Robert Greenhalgh, and Jennie Barnes Pope. *Sea Lanes in Wartime: The American Experience, 1775-1942*. New York: W.W. Norton, 1942.

Ammen, Daniel. *The Atlantic Coast*. Vol. 2 of *The Navy in the Civil War*. New York: Charles Scribner's Sons, 1883.

A Naval Encyclopaedia: Comprising a Dictionary of Nautical Words and Phrases; Biographical Notices, and Records of Naval Officers. Philadelphia: L.R. Hamersly, 1881.

Ancestry and Descendants of Sir Richard Saltonstall, First Associate of the Massachusetts Bay Colony and Patentee of Connecticut. [Boston?]: Printed at Riverside Press for private distribution, 1897. Copy at New England Historic Genealogical Society Library, Boston.

Anderson, Bern. *By Sea and By River: The Naval History of the Civil War*. New York: Alfred A. Knopf, 1962.

Andrews, J. Cutler. *The North Reports the Civil War*. Pittsburgh: University of Pittsburgh Press, 1955.

The Annual Register: A Review of Public Events at Home and Abroad, for the Year 1864. London: Rivingtons, Waterloo Place, Gilbert and Rivington, Printers, 1865. See especially "Naval Action Between the Federal War Steamer the *Kearsage* [sic], and the Confederate Cruiser *Alabama*," pp. 88-93.

The Annual Register: A Review of Public Events at Home and Abroad, for the Year 1865. (Same place and publisher as above, 1866.) See especially, "Arrival of the *Shenandoah* in the Mersey," pp. 162-63, and "The Confederate Cruiser *Shenandoah*," pp. 165-67.

Appletons' Cyclopaedia of American Biography, James Grant Wilson and John Fiske, eds. 6 vols. New York: D. Appleton, 1889.

Archibald, E.H.H. *Dictionary of Sea Painters*. Woodbridge, Suffolk, England: Baron Publishing, for the Antique Collectors' Club Ltd., 1980.

The Argument at Geneva. New York: D. Appleton, 1873. Copy at Portsmouth Athenaeum, Portsmouth, NH.

Arguments...Upon the Bill Distributing the Unappropriated Moneys Paid under the Geneva Award. New York: E. Wells Sackett, 1877. Copy at Portsmouth Athenaeum, Portsmouth, NH.

Ayling, Augustus D., prep. *Revised Register of the Soldiers and Sailors of New Hampshire in the War of the Rebellion, 1861-1866.* Concord, [NH]: Ira C. Evans, Public Printer, 1895.

Badlam, William H. *The Cruise of the* Kearsarge. n.p., 1888. "A Paper Read before the Kearsarge Association of Naval Veterans, Boston, Mass." 12-page pamphlet, copy in Box: "Naval Historical Miscellany," Folder: "John A. Winslow Miscellany." Manuscript Division, Library of Congress, Washington. Badlam was the First Assistant Engineer, USN, aboard the *Kearsarge* during her wartime service.

Baker, George E., ed. *The Works of William Seward.* 5 vols. Boston: Houghton, Mifflin, and Cambridge, MA: Riverside Press, 1884.

Bardwell, John D. *The Isles of Shoals: A Visual History.* Portsmouth, NH: Portsmouth Marine Society, 1989.

Barnes, James. *The Photographic History of the Civil War.* Vol. 6. New York: Review of Reviews, 1912.

Basler, Roy P., ed. *The Collected Works of Abraham Lincoln.* 9 vols. New Brunswick, NJ: Rutgers University Press, 1953.

Baysden, Philip B. *A History of the Marine Barracks, Portsmouth Naval Shipyard, Portsmouth, New Hampshire, 1776-1978.* n.p., ca. 1978.

Bell, Charles H. *The Bench and Bar of New Hampshire.* Boston: Houghton, Mifflin, 1894.

Benjamin, J[udah] P. *Instructions upon Neutral and Belligerent Rights, Prepared by the Hon. J.P. Benjamin, Secretary of State, under the Orders of the President, and Issued by the Secretary of the Navy for the Government of the Cruising Ships of the C.S. Navy.* Richmond, VA: MacFarlane & Fergusson, Printers, 1864. 12-page pamphlet. Copy at Rare Book and Special Collection Division, Library of Congress, Washington.

Bennett, Frank M. *The Steam Navy of the United States.* Westport, CT: Greenwood Press, 1972. Reprint of original 1896 edition.

Benton, Josiah Henry. *Voting in the Field: A Forgotten Chapter of the Civil War.* Boston: privately printed, 1915. Copy at Baker Library, Dartmouth College, Hanover, NH.

Bernstein, Iver. *The New York City Draft Riots: Their Significance for American Society and Politics in the Age of the Civil War.* New York: Oxford University Press, 1990.

Biographical Directory of the American Congress, 1774-1927. [Washington]: U.S. Government Printing Office, 1928.

Biographical Directory of the United States Congress, 1774-1989. [Washington]: U.S. Government Printing Office, 1989.

Blair, Dale James, and Barry Crompton. *The C.S.S.* Shenandoah *in Melbourne*. Melbourne, Australia: The American Civil War Round Table of Australia, 1989. 26-page pamphlet.

Blakeman, A. Noel, ed. *Personal Recollections of the War of the Rebellion: Addresses Delivered Before the Commandery of the State of New York, Military Order of the Loyal Legion of the United States*. Second and Fourth Series. New York and London: G.P. Putnam's Sons, 1897, 1912.

Boatner, Mark Mayo, III. *The Civil War Dictionary*. New York: David McKay, 1959.

Booth, Andrew B., comp. *Records of Louisiana Confederate Soldiers and Louisiana Confederate Commands*. New Orleans, LA, 1920.

Boswell, Charles. *The* America: *The Story of the World's Most Famous Yacht*. New York: David McKay, 1967.

Boyd, David F., comp. *Extracts from the Daily Log Book, U.S. Navy Yard, Portsmouth, New Hampshire, October 15, 1819-December 17, 1929.* "Printed at the UNITED STATES NAVAL PRISON, Portsmouth, New Hampshire, 31 March, 1931." Copies at Portsmouth Athenaeum and Portsmouth Room, Portsmouth Public Library, Portsmouth, NH.

Boynton, Charles B. *The History of the Navy during the Rebellion*. 2 vols. New York: D. Appleton, 1868, 1869.

Brewington, M.V. and Dorothy. *The Marine Paintings and Drawings in the Peabody Museum*. Salem, MA: Peabody Museum, 1968.

Brighton, Ray. *Clippers of the Port of Portsmouth and the Men Who Built Them*. Portsmouth, NH: Portsmouth Marine Society, 1985.

———. *Frank Jones: King of the Alemakers*. Hampton, NH: Peter E. Randall, 1976.

———. *The Prescott Story*. New Castle, NH: Portsmouth Marine Society, 1982.

———. *Rambles about Portsmouth*. Portsmouth, NH: Portsmouth Marine Society, 1994.

———. *Tall Ships of the Piscataqua, 1830-1877*. Portsmouth, NH: Portsmouth Marine Society, 1989.

Brighton, Raymond A. *They Came to Fish*. 2 vols. Portsmouth, NH: Portsmouth 350, Inc., 1973.

Brown, D. Alexander. *The Galvanized Yankees*. Urbana, IL: University of Illinois Press, 1963.

Browne, John M. "The Duel between the *Alabama* and the *Kearsarge*." In *Battles and Leaders of the Civil War*, ed. by Robert Underwood Johnson and Clarence Clough Buel. New York: Thomas Yoseloff, 1956. 4:615-25.

Browning, Robert M., Jr. *From Cape Charles to Cape Fear: The North Atlantic Blockading Squadron During the Civil War*. Tuscaloosa, AL, and London: University of Alabama Press, 1993.

Bulloch, James D. *The Secret Service of the Confederate States in Europe, or How the Confederate Cruisers Were Equipped.* 2 vols. New York and London: Thomas Yoseloff, 1959.

Butler, Benjamin F. *Private and Official Correspondence of Gen. Benjamin F. Butler during the Period of the Civil War.* 5 vols. Privately issued, 1917.

Callahan, Edward W., ed. *List of Officers of the Navy of the United States and of the Marine Corps from 1775 to 1900.* New York: L.R. Hamersly, 1901.

Canney, Donald L. *The Old Steam Navy.* Vol. 1. *Frigates, Sloops, and Gunboats, 1815-1885.* Annapolis, MD: Naval Institute Press, 1990.

———. *The Old Steam Navy.* Vol. 2. *The Ironclads, 1842-1885.* Annapolis, MD: Naval Institute Press, 1993.

Case, Lynn M., and Warren F. Spencer. *The United States and France: Civil War Diplomacy.* Philadelphia: University of Pennsylvania Press, 1970.

The Case of Great Britain...Tribunal of Arbitration. Convened at Geneva Under the Provisions of the Treaty...Concluded at Washington, May 8, 1871.... 3 vols. Washington: Government Printing Office, 1872.

Chadwick, F.E. "The Naval War College." In *Civil War and Miscellaneous Papers.* Boston: Military Historical Society of Massachusetts, Cadet Armory, Ferdinand Street, 1918. 14:341-59.

Cleveland, Mather. *New Hampshire Fights the Civil War.* New London, NH: 1969.

Cogar, William B. *Dictionary of Admirals of the U.S. Navy.* Vol. 1, 1862-1900. Annapolis, MD: Naval Institute Press, 1989.

Commager, Henry Steele, ed. *The Blue and the Gray: The Story of the Civil War as Told by Participants.* 2 vols. Indianapolis, IN: Bobbs-Merrill, 1950.

Committee on Veterans' Affairs, United States Senate. *Medal of Honor Recipients, 1863-1978.* Washington: U.S. Government Printing Office, 1979.

Conn, Granville P. *History of the New Hampshire Surgeons in the War of the Rebellion.* Concord, NH: Ira C. Evans, Printers, 1906.

Cook, Adrian. *The Alabama Claims: American Politics and Anglo-American Relations, 1865-1872.* Ithaca, NY, and London: Cornell University Press, 1975.

Copperhead Minstrel: A Choice Collection of Democratic Poems and Songs, for the Use of Political Clubs and the Social Circle. New York: Feeks & Bancker, Wholesale Agents, 1863. Copy at Houghton Library, Harvard University, Cambridge, MA.

Cushing, W[illiam] B. "The Destruction of the *Albemarle.*" In *Battles and Leaders of the Civil War,* ed. by Robert Underwood Johnson and Clarence Clough Buel. New York: Thomas Yoseloff, 1956. 4:634-41.

Dalzell, George W. *The Flight from the Flag: The Continuing Effect of the Civil War upon the American Carrying Trade.* Chapel Hill, NC: University of North Carolina Press, 1940.

Dana, Richard H., Jr. *A Tribute to Judge Sprague: Remarks of Richard H. Dana, Jr., Esq., at a Dinner Given to the Officers of the* Kearsarge, *In Response to a Toast in Honor of the Judiciary.* Boston: Alfred Mudge & Son, Printers, 1864. 16-page pamphlet. Copy at Massachusetts Historical Society, Boston.

Dear, Ian. *The America's Cup: An Informal History.* New York: Dodd, Mead, 1980.

Delaney, Norman C. *Ghost Ship: The Confederate Raider* Alabama. Middletown, CT: Southfarm Press, 1989.

Dewey, George. *Autobiography of George Dewey: Admiral of the Navy.* New York: Charles Scribner's Sons, 1913.

Dictionary of American Biography. 20 vols. Allen Johnson, ed., vols. 1-3; Allen Johnson and Dumas Malone, eds., vols. 4-7; Dumas Malone, ed., vols. 8-20. New York: Charles Scribner's Sons, 1928-36.

Donald, David, ed. *Inside Lincoln's Cabinet: The Civil War Diaries of Salmon P. Chase.* New York, London, and Toronto: Longmans, Green, 1954.

Edge, Frederick Milnes. *The* Alabama *and the* Kearsarge: *An Account of the Naval Engagement in the British Channel, on Sunday, June 19, 1864, from Information Furnished to the Writer by the Wounded and Paroled Prisoners of the Confederate Privateer* Alabama, *the Officers of the United States Sloop-of-War* Kearsarge, *and Citizens of Cherbourg.* London: Ridgeway, 1864. 48-page pamphlet. Reprinted in *PJ*, November 1, 8, 1879.

————. *An Englishman's View of the Battle Between the* Alabama *and the* Kearsarge. *An Account of the Naval Engagement in the British Channel, on Sunday, June 19th, 1864. From Information Personally Obtained in the Town of Cherbourg, as well as from the Officers and Crew of the United States' Sloop-of-War* Kearsarge, *and the Wounded and Prisoners of the Confederate Privateer.* New York: Anson D.F. Randolph, 1864. 48-page pamphlet. Copy at New Hampshire Historical Society, Concord, NH.

Editors of Boston Publishing Company. *Above and Beyond: A History of the Medal of Honor from the Civil War to Vietnam.* Boston: Boston Publishing Company, 1985.

Editors of Time-Life Books. *The Blockade: Runners and Raiders.* Alexandria, VA: Time-Life Books, 1983.

Ellicott, John M. *The Life of John Ancrum Winslow, Rear Admiral, U.S. Navy.* New York: G.P. Putnam's Sons, 1902.

Elliott, Gilbert. "The First Battle of the Confederate Ram, *Albemarle.*" In *Battles and Leaders of the Civil War*, ed. by Robert Underwood Johnson and Clarence Clough Buel. New York: Thomas Yoseloff, 1956. 4:625-26.

Elliott, Robert G. *Ironclad of the Roanoke: Gilbert Elliott's* Albemarle. Shippensburg, PA: White Mane, 1994.

Estes, J. Worth, and David M. Goodman. *The Changing Humors of Portsmouth: The Medical Biography of an American Town, 1623-1983*. Boston: Francis A. Countway Library of Medicine, 1986.

Everett, Edward. *Orations and Speeches on Various Occasions*. Vol. IV of 4 vols. Boston: Little, Brown, 1868.

Farragut, Loyall. *The Life of David Glasgow Farragut, First Admiral of the United States Navy, Embodying his Journal and Letters*. New York: D. Appleton, 1879.

Faust, Patricia L., ed. *Historical Times Illustrated Encyclopedia of the Civil War*. New York: Harper & Row, 1986.

Fentress, Walter E.H. *Centennial History of the United States Navy Yard at Portsmouth, N.H.* Portsmouth, NH: O.M. Knight, 1876.

Ferris, Norman B. *The Trent Affair: A Diplomatic Crisis*. Knoxville, TN: University of Tennessee Press, 1977.

Field, James A., Jr. *America and the Mediterranean World, 1776-1882*. Princeton, NJ: Princeton University Press, 1969.

Foote, Andrew H. *Africa and the American Flag*. New York: D. Appleton, 1854.

Foster, Joseph. *The Soldiers' Memorial, Portsmouth, N.H., 1893-1923. Tercentenary Edition, with Indexed Record of the Graves We Decorate*. n.p., 1923. Copy at Portsmouth Room, Portsmouth Public Library, Portsmouth, NH.

Fowler, William M., Jr. *Under Two Flags: The American Navy in the Civil War*. New York and London: W.W. Norton, 1990.

Gay, Peter. *Art and Act: On Causes in History - Manet, Gropius, Mondrian*. New York and London: Harper & Row, 1976.

George Blunt Wendell: Clipper Ship Master. Portland, ME: Maine Historical Association, 1949. Copy at Portsmouth Room, Portsmouth Public Library, Portsmouth, NH.

Gibbons, Tony. *Warships and Naval Battles of the Civil War*. New York: W.H. Smith, Gallery Books, 1989.

Gragg, Rod. *Confederate Goliath: The Battle of Fort Fisher*. New York: Harper Collins, 1991.

Greeley, Horace. *The American Conflict: A History of the Great Rebellion in the United States of America, 1860-'65*. 2 vols. Hartford, CT: O.D. Case, 1866.

Griffith, George B. *History of Fort Constitution and "Walbach Tower," Portsmouth Harbor, NH*. Portsmouth, NH: C.W. Brewster & Son, Printers, 1865. 16-page pamphlet. Copy at Portsmouth Room, Portsmouth Public Library, Portsmouth, NH.

Gronberg, T.A., ed. *Manet: A Retrospective*. New York: Park Lane, 1988. Reprinted 1990.

Gurney, C[aleb] S. *Portsmouth: Historic and Picturesque*. Portsmouth, NH: C.S. Gurney, 1902. Reprinted 1981.

Hackett, Frank Warren. *Deck and Field: Addresses Before the United States Naval War College and on Commemorative Occasions*. Washington: W.H. Lowdermilk, 1909. Copy at Portsmouth Room, Portsmouth Public Library, Portsmouth, NH.

————. *The Geneva Award Acts...Decisions of the Court of Commissioners of Alabama Claims*. Boston: Little, Brown, 1882.

————. *Reminiscences of the Geneva Tribunal of Arbitration, 1872, The Alabama Claims*. Boston: Houghton Mifflin, 1911.

Hagan, Kenneth J. *This People's Navy: The Making of American Sea Power*. New York: Macmillan, The Free Press, 1991. Contains an excellent "Bibliographical Essay," pp. 391-411.

Hale, John P. *Frauds and Corruption in the Navy Department: A Speech Delivered by the Hon. John P. Hale of New Hampshire in the Senate of the United States, January 28 and 31, and February 1 and 17, 1865*. n.p., 1865. 32-page pamphlet. Copy at Boston Athenaeum, Boston.

————. *Speech of Hon. John P. Hale of New Hampshire on Frauds in Naval Contracts in the United States Senate, May 23, 1864*. Washington: H. Polkinhorn, Printer, 1864. 16-page pamphlet. Copy at Boston Athenaeum, Boston.

Hanson, Anne Coffin. *Manet and the Modern Tradition*. New Haven, CT, and London: Yale University Press, 1977.

Hayes, John D., ed. *Samuel Francis Du Pont: A Selection from His Civil War Letters*. 3 vols. Ithaca, NY: Cornell University Press for Eleutherian Mills Historical Library, 1969.

Hearn, Chester G. *Gray Riders of the Sea: How Eight Confederate Warships Destroyed the Union's High Seas Commerce*. Camden, ME: International Marine, 1992.

Heilprin, Angelo, and Louis Heilprin, eds. *A Complete Pronouncing Gazetteer or Geographical Dictionary of the World*. 2 vols. Philadelphia and London: J.B. Lippincott, 1911.

Hill, Frederick Stanhope. *Twenty-Six Historic Ships*. New York and London: G.P. Putnam's Sons, Knickerbocker Press, 1903.

History of the Portsmouth Naval Shipyard 1800-1958. n.p., n.d. 24-page typescript, with supplements. Copy at Portsmouth Room, Portsmouth Public Library, Portsmouth, NH.

Hobson, H[enry] S. *The Famous Cruise of the* Kearsarge. Bonds Village, MA: published by the author; printed by Loring and Axtell, Springfield, MA, 1894. 167-page book containing a poem, "Cruise of the *Kearsarge*," pp. 7-103, and "A Reception at Portsmouth, NH, June 19, 1893." Copies at Rare Book Room, Boston Public Library, Boston, and at Mugar Memorial Library, Boston University, Boston.

Holden, Edgar. "The *Albemarle* and the *Sassacus*." In *Battles and Leaders of the Civil War*, ed. by Robert Underwood Johnson and Clarence Clough Buel. New York: Thomas Yoseloff, 1956. 4:628-33.

―――. "The *Sassacus* and the *Albemarle*." In *Personal Recollections of the War of the Rebellion: Addresses Delivered Before the New York Commandery of the Loyal Legion of the United States, 1883-1891*, ed. by James Grant Wilson and Titus Munson Coan. New York: Published by the Commandery, 1891, pp. 96-107.

Holzer, Harold, and Mark E. Neely, Jr. *Mine Eyes Have Seen the Glory: The Civil War in Art*. New York: Orion Books, 1993.

Horan, James D., ed. *C.S.S.* Shenandoah: *The Memoirs of Lieutenant Commanding James I. Waddell*. New York: Crown Publishers, 1960.

Hunt, Cornelius E. *The* Shenandoah: *or the Last Confederate Cruiser*. New York: G.W. Carleton, and London: S. Low, Son, 1867.

Instructions for Navy Yards. Approved by the Secretary of the Navy. Washington: William A. Harris, Printer, 1859. 31-page pamphlet. Copy at Boston Athenaeum, Boston.

Israel, Fred L., ed. *Major Peace Treaties of Modern History, 1648-1967*, with introductory essay by Arnold Toynbee. Vol. II. New York: Chelsea House Publishers, 1967.

Johnson, Robert Underwood, and Clarence Clough Buel, eds. *Battles and Leaders of the Civil War*. 4 vols. New York: The Century Company, 1884, 1887, 1888. Reprint. New York: Thomas Yoseloff, 1956. Various articles, especially on the *Sassacus-Albemarle* and the *Kearsarge-Alabama* battles.

Jones, Virgil Carrington. *The Civil War at Sea: July 1863-November 1865, The Final Effort*. Vol. 3. New York: Holt, Rinehart and Winston, 1962.

Kell, John McIntosh. *Recollections of a Naval Life*. Washington: Neale Company, 1900.

―――. "Cruise and Combats of the *Alabama*." In *Battles and Leaders of the Civil War*, ed. by Robert Underwood Johnson and Clarence Clough Buel. New York: Thomas Yoseloff, 1956. 4:600-614.

Kennedy, Frances H., ed. *The Civil War Battlefield Guide*. Boston: Houghton Mifflin, 1990.

Ketchum, Richard M., ed. *The American Heritage History of the Civil War*. New York: American Heritage Publishing, 1960.

Lewis, Charles Lee. *David Glasgow Farragut: Our First Admiral*. Annapolis, MD: United States Naval Institute, 1943.

List of United States Vessels Sold and Transferred to British Subjects in the Year 1863. n.p., n.d. 12-page pamphlet, apparently published in the Confederate States of America. Copy at Rare Book and Special Collection Division, Library of Congress, Washington.

Long, David F. *Gold Braid and Foreign Relations: Diplomatic Activities of U.S. Naval Officers, 1798-1883*. Annapolis, MD: Naval Institute Press, 1988.

Longfellow, Henry Wadsworth. *The Complete Poetical Works of Henry Wadsworth Longfellow*. Boston: Houghton Mifflin Company, Riverside Press, 1922.

Love, Robert W., Jr. *History of the U.S. Navy, 1775-1941*. Harrisburg, PA: Stackpole Books, 1992.

Lowe, W. Augustus, and Virgil A. Clift. *Encyclopedia of Black America*. New York: McGraw-Hill, 1981.

Maclay, Edgar Stanton. *Reminiscences of the Old Navy*. New York and London: G.P. Putnam's Sons, Knickerbocker Press, 1898.

Mahan, A[lfred] T[hayer]. *Admiral Farragut*. New York: D. Appleton, 1898.

Martin, Charles. "Sinking of the *Congress* and *Cumberland* by the *Merrimack*." In *Personal Recollections of the War of the Rebellion: Addresses Delivered Before the Commandery of the State of New York, Military Order of the Loyal Legion of the United States*, ed. by A. Noel Blakeman. New York and London: G.P. Putnam's Sons, 1897. Second Series. pp. 1-6.

McFarland, Henry. *Kearsarge Mountain and the Corvette Named for It* (1879), 2nd ed. Concord, NH: Rumford Printing, 1906. 35-page pamphlet. Copy at New Hampshire Historical Society, Concord, NH.

McPherson, James M. *Battle Cry of Freedom: The Civil War Era*. New York and Oxford: Oxford University Press, 1988.

————. *The Negro's Civil War: How American Negroes Felt and Acted During the War for the Union*. New York: Pantheon Books, 1965.

McPherson, James M., ed. *Battle Chronicles of the Civil War, 1862*. New York: Macmillan, and London: Collier Macmillan, 1989.

Medal of Honor, 1861-1949: The Navy. [Washington: U.S. Government Printing Office, ca. 1949].

Melville, Herman. *Battle-Pieces and Aspects of the War*. Facsimile reproduction of first edition (1866) with Introduction by Sidney Kaplan. Gainesville, FL: Scholar's Facsimiles and Reprints, 1960.

Merli, Frank J. *Great Britain and the Confederate Navy, 1861-1865*. Bloomington, IN, and London: Indiana University Press, 1970.

Merrill, James M. "Strangling the South: Improvised, often Ineffective, the Blockade Required the Building of a New Navy." In *The Embattled Confederacy* (Vol. 3 of *The Image of War, 1861-1865*), ed. by William C. Davis. Garden City, NY: Doubleday, 1982. 3:102-83.

Miller, Nathan. *The U.S. Navy: An Illustrated History*. New York: American Heritage Publishing, and Annapolis, MD: Naval Institute Press, 1977.

Muir, Thomas, Jr., and David P. Ogden. *The Fort Pickens Story*. Pensacola, FL: Pensacola Historical Society, 1989.

Nash, Jay Robert. *Encyclopedia of World Crime*. Vols. II and III. Wilmette, IL: CrimeBooks, 1990.

Naval History Division, Navy Department, Office of Chief of Naval Operations. *Civil War Naval Chronology, 1861-1865*. Washington:

Naval History Division, Department of the Navy, U.S. Government Printing Office, 1971.

Nevins, Allan, ed. *A Diary of Battle: The Personal Journals of Colonel Charles S. Wainwright, 1861-1865*. New York: Harcourt, Brace & World, 1962.

Nevins, Allan, and Milton Halsey Thomas, eds. *The Diary of George Templeton Strong, The Civil War, 1860-1865*. Vol. 3. New York: Macmillan, 1952.

Nicolay, John G., and John Hay. *Abraham Lincoln: A History*. Vol. 3. New York: Century Co., and London: T. Fisher Unwin, 1890.

Niven, John. *Gideon Welles: Lincoln's Secretary of the Navy*. New York: Oxford University Press, 1973.

Nye, Gideon. *Casual Papers Upon the* Alabama *and Kindred Questions, and, Incidentally, Upon National Amenities*. "First Published in the Hong Kong Daily Press, 1862-1865." Hong Kong: Printed at *China Magazine* Office, 1869. 86-page book of collected newspaper articles. Copy at Houghton Library, Harvard University, Cambridge, MA.

Owsley, Frank Lawrence. *King Cotton Diplomacy: Foreign Relations of the Confederate States of America*. 2d ed., rev. by Harriet Chappell Owsley. Chicago and London: University of Chicago Press, 1931, 1959, 1969. See especially chapter VII, "The Ineffectiveness of the Blockade," pp. 229-67.

Parker, James. "The Navy in the Battles and Capture of Fort Fisher." In *Personal Recollections of the War of the Rebellion: Addresses Delivered Before the Commandery of the State of New York, Military Order of the Loyal Legion of the United States*, ed. by A. Noel Blakeman. New York and London: G.P. Putnam's Sons, 1897. Second Series. pp. 104-17.

Parks, Virginia, Alan Rick, and Norman Simons. *Pensacola in the Civil War*. Pensacola, FL: Pensacola Historical Society, 1978. Fourth printing, March 1991.

Parry, Clive, ed. and annot. *Consolidated Treaty Series, 1648-1918*. 243 vols. Dobbs Ferry, NY: Oceana Publications, 1965-82.

Peters, Harry T. *Currier & Ives: Printmakers to the American People*. Vol. 2. Garden City, NY: Doubleday, Doran, 1931. Reprinted 1976, Arno Press.

Pickett, Gertrude M. *Portsmouth's Heyday in Shipbuilding*. Portsmouth, NH: Joseph G. Sawtelle, 1979.

Pillsbury, Hobart. *New Hampshire: Resources, Attractions, and Its People. A History*. Vol. II. New York: Lewis Historical Publishing, 1927.

Porter, David D. *The Naval History of the Civil War*. Glendale, NY: Benchmark Publishing, 1970. Reprint of original 1886 edition.

Portsmouth Naval Shipyard. *Cradle of American Shipbuilding*. Portsmouth, NH: Portsmouth Naval Shipyard, 1978.

Preble, George Henry. *History of the United States Navy-Yard, Portsmouth, N.H.* Washington: U.S. Government Printing Office, 1892.

Prime, Ralph E. "An Incident Connected with the Alabama Claims Arbitration." In *Personal Recollections of the War of the Rebellion: Addresses Delivered Before the Commandery of the State of New York, Military Order of the Loyal Legion of the United States*, ed. by A. Noel Blakeman. New York and London: G.P. Putnam's Sons, 1912. Fourth Series. pp. 66-78.

Quarles, Benjamin. *The Negro in the Civil War*. New York: Russell & Russell, 1953, reissued 1968.

Quinby, Henry Cole. *The Quinby-Quimby Family of Sandwich, New Hampshire*. New York and Rutland, VT: Tuttle Company, 1923.

Randall, Peter E. *There Are No Victors Here: A Local Perspective on the Treaty of Portsmouth*. Portsmouth, NH: Portsmouth Marine Society, 1985.

Register of the Commissioned, Warrant, and Volunteer Officers of the Navy of the United States, Including Officers of the Marine Corps and Others, to September 1, 1862. Washington: Government Printing Office, 1862.

Richardson, James D., ed. and comp. *The Messages and Papers of Jefferson Davis and the Confederacy, including Diplomatic Correspondence, 1861-1865*. New York: Chelsea House-Robert Hector, Publishers, in association with R.R. Bowker, 1966.

Roberts, Robert B. *Encyclopedia of Historic Forts: The Military, Pioneer, and Trading Posts of the United States*. New York: Macmillan, and London: Collier Macmillan, 1988.

Robinson, Charles M., III. *Shark of the Confederacy: The Story of the C.S.S. Alabama*. Annapolis, MD: Naval Institute Press, 1994.

Robinson, William Morrison, Jr. *The Confederate Privateers*. New Haven, CT: Yale University Press, 1928.

Rogers, Fred Blackburn. *Montgomery and the* Portsmouth. Portsmouth, NH: Portsmouth Marine Society, 1990. Reprint of 1958 edition.

Roland, Charles P. *An American Iliad: The Story of the Civil War*. Lexington, KY: University of Kentucky Press, 1990.

Rowe, John Frink. *Newington, New Hampshire: A Heritage of Independence Since 1630*. Based on the writings of Frederick M. Pickering. Canaan, NH: Phoenix Publishing. Published for Town of Newington in conjunction with Newington Historical Society, 1987.

Rowe, William Hutchinson. *The Maritime History of Maine: Three Centuries of Shipbuilding and Seafaring*. New York: W.W. Norton, 1948.

Schaefer, Rudolph J. *J.E. Buttersworth: 19th-Century Marine Painter*. Mystic, CT: Mystic Seaport, 1975. Includes reproductions of two *Kearsarge-Alabama* sea battle paintings. Copy at Boston Public Library, Boston, MA.

Schneider, Pierre, and the Editors of Time-Life Books. *The World of Manet, 1832-1883*. New York: Time-Life Books, 1968.

Semmes, Raphael. *The Cruise of the* Alabama *and the* Sumter. 2 vols. in 1. New York: Carleton, Publisher, 1864.

Sewell, Richard H. *John P. Hale and the Politics of Abolition*. Cambridge, MA: Harvard University Press, 1965.

Silverstone, Paul H. *Warships of the Civil War Navies*. Annapolis, MD: Naval Institute Press, 1989.

Sketches of Successful New Hampshire Men. Manchester, NH: John B. Clarke, 1882.

Smith, Mason Philip. *Confederates Downeast: Confederate Operations in and around Maine*. Portland, ME: Provincial Press, 1985.

Snow, Edward Rowe. *Pirates and Buccaneers of the Atlantic Coast*. Boston: Yankee Publishing, 1944.

Sobel, Robert, and John Raimo, eds. *Biographical Directory of the Governors of the United States, 1789-1978*. Westport, CT: Microform Review, Meckler Books, 1978. Vol. III. Includes biographical sketches of New Hampshire's Civil War governors: Ichabod Goodwin, Nathaniel Springer Berry, Joseph Albree Gilmore, and Frederick Smyth, pp. 962-65.

Soley, James Russell. *Admiral Porter*. New York: D. Appleton, 1903.

Southwick, Leslie, comp. *Presidential Also-Rans and Running Mates, 1788-1980*. Jefferson, NC, and London: McFarland, 1984.

Spears, John R. *The American Slave-Trade: An Account of Its Origin, Growth and Suppression*. New York: Charles Scribner's Sons, 1900.

Spencer, Warren F. *The Confederate Navy in Europe*. University, AL: University of Alabama Press, 1983.

Stackpole, Everett S. *History of New Hampshire*. Vol. IV. New York: American Historical Society, n.d. [ca. 1916].

Stewart, Edwin. "Address on Admiral Farragut." In *Personal Recollections of the War of the Rebellion: Addresses Delivered Before the Commandery of the State of New York, Military Order of the Loyal Legion of the United States*, ed. by A. Noel Blakeman. New York and London: G.P. Putnam's Sons, 1912. Fourth Series. pp. 162-70.

Still, William N., Jr. *Ironclad Captains: The Commanding Officers of the USS* Monitor. [Washington, DC]: Marine and Estuarine Management Division, National Oceanic and Atmospheric Administration, U.S. Department of Commerce, 1988.

————. *Monitor Builders: A Historical Study of the Principal Firms and Individuals Involved in the Construction of USS* Monitor. Washington: National Maritime Initiative, Division of History, National Park Service, U.S. Department of the Interior, 1988.

Stone, Herbert L., William H. Taylor, and William W. Robinson. *The America's Cup Races*. New York: W.W. Norton, 1970.

Summersell, Charles G., ed. and annot. *The Journal of George Townley Fullam: Boarding Officer of the Confederate Sea Raider* Alabama. University, AL: University of Alabama Press, 1972.

Symonds, Craig L., ed. *Charleston Blockade: The Journals of John B. Marchand, U.S. Navy, 1861-1862*. Newport, RI: Naval War College, 1976.

Tarleton, C[harles] W., comp. *The Tarleton Family*. Concord, NH: Ira C. Evans, 1900. Contains a brief biography of James Neal Tarlton (1811-78), whose family branch used a variant spelling of the Tarleton name, p. 166.

Taylor, Richard. *Destruction and Reconstruction: Personal Experiences of the Late War*. New York, London, and Toronto: Longmans, Green, 1955.

Thompson, Robert Means, and Richard Wainwright, eds. *Confidential Correspondence of Gustavus Vasa Fox: Assistant Secretary of the Navy, 1861-1865*. 2 vols. New York: Printed by De Vinne Press for Naval History Society, 1919.

Thompson, S. Millett. *Thirteenth Regiment of the New Hampshire Volunteer Infantry in the War of the Rebellion, 1861-1865. A Diary Covering Three Years and a Day*. Boston: Houghton, Mifflin, 1888.

Thwing, Walter Eliot. *Thwing: A Genealogical, Biographical and Historical Account of the Family*. Boston: David Clapp & Son, Printers, 1883.

Tibawi, A.L. *American Interests in Syria, 1800-1901*. Oxford: Clarendon Press, 1966.

United States Naval History Division, ed. by James L. Mooney et al. *Dictionary of American Naval Fighting Ships*. 8 vols. Washington: Government Printing Office, 1959-81.

U.S. Navy Engineers. *Memorial of the U.S. Naval Engineers to the XXXVIIIth Congress, First Session*. New York: C.A. Alvord, Printer, 1864. 14-page pamphlet. Copy at Boston Athenaeum, Boston.

Valuska, David L. *The African American in the Union Navy, 1861-1865*. New York: Garland Publishing, 1993.

Vlahos, Michael E. "The Making of an American Style (1797-1887)." Chapter 1 in *Naval Engineering and American Seapower*, ed. by Randolph W. King, pp. 3-29. Baltimore, MD: Nautical & Aviation Publishing Company of America, 1980.

Wait, Horatio L. "The Blockade of the Confederacy." *Century Magazine* 56 (October 1898): 914-28. Excerpted in *The Blue and the Gray*, ed. by Henry Steele Commager. Indianapolis: Bobbs-Merrill, 1950. 2:848-54.

Ward, J. Langdon, ed., comp., and coll. "Geneva Award Miscellaneous." 3 bound volumes of Geneva Award Bill, assorted pamphlets, reprints, and materials, owned by Ward. Deposited at Portsmouth Athenaeum, Portsmouth, NH.

Warley, A[lexander] F. "Note on the Destruction of the *Albemarle*." In *Battles and Leaders of the Civil War*, ed. by Robert Underwood Johnson and Clarence Clough Buel. New York: Thomas Yoseloff, 1956. 4:641-42.

West, Richard S., Jr. *Mr. Lincoln's Navy*. Westport, CT: Greenwood Press, 1957.

Whittaker, Robert H., coll. *Portsmouth-Kittery Naval Shipyard: In Old Photographs*. Dover, NH: Alan Sutton Publishing, 1993.

Wilmerding, John. *Paintings by Fitz Hugh Lane*. Washington: National Gallery of Art, and New York: Harry N. Abrams, 1988.

Wilson, James Grant, and Titus Munson Coan, eds. *Personal Recollections of the War of the Rebellion: Addresses Delivered Before the New York Commandery of the Loyal Legion of the United States, 1883-1891*. New York: Published by the Commandery, 1891.

Winslow, Arthur. *Francis Winslow: His Forebears and Life. Based Upon Family Records and Correspondence During XXX Years*. Norwood, MA: Privately printed by Plimpton Press, 1935. Copy at Dimond Library, University of New Hampshire, Durham, NH.

Winslow, Richard E., III. *Portsmouth-Built: Submarines of the Portsmouth Naval Shipyard*. Portsmouth, NH: Portsmouth Marine Society, 1985.

———. *"Wealth and Honour": Portsmouth During the Golden Age of Privateering, 1775-1815*. Portsmouth, NH: Portsmouth Marine Society, 1988.

Wise, Stephen. *Lifeline of the Confederacy: Blockade Running During the Civil War*. Columbia, SC: University of South Carolina Press, 1988.

Woodward, C. Vann, ed. *Mary Chesnut's Civil War*. New Haven and London: Yale University Press, 1981.

PUBLIC DOCUMENTS

Causes of the Reduction of American Tonnage and the Decline of Navigation Interests...Report of a Select Committee...The 17th of February, 1870. Washington: Government Printing Office, 1870.

Correspondence and Other Papers Relating to the American Civil War, 1863-64. United States of America. Irish University Press Area Studies Series, British Parliamentary Papers. Vol. 17. Shannon, Ireland: Irish University Press, 1971.

Correspondence and Other Papers Relating to the American Civil War and Civil War Claims, 1864-70. United States of America. Irish University Press Area Studies Series, British Parliamentary Papers. Vol. 18. Shannon, Ireland: Irish University Press, 1971.

Executive Documents Printed by Order of the House of Representatives during the First Session of the Thirty-Sixth Congress, 1859-'60. 15 vols. Including Vol. 15: Commerce and Navigation. Washington: Thomas H. Ford, Printer, 1860. Succeeding "Commerce and Navigation" reports in subsequent Congresses, 1861-65.

Executive Documents and Reports of Committees, Printed by Order of the House of Representatives during the First Session of the Thirty-Seventh Congress. 1 vol. Washington: Government Printing Office, 1861.

Executive Documents Printed by Order of the House of Representatives during the Third Session of the Thirty-Seventh Congress, 1862-'63. 37th

Congress, 3d Session. Executive Document no. 1, vol. 3. "Report of the Secretary of the Navy," pp. 1-46.

Executive Documents Printed by Order of the House of Representatives during the First Session of the Thirty-Eighth Congress, 1863-'64. 16 vols. Washington: Government Printing Office, 1864.

Executive Documents Printed by Order of the House of Representatives during the Second Session of the Thirty-Eighth Congress, 1864-'65. 15 vols. Washington: Government Printing Office, 1865.

Executive Documents Printed by Order of the House of Representatives during the Third Session of the Fortieth Congress, 1868-'69. 14 vols. Washington: Government Printing Office, 1869.

Message of the President of the United States, and Accompanying Documents, to the Two Houses of Congress... (variant titles, each containing "Report of the Secretary of the Navy"). Washington: Government Printing Office, 1860-67.

Papers Relating to Foreign Affairs, Accompanying the Annual Message of the President to the Second Session of the Thirty-Eighth Congress. Parts II and III. Washington: Government Printing Office, 1865. American diplomatic documents relating to the *Kearsarge-Alabama* sea battle.

Papers Relating to Foreign Affairs, Accompanying the Annual Message of the President to the First Session of the Thirty-Ninth Congress. Parts I and II. Washington: Government Printing Office, 1866. American diplomatic documents relating to the cruise of the CSS *Shenandoah*.

Report of the Secretary of the Navy in Relation to Armored Vessels. Washington: Government Printing Office, 1864. Copy at Baker Library, Dartmouth College, Hanover, NH.

Revised List of Claims Filed with the Department of State...Known as the Alabama Claims. Washington: Government Printing Office, 1872.

Rives, F. and J. *The Congressional Globe: Containing the Debates and Proceedings of the Second Session of the Thirty-Eighth Congress: Also, of the Special Session of the Senate.* Washington: Printed at Congressional Globe Office, 1865.

Rush, Richard, et al., eds. *Official Records of the Union and Confederate Navies in the War of the Rebellion.* 31 vols. Washington: Government Printing Office, 1894-1927.

U.S. House of Representatives. *Investigation of the Navy Department* printed on spine. 3 vols. *Investigation by the Committee on Naval Affairs. Testimony Taken by the Committee on Naval Affairs.* 44th Congress, 1st Session. Misc. Doc. 170, Part 1, Kittery Navy Yard. Washington: Government Printing Office, 1876. Vol. 1, pp. 1-183. Some scattered material in Vol. 2, Part 5, pp. 643-46, in Boston Navy Yard section, and in Vol. 3, Part 8, *Circular Letter and Answers to Circular Letter*, pp. 108-21.

ARTICLES

Adams, Herbert C.F. "Pirates: The Comedy of the *Caleb Cushing.*" *Civil War Times Illustrated* 20 (January 1982): 26-36.

Alexander, J.W. "How We Escaped from Fort Warren." *New England Magazine* New Series 7 (October 1892): 208-13.

Allard, Dean C. "Naval Technology during the American Civil War." *American Neptune* 49 (spring 1989): 114-22.

Aptheker, Herbert. "The Negro in the Union Navy." *Journal of Negro History* 32 (April 1947): 169-200.

Badlam, William H. "The First Cruise of the *Kearsarge.*" *Civil War Papers.* Boston: printed for the Commandery, 1890. 1:11-24.

Barnard, Joseph. "The Timbers of the *Kearsarge.*" *Granite Monthly* 15 (May 1893): 145-48.

Bradlee, Francis B.C. "The *Kearsarge-Alabama* Battle: The Story as Told to the Writer by James Magee of Marblehead, Seaman on the *Kearsarge.*" *Historical Collections of the Essex Institute* 57 (July 1921): 216-41.

"Brager's Painting of the *Kearsarge* and *Alabama.*" *Scientific American* 11 (October 15, 1864): 249.

Browne, John M. "The *Kearsarge* and the *Alabama*: A New Story of an Old Fight." *The Overland Monthly* 14 (February 1875): 105-11.

"Captain Daniel Marcy." *Granite Monthly* 15 (December 1893): 391.

Chandler, Lloyd H. "The *Portsmouth* - An Historic Ship." *Granite Monthly* 16 (January 1894): 40-47.

———. "Portsmouth, Cherbourg, and Roncador: The Story of the *Alabama* and her Conqueror." *Granite Monthly* 16 (March 1894): 200-209.

Coale, George B. "The Geneva Award and the Insurance Companies." *North American Review* 134 (January 1882): 76-96.

Cooper, David. "Underwater Archaeology." *Pull Together: Newsletter of the Naval Historical Foundation and the Naval Historical Center* 32 (fall/winter 1993): 11-12.

"Cruise of the *Alabama* and the *Sumter.*" Review. From the *Athenaeum* (London). Reprinted in *Littell's Living Age* (Boston) 82 (September 10, 1864): 517-21.

Cutler, Carl C. "Deering and Yeaton, Ship-Riggers." *American Neptune* 3 (October 1943): 123-35.

Davis, Noah. "*Kearsarge.*" *Granite Monthly* 17 (October 1894): 221-22.

Dillon, Richard H. "First Word from *Kearsarge.*" *American Neptune* 19 (April 1959): 126-28.

Dudley, William S. "American Naval Archeology: Past and Prologue." *Pull Together: Newsletter of the Naval Historical Foundation and the Naval Historical Center* 30 (spring/summer 1991): 1-5.

Gilbert, Benjamin Franklin. "Confederate Warships off Brazil." *American Neptune* 15 (October 1955): 287-302.

Goodwin, Frank. "Hon. Ichabod Goodwin." *Granite Monthly* 3 (May 1880): 292-97. Reprinted in *Sketches of Successful New Hampshire Men*, pp. 132-36.

Guérout, Max. "The Wreck of the C.S.S. *Alabama*: Avenging Angel of the Confederacy." *National Geographic* 186 (December 1994): 66-83.

Hackett, William H. "A Reminiscence of the *Alabama*." *Granite Monthly* 6 (August 1883): 382-83.

Hall, Mary T. "False Colors and Dummy Ships: The Use of Ruse in Naval Warfare." *Naval War College Review* 42 (summer 1989): 52-62.

Hanna, William F. "The Boston Draft Riot." *Civil War History* 36 (September 1990): 262-73.

Heffernan, John B. "The Blockade of the Southern Confederacy: 1861-1865." *Smithsonian Journal of History* 2 (winter 1967-68): 23-44.

Holbrook, Francis X. "A Mosby or a Quantrill? The Civil War Career of John Clibbon Braine." *American Neptune* 33 (July 1973): 199-211.

"Hon. Daniel Marcy." *Granite Monthly* 1 (May 1878): 353-57.

"International Committee Protects C.S.S. *Alabama*." *Pull Together: Newsletter of the Naval Historical Foundation and the Naval Historical Center* 30 (fall/winter 1991): 11-12.

"The *Kearsarge* and the *Alabama*." *Scientific American* 11 (July 16, 1864): 42.

Kennett, Rick, B.L. Fuqua, and C.S. Fuqua. "Australia's Stake in America's Civil War." *Naval History* 3 (spring 1989): 50-54.

Kinnaman, Stephen C. "Inside the *Alabama*: Technical Report." *Naval History* 4 (summer 1990): 54-57.

Krein, David F. "Russell's Decision to Detain the Laird Rams." *Civil War History* 22 (June 1976): 158-63.

Laas, Virginia Jeans. "'Sleepless Sentinels': The North Atlantic Blockading Squadron, 1862-1864." *Civil War History* 31 (March 1985): 24-38.

Lambert, C.S. "C.S.S. *Alabama*—Lost and Found." *American History Illustrated* 23 (October 1988): 32-37.

"The Last of the *Alabama*." *Saturday Review of Politics, Literature, Science, and Art* (London) 17 (June 25, 1864): 769-70.

Lathrop, A.J., ed. "Three Years on Board the *Kearsarge*." Diary of Charles A. Poole of Brunswick, ME. *New England Historical and Genealogical Register* 35 (October 1881): 341-43.

Laugel, Auguste. "Les Corsaires Confédérés et Le Droit des Gens." *Revue des Deux Mondes* (Paris) 52 (July-August 1864): 224-48.

Leary, William M., Jr. "*Alabama* versus *Kearsarge*: A Diplomatic View." *American Neptune* 29 (July 1969): 167-73.

Leland, Waldo G., contrib. "*Kearsarge* and *Alabama*: French Official Report, 1864." *American Historical Review* 23 (October 1917): 119-23.

Malloy, Mary. "The Old Sailor's Lament: Recontextualizing Melville's Reflections on the Sinking of 'The Stone Fleet.'" *New England Quarterly* 65 (December 1991): 633-42.

Manning, J.F. "The Geneva Award and the Ship-Owners." *North American Review* 135 (September 1882): 283-97.

Marvel, William. "Answering Lincoln's Call: The First New Hampshire Volunteers." *Historical New Hampshire* 39 (fall/winter 1984): 139-51.

———. "Back from the Gates of Hell: The Deadly Campaign of the Drafted Militia." *Historical New Hampshire* 44 (fall 1989): 104-19.

———. "New Hampshire and the Draft, 1863." *Historical New Hampshire* 36 (spring 1981): 58-72.

———. "The Pride of Portsmouth: The Cruise of the U.S.S. *Kearsarge.*" *Historical New Hampshire* 41 (spring/summer 1986): 1-20.

Merrill, James M. "Men, Monotony, and Mouldy Beans—Life on Board Civil War Blockaders." *American Neptune* 41 (January 1956): 49-59.

Mitchell, S. Weir. "*Kearsarge.*" *Atlantic Monthly* 42 (July 1878): 10.

Newton, Craig. "Inside Semmes." *Naval History* 7 (summer 1993): 6-10.

Nicolosi, Anthony S. "Foundation of the Naval Presence in Narragansett Bay, an Overview." *Newport History: Bulletin of the Newport Historical Society* 52 (summer 1979): 60-82.

"Notes from the Journal of Lieutenant T.A.M. Craven, U.S.N., U.S.S. *Dale*, Pacific Squadron, 1846-49." Introductory biographical sketch of Craven by "C.B." *Proceedings of the United States Naval Institute* 14 (1888): 119-20.

O'Flaherty, Daniel. "The Blockade that Failed." *Civil War Chronicles* (winter 1993): 24-29.

Pelzer, John. "Liverpool and the American Civil War." *History Today* 40 (March 1990): 46-52.

"Permanent Commission of the Navy Department." *Scientific American* 10 (March 12, 1864): 165.

Plowman, Robert J. "An Untapped Source: Civil War Prize Case Files, 1861-1865." *Prologue: Quarterly of the National Archives* 21 (fall 1989): 196-205.

Pratt, Charles Stuart. "*Kearsarge*: Mountain and War-Ship." *Granite Monthly* 51 (April 1919): 160-64. Poem and expanded footnote.

Price, Marcus W. "Four from Bristol." *American Neptune* 17 (October 1957): 249-61.

Roberts, George N. "Hon. Thomas Logan Tullock." *Granite Monthly* 5 (April 1882): 196-207.

Scales, John. "Shipbuilding in Dover and Along the Piscataqua River." *Granite Monthly* 60 (December 1928): 571-76.

Sedgwick, A.G. "The Geneva Award Farce." *Nation* 34 (February 16, 1882): 136-37.

"Sinking of the *Alabama*," with the poem, "The Sinking of the Rebel Corsair." *Harper's Weekly* 8 (July 23, 1864): 466.

Squires, J. Duane. "Some Thoughts on New Hampshire and the Civil War Centennial." *Historical New Hampshire* 16 (December 1961): 1-5.

Switzer, David C. "Down-East Ships of the Union Navy." *United States Naval Institute Proceedings* 90 (November 1964): 82-88.

Tawresey, John G. "The Portsmouth, N.H., Navy Yard." *Historical Transactions, 1893-1943*. New York: Society of Naval Architects and Marine Engineers (1945): 28-30.

Taylor, John M. "The Fiery Trail of the *Alabama*." *MHQ: The Quarterly Journal of Military History. The Civil War: A Special Issue* (1994): 58-67.

———. "The U.S.S. *Kearsarge* versus the *Alabama*: Showdown off Cherbourg." *Yankee* 48 (July 1984): 72-77, 133-38. Includes *Kearsarge* sailor William Alsdorf's eyewitness account of the sea battle.

Underhill, Miriam, arr. "Kearsarge North Regains its Name." *Appalachia* (December 15, 1957): 511-21.

Wade, Arthur P. "The Defenses of Portsmouth Harbor, 1794-1821: The First and Second Systems of Seacoast Fortification." *Historical New Hampshire* 33 (spring 1978): 25-51.

Wait, Horatio L. "The Blockade of the Confederacy." *Century Magazine* 56 (October 1898): 914-28.

Walling, Burns T. "The Wreck of the *Kearsarge*: A Narrative." *Proceedings of the United States Naval Institute* 20 (1894): 671-90.

Williams, Harold. "Yankee Whaling Fleets Raided by Confederate Cruisers: The Story of the Bark *Jireh Swift*, Captain Thomas W. Williams." *American Neptune* 27 (October 1967): 263-78.

Wood, Richard G. "The Two U.S.S. *New Hampshires*." *Historical New Hampshire* [occasional issue], (November 1948): 19-27.

Woodman, John E., Jr. "The Stone Fleet." *American Neptune* 21 (October 1961): 233-59.

NEWSPAPERS

Andover (MA) *Advertiser*

Boston Globe

Charleston (SC) *Mercury*, 1864, including numerous reprints

Chicago Tribune, 1864

Colon Telegram (Colon, Colombia, now Panama); one issue, Friday, February 9, 1894

Exeter (NH) *News-Letter and Rockingham Advertiser*

The Guardian (London)

The Illustrated London News (London, England); one issue, June 25, 1864

Journal des Débats: Politiques et Littéraires (Paris)

Manchester (NH) *Daily Union*

Le Moniteur Universel: Journal officiel de l'Empire Français (Paris)

Nashua (NH) *Gazette*

New Hampshire Statesman (Concord, NH)

New Orleans Daily Picayune

New York Daily Tribune

New York Times
Penny Post (Portsmouth, NH)
Periscope (Portsmouth Naval Shipyard, Portsmouth, NH)
Portsmouth Herald
Portsmouth Journal of Literature and Politics
Portsmouth Chronicle
Portsmouth Times
States and Union (Portsmouth, NH)
The Times (London)
Union Leader (Manchester, NH)
The Watchman, and Wesleyan Advertiser (London), 1864

MANUSCRIPTS

"Abstract Log: U.S. Steam S[hip] *Kearsarge* of Capt Jno. A. Winslow, Commanding." Box: Naval Historical Miscellany." Folder: "Log of U.S.S. *Kearsarge*, 1864." Manuscript Division, Library of Congress, Washington.

Agamenticus. "Complete List of Muster Roll of the Crew of the U.S. Steamer *Agamenticus* on the 6th of July, 1865." 4 pages. Portsmouth Naval Shipyard Visitor Center, Portsmouth Naval Shipyard, Portsmouth, NH.

———. "Log of the United States Iron Clad U.S.S. *Agamenticus*, May 5-June 1865, and stationed at the Portsmouth Navy Yard, Portsmouth, NH." Portsmouth Naval Shipyard Visitor Center, Portsmouth Naval Shipyard, Portsmouth, NH.

Bailey, Theodorus. Notebook. "Memorandum of Prizes taken and sent into Key West by the Vessels composing the East[er]n Gulf Blockading Squadron under the command of Theodorus Bailey, Actg. Rear Admiral." Includes list of prizes and cargoes, 1863-64. ca. 20 pages. Original in possession of Dudley W. Stoddard, New York, and copies in possession of the author, Rye, NH, and of the Portsmouth Naval Shipyard Visitor Center, Portsmouth Naval Shipyard, Portsmouth, NH.

———. Papers. "ZB" File. Naval Historical Center Archives, Washington Navy Yard, Washington. Folder of correspondence relating to Bailey's naval career.

Bartlett, Ezra. "*Kearsarge-Alabama.*" 6-page typescript of 2 letters from Ezra Bartlett, a native of Stratham, NH, to George Bartlett, the first dated, "U.S. Steamer *Kearsarge* off Cherbourg, France, June 14, 1864," and the second, "Cherbourg, Sunday, June 19, 1864," which describe the sea battle and the events leading up to it. Rare Book Room, Boston Public Library, Boston.

[Burnside, Ambrose Everett]. "General Orders No. 13 to Surgeons of Regiments in the Coast Division." Official copy, unsigned, Annapolis, MD, December 29, 1861. 2-page document of "Regulations for

Shipboard Hygiene" for Union General Burnside's command. Gift of Samuel A. Green, M.D., Class of 1851, Harvard University, September 19, 1862. Houghton Library, Harvard University, Cambridge, MA.

Camilla. British Registry Transaction Certificate: 1856-1860, showing the sale and transfer of 64 1/64th shares in the schooner *Camilla*, of Portsmouth, NH, by various owners in England. 1 document. G.W. Blunt White Library, Mystic Seaport Museum, Mystic, CT.

Chandler, William E. "Civil War, U.S. Claims against England, Redfield Commission. Letters to William E. Chandler from his brother, George Henry Chandler, in London, 1862-1868." New Hampshire Historical Society, Concord, NH.

————. Papers. Includes copies of 6 letters from Admiral David Farragut to William H. Shock, fleet engineer at New Orleans, LA, Feb.-Oct. 1864, concerning ship repairs. Manuscript Division, Library of Congress, Washington.

Chapin, John E. "Impact of the Civil War on Maine Shipping and Shipbuilding." University of Maine/Orono M.A. in history, 1970. 166-page photocopy. Copy at Maine Historical Society, Portland, ME.

"Civil War, Fort Constitution." Miscellaneous papers. 1 box. New Hampshire Historical Society, Concord, NH.

"Commandants' Letters, Navy Yard, Portsmouth, NH." Record Group 45, Entry 34, Navy Department. Books (bound volumes): 1860, 1861, 1862, 1863, 1864, and 1865. National Archives, Military Reference Branch, Washington. Original letters in bound volumes, with selected documents microfilmed and sent to the author.

Dempsey, John H. One letter, dated, "U.S. Steamer *Kearsarge*, Brest, France, December 14th, 1863," to his sister. Box: "Miscellaneous Manuscripts, 1856-1864," Folder: "1863." Massachusetts Historical Society, Boston.

DeWitt, Carsten B. "Journal, 1862-1864, kept by Carsten B. DeWitt, yeoman, on board the U.S.S. *Kearsarge*, Pickering, Master, for a naval cruise in search of the Confederate steamer *Sumpter*." 1 vol. Log 433. G.W. Blunt White Library, Mystic Seaport Museum, Mystic, CT.

Dolph, James. Dolph Collection, pertaining to the Portsmouth Naval Shipyard during the Civil War era. Scrapbook of photocopied miscellaneous materials, articles, reports, drawings, and manuscripts. Copies in possession of Dolph, South Berwick, ME, and in possession of the author, Rye, NH.

Doyle, Thomas M., comp. "U.S. Naval Cemetery, 1820-1986. Portsmouth Navy Yard, Portsmouth, New Hampshire." Introductory essay followed by list of gravesites and names of military personnel and dependents interred. 22-page typescript dated "19 August 1986." Copies at Portsmouth Naval Shipyard Visitor Center, Portsmouth Naval Shipyard, Portsmouth, NH, and in possession of the author, Rye, NH.

Eason, Henry. "Journal, Jan. 1858-Sep. 1860, kept by Henry Eason, a seaman aboard U.S. Sloop of War *Marion*, Capt. Brent, during a[n] anti-slaving cruise off the African coast." 1 vol., 105 pages, with pencil illustrations. Log 902. G.W. Blunt White Library, Mystic Seaport Museum, Mystic, CT.

Executive Records. Correspondence and Messages. Papers of the New Hampshire Governors, 1860-1867. Early Documents RG 1, Executive. Boxes 27-33. Department of State, Division of Records Management and Archives, Concord, NH.

Farragut, David Glasgow. 3-page letter in unknown hand, signed by Farragut, Mobile Bay, Alabama, October 5, 1864, to "the Judge of the U.S. Prize Court, Boston." Houghton Library, Harvard University, Cambridge, MA.

Fox, Gustavus V. 1 letter, December 6, 1861, Navy Department [Washington], to "Editor[,] *Boston Journal*." Manuscript 861656, Baker Library, Dartmouth College, Hanover, NH.

Frost, John Eldridge. "Portsmouth Record Book: Records of the South Cemetery." Typescript copy. Copy in Portsmouth Room, Portsmouth Public Library, Portsmouth, NH.

Goldsmith, Reginald E. "Roster of Shop Supervisors." Dated August 1948. 42-page typescript. Copies at Portsmouth Naval Shipyard Visitor Center, Portsmouth Naval Shipyard, Portsmouth, NH, and in possession of the author, Rye, NH.

Goodwin, Ichabod. Papers, 1849-1870. Correspondence and documents of New Hampshire's first Civil War governor (1858-61). 22 items in one folder. New Hampshire Historical Society, Concord, NH.

Greene, Samuel Dana. 1 letter, Hampton Roads, VA, March 14, 1862. Typescript copy in "Papers of the Civil War." Box 2, Phillips Library, Peabody Essex Museum, Salem, MA.

Gregg, James A. 1 letter, Newport, NH, April 29, 1861, to Ichabod Goodwin. Manuscript 861279, Baker Library, Dartmouth College, Hanover, NH.

Hatch, Albert Ruyter. Papers, 1841-93. Correspondence, mostly political and legal, of a prominent Portsmouth lawyer and Democratic politician (1817-82). 3 boxes containing ca. 800 items. New Hampshire Historical Society, Concord, NH.

Hoyt, Martin. "Naval Engagement between U.S.S. *Kearsarge* and the Confederate Steamer *Alabama* in the English Channel 8 Miles off Cherbourg, France, on Sunday, June 19, 1864." 2-page typescript. Civil War File, Langdon Library, Newington, NH.

———. 1 letter. Martin V. Hoyt, U.S.S. *Kearsarge*, Cherbourg, France, June 19, 1864, to "Dear Uncle" [Samuel Hoyt, Newington, NH]. 4 pages. Original at John Paul Jones House, Portsmouth Historical Society, Portsmouth, NH. Copies in possession of Priscilla Hoyt Triggs, great-

great-granddaughter of Martin Hoyt, Hampton, NH, and of the author, Rye, NH.

Joe Hooker. "Journal of a Voyage in Fishing Schooner *Joe Hooker* of York [Maine], Commanded by Edward Low." Fishing log, April 1–September 25, 1864, from York, ME, to the Grand Banks. Phillips Library, Peabody Essex Museum, Salem, MA.

"Letters Received from Commandants of Navy Yards—Portsmouth, N.H." Bureau of Yards and Docks. Record Group 71, Boxes 284-86. (Box 284: Jan. 7, 1859-July 21, 1861; Box 285: Aug. 1, 1861-Dec. 22, 1863; Box 286: Jan. 7, 1864-July 29, 1865). National Archives, Washington.

Lockwood, Samuel. Papers, 1822-85, pertaining to Lockwood's American naval career. Civil War papers include correspondence, orders, log extracts, reports, and signals, with documents related to his blockade service. 2 boxes. Manuscript Group Number 726, with finding aid. Sterling Memorial Library, Yale University, New Haven, CT.

Luce, Stephen B. 1 letter, March 1, 1865, U.S.S. *Pontiac*, to George S. Blake, Newport, RI, regarding conditions in the South toward the end of the Civil War. 4 pages. Ms. Item 10, Naval Historical Collection, Naval War College, Newport, RI.

Mahan, Alfred T. Letter from U.S. Naval Academy Superintendent Commodore George Smith Blake ordering Mahan to duty on the U.S.S. *Macedonian*, May 12, 1863, Newport, RI. Ms. Item 85, Naval Historical Collection, Naval War College, Newport, RI.

Marcy, Daniel. Papers of a Portsmouth shipbuilder and Civil War congressman (1809-93). An extensive collection, containing mostly incoming correspondence, relating to personal, shipping, and political matters, with limited outgoing letters, 1838-81. 8 boxes. New Hampshire Historical Society, Concord, NH.

———. "Telegram, Aug. 31, 1861, from Eastport, ME, to D[aniel] Marcy of Portsmouth, N.H., indicating the vessels *Express* and *Orozimbo* were seized by the Federal Government. Signed by W.L. Frost." 1 document. G.W. Blunt White Library, Mystic Seaport Museum, Mystic, CT.

Martin, Benjamin F. Papers, 1861-66. Correspondence and documents pertaining to Martin's service as a master sparmaker at the Portsmouth Navy Yard during the Civil War. 7 items in 1 folder. New Hampshire Historical Society, Concord, NH.

Military Records. Civil War Period. Early Documents, RG XII, Boxes 18, 30, 34, and 35. Department of State. Division of Records Management and Archives, Concord, NH.

Morning Glory. "Scattered papers, 1855-1860, of ship *Morning Glory* of Portsmouth, N.H., Hiram H. Hobbs, master, including correspondence, disbursements, charters, Lloyd's inspection, bottomry bonds, repair bill, bills of lading, average bond, and loss inventory." 31

pieces, including an 1860 Ichabod Goodwin letter. G.W. Blunt White Library, Mystic Seaport Museum, Mystic, CT.

Morris, Francis. Various U.S. Navy papers, certificates of appointment and discharge, and photographs. Includes a photograph of USS *Ossipee*. Manuscript Collection 45, Naval Historical Collection, Naval War College, Newport, RI.

Morse, J.P. 1 letter, "Fort Monrow [Monroe, VA], March 13th, 1862." Original and typescript copy in "Papers of the Civil War," Box: "Naval-Miscellany." Phillips Library, Peabody Essex Museum, Salem, MA.

"Navy Yard, Portsmouth, NH." Folder: "ZE." Naval Historical Center, Washington Navy Yard, Washington. 44-page manuscript of Yard's history, 1800-1860.

Nelson, George, A., comp. "Early U.S. Customs Records and History, Portsmouth, N.H." 6 vols. Bound typescripts. Copies at Joseph P. Copley Library, Portsmouth Athenaeum, Portsmouth, NH.

"News Release No. 864/17, 25 March 1987," pertaining to the possible salvage of the U.S.S. *Kearsarge*, and "The *Kearsarge* Project: Executive Summary." 9-page typescript copy, in possession of the author, Rye, NH.

Parrott, Enoch Greenleafe. Letters and Papers, 1780-1874. 2 boxes, 11 folders, comprising 230 pages. Beinecke Rare Book and Manuscript Library, Yale University, New Haven, CT.

Perkins, George Hamilton. Papers. 12 bound vols. New Hampshire Historical Society, Concord, NH.

Pickering, Charles Whipple. Lettercopy books, 1860-64. Incoming and outgoing letters, mostly pertaining to Pickering's service aboard the USS *Kearsarge*, as the ship's first commander. 3 vols. New Hampshire Historical Society, Concord, NH.

Poole, Charles. "Charles A. Poole's Journal of the Cruise of the United States Steam Sloop *Kearsarge*, In Se[a]rch of Rebel Privateers in 1862, '63, '64." 2 vols. Logs 431-32. G.W. Blunt White Library, Mystic Seaport Museum, Mystic, CT.

Pope, John. Papers. "ZB" File. Naval Historical Center Archives, Washington Navy Yard, Washington. Folder of correspondence relating to Pope's naval career.

Portsmouth Naval Shipyard, Civil War Papers, 1861-65. Portsmouth Naval Shipyard Visitor Center, Portsmouth Naval Shipyard, Portsmouth, NH. Miscellaneous documents.

"Portsmouth, New Hampshire: Records of the Bureau of Customs." 12-page typescript inventory of the U.S. Customs Service records, with many entries pertinent to the Civil War era. Record Group 36. Among the most important are: "Letters Received, 1801-1900" (Entry 315); "Letters Received from British Consuls, 1849-1869" (Entry 317); "Letters Sent, 1789-1899" (Entry 318); "Records of Entrances and Clearances, 1789-1918" (Entry 320); "Marine Protests, 1837-74"

(Entry 334); "Impost Books, 1792-1907" (Entry 337); "Records of Fees Collected, 1838-72" (Entry 351); "Quarterly and Monthly Statistical Returns, 1829-1884" (Entry 364). National Archives, Washington.

"Portsmouth Navy Yard (NH), 1815-1955." Computer printout inventory of National Archives records, with many entries pertinent to the Civil War Era. Record Group 181, Naval Districts and Shore Establishments. Among the most important are: "Fair Copies of Miscellaneous Letters Sent. April 2, 1823-September 25, 1867." 5 vols. (Entry 2); "Miscellaneous Letters and Telegrams Received, Aug. 1818-Jun. 1902." 21 vols. (Entry 7); "Copies of Letters and Endorsements Sent to the Secretary of the Navy, Apr. 9, 1823-Dec. 20, 1911." 22 vols. (Entry 8); "Letters, Telegrams, Circulars, and Orders Received from the Secretary of the Navy, Aug. 29, 1815-Apr. 29, 1902." 17 vols. (Entry 10); "Copies of Letters and Endorsements Sent to the Bureau of Construction and Repair, Sep. 9, 1842-Dec. 27, 1911." 23 vols. (Entry 15); "Letters, Telegrams, and Circulars Received from the Bureau of Construction and Repair, Sep. 1842-Feb. 1902." 39 vols. (Entry 16); "Copies of Letters and Endorsements Sent to the Bureau of Equipment, Nov. 12, 1862-Jun. 30, 1910." 14 vols. (Entry 17); "Letters and Telegrams Received from the Bureau of Equipment, Nov. 14, 1862-Apr. 2, 1902." 24 vols. (Entry 18); "Copies of Letters and Endorsements Sent to the Bureau of Medicine and Surgery, Oct. 28, 1842-Nov. 16, 1911." 5 vols. (Entry 19); "Letters and Telegrams Received from the Bureau of Medicine and Surgery, Oct. 21, 1842-May 9, 1902." 3 vols. (Entry 20); "Copies of Letters and Endorsements Sent to the Bureau of Navigation, Sep. 13, 1862-Dec. 29, 1911." 19 vols. (Entry 21); "Letters, Circulars, and Telegrams Received from the Bureau of Navigation, Sep. 11, 1862-Jun. 5, 1902." 10 vols. (Entry 22); "Copies of Letters and Endorsements Sent to the Bureau of Ordnance, Sept. 14, 1842-Dec. 28, 1911." 10 vols. (Entry 23); "Letters, Circulars, and Telegrams Received from the Bureau of Ordnance, Sep. 10, 1842-Jul. 17, 1901." 13 vols. (Entry 24); "Copies of Letters Sent to the Bureau of Provisions and Clothing, Sep. 7, 1842-Feb. 24, 1889." 5 vols. (Entry 25); "Letters, Circulars, and Telegrams Received from the Bureau of Provisions and Clothing, Sep. 2, 1842-Jan. 23, 1892." 7 vols. (Entry 26); "Copies of Letters and Endorsements Sent to the Bureau of Steam Engineering, Aug. 30, 1862-Dec. 29, 1911." 13 vols. (Entry 27); "Letters and Telegrams Received from the Bureau of Steam Engineering, Aug. 23, 1862-May 19, 1902." 16 vols. (Entry 28); "Copies of Letters and Endorsements Sent to the Bureau of Yards and Docks, Sep. 6, 1842-Dec. 30, 1911." 20 vols. (Entry 31); "Letters, Circulars, and Telegrams Received from the Bureau of Yards and Docks, Sep. 3, 1842-May 1, 1902." 32 vols. (Entry 32); "Copies of 'Orders' (Letters, Memorandums, and Endorsements) Sent to Yard Officials and Heads of Departments,

Sep. 21, 1832-Dec. 28, 1911." 57 vols. (Entry 36); "Letters, Reports, and Memorandums Received from Yard Officials and Heads of Departments, 1857-1902." (Entry 37); "Circulars of the Bureau of Equipment and Recruiting, Feb. 24, 1863-March 22, 1889." 1 vol. (Entry 51); "Reports of Surveys and Boards, Jan. 9, 1836-Jun. 5, 1861." (Entry 56); "Film Aperture Cards of Ship Plans, ca. 1840-1923." 194 items (Entry 57); "Letters and Telegrams Received by the Inspector of Ordnance (Ordnance Officer), Sep. 1864-Dec. 1867." (Entry 66); "Bureau of Yards and Docks, Captain of the Yard (Executive Officer), Letters, Circulars and Orders Received, Jun. 1860-Sep. 1891." 2 vols. (Entry 71). National Archives-New England Region, Waltham, MA.

Preble, George Henry. "Rough Mss. of a History of the U.S. Navy Yard, Portsmouth, New Hampshire. Prepared by Order of the Hon. Secretary of the Navy with the direction of the Chief of the Bureau of Yards and Docks, by Geo. Henry Preble, Rear Admiral, U.S.N., 1876-1877. The revised and corrected copy was forwarded to the Hon. Secretary of the Navy from Callao, Peru - Nov. 1877. Geo. Henry Preble, Rear Admiral, U.S. Flagship *Omaha*, Callao, Peru, Nov. 28, 1877." A written draft of Preble's study of the Portsmouth Navy Yard, eventually published in 1892, six years after its author's death. The bound manuscript also contains photographs, lists, tables, and 7 pasted-in 1876-77 Benjamin F. Chandler letters. New Hampshire Historical Society, Concord, NH.

————. Collection. Portsmouth Naval Shipyard Visitor Center, Portsmouth Naval Shipyard, Portsmouth, NH. Documents and letters.

Purington, David. "The Civil War Era." 6-page typescript essay. Copies in Dolph Collection and in possession of the author, Rye, NH.

Quinby, Austin H.F. "Cruise of the *Kearsarge*." Morocco-covered volume containing 121 numbered pages of Quinby's transcription of official reports and an additional 204-page personal log of his service as a U.S. Marine aboard the USS *Kearsarge*, 1862-64. Handwritten poems and pasted-in newspaper clippings at the end of the book. A superb personal account of life at sea and of the 1864 battle. Phillips Library, Peabody Essex Museum, Salem, MA.

Roe, Francis Ashbury. Papers. Collection of a Union Rear Admiral, including a 10-page typescript recollection, "*Sassacus* and *Albemarle*, May 5, 1864, Sounds of North Carolina," written in 1899, and undated newspaper clipping, "The *Sassacus*' Fight: Brave Attack of Roe's Ship Against the *Albemarle*, the Horrors of a Naval Hand-to-Hand Fight Described by the Ship's Surgeon," by Edgar Holden, M.D. Manuscript Division, Library of Congress, Washington.

Saltonstall, William G. "Autobiography and Reminiscences." 32-page typescript, with manuscript insertions, written in 1886. 1 box. MS. N-146. Massachusetts Historical Society, Boston.

Scofield, Walter K. Papers, including Civil War diaries and medical memorandum books of a Union naval surgeon serving on blockade duty and in naval hospitals. 3 boxes. Manuscript Group Number 437, with finding aid. Sterling Memorial Library, Yale University, New Haven, CT.

Spinney, Daniel H. Commentary and Identifications. Extensively marked copy of 1867 *Portsmouth Directory Containing the City Record, and the Names of the Citizens, with Business and Street Directories*, by Dean Dudley. Portsmouth, NH: For sale by James F. Shores, Jr., 1867. Original owned by Mrs. Garland W. Patch, Portsmouth, NH; photocopy in possession of the author, Rye, NH.

Stewart, Charles Samuel. "Letters to his Children, written during the Blockade of the Gulf Ports: 1861-1862. Originally 33 pieces, now wanting Nos. 4 and 9." Manuscript letters written aboard blockading vessels. Houghton Library, Harvard University, Cambridge, MA.

Stowell, David Porter. Diaries. Journal and Medical Notes, 1858-62, aboard the ship *Orion*. 1 vol. New Hampshire Historical Society, Concord, NH.

Thomas, Charles M. Papers, 1862-1905. Notebooks from the U.S. Naval Academy, cruise journals from U.S.S. *Shenandoah* and Civil War imprints. Ms. Coll. 61. Naval Historical Collection, Naval War College, Newport, RI.

Tobey & Littlefield. As per J.V. Hanscom. 1 letter, May 30, 1864, to S.M. Pook, "U.S. Navy Yard, Kittery." 1 page. Portsmouth Naval Shipyard Visitor Center, Portsmouth Naval Shipyard, Portsmouth, NH. Copy at Portsmouth Athenaeum, Portsmouth, NH.

Tomblin, Barbara B. "From Sail to Steam: The Development of Steam Technology in the United States Navy, 1838-1865." Rutgers, the State University of New Jersey/Brunswick, Ph.D. dissertation, 1988. 396-page Xerographic copy, No. DA8914272, University Microfilms, Ann Arbor, MI.

Tucker, Richard Hawley. Papers. Correspondence of prominent Wiscasset, ME, shipbuilder. 13 letters from James N. Tarlton, Portsmouth, NH, 1861-62. Originals at Hawthorne-Longfellow Library, Bowdoin College, Brunswick, ME. Typescript copies in possession of Jane S. Tucker, Wiscasset, ME.

"U.S. Navy, 1775-1910, PI - Industrial Activity, 1819-1870. Portsmouth, N.H." Navy Department. Record Group 45. Folder 3: "Paymaster's summary statement of receipts and expenditures." Folder 4: "Navy Agent's summary statements of receipts and expenditures." National Archives, Washington.

"U.S. Navy Yard, Kittery, Maine." Logbooks. Four pertain to the Civil War era ("Dec. 27, 1860 to May 13, 1862"; "May 14, 1862 to June 28, 1863"; "June 29, 1863 to Oct. 19, 1864"; and "Oct. 20, 1864 to Nov. 12,

1865"). Portsmouth Naval Shipyard Visitor Center, Portsmouth Naval Shipyard, Portsmouth, NH.

Victoria. "Journal of a Voyage in Fishing Boat *Victoria* 10 42/95 tons of [York] Maine, Commanded by Hiram Tobey." Fishing Log, April 6–August 30, 1863, from York, ME, to the Grand Banks. Phillips Library, Peabody Essex Museum, Salem, MA.

Wainwright, William. "Journal, 1861-1864, kept by William Wainwright on board the U.S.S. *Kearsarge*, Captain Charles W. Pickering (until Mar. 28, 1863), and Captain Winslow (from Apr. 5, 1863), commanding for a Naval Cruise. Made 87 ports-of-call, and spoke 5 vessels." 2 vols. Log 429. G.W. Blunt White Library, Mystic Seaport Museum, Mystic, CT.

Welles, Gideon. Papers. ca. 15,000 items. Manuscript Division, Library of Congress, Washington. On microfilm with finding aid.

Woodbury, Jesse P. 1 letter, February 3, 1863, USS *Passaic*, Warsaw Sound, Georgia, to Charles Woodbury. Charles and Levi Woodbury Papers. Manuscript 14, Portsmouth Athenaeum, Portsmouth, NH. Discusses the Emancipation Proclamation from aboard a blockading vessel.

Woodbury, Levi. Family papers. Collection includes the papers of Levi Woodbury; his son, Charles Levi Woodbury; and his (Levi's) daughter, Virginia L. Fox, wife of Gustavus V. Fox. Collection includes "a lengthy diary kept by Woodbury's daughter, Virginia L. (Woodbury) Fox, 1860-1878, and her general correspondence, 1862-1890." Manuscript Division, Library of Congress, Washington. Collection microfilmed. 16 linear feet.

Yeaton Family. Papers, 1752-1956. Incoming correspondence especially involving William Harper Yeaton of Stratham, NH, pertaining to service aboard the USS *Kearsarge*, 1862-64. 20 items in 6 folders. New Hampshire Historical Society, Concord, NH.

UNPUBLISHED STUDIES

Winslow, Richard E., III. "Frank Jones of New Hampshire: A Capitalist and a Politician during the Gilded Age." Unpublished master's thesis, University of New Hampshire, Durham, NH, 1965.

BROADSIDES

"Joint Resolution of the City Council," issued by the "City of Portsmouth, NH." Resolutions pertaining to the assassination of President Abraham Lincoln, and to the premature and erroneous report of the murder of Secretary of State William H. Seward. Dated April 15, 1865. Copy. Broadside Portfolio 94, No. 9. Rare Book and Special Collection Division, Library of Congress, Washington.

"Rates of Dockage and Wharfage, Established by the Proprietors, Agents, and Lessees of Wharves for the City of Portsmouth, NH...January 1,

1864." [Portsmouth, NH?]: 1864. Boston Athenaeum Library, Boston Athenaeum, Boston.

"The Sinking of the Pirate *Alabama* by the US Gunboat [Steam Sloop] *Kearsarge*, Captain Winslow, June 19th, 1864," by Silas S. Steele. New York: Published by Charles Magnus, ca. 1864. Catalog number MH 0.84, Box 2, Folder 34, Phillips Library, Peabody Essex Museum, Salem, MA.

"Welcome Song, Dedicated to the Commander, Officers and Crew of the U.S. Sloop-of-War *Kearsarge*, on her Arrival at Charlestown Navy Yard, Nov. 7, 1864," by Phineas Stowe, Pastor of the First Baptist Mariners' Church, Boston. Boston: W & E Howe, Printers, 1864. With signature, "Jno A. Winslow, Captain, *Kearsarge*, Nov. 14th 64." Peabody Essex Museum, Salem, MA.

Appendix

The Civil War Display at the Yard's Visitor Center

THE RICHNESS OF THE PORTSMOUTH Naval Shipyard's heritage has not been neglected. In 1985, largely through efforts of Bea Lammers, wife of the shipyard commander at the time, a group of active and retired Yard employees, naval personnel, and area volunteers established the nonprofit Portsmouth Naval Shipyard Historical Foundation. Its goal was to collect, house, and preserve the Yard's artifacts, photographs, logbooks, documents, and related items. Foundation members scoured the Yard to acquire significant objects ranging from a single document to a fire engine.

To display the collection (except for the fire engine, which remains at the Yard fire station), Shipyard Commander Lennis L. Lammers made space available in the small structure that was once the Yard's powder house. From this fledgling beginning, the project has never looked backward, having been strongly supported over the years by subsequent Yard commanders: Captain Peter Bowman, Rear Admiral Lewis A. Felton, and Captain Lance Horne. In addition, the general public, the city of Portsmouth, the town of Kittery, and the United States Navy have generously come forth with donations of artifacts and funds. With such backing, the Portsmouth Naval Shipyard Visitor Center (the current name, replacing the original organizational title of the PNSY Foundation, which continues to be active in its important role as a Friends group) has expanded into progressively more accessible and more spacious quarters.

During Captain Bowman's tenure, the facility was housed in two first-floor rooms in the old Marine Barracks. Later, Felton authorized that half of Building 156 be used as a museum, with the other half remaining as living quarters for enlisted submarine crews. More recently, Horne oversaw the restoration of two conference rooms on the third floor of Building 86, the site of the 1905 Russo-Japanese Peace Treaty. This historic venue is open to the public.

On December 7, 1991, the fiftieth anniversary of the bombing of Pearl Harbor, Admiral Felton officiated at the opening of the greatly enlarged Visitor Center in Building 156. The center serves not only to display the collected memorabilia but also to interpret the Yard for the naval community and the general public. Since its inception, the center has become the focal point for exhibits, conferences, receptions, historical research, and related activities. The Civil War era figures prominently in three wall-display cases, a six-foot model of the USS *Kearsarge* built by the inmates of the naval prison in 1936, and more—everything from spikes, uniforms, and an oil portrait of Farragut to a soup cup with "U.S.N." stenciled in blue on the side. Dressed in regulation naval uniforms of the period, Civil War Round Table groups often come to view exhibits and to "refight" sea battles.

Visitor Center Director James Dolph and his staff conduct walking and bus tours of the Yard and also present programs to audiences throughout the area. Quarters "A" and other buildings—several steeped in Civil War associations—have been added to the National Register of Historic Places. Archaeological digs are slated to begin. These various activities thus ensure that the Civil War era, together with other aspects of the Portsmouth Naval Shipyard's history, will be permanently preserved and interpreted for future generations

Index

413

Peabody, Samuel Endicott, 171
Pearson, Capt. George F. (Navy
    Yard commandant), 7 (ill.), 15,
    17-18, 19, 29-31, 32, 34, 35, 36,
    37-38, 40, 42, 43, 45, 47, 48, 49,
    55, 58, 59, 78, 79, 80-81, 82, 84,
    85, 93-94, 95-96, 98, 108-9, 110,
    111, 112, 115-17, 132, 142-43,
    148, 149, 150, 156, 175, 180, 194,
    197, 198-99, 200, 201, 204, 205,
    211, 215, 217, 225, 226-28, 229,
    230, 231-32, 258-60, 268, 323
Pease, Joachim, 255
Peirce's Island, 33
Pendergrast, Lt. Austin, 103
Penguin, USS, 134-35
Penny Post (Portsmouth), 325
Pensacola (FL) Navy Yard, 20, 156
Peri, 66
Perkins, John H., 207-8
Perry (ship), 59
Perry, Oliver H., 76-77
Peru (schooner), 77
Petersburg (VA), 284
Pettigrew, William, 21
Philadelphia (steamer), 103
Philadelphia Ledger, 274
Philadelphia Navy Yard, 205
Philadelphia North American, 256
Phillips Exeter Academy (NH), 45
Pickering, Comdr. Charles W., 87,
    98-101, 323
Piscataqua River (ME/NH), 2, 5
Piscataqua, USS, 322
Planter (ship), 196
Plymouth (NC), 283
Pocahontas, USS (gunboat), 158
Pollard, William, 229
Poole, Charles A., 244
Pope, Capt. John (Navy Yard com-
    mandant), 7 (ill.), 8, 323
Pope, Jennie Barnes, 291, 321
Port of Portsmouth: arrivals and
    departures, 4; decline of com-
    merce, 288; history, 2; reputation

of, 2; shipbuilding in, 2. *See also*
    Portsmouth (NH); Portsmouth
    Navy Yard
Port Royal (SC), 230-31, 280
Porter, Capt. (later Adm.) David D.,
    141, 274, 276, 313, 323
Portfire (steam tug), 310
Portland (ME) *Advertiser,* 219
Portland (ME) *Press,* 178, 220
Portland (ME), 177-78
Portsmouth (NH), 6, 87; decline of
    shipbuilding, 3, 23-24, 130, 319;
    1860 population, 2; 1864 fire,
    228; harbor security, 192-97;
    importance of shipping, 3, 4. *See
    also* Port of Portsmouth;
    Portsmouth Navy Yard
Portsmouth Chronicle: citations, 3,
    4, 12, 18, 20, 29, 31, 32, 33, 34,
    35, 36, 40, 42, 44, 49, 52, 53, 61,
    62, 63, 66, 75, 77, 78, 83, 85, 87,
    90, 91, 93, 94, 95, 96, 97, 98, 99,
    100, 105, 106, 108, 110, 111, 122,
    124, 132, 133, 133, 136, 144, 148,
    151-52, 155, 159, 162, 164, 165,
    166, 172, 173, 174, 175, 178, 180,
    183, 185, 186-88, 189, 192, 194,
    196, 198, 199, 201-4, 205, 206,
    209, 212, 216-17, 218, 220-21,
    227-28, 230, 232, 234, 235, 236,
    237, 239, 241, 249, 252, 254, 257,
    258, 260, 263, 264, 266, 268, 271,
    273, 277, 278, 280, 281, 285, 287,
    289-90, 293, 294-95, 296, 299,
    301, 304, 305, 306, 307, 309, 310,
    313, 315, 319, 321, 329-30
Portsmouth draft riot (1863), 161,
    181, 232, 301. *See also* Draft
Portsmouth Harbor, 39 (ill.); protec-
    tion of, 38. *See also* Fort
    Constitution; Fort McClary; Fort
    Sullivan
Portsmouth Journal: citations, 1, 2,
    3, 6-7, 13, 22, 27-28, 31, 36, 53-
    54, 67, 69, 71, 73, 83, 85, 94, 95,

About the Author

WITH THIS FOURTH BOOK in his twelve-year association with the Portsmouth Marine Society (PMS), Richard E. Winslow III (no relation to the famous *Kearsarge* commander) continues to cover the New Hampshire waterfront. His latest effort combines three of his interests—Portsmouth, the Civil War, and the United States Navy—and also builds upon his earlier PMS books: *The Piscataqua Gundalow: Workhorse for a Tidal Basin Empire* (1983), *Portsmouth-Built: Submarines of the Portsmouth Naval Shipyard* (1985), and *"Wealth and Honour": Portsmouth During the Golden Age of Privateering, 1775-1815* (1988).

Born in Boston in 1934, Winslow has lived in the Portsmouth area intermittently since 1938, permanently since 1981. He received undergraduate and graduate degrees from Union College, the University of New Hampshire, the University of Maryland, and the Pennsylvania State University. As a visitor to the Portsmouth Navy Shipyard since 1941, and frequently as a "Navy Junior" during his father's tour of duty as a supply officer from 1957 to 1960, Dick has witnessed much of the Yard's recent history first-hand.

In reconstructing the Civil War era, Dick has toured not only the Yard on numerous occasions, but also harbor forts, buildings, cemeteries, and sites. His memberships in the Portsmouth Athenaeum, the Portsmouth Public Library, the Portsmouth Naval Shipyard Visitor Center, and the Civil War Round Table of New Hampshire have led to resources and professional contacts that have enriched this study.

One totally unexpected pleasure for Dick while conducting his investigations for this book involved the controversy swirling around the origin of the naming of the USS *Kearsarge*. Prompted by a conscientious sense of duty to cover either possibility, he ascended both peaks—Mount Kearsarge, near Warner, and Kearsarge North, in the North Conway area—as part of necessary research. He hopes, with similar justification, to head for the waters off Cherbourg, France.

When not engaged in writing histories for the Portsmouth Marine Society, Dick enjoys such other water-related activities as canoeing, kayaking, swimming, and researching the lives and literary careers of sailor Herman Melville and paddler Henry David Thoreau.

Log of the U. S. Navy Yard, Kittery, Me.

State of the Weather, Friday Sepr 20 1861.

Light S. Wind Cloudy Clear

Mechanics, &c. employed as follows:

Total number of Mechanics and others employed this day,

Carpenters	555	On Ossipee Kearsage Side Wheel Steamer Pecham Contingent
Carpenters' Lab'rs, &c.	559	Miss: Ossipee Kearsage Sidewheel Steamen
Carpenters' Apprentices	6	
Calkers	89	Ossipee Kearsage
Calkers' Lab'rs&R'u'rs	17	Ossipee Kearsage
Boat Builders	16	Kearsage
Mast Makers	20	Kearsage
Mast Makers' Laborers	1	Kearsage
Joiners	81	Miss Ossipee Kearsage Side Wheel Steamer Pecham
Joiners' Laborers	11	Ossipee
Smiths	914	Ossipee Kearsage Side Wheel Steamer Ordnance Contingent
Sawyers	19	Ossipee Side Wheel Steamen
Painters	12	Kearsage Side Wheel Steamer Ordnance
Painters' Laborers		Ordnance
Gun Carriage Makers	40	Miscellaneous Kearsage Ossipee
Sail Makers	20	Ossipee
Sail Makers' Laborers	1	